COMPLETELY
MAD

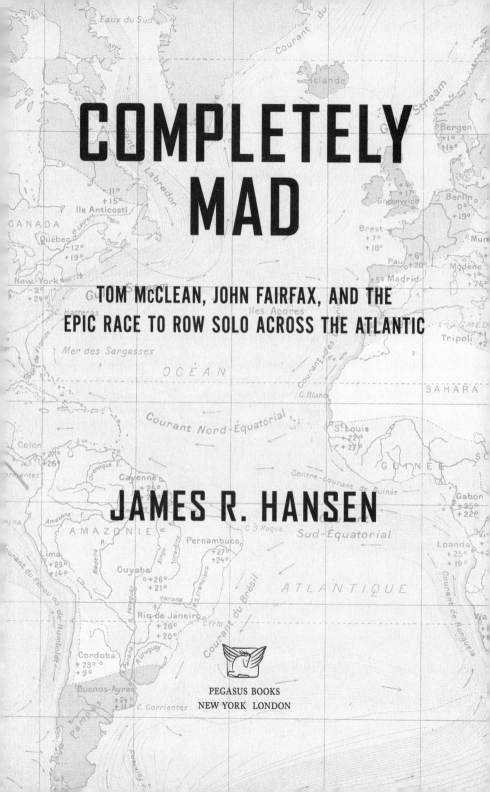

COMPLETELY
MAD

TOM McCLEAN, JOHN FAIRFAX, AND THE
EPIC RACE TO ROW SOLO ACROSS THE ATLANTIC

JAMES R. HANSEN

PEGASUS BOOKS

NEW YORK LONDON

COMPLETELY MAD

Pegasus Books, Ltd.
148 West 37th Street, 13th Floor
New York, NY 10018

Copyright © 2023 by James R. Hansen

First Pegasus Books paperback edition July 2024
First Pegasus Books cloth edition July 2023

Interior design by Maria Fernandez

Library of Congress Cataloging-in-Publication Data is available.

Paperback ISBN: 978-1-63936-693-4
Hardcover ISBN: 978-1-63936-417-6

10 9 8 7 6 5 4 3 2 1

Printed in the United States of America
Distributed by Simon & Schuster
www.pegasusbooks.com

In Memory of the Great Ocean Rower

Don Allum

(1937–1992)

And all the other "completely mad" adventurers

who bless and honor the human experience

From the Apollo 11 Astronauts

To John Fairfax:

May we of Apollo 11 add our sincere congratulations to the many you have undoubtedly already received for your bold and courageous feat of rowing alone across the Atlantic. We who sail what President Kennedy once called "The new ocean of space" are pleased to pay our respects to the man who, single handedly, has conquered the still formidable ocean of water. We find it an interesting coincidence that you completed your arduous voyage here on earth at a spot very near the one from which we started our voyage to the moon. And that you arrived at your destination quite near the time that we reached ours. Yours, however, was the accomplishment of one resourceful individual, while ours depended upon the help of thousands of dedicated workers in the United States and all over the world. As fellow explorers, we salute you on this great occasion.

The Apollo 11 Astronauts

Neil Armstrong

Michael Collins

Edwin A Aldrin Jr.

> —Telegram from the Apollo 11 astronauts in quarantine inside the Lunar Receiving Laboratory at the Manned Spacecraft Center in Houston, Texas, to ocean rower John Fairfax, July 30, 1969

"More than twice as many people have walked on the Moon as have soloed the Atlantic Ocean in a rowboat."

> —Statement from the Ocean Rowing Society International, 2019

"The first ocean rows were done under conditions that were not much different from the days of Columbus."

> —Geoff Allum, trustee of the Ocean Rowing Society International and cousin to Don Allum (1937–1992), the first person to row the Atlantic in both directions, and still the only person to have rowed both ways solo

Contents

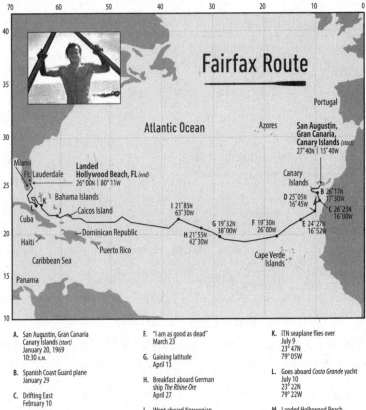

Fairfax Route

Atlantic Ocean

Portugal

Azores

San Augustin, Gran Canaria, Canary Islands *(start)*
27°40N | 15°40W

Miami

Ft. Lauderdale

Landed Hollywood Beach, FL *(end)*
26°00N | 80°11W

Canary Islands

Bahama Islands

B 26°17N 17°30W

D 25°05N 16°45W

Caicos Island

C 26°23N 16°00W

Cuba

I 21°85N 63°30W

E 24°27N 16°52W

Dominican Republic

G 19°32N 38°00W

F 19°30N 26°00W

Haiti

H 21°55N 42°30W

Puerto Rico

Caribbean Sea

Cape Verde Islands

Panama

A. San Augustin, Gran Canaria Canary Islands *(start)*
January 20, 1969
10:30 A.M.

B. Spanish Coast Guard plane
January 29

C. Drifting East
February 10

D. Went aboard passing tanker *Bulford* for a shower
February 15

E. Went aboard passing Russian ship *Talsy*
February 24

F. "I am as good as dead"
March 23

G. Gaining latitude
April 13

H. Breakfast aboard German ship *The Rhine Ore*
April 27

I. Went aboard Norwegian ship *Bay Ross*
June 6

J. Goes ashore on Cay Verde
June 29
22°02N
75°12W

K. ITN seaplane flies over
July 9
23°47N
79°05W

L. Goes aboard *Costa Grande* yacht
July 10
23°22N
79°22W

M. Landed Hollywood Beach, Florida *(end)*
July 19, 1969
1:45 P.M.

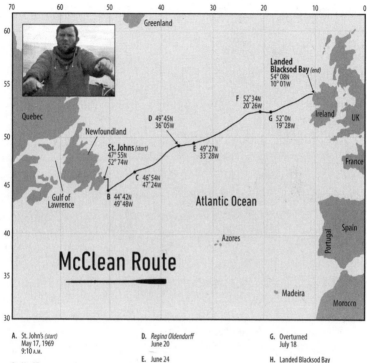

| 70 | 60 | 50 | 40 | 30 | 20 | 10 | 0 |

Greenland

Landed
Blacksod Bay *(end)*
54° 08N
10° 01W

F 52°34N
20°26W

Quebec

D 49°45N
36°05W

G 52°0N
19°28W

Ireland UK

Newfoundland

St. Johns *(start)*
47° 55N
52° 74W

E 49°27N
33°28W

France

C 46°54N
47°24W

Atlantic Ocean

B 44°42N
49°48W

Gulf of
Lawrence

Azores

Portugal Spain

McClean Route

Madeira

Morocco

A. St. John's *(start)*
May 17, 1969
9:10 A.M.

B. May 27

C. Rio Alfusqueiro
June 3

D. *Regina Oldendorff*
June 20

E. June 24

F. Hansa
July 14

G. Overturned
July 18

H. Landed Blacksod Bay
July 27
7:15 A.M.

Prologue

This is not *a* true story. It is *two* true stories. Two true stories that have never been told as one, though they deserve to be.

One sweeping saga involving two extraordinary—and extraordinarily different—adventurers, Tom McClean and John Fairfax, having only two things in common: the Atlantic Ocean and the ambition to cross it in a rowboat . . . alone.

Just one man, one small boat, and a pair of oars.

They raced across the Atlantic solo during one of humankind's most epic years. It was 1969, and each rower finished his remarkable transoceanic journey within just a few days of the historic first landing on the Moon by Apollo 11 on July 20.

The two oarsmen took very different routes across the sea. McClean, a twenty-six-year-old British paratrooper, set out from St. John's, Newfoundland, on May 17 and landed at Blacksod Bay on the remote northwest coast of Ireland on July 26. Moving from west to east, his crossing took 70 days. McClean's was the first solo row ever across the Atlantic in that direction. Fairfax, a 31-year-old profligate gambler, playboy, and former whiskey and gun smuggler (read: pirate), had a head start, and he would need it. He left from San Agustín in the Canary Islands off the coast of Africa on January 20, 1969, and landed at Hollywood Beach north of Miami, Florida, on July 19. Fairfax's east-to-west crossing took a torturous 180 days and was the first solo row crossing of the Atlantic in that direction.

For both men, crossing the ocean meant thousands of miles of back-breaking effort, exhaustion, and bodily wear, tear, and injury. Vicious storms, gale winds, high waves, and sharks would all attack them. More than once their rowboats capsized. Battered beyond belief, hands blistered and bloody, almost continuously soaked to the skin, and fighting against mental and physical lethargy, both oarsmen rowed on, never seriously doubting a final success. What made the dogged determination of both men so incredible was the fact that neither man had any previous experience as an ocean rower, and McClean, worse yet, knew almost nothing about the sea or seamanship. He set off into the North Atlantic anyway.

Completely Mad tells an intertwined story of the two astonishing journeys and the two uncommonly extraordinary men who were crazy enough to make them. What sort of person rows a boat solo across an ocean? Who would even consider taking on that sort of frightful and highly perilous challenge? Is it someone with a suicide wish? Is it a person out of balance mentally or emotionally? Is it a pure glory seeker? A daredevil? Is it a narcissist pining to be famous? Who possibly? Why in the world?

As a research scholar specializing in aerospace history I have learned a lot about people who risk their lives in perilous pursuits. I have spent five decades of my life studying in depth the lives of test pilots and astronauts. I am therefore quite familiar with the motivations of the rare breed of men and women whose driving passion is to fly experimental airplanes at great speeds, through fantastic maneuvers, to great heights, and ultimately even taking some of their craft to the edge of the atmosphere and beyond into space. I have studied their background stories, their personalities, and their ambitions, as well as their mindsets, emotional dispositions, and psychologies, and I have come to understand how far some human beings—perhaps those with the ineffable "right stuff"—will push their bodies and minds, their capabilities, and their goals in order to pioneer epic expeditions into the unknown. I had the great good fortune of writing the authorized biography of just such a man, Neil Armstrong (*First Man*, 2005), who, with his Apollo 11 crewmates Michael Collins and Buzz Aldrin, committed their flying careers—and their very lives—to an ultimate destination: a half-million-mile trip from Earth to the Moon and back. That sensational lunar goal was achieved not just at great cost to the nation, but, as we have found as we have delved more deeply over the years into the personal stories of the astronauts, also to themselves and their wives and children. After all, wasn't going to the Moon the most dangerous mission of all time?

I had always thought so until I thought about what it would take to row a boat solo across an ocean. Now *that* sounded truly crazy! If given a choice of going to the Moon with two other trained professionals, in a spacecraft as roomy as a large automobile, with a whole team of experts back at Mission Control in Houston overseeing virtually every step of the trip, or rowing a small boat across the Atlantic Ocean by myself, requiring as many as 24,000 oar strokes per day, which would I choose?

Hands down, I'm going to the Moon!

Were John Fairfax and Tom McClean mad? Were they actually suffering from some clinical condition? Certainly, a number of people back at the time, when John and Tom told them of their plan to row the Atlantic solo, said to them, "Alone?! You're daft, man! You must be completely mad."

This book offers no formal psychological study of John Fairfax or Tom McClean, as interesting as that might be. My son Dr. Nathaniel Hansen is an MD psychiatrist, but I am not. Although as part of my background research for this book, I reviewed a great deal of the scientific literature dealing with the psychology of mountain climbers, bullfighters, automobile racers, and participants in such extreme sports as free climbing, BASE jumping, volcano surfing, wingsuit flying, para-skiing, high-lining, and other highly dangerous, physically hazardous, and life-threatening pursuits of athletic and human performance, I have made no serious attempt to make systematic use of any formal psychological theories in my analysis of the two men. Nonetheless, my book illuminates a great deal about the personalities and characters of Fairfax and McClean, as extremely different as the two men were—as close to the opposite ends of the human personality spectrum as two adventurers with the same incredible goal in mind could possibly be.

It will not be in any theory of psychology but in the actual words and deeds of Fairfax and McClean that readers will discern the emotional makeup, mental states and processes, thought patterns, drives and ambitions, motives for action, beliefs and values, ethics and egoisms, attitudes and prejudices, essence of intellect, sense of identity, moods and feelings, and emotional makeup of the story's two protagonists. By the end of the remarkable tale, readers should feel that they have developed a good understanding of the highly contrasting nature of the two men who first crossed the Atlantic Ocean solo in a rowboat. And perhaps we will come to the understanding that it's not one particular "type" of person that takes these crazy risks and can do these amazing feats, but a strange confluence of traits and temperaments that sometimes, in certain combinations, yield a peculiar kind of magic.

Of course, neither Fairfax nor McClean ever considered himself truly mad—though there were moments on the Atlantic when things were going so terribly for them that they were not so sure. Maybe they were a bit crazy for taking this on, they could occasionally admit to themselves. But both men were always determined—rather absolutely—to press on.

The narrative penetrates deeply into who they were and what drove them to dare such an extreme, mortally risky endeavor. It explores not only what their extraordinary ocean crossings meant to the protagonists but also what their individual journeys illuminate about them in high contrast as fundamentally different types of men. In this vein, there is also analysis of what their passages—across the ocean and across life in general—signify about some of the male attitudes and masculine values that were prevalent in Western societies—for good or ill—during the middle decades of the 20th century.

As I was immersed in the story of McClean and Fairfax, the Homeric nature of their stories became clear to me. Just as Odysseus was the subject and the center of Homer's great poem, *The Odyssey*, McClean and Fairfax are the alpha and the omega of this epic tale.

Some commentators have called Odysseus "the first modern man"; other scholars have labeled him "The Untypical Hero." Similar rubrics can be applied to Tom McClean and, even more so, to John Fairfax. In responding to their call to adventure, both were self-assured and self-actuated. To achieve what they came to regard as the paramount mission of their early adulthood—that was, to battle past one's personal and local limitations, win a victory over nature, and prove mastery over oneself, thereby becoming a personage of not only local but also world historical import—McClean and Fairfax pitted themselves, figuratively and literally, against a host of monsters, sirens, nymphs, angry gods, foreboding ill winds, screaming gales, mysterious murky mists, shark attacks, drownings, and collisions with passing ships. In their innate need to overcome such threatening and potentially deadly circumstances and emerge at their destinations victoriously, the two men were similar. But in virtually everything else about McClean and Fairfax and their common yet so uncommon personal sagas, they could not have been more different.

One of the book's clear conclusions is that Fairfax and McClean undertook their epic voyages for very different reasons—reasons that flowed from who they were and what their lives up to the time of their great journey had made them. It is impossible to imagine two men who were seeking to do the same sort of "crazy" thing ever being more different than Fairfax and McClean. Or how their two crossings of the Atlantic Ocean, occurring with virtual simultaneity in 1969, could have been of such tremendously different character. Impossible to imagine, that is, until one understands the deeply different social and cultural settings out of which the two men as boys and young men had developed their values and ambitions. During the writing of the book, in fact, I seriously considered using *The Paratrooper and the Playboy* as its title, in order to feature the tremendous contrast between the two adventurers.

In the end, I determined that *Completely Mad* was a better title to use—not to suggest any sort of clinical madness inherent to the two ocean rowers but to capture the incredulous popular attitude of the general public when it came to individuals like Fairfax and McClean who attempted such extreme, mortally dangerous feats. What the title conveys, as a colloquialism, is the sense of amazement, awe, disbelief, and even borderline scorn that we human beings feel when we confront the audacious daring of such seemingly impossible challenges that only a few of our kind would ever venture to try. Whether that sense of skepticism of fantastic individual risk-taking and daring performance was stronger in Western society and culture 50 years ago than it is today is debatable—and worthy of further study. But there is no question that most people who heard about the solo transatlantic rows of Fairfax and McClean in the summer of 1969 felt that both men had to be "completely mad."

Although not a race between them in any way official or declared, both men clearly committed their heart and soul to a solo ocean crossing with the idea of being the very first to do it. Otherwise, if they couldn't have been first, they would never have bothered to do it. Their two stories, as remarkably dramatic as they were individually, when woven into a tale of two men of deeply contrasting characters and divergent approaches both making it alone across the ocean, rank as one of the most fascinating personality-driven adventure stories of all time. Historically the "race" between Fairfax and McClean deserves to be remembered as another great saga of the year 1969, one of even more awesome individual daring and commitment than the monumental trip of astronauts Armstrong, Collins, and Aldrin across the vacuum of space to the Moon.

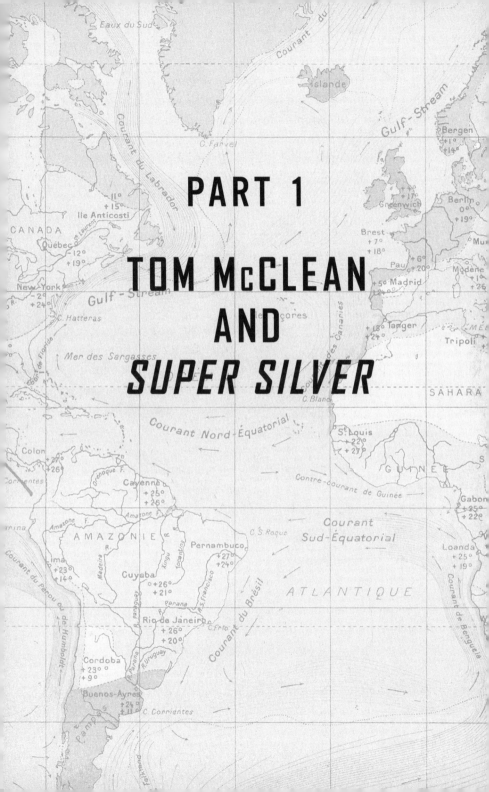

PART 1
TOM McCLEAN
AND
SUPER SILVER

1

Oars through the Harbor

It was a long smooth pull through the placid harbor waters. Twenty-six-year-old Irishman Tom McClean, all 5'6" of stoutness, bent his back in what was a not-too-regular rowing rhythm as he concentrated on getting a feel for his boat. He had dubbed his vessel *Super Silver*, the result of a deal of $1,000 from the Gillette UK company, which was launching a new razor by that name. Tom himself simply called his rowboat *Silver*.

At this stage the boat meant little more to McClean than a conglomeration of plywood, oak frame, nylon canvas, glue, and epoxy resin from which came an assembly of hull, floors, planking, gunwales, oarlocks, and bows. It wasn't that he disliked his rowboat; he was unsure how well it would perform for him. How would the boat do in the rough open ocean? How would it stand up to the serious, even life-threatening challenges that were sure to come? Could *Silver* stand the strain? Could it take him all the way home, the full 2,000-plus miles from Newfoundland to Ireland? He liked the look of his boat, but there was no reason yet to love it, and he didn't.

It was 8:45 A.M. Saturday, May 17, 1969. Tom had wanted to be in the water with *Silver* at least 45 minutes earlier. But the large crowd of interested spectators and well-wishers on the quay at St. John's Harbour that weekend morning made a prompt departure impossible.

"Half the world and his wife were there to see me go," Tom remembers. A conflux of maritime Canadians estimated at over 200 had come down to the wharf to watch the chap—who they had heard, accurately, was an active-duty British soldier on leave from his commando unit—take off to cross the ocean in a rowboat.

The onlookers applauded his arrival and cheered loudly as he made his way through them and down to his boat. One rascal handed him a girlie magazine: "There you are, sir, that'll give you something to keep you heading for home!" Making it down to the dock where *Silver* was tied up, a bearded man that Tom had every reason to think was a veteran fisherman handed Tom a bottle of whiskey. "Christen the boat with that," he shouted for all to hear. Immediately Tom did just that, cracking the bottle and, in an act of ultimate sacrifice in a place where whiskey was currency, pouring out every last drop of the precious liquid over the bow. He answered a few questions asked by local newspaper reporters, and to please a local television cameraman he made a fist and punched the air a few times with it. One man asked if he could have a picture taken with Tom in *Silver*, a request that, in his shyness and his hurry, Tom politely declined.

Surrounded by folks—even teenagers—who knew quite a bit more about boats and being on and around the ocean than he did, because they had been born and bred into an intimate marriage with the sea, Tom suddenly felt terribly self-conscious. The people of coastal Newfoundland were among the very best boatbuilders, boat handlers, and fishermen in the entire world. Their proximity to the Grand Banks, a series of underwater plateaus southeast of the island of Newfoundland, on the North American continental shelf, gave them ready access to one of the world's richest fishing grounds, supporting Atlantic cod, flounder, halibut, swordfish, haddock, redfish, capelin, pollack, and other so-called groundfish, as well as shellfish, seabirds, and sea mammals. For generations the way of life, economy, and culture of Newfoundland and the other maritime provinces depended on the bounty of the sea. Mountains of shellfish were hauled in regularly by trawlers: snow crab, shrimp, lobster, sea cucumbers, and scallops. Many a day, mackerel and herring filled up the fishermen's nets. Into the early twentieth century there had been whaling, and even into the 1960s, though increasingly controversial (and to be outlawed by a number of national and international laws and treaties), there was large-scale commercial harvesting of harp seals and other sea mammals as well as the hunting of sea birds.

Though Tom McClean chose to embark from Newfoundland primarily due to its location and the shorter distance across to Ireland from there, it was not at all irrelevant to him that the Newfoundlanders knew their boats, and they loved their boats. The type of boat that Tom was using for his Atlantic crossing was of their own special creation—one could even call it their pride and joy. The Newfoundland dory had been used as the traditional fishing boat on the Grand Banks since the early 19th century. The boat, also called the Banks dory, was a small, open, narrow, flat-bottomed, and slab-sided boat with a particularly narrow transom and long overhangs at the bow and stern. It was a simple enough but extremely well-conceived design, perfected over the decades, that helped lift the boats *over* the waves. Inexpensive to build, the dories were stacked inside each other—some 30 to 40 of them—and stored on the deck of a larger fishing vessel, which functioned as a mother ship. The dories were then lowered one at a time off the mother ship, usually with one man per boat who was equipped with as many as 500 hooks with lines. The fishermen of Newfoundland would stay at sea for weeks at a time in all types of weather, going forth and back from the mother ship. The heavier the dories became with loaded catch (up to about a half ton limit), the more stable the dory actually became.

The Newfoundlanders had forgotten more about dory operation than McClean could have possibly learned in the few months that he had been building and practicing in his—and Tom knew that the people of the wharf at St. John's knew it . . . and suspected that he knew that they knew.

Tom's boat was also a dory, but it had been built in England, not Newfoundland. His was a Yorkshire dory. The Yorkshire dory was basically similar to the Newfoundland dory. Both featured a keelless design that enabled the dory to ride the sea rather than attempt to fight it. Built by Bradford Boat Services in West Yorkshire, the dory that was to become

Tom's *Silver* was handcrafted from top-grade plywood on an oak frame. Its hull was covered in tough nylon canvas sheeting that was woven and glued onto the plywood with epoxy resin. The nylon sheathing made the exterior of the boat quite tough. If the boat took a big impact, it might crack the marine ply hull, but the nylon sheathing would stretch under impact rather than break, adding protection from the boat leaking. With the help of carpenters working at the army base in Hereford where Tom was stationed, Tom altered the boat by having her gunwales raised nine inches and by fitting "turtle decking" fore and aft over watertight compartments containing blocks of polystyrene for additional buoyancy.* Freshwater in two-gallon containers was placed under a false floor, protecting the water for drinking and adding ballast. There was no cabin, but Tom gave his boat a small canvas shelter stretched over a metal U-frame. Under the canopy Tom left a space measuring two feet seven inches at its highest center point, about four feet wide and three feet long. The space was not all for Tom and his food supply. It also served to shelter his chronometer, his radios, and an inflatable rubber dinghy loaned to Tom by the RAF.

The sheltered space left for Tom himself gave him nowhere near the protection from the salt air and freezing cold that he hoped for. One "touch of luxury" that he intended for his trip was to sleep on an "air bed" that could be packed into the space, but that didn't work out nearly as well as he planned. "I had to lay it fore and after leaving about three feet of my body sticking out in the open." His only choice was to "make the best of it." In the preparation stage Tom had not even thought of the possibility of frostbite attacking his feet, but attack it would, to the point that his feet were so swollen he couldn't wear his boots for days on end.

---

*   *Turtle decking* is a term applied to a weather deck that is rounded over from the shell of a boat so that it has a shape similar to the back of a turtle. The upper deck of the vessel thus has a pronounced curve from its centerline down to the sides. The purpose of turtle decking is to assist overboard the flow of any seawater shipped over the bows.

In key respects, Tom's dory copied the design of the *English Rose III*, the dory that in the summer of 1966 had taken his fellow British paratroopers John Ridgway and Chay Blyth on their historic two-man crossing of the Atlantic, though, at 18 feet, *Silver* would be two feet shorter. It was the ocean crossing of *English Rose III* by Ridgway and Blyth that first gave Tom the notion that a person could row the Atlantic solo—a crazy notion for anyone, but especially for someone who at the time the idea hit had not only done zero ocean rowing but had hardly done any kind of rowing at all.

Though the two boat types were similar, the experienced Newfoundlanders could quickly spot the differences between Tom's dory and their own. The hulls weighed much the same, but the Newfoundland dory was made of wide boards of wood and was a completely open boat with no turtle decks holding buoyancy compartments. Regarding the raised deck and gunwales reinforced with oak, they could see what Tom had done to substantially beef up his dory for the ocean crossing—and rightfully so. Their own dories, because they needed to be launched and retrieved from the mother ship many times between fishing trips, needed to be kept as basic and lightweight as possible.

As curious as the crowd on St. John's quay was, picking out and conversing among themselves about the special features of Tom's dory, they were even more curious to learn how such a barmy British soldier and inexperienced seaman would handle his boat. That was certainly what the majority of the local fishermen were waiting to see. None of them had yet witnessed him row a single stroke. The only rowing that "this trooper" had done after he got to St. John's via an RAF transport from England was at dusk the previous evening when—Tom made sure—nobody was around. And then all he did was move *Silver* a few yards from one side of the dock to the other side of the dock, readying it to head "off" in the morning.

Sensing Tom's nervousness, several people in the crowd—men, women, and children—shouted out what they believed to be vital last-minute pieces of advice:

"Our Newfoundland has miles of tricky coastline, be warned!"

"You have to watch for the draw of the land, young man! It's a compelling force that will try to drag you back and dash you against our jagged rocks."

"Once you're through those narrows, son, keep pulling. Get away from that coast. Don't stop rowing until the land is out of sight."

"Sailors want wind, sir, rowers don't."

"Why didn't you give yourself a sliding seat? That way you could put more of your back and abdomen into your strokes and not so much into your arms!"

"Don't grip your oars too tight, not even in strong winds or big waves! That'll tire out your hands and body more than anything!"

"Stay relaxed and calm even in the fiercest winds!"

"Don't ever get scared out there, boy! If you do, you're a goner."

"Feel the water on each blade of your oar! In difficult seas you'll only control the boat when the blades of your oars are in the water."

"In rough seas don't use long strokes. Shorten your stroke by a quarter to a half."

"If you work your way upwind of your mark, turn to take the waves on the stern quarter. A zigzag course will avoid settling into the trough."

"You'll be lucky, lad, to make it through the Labrador Current!"

"Watch for icebergs! There's likely to be a few out there!"

"Don't go into the water unless you absolutely have to, young man! It's damned cold, and the fog can be so bad you might never see your boat again!"

"The foggiest place in the world is the Grand Banks!"

"You can count on the weather being treacherous. It almost always is in the Banks."

A lot of that advice seemed pretty solid to McClean, but it was not the time for a course in Newfoundlander boating wisdom. Looking at his watch, Tom said to the crowd: "Well, it's no good hanging around. I might as well start now so that at least I'll be out of the harbor by dark!" That wisecrack got laughter all around. It helped Tom to relax.

Scanning the wharf, he saw some of the friends he had made in the few short days he had been in St. John's. There was Jack Robbins, an officer with the Royal Canadian Mounted Police who had allowed Tom to stay in the Mounties barracks, enjoy the freedom of the mess hall, and showed him some of the sights around the city, including a trip up to the old tower on Signal Hill overlooking the entrance to the harbor from where radio pioneer Guglielmo Marconi had transmitted the world's first transatlantic cable message in 1907.

Tom also picked out the unmistakable head of "Big Ed" Gedden, the man from Furness Withy, the firm that had received shipment of *Silver* in St. John's, who had watched every minute of the loading of Tom's dory like a hawk. Big Ed had come quayside two or three times a day to run a casually expert eye over *Silver* and deliver his verdict. On one of those visits, Ed had growled, "Where are your gloves?" Tom showed him two pairs, one woolen and the other leather. "Useless," Ed rumbled. "You might as well have none in that cold out there. What you need is Portuguese fishermen's gloves. Wool soaked in cod oil. Used out on the Banks. They last forever, and when you get them wet, just wring them out, put them back on, and they'll still keep your hands warm." A half hour later Big Ed was back with a pair of the Portuguese mittens. Tom still uses that same pair to this day.

Tom also spotted the three teenage boys who had run up to him on the docks and "who wouldn't rest until I allowed them to help me." In a biting wind the boys—Patrick, Harold, and George—helped Tom load and stow all his stores in the various nooks and crannies of the boat "as if their lives depended on it." Even in St. John's it was thought that there should be a guard on such a vulnerable boat at night. Tom told the boys that he would sleep aboard, "but the kids would hear nothing of that; I needed all the sleep I could get, they insisted." The teens mounted two-hour watches, one of them dashing home to get an air pistol. The Mounties even got into the act, asking the boys in the early dawn what they were up to and ensuring they were "about legal business."

"Such was the spirit of the place," Tom reflects fondly.

And, of course, standing close by and with tears brimming in their eyes were the members of the Squires family. Jack the Mountie had introduced Tom to them at a church service: husband Harold, a local civil servant; his wife, Jean; and children Elizabeth, Robin, Ann, Jeannie, and David. Being an orphan from infancy and living in an orphanage until age 15 and in the care of that orphanage until age 17½, when he joined the British Army, Tom had benefited only a couple times in his life from anything like genuine family life. But in the short time they had known each other, the Squires family took in Tom like he was one of them. The night before he left for his Atlantic crossing, Jean Squires had prepared an enormous going-away dinner for Tom, "which I literally wolfed down."

David Squires, twelve years old, asked Tom how he felt about taking on the ocean. "Just like I did before a parachute jump," said the paratrooper.

"What were the chances you could die from jumping in a parachute?" queried David.

"We were told in the Parachute Regiment that there was a four to one chance of surviving our first jump unscathed," Tom answered.

"Those are pretty good odds, huh," said David. "I imagine the chances of your making it all the way across the ocean are a lot worse."

"Well, we'll see" was all the trooper managed to answer.

Tom slept that night at the Squires home. For breakfast they fed him an enormous meal of eggs, bacon, and toast; Tom drank three huge cups of tea. The Squires family was truly sad to see him go. Before leaving the house, Jean gave him a flask of tea and a large batch of sandwiches—"it looked enough to last a month."

On the quay, again spotting Jack the Mountie, Tom couldn't help but notice the special caring look the splendid policeman was giving him. Tom thought back to the church service Jack had insisted that he attend with him. "Me? Church?" Tom had thought to himself. The orphanage had choked virtually all traces of formal religious belief out of him. At first Tom made the excuse that he had not packed a formal shirt or suit and therefore was not fit for going to church. "No problem," replied Jack. "We can find clothes at the barracks that should fit you." At 5'6" Tom doubted that. Most of the Mounties were close to six feet or taller. But Jack found a man who was just two inches taller than Tom. The jacket was long, the trousers had to be rolled up at the ankles, and the shirt covered Tom almost to his knees, ballooning around him like an air-filled tent. The shoes were very tight. All kitted out, Tom deserved the good-natured grin that Jack gave him. But Jack gave him no choice. He figured that a man who was going to leave in the morning to row a boat across the ocean "bloody well ought to pray."

And in church, Tom, the apostate, did pray. It was a prayer for God to let him get on his way.

◆

"Let go the mooring lines," Tom finally was able to shout at 8:45 A.M., a little louder than he intended. Tom, inside *Silver*, was more than ready to leave, to take on the monumental challenge he had chosen for himself.

A dozen strokes of his oars through the harbor, McClean looked around for the last time.

"There were a few sad eyes amongst that crowd." Tom recalls. But he noted even more the grave worry etched on their faces, very concerned for his fate. "I'll never forget all those watching faces as I rowed out for the open sea. No question that many of them thought they were watching the departure of a man who would never see land again." Many of them also thought that the man leaving in that boat was "completely mad."

Shrugging off the shivers, Tom told himself: "Well, we'll just have to wait and see. One thing for sure: I'll find out before they do."

2

Blow Me East

McClean headed for the narrows—the immediate exit from St. John's Harbour to the Atlantic Ocean. On each side of the tight channel, heavy dark cliffs lowered themselves to sea level and became a huge jumble of jagged rocks. Around them the water foamed and swirled, breaking each striking wave into angry clouds of white spray before dividing and skittering back, as if trying to rejoin the receding swell.

Newfoundland had miles of coastline like this. Tom had been warned about it. Old fishermen who had risked their lives for years around these shores had cautioned him about what they called "the draw of the land"—an all-compelling force that tried to drag you back, to dash you in savage triumph on those treacherous rocks.

Still with Tom was a small flotilla, about eight in all, of fishing launches, which kept company with him into the open sea. Some boats were carrying reporters and TV cameras. Others were carrying the plainly curious. Except for the sound of the chugging engines of their boats, they too were silent. To Tom, they all "looked so bloody gloomy." He stopped rowing just long enough to give the nearest boat a wave and yell: "Cheer up, you're not going all the way like I am!"

A raised hand or two in response was the only answer. Not until months later did Tom discover that his rowing style was the cause of the gloom:

"He's digging his oars too deep."

"His hands are too close together."

"Holy cow—he won't clear land by next weekend, not rowing like that!"

Tom was only too glad he did not hear all the muttered comments. He didn't need anyone telling him that he was a raw novice when it came to handling boats: "I had long ago made up my mind that what I didn't know I would just have to learn, on the spot, when it counted most. Believe me, the will to survive is a powerful tutor. In any case, I would rather have sunk like a stone, there and then, than ever think of turning back."

Then he was through the narrows and in the open sea at last.

Silver was grabbed by a huge twisting swell. She slewed and rolled in uncontrollable, ponderous, lurching movements like a bucking bronco trying to unseat its rider in slow motion. Each gunwale dipped in laborious, seemingly never-ending arcs as she heeled from side to side. Tom was pulling with all his strength with both oars in the water but making no headway at all. *Silver* seemed to stop dead as the incoming swell tipped her bows skyward and tried to slide her backward into the bottom of the trough from which she had just climbed.

Within seconds the next swell swung the dory around almost broadside on to the incoming water, leaving Tom with the impression of trying to row along the side of a hill with one oar jammed in the ground, the other waving aimlessly in the air. Tom was "somewhat stunned" that he didn't seem to be getting much help from the outgoing tide. He had left St. John's on the turn of the tide, intent on dragging every ounce of advantage from it to get beyond the rocky coastline. Instead, he felt as if he was fighting an incoming tide all the way: "It seemed a hell of a way to start my grand adventure. I felt quite a clown."

Sweat poured off him as he wrestled to keep *Silver* on as even a course as possible. Before starting he had donned a thick woolen shirt, two sweaters, jeans, and a suit of oilskins. Although the sun was bright in a cloudless sky, the temperature at St. John's had only been 43°F, 11 degrees above freezing. Now he was dripping.

Each lurching movement of his boat had his body, from the haunches up, twisting from side to side and backward and forward in a continuous pendulum movement, while the muscles in his legs became rock hard with tension as he braced them against the floorboards.

Just three-quarters of an hour out and already one of Tom's pet schemes to provide himself with a spot of comfort was crumbling. Before leaving he had combed the shops at St. John's to find a wedge-shaped plastic cushion to lash to his thwart.* Now he knew it was no good: "It had me sitting too high, leaving me with the sensation that I was squatting above the level of the gunwales with a bird's-eye view of the water." The real trouble, however, was that no matter how tightly it was lashed, there was still movement. *Silver* would roll one way, the cushion another, and his body yet another. It was no good. It would have to go. "I would just have to squat on hard wood all the way."

Tom stopped rowing long enough to lash the cushion, throw it into his little shelter, and strip down to shirt and jeans. He told *Silver*: "Now let's get down to it!" Gradually, things began to go right. The wind, which had been northwest when he set out, swung around to the west, letting him get used to his boat's movement: "At last I felt as if I belonged to her, and she to me. I actually felt we were moving as one. Slow . . . but moving in the right direction. East."

Eight or 10 miles out, the accompanying boats began turning back to St. John's. One by one they circled Tom and their occupants shouted "Good luck!" and headed for home. The paratrooper–turned–ocean rower watched as they rolled off in the swell. Sliding into trough after trough of the sea, they disappeared from sight until the next swell carried them into view again like some wild conjuring trick. As they bobbed up and down, Tom realized that he must be presenting exactly the same picture to them.

In a short time, there was only one boat left, a man alone in his launch. Tom saw that it was Bob Ivery, a St. John's carpenter who had kindly helped to put the final touches on *Silver*'s woodwork before putting her into the

---

*   *Thwart* is the nautical term for the transverse seat across a boat stretching from gunwale to gunwale.

water. Ivery waved, then he, too, turned for harbor. It was a full five minutes before Tom realized he had stopped rowing to watch Bob motor away. Tom shook himself and got on with what he was out there to do. Row.

Alone at last? Not quite. About half an hour later a frigate of the Royal Canadian Navy steamed past Tom about 100 yards off his port side. They clearly knew what Tom was doing there: "The lads lined the rails to wave and the wind carried the tail end of their shouts to me, but I could not make out what they were saying." Then, with a breezy *toot-toot-toot* of her siren, the ship headed north on what Tom supposed was ice patrol.

He rowed until four o'clock in the afternoon. He could still see what he thought was the outline of land, but he figured he was far enough now to be reasonably safe from coastal hazards. He poured tea from the flask Jean Squires had given him and munched steadily through the great pile of sandwiches she had made: "I was happy to find that my appetite had not been affected in any way at all. I had thought I might be sick. But luckily there had not been the slightest sign of queasiness."

Sipping the tea, he stared out at the fading daylight and took stock of the situation. The sea was getting rougher. *Silver* was beginning to be thrown about a bit, and the temperature had dropped to 40°F. The wind had swung around yet again and was driving the dory south. Tom decided the best thing to do was put out the sea anchor and get his head down.*

---

* A sea anchor is a device whose principle is to stabilize a boat and limit its progress through the water. It's not actually an anchor; it is more of a drogue or drag device. Rather than tethering a boat to a seabed (which is impossible for a small boat at typical ocean depth), the sea anchor provides a bridling system, providing drag, thereby acting as a brake. The sea anchor (sometimes called a para-anchor) can be used for various good purposes: it can prevent a vessel from turning broadside to the waves and being overwhelmed by them; it can help to stop a boat; it can stop a boat from turning into an unstable position; it can help a boat ride out a storm; it can help control drift; it can stabilize a boat for repair work and pumping-out operations; it can give the boatman (especially needed if he is a rower) a time-out, the chance to get some rest; and it can help a boat make a safer landfall. Modern sea anchors are usually made of synthetic fiber or cloth, shaped like a cone or small parachute and rigged so that the wider end of the anchor leads while its narrower end trails. When deployed, the sea anchor floats just under the surface, and the water moving past the sea anchor keeps it filled.

It was five o'clock in the morning before Tom opened his eyes again. He was sick: "I thought it would overtake me, but I didn't know whether it was seasickness or just a result of the built-up excitement of the last couple of days." He draped himself over *Silver*'s side and hung there until he felt empty. Finally managing to lift his head, he stared across the sea through streaming wet eyes. Something seemed to be missing. At first he couldn't understand what it was. Then light dawned. The land was completely out of sight.

His bout of sickness was only the beginning of the alarming initiation ceremony to the discomforts of the Atlantic. A slight pricking feeling spread across the palms of his hands. As the hours passed, each stroke of the oar seared into his hands as if the skin was wearing paper thin. Then the blisters began to balloon. There were three on the palm of each hand. He could feel them growing larger as he rowed. By midday they were so swollen that the handles of the oars felt as if they had doubled in thickness. Tom could hardly clasp his fingers round them.

Some drastic first-aid treatment was called for: "I bit through each blister in turn, carefully nicking a hole as near the middle as possible, with the corners of my eye teeth, then squeezed out as much water as I could. Then I plunged my hands in and out of a bucket of water several times to try to pickle the dead skin into some state of firmness in order to protect the patches of raw flesh underneath." His hands stung like the blazes, but at least the oars felt normal size once more.

◆

Monday morning, May 19. Tom woke just after dawn to below-freezing temperatures and *Silver* covered from stem to stern with a layer of thick frost. He sat up with the sleeping bag tucked tightly under his chin and, pulling aside the canvas front of his little shelter, looked around *Silver* as she glistened in the dull morning light. In Tom's recollection, "It was like sitting in the middle of a birthday cake."

Enveloped in a slight fog, Tom wondered where he could be. He had not yet bothered to fix a position and decided to let it slide for another day or two. His compass told him he was heading east, and that was all that mattered for the moment.

He sat for quite a while with *Silver* rocking gently in a 10 MPH breeze. In the distance to the north, he spotted a couple of whales, but either they did not see him or considered him and his little boat unworthy of their attention, for they kept going on their chosen course until they vanished from sight.

It was a lonely day, the first of many. Tom saw no ships, no birds, no planes. There was, however, a brush with domesticity that was quite out of touch with Tom's ocean adventure: a child's plastic potty came drifting past, bright yellow. He watched it as it bobbed away into the distance and pondered that, out in the middle of the Atlantic, the big event of the day can very well be seeing some totally unexpected, incongruous, and otherwise everyday object. As he rowed he kept thinking about that yellow potty. Where could it have come from? How old was the child? A boy or a girl? What sort of home was he or she growing up in? They were natural questions for a person to ask who had grown up an orphan.

There was little time for reverie. The strongest winds he had yet experienced had been building up through the night. The wind whipped through the locking holes in the telescopic radio, its aerial whistling like a demented steam kettle. The most Tom managed was an extremely erratic session of catnaps. For the first time *Silver* was being really knocked about. The sea thudded into her, shaking her so much that the vibrations didn't have time to fade away before the next lot of water attacked. She spun, bounced, and rocked. Waves broke over her every 15 to 20 minutes. Huge waves, each one loading flimsy little *Silver* with somewhere near 40 gallons of water.

That night was a living nightmare. It was pitch-black, relieved occasionally only by the slight illumination afforded by the swirling phosphorus shining a ghostlike green on the water. That was the only means Tom had of visually checking the level of water inside the dory and deciding when to pump. He completely lost count of the number of times he crawled out of his shelter to go to work on those pumps. Finally, he just kneeled on his bundled-up sleeping bag in the shelter entrance holding the pump handles and ready to pump at a moment's notice. Never did a night seem so long. Tom now propped himself up, his chest heaving with the effort of pumping. The blood tingled as it raced through his arms. His overheated body felt as if it was steaming against the bitter night air.

Hours later, or so it seemed, a faint moody gray light appeared around Tom. It came from the walls of ocean waves, topped with white fury, racing toward him and becoming visible against the sky. Not until dawn arrived was Tom able to see exactly what was happening. It was a toss-up whether or not he would welcome a freak of nature that could plunge him back beneath the cover of the ink-black night. This was his first taste of what he came to know as "the Atlantic's favorite sport": playing squash with the smallest boat it could find.

Tom had been a physical person all his life, relying mainly on his strength and willpower to cope with whatever situation came his way. But this was something he had no experience with. Never had he felt quite so utterly helpless. *Silver* was in the grip of winds of at least 50 MPH, and Tom said there was "absolutely nothing I could do . . . except pump for my life." Rolling toward him, under him, over him, and past him were 40-foot-high waves, a never-ending avalanche of water. Awesome, unnerving, terrifying . . . it was all that and more. Yet the strongest feeling Tom had was that of being hypnotized by this fantastic show of nature's power.

"I wasn't exactly frightened," Tom relates, "but I reckon I would have become well and truly scared if I had sat there too long just looking at the sea. The extraordinary thing was the difficulty I had in forcing myself not to look." Those heaving, rushing waters dragged at his eyes like a magnet.

Foolishly, he decided that if he tried rowing for a bit his mind would be too fully occupied to worry about the sea, and he would find welcome relief in the pure physical effort. For nearly an hour he pushed himself in this futile and frantically unequal contest of man against the sea. Twice, probably the only times the oars really entered the water, Tom was "within an ace" of having the oars snatched from his grasp. He became obsessed with the idea that to lose one oar would be a disgrace, but to lose both . . . that would "stamp him as an idiot" even though *Silver* carried two extra pair. He shipped the oars (that was, placed them in their rowlocks) and lashed them down as tightly as he could. "I imagine a more experienced seafarer would never have bothered in the first place," concedes Tom. "He would wisely have conserved his energy rather than expend it in such a useless manner."

For the first time Tom began to realize what was meant by the term *seamanship*. Yet, he wondered, what more could the best sailor in the world have done? The answer would surely be nothing more than wedge himself in the bottom of *Silver*, wait, and hope for the best. He was beginning to learn.

Silver was now running before the wind. She was fairly zipping along and, with a following wind, was not taking nearly so much water inboard. But it was a wind from the north, driving Tom hard to the south and far off his eastward course. He cursed the unfriendly wind. "If you have to blow, blow me east!" he yelled into the storm as he watched his compass needle quivering relentlessly toward the south.

He bitterly resented every yard that was off his eastward course. For every yard would have to be regained, fought for, and bought back. And the price he would have to pay would be time, invaluable time. Every yard was a knife thrust to his ambition to be the first person to row the Atlantic single-handed.

Every yard was a bonus to John Fairfax, somewhere far to the south of him.

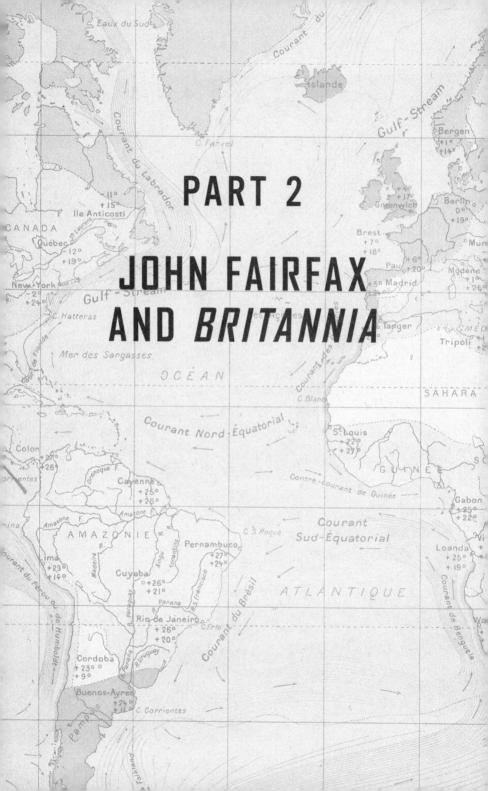

PART 2

JOHN FAIRFAX
AND *BRITANNIA*

3

Betting on the Trades

B y the time Tom McClean and his *Silver* left St. John's Harbour on May 17, 1969, and entered the open sea, John Fairfax in *Britannia* had already been in the Atlantic for 117 days. One would think that, in terms of there being any sort of race between McClean and Fairfax to cross the Atlantic first, Fairfax would be the hands-down winner. After all, McClean estimated that it could take him 100 days to row the North Atlantic from Newfoundland to the British Isles, meaning an arrival in late August. At the very best, he felt he might make landfall in Ireland in 70 days, resulting in an arrival in late July.

But crossing the ocean, any ocean, was a very chancy thing. Without warning or apparent cause, any one of thousands of things could go wrong—with the boat, with the rower, with the weather, with the winds, with the current, with the supplies—and likely *would* go wrong, individually or in cursed combination, multiple times, no matter what sort of vessel and how well designed, let alone a rowboat. There was absolutely no certainty that Fairfax would make it across the Atlantic successfully—or that McClean himself would manage it—no matter how willful and determined each man was.

Plus, Fairfax had a long way to go, much farther than McClean.

Originally, Fairfax had planned to row from Newfoundland to England. That was his intention in April 1968, when he first got truly serious about making the voyage. Given all the preparations that would need to be made, the timetable was very strict. The latest he could start and then have three months of fairly steady westerly winds was June. After that, according to the *Atlas of Pilot Charts*, the winds would become more and more variable, increasingly coming from the east and northeast. "To start from scratch and be ready in three months' time," Fairfax came to understand, "was a forlorn hope." But waiting a whole year until June 1969 was for him "an unbearable thought."

Fairfax committed to an alternative plan. Instead of crossing the Atlantic from west to east, thereby taking the shortest route possible involving a launch from Newfoundland, he would row east to west, from the Canary Islands to Florida. It was a much longer route, nearly 4,000 miles as the crow flies—and likely a few hundred miles more than that in actual navigation. That was twice as far as Newfoundland to the British Isles, which was roughly 2,000 miles. Once committed to the alternative, John took delight in how the new scheme double-dared him: "The disadvantage was obvious, but so was the challenge. After all, nobody had ever tried to row that way, and I could become not only the first person to row the Atlantic single-handed, but the first to do it from east to west."

His alternative routing actually made a great deal of sense. First and foremost, he could make his departure from the Canary Islands the coming January—in the middle of winter—rather than waiting six more months. The island of Grand Canary, located in the archipelago 93 miles off the northwest coast of Africa, enjoyed mild winter weather—in January, a mean temperature of 64.2°F, with 184 days of mostly sunshine, and a mere inch of monthly rainfall. Grand Canary also had some great resorts, with long beaches, dunes of white sand, and great Spanish food. Always a fan of the good life, John liked the idea of spending a few days at a comfortable resort relaxing and sunbathing with his girlfriend prior to starting his trip.* Besides, the island's capital city, Las Palmas, as well as being famous for its annual *carnaval*, had been the first stop of Christopher Columbus's expedition on his way back from the Americas in 1492. John liked the symmetry of that: Christopher Columbus and John Fairfax in the same sentence.

It was not just that the jumping-off point would have nice weather. So would the route of the entire trip—at least in theory.

Traveling at latitudes that were generally 25 to 35 degrees to the south of the Newfoundland route, Fairfax could rightfully expect his weather and sea surface temperatures to be considerably warmer. Although ocean temperature is affected by a number of factors (including air masses in the atmosphere, winds, currents, and depth of the water), latitude is the primary factor, with the temperature of the surface water gradually decreasing from the equator toward the pole at a rate of 0.5°F per degree of latitude. A 35-degree difference in latitude between Fairfax's Canary Island route and the Newfoundland route could thus be expected to produce a difference in water temperature of 17 to 18 degrees. In terms of latitude, Miami was 100 miles south of Grand Canary, so John would not be taking *Britannia* northward, except for some possible navigational adjustments. In the month of January, the difference between John's southern route and the Newfoundland route—in terms of surface water temperature—could be as much as 30 degrees. No frosty seas or icebergs for him. The difference in air temperature would be even greater. All considered, crossing the Atlantic from the Canaries should make the experience significantly more pleasant for the rower and a great deal more accommodating for the boat, all the equipment and supplies, and everything else involved—*should* being the operative word.

---

* Fairfax's girlfriend was 21-year-old Sylvia Cook (born 1947). Much more will be written about her later in this chapter and throughout the book, as she plays a major role in Fairfax's story.

An ostensibly even greater advantage of the southerly routing was the way it would take advantage of the trade winds, or trades. The trades had been the driving force for sailing across the Atlantic ever since the Portuguese and Spanish began plying the ocean in the 15th century. Put simply, Earth's rotation causes air to slant toward the equator in a southwesterly direction in the northern hemisphere and in a northwesterly direction in the southern hemisphere. Expressed conversely, this Coriolis effect, in combination with zones of high pressure, causes the trade winds to blow mainly from the northeast in the northern hemisphere and from the southeast in the southern hemisphere.* (The trade winds prevail only in a zone from about 30 degrees north to about 30 degrees south of the equator. Get outside of that 60-degree belt of latitude—sometimes called the horse latitudes—and the trade winds vanish.)

Known to sailors around the world, the trade winds and associated ocean currents have helped ships sail from European and African ports to the Americas for over 500 years. (Likewise, the trades have hastened ocean voyages from the Americas toward Asia.) By starting his crossing on Grand Canary Island and heading west, Fairfax's plan was to get as quickly as possible into the prevailing westward-driving action of the Atlantic trade winds. For *Britannia*, that would mean being carried along nicely, most of the time, with the breeze; for Fairfax, it meant he shouldn't be undergoing the torture of rowing against strong headwinds—*shouldn't* this time being the operative word.

Unfortunately, the operational dynamics of the world's winds are not that simple or reliable, and certainly not always predictable—not even the trades. In the ocean route westward that Fairfax proposed to make from the Canary Islands, he might easily encounter cold fronts, squalls, storms, and the effects of such nebulous phenomena as wind shadows

---

*   The rotation of Earth deflects the atmosphere, resulting in curved wind paths. This deflection, called the Coriolis effect, sets up the complex global wind patterns that drive surface ocean currents. It is named after the French mathematician Gaspard-Gustave de Coriolis (1792–1843), who studied waterwheels to understand the transfer of energy in rotating systems.

and acceleration zones, which extend a long way from the Canaries and can foul up the considered plans of even the best prepared mariner.* Not even professional meteorologists understood these phenomena very well. Fairfax himself was completely unaware of them when he launched his rowboat into the Atlantic from Grand Canary on January 20, 1969.

In addition, his rowboat, *Britannia*, was a Fairfax advantage. Designed by renowned naval architect Uffa Fox, England's leading—and at age 69, most experienced—designer of small boats (and Prince Philip's yachting companion), *Britannia* was a superior vessel, absolutely the best rowboat money could buy.† It incorporated a number of advanced features.

---

*   Leaving the Canary Islands, the wind blowing from the northeast is not always as stable in force and in direction as many sailors believe. There are mountains on the Canary Islands that reach as high as 3,700 meters (over 12,000 feet); the snow-covered peak of the Teide volcano on the island of Tenerife stands 3,718 meters (12,198 feet) high. The wind has to "bypass" these great heights, either by passing above or around the sides of the islands. Such a flow of air mass creates disturbances that modern meteorologists can spot quite well on pictures from satellites. The disturbances can include "wind shadows" of light yet contrary winds as well as "acceleration zones" between the islands. Today's yachtsmen and skippers try to pass a long way from the Canaries to avoid these big wind shadows, which are followed by strong accelerations. Much has been learned about such "anomalies" since 1969; certainly, John Fairfax was completely unaware of them when he launched his crossing from Las Palmas in January of that year.

†   Before Uffa Fox was recommended to him, Fairfax had never heard of him, an indication of how unconnected John was to British seamanship generally when, in late 1966, he first started contemplating his solo trip across the Atlantic. Fox was suggested to Fairfax by the London correspondent of an Argentine daily paper, George Marin. (As we shall see in a later chapter, though born of an English father and a Bulgarian mother, Fairfax was born in Rome, Italy, and grew up in Buenos Aires, Argentina.) Following up on Marin's advice, Fairfax sought Fox out at the London Boat Show held annually at Earls Court Exhibition Centre in Kensington. Fairfax recalled that first meeting: "As was to be expected, (Fox) was dispensing advice to a crowd of boat lovers on one of the technical stands. I wanted to talk to him alone so hung about for a while, summing him up. . . . To beat around the bush with a man like Uffa would have been a serious mistake; so the moment he was left alone, I introduced myself and told him straight-away that I had the intention of attempting to become the first man to row the Atlantic single-handed, had come far to do it, had no money and no boat, and would he help? How I went about it I cannot remember, but I do remember the general feeling of dry emptiness, with the tingling of cold sweat somewhere along my

Notably, the boat was self-righting, a major attribute that Fox adapted from his earlier pioneering design of a self-righting lifeboat. Indeed, during sea trials, *Britannia* proved that if capsized, she could right herself in two seconds. The boat was also self-bailing. If swamped, she was dry in 30 seconds, the water sluicing down self-bailing slots "almost as fast as the eye could follow." She was also highly stable: two men could stand on her gunwale and *Britannia* would only tilt a few inches. In turn, the boat was extremely durable. Rather than being constructed from simple oak planking, *Britannia* was made of a molded marine-grade double-diagonal mahogany, which was also resistant to rot and mold. Too, she featured a protective covering for the pilot and for storage of equipment and supplies. At a length of 24 feet, she was relatively commodious (McClean's boat was 20 feet long). Furthermore, Fox replaced the traditional fixed seat with a sliding seat (a feature now common to all modern ocean rowing boats), which allowed the rower to work more efficiently.

In its glistening coat of fluorescent orange paint, *Britannia* was a strikingly beautiful boat, an elegant combination of form and function.

---

back, as I finished and braced myself for the inevitable question I knew would come, why did I want to do it? A question I would not, could not, answer. Not then or there. With a tinge of scorn which set my blood on fire, he asked, 'Row the Atlantic single-handed, eh? And what on earth makes you think you can do it, my boy?' Gripping the edge of the table so hard it hurt, I leaned forward and told him, 'Mr. Fox, I don't need the earth to tell me what I can do. I know.' He frowned, and for a second or two, as he stared at me without batting an eyelid, a glimmer of ice replaced the naughty sparkle in his eyes, and I had a glimpse, behind the benevolent façade, of the steel the man was made of. A second or two and the flicker of mischievous amusement reappeared, with a huge smile and a sea of wrinkles in the weather-beaten face. He slammed his fist on the table and said, 'Right! I know exactly what kind of boat you will need, and I will design her for you'" (Fairfax, *Britannia*, 24). It took a few months, but Fox kept his promise, sending him a long letter dated March 20, 1967, describing the design of what became *Britannia*, including detailed blueprints and a sketch of what the boat would look like. It took even longer for Fairfax to arrange for Fox to be paid for his design and for the boat to be built (by Wilf Souter of Cowes, England) and paid for. Ultimately, payment for both was provided by a banknote from one of the major sponsors for Fairfax's expedition, Yorkshire businessman Martin Cowling.

Although his feelings about the boat would grow ambivalent after encountering difficulties while crossing the ocean, Fairfax initially found *Britannia* easy to handle and a pleasure to row. Before leaving from Grand Canary he told reporters, "I could take such a boat to hell and back without either of us being the worse for it."

In preparing for his expedition Fairfax benefited from the help of other experts. One of them was Archie de Jong, a "developmental physicist," i.e., nutrition expert, at Horlicks, a long-established British manufacturer of various powdered and dehydrated foods, ranging from its flagship malted milk to instant noodles, confectionery, and breakfast cereal. With Horlicks, Archie de Jong had provisioned a number of polar and desert expeditions and most recently had helped supply food for the tragic attempt by London journalists David Johnstone and John Hoare in the summer of 1966 to row the Atlantic. Fairfax was not without his superstitions and Horlicks's involvement with the Johnstone and Hoare disaster was nearly enough for John to reject their food, but being offered a plentiful supply of it free of charge (in return for the publicity) changed his mind.

De Jong calculated that Fairfax would need 3,600 calories a day to stay fit. Horlicks packaged the rations in 100 individually sealed plastic bags, each weighing 2.5 pounds, for a total of 250 pounds. One package contained a day's full ration: a hot breakfast, a cold snack, and a hot main meal. The food required little preparation, and all of it, in an emergency, could be eaten uncooked.* Supposedly, this supplied a balanced diet while

---

*   Each one-day pack of Horlicks food contained: one 2.5-ounce vacuum-packed block of oatmeal, one 2.81-ounce tin of Holsteiner meat paste (or Spam paste), one 2-ounce vacuum pack of cheese, two 2-ounce envelopes of Materne fruit bars, two 0.75-ounce envelopes of Enerzade glucose tablets, one 0.75-ounce packet of Horlicks tablets, one 2.5-ounce vacuum-packed meat/vegetable bar (three varieties: beef, mutton, and steak and kidney), one 2-ounce envelope of potato powder or rice (45 packs contained potato powder and 45 contained rice), one 0.5-ounce polyethylene bag of salt, two 3-ounce vacuum packs of biscuits, two tea bags, one 1-ounce envelope of instant skim milk powder, one 2-ounce envelope of glucose/lemon drink powder, one 1.25-ounce envelope of Horlicks chocolate powder, two envelopes of instant coffee, and six cubes of sugar.

being tasty enough. The total weight of the rations was relatively light, and it would all be easy to cook and to stow.

But, if Fairfax at times during his voyage became a bit ambivalent about his boat, he would grow downright bad-tempered about the Horlicks food. It meant eating exactly the same things, day in and day out, for 100 days. By the second week of his voyage, John grasped what he called "the appalling implications" of this sameness. Archie de Jong had warned John that he would "probably hate his guts" long before the trip was over—and, although he did not come to hate Archie, he quickly learned to detest his food.

◆

John Fairfax had hoped that, by his 117th day at sea, he and *Britannia* would be well past the 70° line of west longitude, breezing past the islands of Turks and Caicos and quickly approaching the Bahamas. From there the distance to Miami would be only 500 to 600 miles. At a rate of 40 miles per day, he could make Florida in two weeks or less. That would put him safely on land by June 1, the official start to the Atlantic and Caribbean hurricane season. It had always been Fairfax's plan to beat any possibility of getting caught in one of the early summer's violent tropical storms.

But Fairfax was nowhere close to the West Indies, let alone the Bahamas. Nor was he anywhere close to being past 70° west longitude. His position on May 17—the day that Tom McClean, unknown to John, started his Atlantic trek from St. John's—was 22°54'N and 54°46'W. Those coordinates meant that *Britannia* was still over 1,500 miles from Miami, three times farther than he wanted to be.

What had happened to slow down Fairfax?

His voyage had started smoothly enough. Taking the advice of local fishermen, he had arranged for *Britannia* to be towed down from Las Palmas, on the north side of Grand Canary, some 35 miles to the beachside village of San Agustín on the southeast coast. Leaving from San Agustín with the benefit of a light southwesterly breeze behind her,

Britannia, even plodding along at a two-knot pace, managed to round the Maspalomas lighthouse at the southern tip of the island within a few hours. So content was Fairfax with the comfortable start to his journey that, in the hot sun of the early afternoon, he decided to have "a little rest." A "kind soul" had dropped a long-necked bottle of beer on deck just as he pushed off from San Agustín; it was a bottle of Tropical Premium, the beer of choice on Grand Canary, brewed in Las Palmas, and noted for its amber color and taste of butterscotch and malt. "To be on our own at last," thought John, "called for a celebration." He drank his fill of the tasty beer and "let *Britannia* have the dregs." For the next few hours, John took a siesta, simply letting the boat drift. By late afternoon they had skimmed along enough, with little rowing, to clear the island.

As sunset approached, the wind increased to Force 3 and then to Force 4, still coming from the southwest but accelerating to between 8 and 17 miles per hour; according to the Beaufort scale, that range indicated "a moderate breeze."* With small waves starting to crest and break as whitecaps (known to sailors as "white horses"), John decided to shift *Britannia* onto a northwesterly course, thereby keeping the waves more or less abeam—that was, at a right angle to the fore-to-aft line of his boat. "It was the best of a bad choice," John wrote in his log. It was John's first awareness of just how "grossly overloaded" his boat was, weighing, as it did at the start of the trip, over 2,000 pounds.

But to get into the trade winds, John couldn't let *Britannia* wander too far north; he needed to make her run on a southerly course. As the wind increased in force and started to move on her bows, *Britannia* did not adjust well to the new course. In his log John described this as "our first clash of wills," with the boat's will mostly winning: "Bending to the oars with all I had, sweating, cursing, changing the position of the dagger board, trailing a warp, pulling on the port oar alone—try as I might, I

---

*   Created by British Admiral Sir Francis Beaufort (1774–1857) in 1805, the Beaufort scale was one of the first scales to estimate wind speeds and their effects. Beaufort developed the scale to help sailors estimate the winds via visual observations. The scale starts with 0 and goes to a force of 12. The Beaufort scale is still used today to estimate wind strengths.

could not make her change her mind. Eventually, so drained out I could not even spit, I had to surrender. *Britannia* insisted that if she was going to head anywhere, it would be either southeast or northwest. She loved being broadside to the weather."*

John's main concern was getting as far away from the Canaries as possible. If the boat drifted to the northwest, there were other islands out there: Tenerife, La Gomera, El Hierro, and La Palma. The last thing he wanted was to crash in the middle of the night into a rocky shoreline. So very slow had *Britannia*'s progress been during its first day on the sea that John, looking over his shoulder, could still see the dark, rugged silhouette of Grand Canary on the rear horizon. He guessed that *Britannia* was no more than 15 miles from piling up on its cliffs. If the wind somehow switched to a westerly, that would become a real threat.

Highly frustrated, Fairfax wondered, "How on earth have I got myself into this mess?" Already he was aching, tired, and fed up. Uffa Fox's design of the rowboat was undeniably excellent. Ocean water was shipping into her by the bucketful, but *Britannia*'s ingenious self-draining system was working to perfection. That didn't stop John from getting wet, however, nor did it make it any easier for him to row through the choppy backs of five- and six-foot waves. By the second day of the voyage, John was already thinking he might be better off dumping overboard at least a third of his stores, lightening the boat's weight, and rely more on catching fish for food. If *Britannia* wasn't so damn heavy, he would have a better chance going in the direction that he wanted: west. Also, as quickly as possible he wanted to get out of the shipping lane that ran along the African coast. *Britannia* had no navigation lights. All John had to show himself to approaching ships was the glow of a rather powerful

---

*   A daggerboard (or centerboard) is a small removeable board that can be lowered into the water (usually through a trunk) to serve as a keel. Its purpose is to balance the force of the wind on the sails. With a daggerboard, *Britannia* had a better chance to "sail" upwind and avoid simply being blown sideways. "Trailing a warp" refers to dragging a rope or line (a warp) off the stern. It is a technique that can be helpful in holding the stern into the wind or turning the boat.

flashlight he had brought aboard for that purpose—but with a limited number of batteries.

To obviate the chances of getting hit—most likely, fatally—by a ship, Fairfax settled on staying awake and rowing almost nonstop throughout the night and sleeping during the day. A change of the wind to a northeasterly on day 3 made his rowing much easier. On his fifth day (January 25), however, he strained a muscle in his back: "At first I thought nothing of it, but gradually the pain increased, finally becoming so agonizing that I could not row any longer." As the wind remained favorable, John just let the boat drift to the southwest. He crawled into what he initially called his "cubbyhole"—and would later refer to his "rathole"—under the boat's seven-foot-long inflated rubber self-righting chamber. Curling up in that space, he "allowed himself the luxury of 8 hours' undisturbed rest."

As challenging as the opening leg of his ocean crossing had proven to be, it was about to get nastier. The weather became colder, tightening John's aching back muscles to the point where he could hardly move. Worse, the wind had not only intensified; it had changed direction. It was now blowing from the southeast at speeds from 13 to 24 miles per hour (Force 4–5). He had no choice but to row. Forcing himself to stay on the oars for 5 to 10 minutes at a time, alternately biting on a piece of wood and screaming his head off into the wind, John did what he could to wrestle *Britannia* as westward as he could. His only success, truly, was aggravating his muscle pain into "a hot burning" deep in his back. Through his off-and-on schedule, John managed that day a grand total of two hours on the oars.

It was not until his ninth day at sea, Wednesday, January 29, that his back felt noticeably better. But his mood could not have been blacker, for his position was 26°17'N, 17°30'W. That meant that *Britannia*, since leaving Grand Canary, had traversed only 143 miles, an average of less than 16 miles per day. "Bugger all!! Most disappointing," Fairfax noted in his log. "True, I have not been able to row properly for the last few days and the wind is blowing from the wrong direction, but still hard to take. I must try to do 40 miles per day at all cost." The situation was so bad that John felt he had to deploy his drogue sea anchor just to prevent being blown back to Africa—an awful irony made worse by the fact that an airplane from the Spanish Coast Guard practicing "search and find" exercises made a few low passes over *Britannia* to see if it was in need of emergency help.

The next day things deteriorated. It had not been propitious for Fairfax when the wind was coming from the southeast, pushing him farther north than he wanted to go. But then, on day 10 (January 30), the wind stopped almost completely. In his log John noted: "This is bad. If the wind doesn't blow from the northeast, I will spend a lot of time around here." "Around here" was still in the vicinity of the westernmost Canaries—specifically only 20 miles to the southwest of the island of El Hierro. "Because of clouded horizon," John logged, "cannot see any sign of it, but if my fix is correct, should be there. I have promised myself not to be angry at the sea. Nobody asked me to come, and the sea is doing what it always has done; too bad if I don't like it. It will probably take me four months to reach Florida," but "I intend to win this battle, and the only way to do it is to arm myself with patience. I feel tired, a little depressed, but otherwise O.K."

By the evening he got his wish for a change in the wind. Unfortunately, it wasn't a trade wind. Just the opposite. It was a Force 5 wind that sprang directly from the west, conjuring waves of four to eight feet. It was the sort of wind that would definitely be pushing *Britannia* back toward Africa if it kept blowing—and there was little Fairfax could do about it. "Impossible to continue," John wrote that night. "Have to."

Wind from the west, so contrary to the trades, continued not for one or two days but for 14 days straight—two full weeks. Most days the breeze stayed at Force 4–5. John's log entries showed a growing sense of desperation:

January 31:   "Attempted to row, but impossible. Forced to lie to drogue all day. Two drogues. Sighted Hierro (the farthest south and west of the Canary Islands) in the afternoon. Could not do a thing all day."

February 1:   "Heavy swell and spray. Could not move. Situation bad.
                Have exhausted supplies for two weeks without getting
                anywhere; if the wind does not change, afraid I will not
                have enough stores to make it to Florida."

February 2:   "I am rowing like a slave only to keep more or less the
                same position, but gradually losing ground. It is just not
                possible for one man to row against winds Force 3, 4,
                and 5 without losing ground, as one must rest, and it is
                inevitable to drift back. This cannot go on forever, but
                it is very trying all the same."

February 3:   "Another day of the same. Too tired to write."

February 4:   "I will finish in Africa at this rate. Have not slept for
                two days. Absolutely dead. Rowed 10 hours."

February 5:   "Is this a joke? Where are the trades? I have had nothing
                but southwesterlies and westerlies since leaving San
                Agustín. I won't be able to fight against them very
                much longer. Every time I pull the oars now the boat
                seems to weigh 10 tons. I never thought one could get so
                tired—but as long as this wind blows, resting is out of
                the question."

February 6:   "Down to Force 2–3. Not so bad, at last. Still from the
                wrong way, but at least I can try to go south a bit."

February 7:   "Wind from the northwest, Force 2–3. Rowing south,
                but too tired to take full advantage of this change of
                wind. Come what may, tonight I intend to sleep at least
                8 hours at a stretch. There is a limit to what one can do,
                and I think I have reached mine."

February 8:   "Damn wind changed during the night to west, Force
                4–5, and drogue, naturally, fouled up. The gods know
                how much we have drifted!"

February 9:   "Winds from the northwest, but mainly west, Force 3–4.
                Heading south but drifting toward east. Progress very
                slow. Rowed 10 hours."

February 10:   "Fighting on. Position at noon 26°23'N, 16°00'W.
                  (On January 29, *Britannia*'s position was 26°17'N,
                  17°30'W, indicating that she was 143 miles from Grand
                  Canary Island. This new reading fixed her position only
                  97 miles from Grand Canary, meaning that, in 13 days
                  of rowing, she had lost 46 miles. Basically, she had done
                  a curlicue.) Am O.K. physically, but morale very low.
                  All this rowing to make an average of 5 miles per day,
                  and even this south instead of west, is very depressing.
                  However, the wind must change. I will try to go as far
                  south as 20 North Latitude and then hope for better
                  luck. At this rate it will take me a hell of a long time to
                  get there—but by the gods, I will do it. Rowed 10 hours."

February 11:   "Winds from northwest. Makes for awkward rowing and
                  is pushing us toward the African coast. Very bad day.
                  All the time at night we are afraid of being run down
                  by some ship."

Finally, blessedly, on Wednesday, February 12 (day 23), Fairfax
got a break. The wind shifted to the northeast. "Can't believe it!" John
exclaimed in his log. Better yet, it was also a Force 4 wind, which gave
Britannia quite a kick in the butt. As naturally changeable and vexatious
as he knew that wind, weather, and ocean could be, John gave in to a
superstitious feeling, recording in his log: "I just threw away a mirror I
had broken the day of my back injury, finally deciding it was a bad thing
to have it on board. One hour afterward, the wind came up from the
northeast. I must be getting superstitious in my old age. God damn it
all, let's row."

Row he did. For five days the winds came from the northeast and
the east—sometimes weak (Force 1, 2, and 3) but still very helpful. By
February 16, he had reached a position of 25°05'N, 16°45'W, which
meant he was at the same latitude as Florida though still was not back
to where he had been on January 29 due to the strong westerlies blowing
him back. His situation was enormously frustrating: "All these days,

nearly a month now, and I am still making no progress—just trying to get back to where I was nine days after leaving San Agustín! True, I am 120 miles south of that position; but I am aiming west. Not south, and this is very depressing."

For the first time during his trip, Fairfax began to feel a loneliness, which was a very unusual feeling for him. Even more fundamentally, he became atypically contemplative, questioning why he had ever decided to cross the ocean by himself in the first place: "What the hell am I doing here? Money? No, people don't do this sort of thing for money, certainly not me. There are far easier ways. Glory, then? Perhaps a bit of that. Or am I trying to prove something? To myself or others? Surely not to others. And to myself? What can I prove to myself that I don't know already? What, then? Maybe I will find the answer before the journey is finished. And maybe I won't. What does it matter?"

John was not a religious man, at least not in the conventional sense of the modern world. Although ostensibly raised in Italy and Argentina by his mother as a Roman Catholic, he was, if anything religious, a pagan in the Romantic sense of the word. It wasn't that he actively believed in the pantheons and rituals of ancient cultures or the personification of nature as full of divine life. But he did make frequent references to the gods of ancient Greco-Roman culture, took delight in sensual pleasures and material well-being, and regarded the human experience—at least *his* human experience—as essentially an existential—and potentially heroic—struggle against Nature with a capital *N*. In that regard, Fairfax saw himself very much as a Homeric figure, a modern Odysseus, a man of intellectual brilliance, guile, and versatility who was in a virtual contest with the gods and everything they could throw at him: storms, monsters, temptations, challenges, seductions, betrayals, hardships, deprivations, egotism, pride, and insolence.

His logbooks are full of epic neo-Homeric struggle, no more so than his entry on February 16: "There is not a single thing I regret, whatever the outcome. I am doing what I have always loved to do, being part of and fighting against Nature. That is what it is. I know She doesn't care, but look at the beauty of it all! Vast, cruel, indifferent to whether I am here or not, or anybody else for that matter, but who cares? I have accepted Her challenge, and in trying to beat Her in such a primitive way I am doing more than thousands, millions of men have done before me, and will go on doing. Fighting Nature at her rawest! Could there be a more beautiful thing?

"Whether I win or lose is beside the point. What matters is the struggle—uneven, yes, but well worth fighting for. Insignificant, little as I feel at the moment, I cannot but feel proud of myself, and if I end at the bottom of the sea, it won't make any difference. I shall give as much as I can take. The sea can certainly break, destroy me, if such is his whim, but bend my will, conquer me? Never! And if those are bold words, let them be so.

"I love you, Sea, and if I soon will be cursing you again, at least tonight we are at peace with each other. Let us enjoy it, and hell take tomorrow. After all, whether you care, or like it, or not, you are part of me, and I might soon become part of you."

4

Goddess Venus

I n his logbooks, as well as in his everyday parlance, Fairfax made extraordinarily frequent use of pagan expressions, such as "by Jove," "by Jupiter," "by all the gods," "from the gods," "ye gods," and "what in the name of a thousand gods." He also made numerous references to Neptune, Olympus, Hades, and other names and places derived from Greco-Roman mythology. John even dreamed in classical images. One night deep into his trip across the Atlantic, he dreamed he was fighting a "most terrifying hurricane." The battle between him and the violent storm, in his dream, went on for three days and nights. "I was definitely winning," he wrote in his log, "when the bitch, in despair, asked Juno (the goddess of marriage and love), who hates my guts, to help, and she went to Jupiter (Juno's husband) asking him a favor, without saying what, and the doddering old goat, to get rid of her, said yes.* She asked him to strike me down with his lightning—and having promised, he had no choice but to do so. Down came a bolt, and with, the end."

---

* The goddess Juno was the Roman equivalent of the Greek goddess Hera, wife of Zeus, who was the god of sky and thunder and king of all the gods on Mount Olympus. Jupiter, also known as Jove, was the Roman iteration of Zeus. The offspring of Jupiter and Juno were Mars, Vulcan, Bellona, and Juventas. Juno's siblings were Neptune, Pluto, Vesta, and Ceres. Of course, Jupiter, her husband, was also her brother.

The dream continued, but changed venue to Norse mythology: "The fallen hero was floating between sea and sky, and another battle, this one for my spoils, raged around me, and although I was dead, I could hear and see it all. No less than mermaids and Valkyries were fighting over me—the mermaids striving to take me down into the abyss, the Valkyries into Valhalla. I prayed for the Valkyries to win, and as I did so, Brünnhilde galloped by and, without stopping, snatched me away, and we went up into the clouds.* Although magnificent in her warlike beauty, she was ice to the touch, and I suddenly found myself screaming for my beloved, my goddess, my Venus, to come and take me away. Could she beat the formidable rival? Don't know how she managed, but suddenly I found myself in her arms, enveloped in the incredible softness of her body, and she took me to Olympus, where all the gods had gathered to hail and greet me. And we sipped nectar and the nymphs danced and sang for us, and then we made love, and I wished I could happily stay dead forever after."

A spray of cold water coming over *Britannia*'s bow splashed in Fairfax's face, awakening him. Looking up, he saw a flash of lightning, in which he swore he could see Juno's face contorted in a wicked grin. Noticing the aerial for his Marconi radio pointing like a dark finger to the sky, he worried, just coming out of his dream, that Jupiter might be tempted to throw a lightning bolt right at it. "So, I got it down as fast as I could and, cringing like a little mouse, hid myself in my hole."

---

*   In the Norse tradition, Brünnhilde (or Brunhild) was a "shieldmaiden" or Valkyrie, a powerful warrior-cum-angel who chooses who dies in battle and who lives, and then takes the chosen dead to Valhalla, the afterlife hall of the heroically slain. Clearly, John Fairfax knew his mythology. Some of his knowledge of Brünnhilde and Norse/Germanic mythology likely came from his love for Richard Wagner's opera cycle *Der Ring des Nibelungen*. The *Nibelungenlied* introduces Brünnhilde by saying: "There was a queen who presided over the sea / Whose like no one knew of anywhere / She was exceedingly beautiful and great in physical strength / She shot the shaft with bold knights—love was the prize." Fairfax loved opera and sometimes sang parts of his favorite arias during his voyage, especially the aria from Mozart's *The Marriage of Figaro* in which Figaro vows revenge on the Count Almaviva for plotting to seduce Figaro's wife ("Se vuol ballare, signor Contino"). On the other hand, Fairfax hated "bloody pop music," especially the Beatles.

"What the hell is wrong with me?" he asked his log. "Am I cracking up like an old woman? By all the gods, if I get it, I know what it will be like now. What more could a mortal man ask?"

"Sweating and sweating" like he had never done before, he wondered: "Does anyone think I should have my dreams psychoanalyzed?"

A rhetorical question, most likely. But perhaps not. For it is not just his dreams that should be analyzed, it should be his logbooks and all of his writings, complete. Perhaps his entire life story.

Any psychoanalysis of John Fairfax—certainly any profile based on what he so candidly shared in his logbooks while crossing the Atlantic—should begin with John's devotion to "my beloved, my goddess, my Venus." In his logs he alludes to Venus no fewer two dozen times. None of the allusions are mere references to the goddess but rather a streaming invocation of his abiding love for her, a calling upon her for protection and inspiration, an entreaty for aid and guidance, and a prayerful statement of trust that the goddess will be there for him no matter what difficulty he might be facing.

On the surface, it might seem that Fairfax depended on Venus purely as a bright-in-the-sky planetary body by which to help navigate his course across thousands of miles of ocean. His main way of identifying *Britannia*'s position was, of course, sextant readings. Usually he took sightings once every three days, either at dusk or at dawn. A three- or four-star fix on the brightest equatorial stars in the Western Hemisphere—usually looking for Arcturus (Boötes), Gienah (Corvus), Markab (Pegasus), Alpheratz (Andromeda), or Sirius (Canis Major)—would then give John his position right away. In between his sextant readings, he was "perfectly satisfied to guess our position," seldom erring, he judged, by more than 30, or at most 40 miles.* As John's overriding navigational interest was

---

* Fairfax made his estimates on the basis of the age-old technique of dead reckoning, which judged a position based on a knowledge about the direction and distance that a vessel had traveled from a known point. Veteran sailors sometimes referred to this method as "navigation by esteem." Fairfax felt his estimates being off by only 30–40 miles was quite good, given that a highly accurate knowledge of course, speed, and leeway is impossible in a rowboat.

steering *Britannia* in a westerly direction (while attempting to lose as little latitude as possible), he rarely bothered with the time-honored operation of shooting the sun at its meridian (noon), in spite of its relative simplicity compared with other sightings. For him it was usually good enough to know he was heading west rather than know precisely where on what westward line he was located.*

In his navigating, spotting Venus, the second brightest natural object in the night sky after the Moon, was easy and could be helpful; on rare occasion, the planet was even visible to the naked eye in broad daylight. Because Venus is so bright and casts a steady light—unlike stars, whose light once it gets to Earth scintillates ("twinkles")—it is often possible for navigators to shoot Venus (or one of the other two of the three so-called navigational planets: Jupiter or Mercury) just after dusk or rising in the east a bit before dawn.† Sometimes John used his sextant to shoot Venus in conjunction with a couple of stars or with the Moon, but not often. The most useful thing that his Venus readings did was help John hold *Britannia* on course. With it shining so brightly, it was a great way to hold a steady direction. He especially loved to look at the planet when it told him he was indeed heading west.

But Venus meant significantly more to Fairfax than a navigational guide. He expressed his own love for the Roman goddess of love and beauty over and over again in his logbook, connecting it for his own need for the love of a woman—clearly, a woman who vexed him:

January 30: "Soon Venus, my goddess, will be out for a shot. Terrible this lack of feminine company."

February 19: "Where are you, Venus? You, the most brilliant, beautiful body in the sky, have you forgotten me? I haven't made any sacrifices to you for a month now, but what do you

---

* For a true positional fix, Fairfax needed to make at least two observations with his sextant, giving position lines that crossed.

† The planet Venus lies within Earth's orbit, thus never appears to be far from the Sun. Because of its routine dual appearance at dawn and at sunset, the ancient Egyptians and ancient Greeks believed Venus to be two separate bodies, a morning star and an evening star, and gave separate names to each.

expect? I am in the middle of the Atlantic, on my own, in case you haven't noticed; what can I do? Just give me a hand and I promise you the most beautiful orgy I can think of at the other side. You are my star; you have never failed me yet. Why now? Come on, old girl, give me a hand and I will beat the sea."

February 25:   "Come on, Venus, make an effort. I need strong winds from the east. Stop playing about and send them."

March 9:   "I am feeling very sad and depressed today, really blue, for the first time since leaving. Think I need a girl bad. London Traffic (radio station) is the only female voice I hear when I call London. She's got a beautiful voice, or at least, it seems so out here, and I keep dreaming of her whispering in my ears not 'Hello *Britannia*' but nice, indescribable things. I have not asked her name yet—sort of want to keep it in mystery—but I think I will ask her next time and invite her to dinner when I return to London. I only hope she is not some old, ugly bitch with a sweet voice. If only she was like my goddess."

March 24:   "Can't believe it, but there it is again: wind from the northwest, Force 5–6. How the hell is one supposed to go on like this? What have I done to you, Venus, and all the gods alike, to deserve this?"

April 7:   "Florida is so far away still, but Venus is helping me. She came to me last night, resplendent in her naked beauty. She promised me that as long as I keep fighting, I would get to Florida, and even predicted a date—June 27. I write it down at this stage, when everything is so uncertain that I could not even predict the month, let alone the date, of my arrival, so as not to forget. *She predicted something for me years ago, when I was 13 years old* [author's emphasis, for later reference], only I didn't believe it, and when it came true I could have shot myself for a fool."

April 13:   "Venus—my adorable, beautiful, gorgeous Venus—you
             are the greatest! Keep pushing for me, keep pushing,
             and we'll make it. . . . Keep rowing, God damn it all, and
             we'll make it, by the gods!"

May 4:   "I shouldn't have mentioned the wind at all yesterday.
             Somehow I get the feeling that every time I do, some-
             thing happens. Is Venus playing with me?"

May 28:   "The sea—I've decided she's a frigging female—has it
             against me in the most stupid way. Time by now she
             realized that she hasn't got a hope in hell of tiring me out
             to the point of giving up. If it takes me a year, I'll get to
             Florida. The only way she can stop me is by sending me
             to the bottom in a hurricane. So, let's have it—either send
             me one, or stop this nonsense and let me have some fair
             winds. God damn it! What's the use?! Females! Bah!"

Fairfax would later add an addendum to his log entry of May 28:
"Females! I have been asked many times what it was like to spend six
months alone at sea without even the soft purrs of a doe-eyed little thing
to keep my mind off rowing. 'Well,' I say, 'If you don't see, or hear, or
smell them, then you don't miss them.' Rot! The honest truth be told, I
could have ravaged all of King Solomon's harem twice over, and still gone
back for more. When I think of all those magnificent, burning sunsets,
those beautiful, warm, starlit nights—ye gods, and all I had to rest my
weary hands on was a bleeding pair of oars! Let me tell you, at those
times, knowing that my beloved Venus waited for me, somewhere in the
mysterious recesses of her cloudy alcove, was no consolation, none at all.
But what's the use. Females—wow!"

On June 1, Fairfax was very ill, with high temperatures and "feeling
weak as a baby." He was vomiting over the side when a tiger shark,
"looking very mean," started making circles around *Britannia*. Like a
madman, John pulled out his knife, dived at it, and swam some distance
after the fish. Fortunately, the fish swam away. When John came to his
senses, he was on top of a swell some 500 yards away from his boat, which

was drifting even farther away. "There was barely a whisper of wind," John logged, "otherwise I would never have been able to catch up with her. Venus really must have looking after me." (Whether this actually happened or John was delusional due to his high temperature or he was just making up a good yarn is uncertain. There are some events described in his log that seem very unlikely to have happened, such as his entry on April 28 describing how he "hitched a short ride" on the back of a whale.)

June 12:   "Squall after squall is my lot. At home must be winter now, and *my mum is probably sitting in front of the fireplace thinking about her crazy son* [author's emphasis]. It is not a thing I yearn for very often, but today I really wish I were home, lying in front of that very fireplace—a glass of wine punch in my hand; a beautiful woman, utterly naked, overwhelmingly erotic, gorgeous neck, desire-bearing breasts, sprawled all over me, purring. Gee, how many times have I done so. Oh, Venus, how I adore you for encompassing all my desires: love, beauty, desire, sensuality, sex, prosperity, and victory! I must be indeed crazed. Dearest beloved goddess, could I be your Aeneas?"*

Clearly, John Fairfax was a deeply complicated man whose ambition to cross the Atlantic alone—and his ultimate success in doing so—can only be understood in the context of his remarkable background story.

---

*   In Greco-Roman mythology, Aeneas was a Trojan hero and demigod, the son of the Trojan prince Anchises and the goddess Aphrodite (Venus). Although mentioned in Homer's *Iliad*, Aeneas receives much fuller treatment in Roman mythology, most extensively in Virgil's *Aeneid*, where he is cast not just as an ancestor of Romulus and Remus, the founders of Rome, but as the first true hero of Rome. It is not known how familiar John Fairfax was with any literary or artistic depiction of Aeneas (or Venus, for that matter), but his reference here to Aeneas is illuminating. Not only was Venus the mother of Aeneas, according to many classical scholars the goddess was also the clear object of her son's Oedipal desire. See Kenneth Reckford, "Recognizing Venus: Aeneas Meets His Mother," *Arion: A Journal of Humanities and the Classics* (3rd series) 3, no. 2/3 (Fall 1995–Winter 1996): 1–42.

5

No Boy Scout

John Fairfax was born in Rome, Italy, on May 21, 1937. His mother, Mara Penev, was a Bulgarian émigré; his father, Kenneth Fairfax, was an Englishman who worked in Rome for the BBC.

Very little is known about his mother, as John never publicly offered details about her or her life, though he mentioned her frequently, if always briefly, in his writings. What is known about Mara Penev is that she was born in 1918, came from a family of Bulgarian intellectuals and socialites, and was raised in a large home in a suburb of Sofia, Bulgaria's capital. Her family was wealthy, as evident by the fact that the Penev women chose their clothes from a selection of the newest Paris fashions that was delivered directly to their home in large trunks twice a year. Mara's father, whose given name is not known, is believed to have been a member of an elitist group called Zveno ("A Link in a Chain"), which drew its membership from intellectual, commercial, and antiroyalist military circles and advocated a "national restoration" through a Mussolini-like fascist regime. In 1934, Zveno leaders led a peaceful coup d'état that installed as prime minister a formerly discredited right-wing politician (Kimon Georgiev), suspended the parliamentary constitution, and suppressed all political parties and trade unions. The new regime was short-lived, however, and, with its fall, came a purge of Zveno. Filling the power vacuum was the king of Bulgaria (Boris III) in association with a weak parliament. With his country now in the hands of a monarchical dictatorship, Mara's father expatriated to Mussolini's Italy, taking his family—and as much of his wealth as he could manage—to a new home in a suburb of Rome.

Mara first met John's father, Kenneth Fairfax, at the University of Paris when she was only 16, while the family was still ensconced in Bulgaria. She had been allowed to attend the university at such a young age because her older male cousin, Janko Peneff, was studying medicine there—and also because it was safer for her to be there during Bulgaria's coup in 1934.

Mara was an extremely intelligent woman who eventually learned to speak five languages: Bulgarian, French, Russian, Italian, and Spanish (though she tended to mix up the Italian and the Spanish). She was also exquisitely beautiful. With short curly blond hair, sparkling blue eyes that darted flirtatiously around a room, a small upturned nose, and a shapely petite frame that was very quick in its coquettish movements, pictures of her as a young woman could be compared to the American film actress of the 1950s and 1960s Kim Novak. Mara dressed in a very feminine way, in lots of pinks, lots of lace, and plenty of frills. In terms of her blond and blue-eyed looks, she appeared the very opposite of Bulgarian women with Roma blood in them whose looks were generally darker and more Mediterranean. The fact that Mara could *not* be mistaken by anyone for a Romani delighted her, for Mara was, according to those who knew her in later years, "very racist." Also, disguised to many by her very feminine appearance, she was a "woman of steel."[†]

---

[*]   During World War II, Bulgaria, as an ally of Germany, would introduce several restrictive laws against the Roma. The Roma were denied access to the central parts of Sofia, forbidden to use public transportation, and given smaller food rations than the rest of the population. In some areas, they were forcibly converted to Christianity. Roma were forced to work for the state, and marriages between non-Roma Bulgarians and Roma were outlawed. Interestingly, although Bulgarian Roma, together with Bulgarian Jews, were put in camps in Bulgaria, neither group was deported to concentration camps in Germany. Perhaps that was because Bulgarians had grown up with Armenians, Greeks, and Roma and had less virulent prejudice against them. The Jews and Roma who lived in territories occupied by the Bulgarian army, however, were sent to concentration camps, as the army was an ally of Nazi Germany and Fascist Italy. Though the Roma death rate in Bulgaria during the war was one of the lowest in Europe, Roma, to the end of the war and beyond, were nonetheless the targets of purposeful, if inconsistent, restrictive state policy.

[†]   Sylvia Cook to author, email interview, October 20, 2020.

Even less is known about John's father, Kenneth Fairfax, who married Mara Penev after getting her pregnant when she was 18 years old, in 1936.

John came to believe that his father was descended from the English noble and peer Sir Thomas "Black Jack" Fairfax (1612–1671), one of Oliver Cromwell's greatest generals during the English Civil War, but that may have been John's wishful imagination, of which he had plenty. Kenneth was working for the BBC in Rome when World War II broke out in September 1939. He returned to London immediately and kept working for the BBC throughout the war. But that is not the story that Mara told her little boy. She told him that his *bashta* ("father" in Bulgarian) had joined the RAF and become a pilot. When Allied aircraft came bombing Italy in 1943 and 1944, she reassured her son that his father would never let any plane drop bombs on his loved ones.

Whatever went on with Kenneth during World War II, Mara and John stayed in Rome. According to John's telling, he and his mother were interned until the liberation of central Italy by the Allies in the fall of 1944, as were all other foreign nationals living in the country. Whether Mara's mother and father were interned with her and her son is not known—nor are any details of their living conditions in the internment camp or even the exact camp which they were in. For that matter, it is only John's version of his life story that testifies he and his mother were interned at all. It is known that Mara's cousin, Janko, who had graduated from the Sorbonne with his medical degree and whom John called "Papa Janko," was not interned and had a private practice in Rome during the war, specializing in treating venereal disease for both Nazi and Italian officers as well as for Vatican personnel. According to John, Papa Janko was a highly eccentric man who became a millionaire after the war. (John told the story that Dr. Janko Peneff, during the war, stuffed his curtain roads with gold coins, thinking that was the safest thing to do with his money. Also, Papa Janko reputedly trod the streets of the fashionable parts of Rome wearing a shabby old raincoat so he wouldn't be recognized while he attached posters to lamp posts advertising his discreet medical services.)

Someone who got very intimate with the adult Fairfax, Sylvia Cook, remembers John telling her that "the interns got special privileges with regard to food, et cetera. It seems to have been a pretty liberal kind of internment because John told me one story, which I heard repeated to others, of himself and a friend scrumping apples by climbing over the wall of what turned out to be Mussolini's garden. They were caught, told off, put in a room for a couple of hours, and then told to go home. Whether he had climbed a wall to escape from the internment, or whether he and his mother were free to come and go, I have no idea."

All circumstantial evidence considered, it seems at least a reasonable possibility that Mara and her son did not actually live through the war in an internment camp, nor did Mara's parents, given her father's role in the Zveno regime and the family's active support of Mussolini.

John never saw his father again after Kenneth returned to England in 1939, when John was only two and a half years old. Mara told her son that his father had been killed in action with the RAF, and thus John grew up thinking his dad was a war hero. Kenneth did not return to Rome after the war even to dissolve the marriage—apparently he managed that elsewhere. Not until many years later, on the eve of John's Atlantic crossing in 1969, did Mara tell her son the truth. She began by saying she had "something very serious to tell him." She then revealed that Kenneth Fairfax had not been killed in the war but was still alive and serving in London as the director of the BBC Overseas Service. Apparently Mara believed that John would be mixing with journalists and the press before and after his ocean voyage, and she didn't want him finding out that way.

Upon hearing this revelation, John felt an urgency to meet his dad. He arranged to meet him for a drink at his father's gentleman's club on St. James Street in London. The meeting did not go well. John was desperately in need of money for his Atlantic expedition, but it was not for that purpose he wanted to see his father. But that's what the father thought John was after and sternly told him that it was "no good" of him to be coming begging for money after all the years separating them. Kenneth had remarried years ago, had a new family with children, and, as far as he knew, John might not even be his son (possibly because he was aware that Mara had at least one abortion before John's birth). John was devastated. The meeting "absolutely gutted" him.

There was no further contact of any sort between father and son. Kenneth died in the 1970s.

Not having a strong male figure in his life while growing up undoubtedly affected John. As an only child who was doted upon and spoiled rotten by his vivacious young mother, John, by his own admission, became brash and ill-behaved, "a horrible kid," and "an opinionated little brat." (Into old age, Fairfax would not like children to be anywhere around him because they reminded him of "myself as a kid.")

One can only guess what Mara did during the war. It is highly unlikely that she held a job, as the haughty young lady thought jobs were for what she called "the people people" and certainly not for "we people"—a snobbery and prejudice that John also came to hold. Mara had many boyfriends, all of them presumably Mussolini supporters, as she held to the same ideological opinions as her father, and went to parties, celebrations, and other events always escorted by some good-looking Italian, German, or Bulgarian expat.

Mara cultivated political connections within the fascist regime. In published accounts of Fairfax's biography as well as in obituaries, it has been written that John's mother, in early 1943, arranged for his early admittance into the "Italian Boy Scouts." The problem with this statement is that the official Boy Scouts organization—established in Italy in 1922 in association with the World Organization of the Scout Movement—was suppressed by the fascists when Mussolini came to power that same year. In its place came the Opera Nazionale Balilla, known to most simply as Balilla, which was the nickname of a legendary boy-hero from Genoa who had inspired Italy's fight against the Austro-Hungarian Empire in World War I. (Until 1915 Italy had been part of the Triple Alliance, with Germany and Austro-Hungary.) Essentially, the ONB was a paramilitary youth organization. In 1937 it was absorbed into the Gioventù Italiana del Littorio (GIL), with it and the Balilla together becoming the youth section of the National Fascist Party.

That had to be the "boy scout" group that Mara enrolled her son in 1943—an organization designed as Fascist Italy's version of the Hitler Youth. Besides preparing boys for duty in Mussolini's National Republican Army, the GIL (which translates as the "Italian Youth of the Lictor'*") indoctrinated the minds of the nation's youth, taking charge of all activities initiated by schools, holding "Fascist Saturdays," and setting up summer camps. As a member of the GIL, John ("Giovanni" in Italian—John did not learn to speak English until years later) would have worn a full uniform adapted from Mussolini's "Blackshirts": black shirt, fez, gray-green trousers, black Fascist Party emblems, and azure handkerchief (the national color of Italy). During military exercises, the boys were armed with scaled-down versions of the Italian Army service rifle.

Looking back as an adult, John imagined that his mother sent him into the GIL partly to instill some stricter male discipline and partly to get him out of the city and into nature. Like the Boy Scouts, the GIL offered a rigorous test of a boy's ability to master survival skills. He learned to cook, build fires, and track and trap wild game. "Because I was the youngest, the pressure was on me to prove myself," John later reflected, "and I did." Not only did he find that he had "a taste for outdoor adventure," he also discovered that he excelled in many areas. He earned dozens of merit badges, often finishing first in whatever test or performance trial was put before him.

Although John's physical prowess matched and even outpaced boys a couple years older than him, his emotional maturity lagged. The GIL

---

*   A lictor was a Roman civil servant who was an attendant and bodyguard to a magistrate who held *imperium*, an important form of governmental authority. According to Roman legend, the lictors were instituted by Rome's first king, Romulus, who appointed 12 lictors to attend him. Historians of ancient Rome believe the institution of the lictor may have originated with the Etruscans. Another indication of how the Fascists tried to revive and tap into a fascination with ancient Rome can be seen in the Figli della Lupa (Children of the She-Wolf), which was a special section of the ONB whose name alluded to the mythical role of Romulus and Remus in the original formation of Rome. Boys six to eight years old were placed in this section of the ONB, making it likely that young Fairfax was first placed in it.

came to an end with Fascist Italy's surrender to the Allies on May 2, 1945, with the international Boy Scouts organization eventually coming back to life in the country. In 1946, when John was nine years old, an incident during a scout camping trip led to his dismissal. "We were up in the mountains," Fairfax recalled, "and we stayed the first night in a hut." Inside the hut John got into an argument with another boy over a blanket and lost his temper: "I went and got the pistol I knew our leader kept in his gear. I stood outside and started firing at the hut, where the boys were sleeping. They were military bullets and they penetrated the wooden hut like it was made of paper." Years later, John laughed about it dryly: "It was a miracle I didn't kill someone."

After John emptied the revolver, the troop leader rushed out and grabbed it from him. Livid, he slapped John, who responded by kneeing him in the groin: "That really made him mad, and he proceeded to kick the shit out of me." The next day, the scouts held a special ceremony just to drum John out of the corps. He was stripped of his merit badges and sent him home in disgrace. In John's view, the dismissal was a catalyst for him becoming even more of a loner. His indulgent mother chalked it up to Johnny just being "incorrigible."

In July 1947 Mara, now divorced, took her 10-year-old son John from their home in suburban Rome to the port of Genoa, boarded the MS *Vulcania*, made the voyage on the Italian ocean liner through the Mediterranean Sea and across the South Atlantic, disembarking two weeks later in Buenos Aires to start a new life in Argentina. It might seem that Mara was taking her boy on a long and lonely path to a strange and far-away land where mostly Spanish was spoken, but John's young mother, still only 31 years old, was well aware that their new country was rich with Italians and Bulgarians—and had been for some time.

The wave of departing Italians for Argentina that crested in the years right after World War II was hardly the first such exodus. Between 1880 and 1900, some 830,000 Italians traversed the Atlantic to take up a new life in the South American country; from 1901 to the end of World War I in 1919, over a million people emigrated from Italy to Argentina; and from 1920 to 1930, another 542,000 made the exchange. Thus, in 50 years' time, roughly 2.4 million Italians moved to the fourth largest country in the Americas and the second largest in South America (after Brazil). Although the dominant language and culture of Argentina remained Spanish, Italians came to rank as the largest ethnic group in Argentina with over half of the country's population having some degree of Italian ancestry. The *paisan* brought with them enormous and justifiable pride in the greatness and antiquity of Italian culture and history—its language, customs, cuisine, arts and architecture, literature, and traditions—revered as it had been around the world for many centuries.

Of course, the character of Italian migration to Argentina—or anywhere else in South America—following the victory over fascism in World War II made the entire enterprise a little different. Thousands of Nazis, other fascists, and wartime collaborators were looking for a new home, a new identity, a place to preserve their wealth (much of it stolen from Jews and other European citizens during the Holocaust), and an escape from war crime trials. Argentina, which had favored the Axis in the war because of its close cultural ties with Italy, Spain (still ruled by the fascist Francisco Franco), and Germany, welcomed many of them; in fact, the authoritarian regime of General Juan Perón in Argentina went to great lengths to secure their arrival, even sending agents to Europe to ease their passage, provide travel documents, and in some cases even cover their expenses. Among the former leading Nazis who secretly made their escapes to Argentina (some later captured, some not) were Adolf Eichmann, Sándor Képíró, Josef Mengele, Ante Pavelić, Erich Priebke, Eduard Roschmann, Hans-Ulrich Rudel, and Dinko Šakić.*

---

* During World War II, Argentina had been full of Nazi spies, and Argentine officers and diplomats held important positions in Axis Europe. Juan Perón himself had served as military attaché to Mussolini's Italian army in the late 1930s. The dictatorship that came to power in Argentina following a military coup in June 1943 was a big fan of fascist trappings: spiffy uniforms, parades, rallies, and vicious anti-Semitism. Argentina would eventually declare war on the Axis, but not until a month before the war ended and then partly as a ploy to get Argentine agents in place to help Nazi and Italian fascists escape after the war. In the late 1940s, under Perón's leadership (he became president in June 1946 after serving as minister of war and vice president) the government quietly allowed

Along with the Italians, there had been a concurrent Bulgarian diaspora to South America, again most strongly into Argentina, where over 20,000 Bulgarians arrived following World War I, many of them settling in and around Buenos Aires. Another wave of Bulgarians came after World War II, with the Bulgarian émigré population climbing to over 50,000.

Why Mara Penev decided to emigrate to Argentina in 1947 is not exactly known. She may simply have been looking for a new start for her and her son, and with Argentina being the home to more and more people of Italian and Bulgarian descent, it might simply have made sense for Mara to take John there. She might even have had friends or family members who had already moved there or were planning to transplant there soon.

On the other hand, Mara and her family, her boyfriends, and her entire social circle in Rome had been tied in one way or another to Mussolini's fascist regime. By moving to Argentina, she may not have clearly understood that she was moving to a country whose government and society under the Perón regime would not be very different from what the Italians had experienced under Mussolini; on the other hand, Mara may have known that very well—and that was the reason she was moving there. We just don't know. The one thing that John did relate later in life about their emigration was that his mother was unable to get "papers" for them to move to the United States, Canada, or Australia, so they ended up going to Argentina.

Mara's emigration situation, to get out of Italy, was complicated. There is little doubt she had associated with fascists and was likely one

---

entry of a number of Nazi fugitives, over 300 of them, into Argentina. The most infamous of these war criminals was Adolf Eichmann, who was kidnapped in Argentina by the Israeli Mossad in May 1960, brought to trial in Israel, and executed in 1962. On Argentina in World War II, see Isidoro J. Ruiz Moreno, *La Neutralidad Argentina en la Segunda Guerra Mundial* (Buenos Aires: Emecé, 1997). For a broader treatment of the complex historical nexus between Italy fascism and fascism in Argentina, see Federico Fichelstein, *Transatlantic Fascism: Ideology, Violence, and the Sacred in Argentina and Italy, 1919–1945* (Durham, NC: Duke University Press, 2010).

herself. One of her closest boyfriends in Rome during the war was a Bulgarian by the name of Sasha (a diminutive of Aleksandar). Back in Bulgaria he had been deputy head of the secret police used by the Zveno regime, and after the regime's collapse, Sasha became one of the top political criminals on King Boris III's most wanted list. As for John's own political ideas as he matured, he never mentioned anything about having Nazi sympathies or connections, but it is nonetheless clear that he held similar right-wing views.*

Mara apparently financed her family's new life in Buenos Aires by helping to smuggle Old Master paintings out of Italy to Argentina and selling them on the black market. There is evidence that Mara, with Sasha's help and most likely the help of some others, had been stealing valuable paintings during fascist confiscations of Jewish property while the war was still going on, squirreling them away to a safe place, and then finding a secure way to ship them to her in Buenos Aires.

No surprise, given his mother's example, that John Fairfax, as he grew up in Italy and Argentina, would come to lead an adventurous life involving a high degree of impulsivity and risk seeking, thrill seeking, and

---

* Sasha (whose last name is unknown) fled Bulgaria in 1937 and crossed the Alps on foot in winter. There waiting for him, to help him get to Rome and get set up with a new life, was Papa Janko, Mara's cousin, who was helping a number of Bulgarians flee their own country for Mussolini's Italy. When Kenneth Fairfax left for London in 1939 with the start of World War II, Sasha stepped in to become Mara's protector. Now along with Sasha and her cousin Dr. Janko, she, too, helped bring Bulgarian refugees into Italy. Although she never married him and enjoyed many other men friends throughout her life, Mara stayed deeply involved with Sasha until his death in the late 1970s. One of the chief reasons that Mara and John could emigrate to nowhere but Argentina surely stemmed from the darkness of Sasha's records as a fascist.

We know a few other important things about John's mother that reflect on her connections to fascism. When she arrived in Buenos Aires, with her she had a great deal of jewelry, some fine paintings, a collection of silver, and a number of antique artifacts. She had enough money to buy a half-acre plot of land in a pleasant suburb of Buenos Aires. There Sasha, with his own hands, built for her a very pleasant bungalow. Mara suffered no economic hardship and was surrounded by Bulgarian neighbors who helped each other out with their housebuilding.

ready participation in dangerous activities, replete with cutting corners, direct flirtations with suicide and death, disinhibition and rejection of norms, highly questionable ethical behavior, and the desire to pull off never-before-seen tricks or stunts.

Unfortunately, we also do not know a great deal about John's preteen years in Buenos Aires. Enrolled in a school run by Catholic nuns and then, at age nine, at the Lycée Français Chateaubriand ("Liceo Chateaubriand" in Italian), a French international primary and secondary school with two campuses in Rome, John was a poor and disinterested student. Looking back, he considered himself a boy that was a "bright and impassioned dreamer." Approaching his teen years, he came to love reading tales of adventure. Significantly for his future, the one book he "devoured" was *Voyagers Unafraid*, which featured a chapter titled "Row, Sailor, Row," a vivid account of the historic voyage of George Harbo and Frank Samuelsen, Norwegian-born Americans who in 1896 were the first to row across the Atlantic Ocean. "What an awesome ordeal they had lived through!" John would later reminisce. "Their reward had been the satisfaction of getting out of it alive, of having won, by sheer determination, willpower, endurance, against all the odds, proving once more what man can do, the vital flame that burns in him that enabled him to become a man in the first place, through the ages and before, when there was nothing!"

John kept a *Reader's Digest* version of the book's account of the amazing Harbo-Samuelsen ocean journey under his pillow, reading and rereading it, "my boyish imagination lit by a fury of sparks which burned and glowed till I was all but consumed by it." He remembers the exact moment "An ideal was born." One day he too would row the Atlantic, he told himself. But he would do it *alone*. "I knew right then that I was going to do it. I just didn't know when." He went to his mother and told her of his vow. Mara kissed his forehead, put her two hands on his cheeks, looked deeply in his eyes, and told him that it was, indeed, his fate to make that journey. But no, he would not make it alone. She would be there with him, always, in her "infinite love" for him. She would be his Venus.

Mara apparently gave John a lot of freedom and independence—either that, or he was unusually rebellious and disobedient, because, at age 13, he left home. He had been attending a private boarding school run by the Jesuits, the San Salvador, a formal and classical education (taught in Spanish, which became his mother tongue) that he hated, so John ran away much more from the school than his home per se. In what would become characteristic of his craving for excitement and desire for an absolute freedom, John did not run away just to a friend's house. Or find a job at the nearby deep-water port in La Plata. Or buy a horse and ride to San Antonio de Areco to become a gaucho. No, what John wanted to do was live in the jungle. "I wanted to go to the Amazon and live like Tarzan," he later told his mother." Apparently, she never tried to stop him or bring him home. She knew that her boy, from an early age, could not control his impulses and "had a fixation to be one with nature."

How exactly he got there is unknown, but John ended up in the region of Misiones, known as "Argentina's jungle province." Sticking out like a crooked finger from the northeastern corner of the country and surrounded by Brazil to the north, east, and south and by Paraguay to the northwest, the Misiones province, though not technically a part of the Amazon rain forest, is very much like it. Dominated by the Paranaense Forest, one of the world's largest remaining pristine forests, Misiones has a humid subtropical climate with no dry season and abundant rainfall throughout the year. Its average summer temperature (December to February) exceeds 90°F. Three big rivers run through the region: the Paraná, Uruguay, and Iguazú. Located in the northwest corner of the province, bordering Brazil, are the spectacular Iguazú Falls. Considered one of the seven natural wonders of the world, the waterfalls at this point on the river have 275 drops, the largest being 269 feet, equivalent to a 25-story building.

One can only imagine how intoxicating—and perilous—it must have been for a 13-year-old boy, on his own, to be experiencing everything the Misiones had to offer. Within the wondrous natural environment, John also found one of the world's most incredible arrays of wildlife and other biodiversity: 150 species of mammals, 564 species of birds, 60 species of fish, 116 species of reptiles, 68 species of amphibians, and thousands of plant and fungi species. It was one of the best habitats for jaguar and ocelot (a medium-sized wildcat characterized by solid black spots and streaks on its coat) in the world.

John would stay in the Misiones for three to four months at a time. He lived off the jungle, became a proficient hunter, and occasionally bartered with the indigenous peoples of the region, especially the Mbyá-Guaraní, Lule, Pilagá, and Tonocote, aboriginal groups that had inhabited eastern Paraguay and parts of southeast Brazil and northern Argentina long before the Portuguese or Spanish arrived in South America. "There were days when I nearly starved," John remembered years later, "but I learned how to survive from the natives and from peasants I encountered. They all knew me—I was the young, crazy Gringo." Mostly he hunted jaguar and ocelot, using bow and arrow adapted from the Mbya-Guarani as his weapon of choice and sometimes as part of a hunting party of local tribesmen. He also had a spear to use and somehow he had also gotten his hands on a pistol. When a good number of precious animal skins were in hand, John would return to Buenos Aires. One assumes that he received some sort of formal schooling in the big city through his high school years, but that is not certain. Apparently he returned to the Misiones region a number of times.

There was an intensely romantic side to young John Fairfax—a dangerously romantic side that exaggerated and mythologized extravagant risk-taking. When he was 20, while attending university in Buenos Aires (another Jesuit institution), he fell hopelessly in love with a girl he met at a club. When the young lady ended the affair, John was so devastated he couldn't imagine going on. In a manner fitting a daring adventurer and wild romantic, he decided to go back into the jungle and commit suicide. "I was going to let a jaguar attack and kill me. I had a spear and a gun with me, and my plan was to use the spear when the jaguar attacked. Since I was not good with a spear, I would be killed. But when the jaguar came at me, instinct took over and I grabbed the gun and killed it."

He never made another explicit suicide attempt, although a death wish never seemed to be far out of his subconscious. John would do a great number of highly dangerous, life-threatening things for the rest of his life—including rowing the Atlantic Ocean solo.

Promising himself never again to suffer such emotional pain or depression, and being the sort of person never to "go small" when he could "go big," John decided that the best way to forget the girl was to leave the country and travel the world. He told Mara about his decision. As much as his mother hated to see him go, she gave him $10,000 for his trip (money that Papa Janko had provided for John's college education), which was a modest fortune in 1959, showered kisses on her boy, and tearfully bid him farewell. John took a ship to New York City. There he bought a new two-door Chevrolet Bel Air sedan and drove cross country to San Francisco, where he sold the car.

On Morton Street, in San Francisco's popular red-light district, John found his next great love—"the most tantalizing Chinese call girl that ever lived." Her name—at least the name she told to John—was Taffy Song. Night after night John paid to be with Taffy. There was such "vulnerability" in the woman's eyes. Her body when naked was "bewitching," her breasts "small and firm" but "so responsive to (his) touch." Her mane of hair was "constantly moving, glittering long, silky, dark, and sleek." She had "those double-eyelids so characteristic of classically beautiful Chinese women," with "a crease in the small flap of skin that covered the eyelids." Her skin was "fair, not tan." She moved "slowly, gently, but athletically." "Ah, what a fortnight!" John came to remember. "After a most unfortunate love affair I was on a pilgrimage, hoping that time and distance would eventually heal my shattered heart."

Taffy Song didn't cure John, "but she did try, ever so hard." Actually, it may have been John's attitude about women and love that needed curing: "I shall never forget the agonizing sorrow in her little face, her sad smile when, the last of my $2,000 gone, she bid me goodbye and good luck. Women? What would I do without them!"

His idea had been to travel the world, but now he was stuck in California, penniless. He decided to return to Argentina, but how to get there? He couldn't very well ask his mother for more money; he didn't want her to ever see him as an abject failure. Perhaps he could take a job on a freighter heading to Rio? But hard work like that had no appeal for him. So, thinking more adventurously, he hijacked a bicycle and started pedaling south. All he had to do to get back to Argentina was pedal long enough, right? He could do it.

Two months and 3,000 miles later, he reached Guatemala. Fed up with pedaling the bike, especially on all the potholed roads and muddy pathways in Mexico and Central America, John sold the bike, stuck out his thumb, and began hitchhiking. Through Honduras, Nicaragua, and Costa Rica, it took a month for the vagabond to travel the 800 miles south to Panama. There he fell in with a group of artists and other vagabonds. He stayed on the beaches of Panama for some ten weeks, catching the odd fish, grilling it over an open fire, drinking lots of cheap wine, and making love to "the occasional stray bird." Most of the time he spent on the white sand beaches of San Blas, an archipelago on the north coast of the Isthmus of Panama, east of the Panama Canal, where the island habitats were pristine, mass tourism was nonexistent, and life was dominated by the local Kuna people. "It was my beatnik phase," laughs John. "For three months I was a bum."

His next destination was the Amazon, his ambition to go up the world's longest river from its headwaters in Peru and Ecuador through Columbia and Brazil to its outlet into the Atlantic Ocean. Reaching the Amazon at Tabatinga in the far southeastern corner of Columbia, he took a job on a boat that didn't make it very far out of port. Its crew—"a bunch of unsavory characters" who were on the verge of mutiny—made Fairfax, the only person on the crew who could read, their spokesman. Enraged, the river boat captain, who was a veteran of navigation on the Amazon, threatened John's life. Taking the threat very seriously, John quickly got far away from anything to do with the river. In fact, he fled all the way back to Panama, where he knew he had good friends.

His life sounding more and more like a cheap adventure novel, he met a man back in Panama who was one of the region's biggest smugglers—an honest-to-goodness modern pirate. John got to know him only as Captain Z: "a smuggler, sailor, forger, and adventurer extraordinaire" and a "brutal, non-nonsense soldier-of-fortune" who took young Fairfax "under his piratical wing" and made "a trusted lieutenant" out of him. "Sure, I'd like to try my hand at smuggling," John told him.*

Captain Z's response was "to take me to a whorehouse and put me in bed between two whores. He said if I survived the night and the women approved of me, then I could work for him. I got so drunk that I didn't remember anything, but I survived and must have gotten their approval because I soon became the captain's right-hand man." Within a year John was captain of one of Captain Z's "fast boats." He piloted them all over the Caribbean, Central American, and South American coasts, smuggling guns, whiskey, and cigarettes. But no drugs—Captain Z would not touch drugs. Not only did John learn a great deal about boats and maritime navigation, but he also made a lot of money—according to John, "my first million." It was money that didn't last long, however, for pirates "spent hard and fast, easy come, easy go."

It was the most exciting period of his life, full of intrigue, contraband, danger, women, and loot, but also hard chores, difficult assignments, near-impossible tasks, and nonstop frenzied work: "I never knew what thrills the next day would bring. I simply lived through every one as if it were my last—which, with Captain Z ruling them out for me, might well have been so." He taught John a lot of "painful, untrimmed truths," about others and about himself. "I was his favorite," John recalled, "and the price I had to pay was to prove myself to his satisfaction. There was no arguing with him, either. When he wanted something, whether for a reason or just for kicks, he got it, and that was that." If John made a mistake, Captain Z made him pay for it—literally, in cash, not just what he was owed but "then some."

---

* In his autobiographical book *Britannia*, Fairfax refers to the Caribbean smuggler for whom he worked only as "Captain Z." But in his "Notes on Biography," dated October 11, 1967, which John wrote at age 30 about his life while residing in London, he referred to "Captain B." Sylvia Cook believes that "B" stood for Batista.

"What a man, Captain Z! Hard as nails: only nails will bend, he wouldn't." One of the most important lessons he taught John was that "one always pays for one's mistakes." John learned that "a man never knows what may happen to him; he must always be able to know, regardless of his condition, what he can or cannot do. As long as you have a will to drive you on, there is no such thing in life as giving up something you have to do just because it proves to be painful or difficult." The captain's motto was "Never give up."

In the four years that John spent with Captain Z, those three words were "imprinted on my mind in blood, sweat, and tears."

The captain's last words to him were: "I have made half a man out of you. The other half you must make yourself."

Those words would come back to him often when sitting at the oars of *Britannia* crossing the Atlantic Ocean.

It was not easy for John to get away from the pirate life. It literally took a getaway. And a betrayal of Captain Z.

John's motive for leaving was "pure enough": money. A rival Caribbean smuggler who had reason for wanting revenge against Captain Z came to Fairfax with a deal. The plot involved arranging a hijacking of a ship and its cargo owned by Captain Z that John was piloting. "The guy said I could keep the money—$60,000—all he wanted was to screw over the big guy." When they arrived at the site that had been set for the hijacking (John would never say where other than somewhere in Panama), police and other authorities were waiting—apparently paid off by Captain Z and notified in advance about the hijack scheme. John was the only member of his four-man crew to get away. "I had been prepared for that day for a long time," he would say. "I had my mask, flippers, and false passport all set to go. I swam five miles to get away. The others didn't have a chance."

For two weeks John hid out in a whorehouse—houses of ill repute being a rather constant theme in his life. Getting a hold of a small boat, he skippered it to Jamaica, where he worked as a fisherman for a year and learned how to speak English. Then he chanced a return to Panama.

This resulted in him getting involved in a shootout. He left the country with only the clothes on his back.

It had been six years since he had been home to Argentina, and he missed his mother. Rather than traveling by ship, air, train, or some combination of the three, John chose to go by horseback. He thought that a leisurely pace over the 3,300 miles of his trip (as the crow flies) would give him plenty of time to sort out his life. He arrived home having asked himself myriad questions but arriving at no solid answers. His mother wanted him to become a businessman. To humor her, he took a job that Mara arranged for him managing a mink farm on the outskirts of Buenos Aires. "I was given full authority to overhaul the place, get things going, liven it up. The farm was losing money, and I was supposed to find out why and change that. Well, the trouble was that when I got the job the old administrator was still there, and until they found a way of getting rid of him, I was provisionally assigned the job of keeping an eye, not on the minks but on the pigs. They had a small pig farm on the side." The owner asked John, "I don't suppose you know anything about pigs?" "Yes, of course, I do," John replied.

Of course, he didn't: "Most of the sows were pregnant, and I fed them with raw potatoes, which you are not supposed to do—apparently it was like poisoning them. So, most of them died."

John was removed from overseeing the pigs and given the job of ridding the fields of weeds. The best way of doing that, he thought, was by fire. If not the best, at least the quickest. He remembered: "Everything was going fine till, unfortunately, the wind started blowing from the wrong direction and the fire got somewhat out of hand when a few sparks flew onto the wrong fields. It was harvest time, and I was not sure what the stuff was—wheat, I think—but, in any case, it burned spectacularly. They told me the glow could be seen for miles. It must have been beautiful. I was far too busy to appreciate it myself. They still remember me in those parts. They call me 'Nero.'"

In a nutshell, the job on the mink farm didn't work out: "I burned up the place and got fired."

It was John's last real job.* He was cut out for bigger things—for heroic acts and great adventures. As his beloved Venus had confirmed years before, it was his fate.

---

*   Fairfax was employed very briefly after he moved to London in 1967. Arriving there "somewhat lost and penniless," he walked into an employment agency and ended up working, for a few weeks, as a dishwasher in a Knightsbridge restaurant. Typically for Fairfax, even that difficult time in his life possesses a fascinating aspect to it: the restaurant's name was French (the Pierrot Gourmand), the owner Dutch, the chef English, the waiter Yugoslavian, the singer Russian, and then John, a mixture of English, Italian, and Argentinian. The manager of the restaurant was Turkish, though that by itself was one of the least interesting things about him. Bulent Rauf (1911–1987) was an ex-millionaire, ex-archaeologist, ex-professor of literature, and ex-husband of Princess Faiza, the sister of the late King Farouk of Egypt (who died in 1965). Bulent Rauf, after leaving the restaurant business, which didn't take long, gained considerable repute as a mystic, author, and, in an era of a number of internationally famous gurus, spiritual teacher. In 1975 Rauf started the Beshara School for Esoteric Education, located at Chisholme in the Scottish Borders, which attracted hundreds of students from all over the world. While Fairfax worked at the Pierrot Gourmand, he had a number of conversations with Rauf about "the problems of the world." During their chats, according to John, he learned a little about the Islamic concept that Rauf was then developing concerning "the one Absolute Unity of all existence" (*tawhid*). What appealed to Fairfax was Rauf's notion that each person is taught about God's truth and justice directly through their own life with no intermediary; that corresponded perfectly to John's character and lifestyle. Rauf's approach to the "absolute unity of existence" and the perfectibility of man became especially well known after the British Sufi mystic and author Reshad Field portrayed Rauf as the main character—Hamid—in his 1977 book *The Last Barrier: A True Story of a Journey into Reality*, which became a classic.

6

Shark Attack, Passing Ships, and Sylvia

ohn was at peace with the sea for five days. From February 12 through February 16, 1969 (days 23 to 27), he enjoyed favorable, if mild, winds from the northeast and the east. Rowing 10 hours for four of those days and 12 hours the other, he made some real progress westward for the first time. On the evening of Sunday, February 16, he wrote in his log that "if the wind holds, tomorrow I hope to reach 18° West Longitude." That would finally get *Britannia* back to where it had been on January 29, before the strong westerlies blew it back toward Africa.

He was awakened well before dawn on February 17 and immediately launched into his strongest cursing of the Atlantic since the start of his voyage: "Bloody bastard! Didn't lose any time, either, did you? What do you expect to achieve by this? Make me lose more time, that's all. Damn everything to hell and back!"

A gale had hit *Britannia*. Winds of Force 4–5 came at the boat again from the southwest, increasing to Force 6–7. Force 7 meant nearly 40 miles per hour. Waves crested at 15 feet. There was nothing John could do but deploy the drogue. Had the wind been coming from the northeast or east, he could have tried to run before it, but as it was from the west, he could only curse more and louder. It was "a very bad night" and what made things worse was that the blasted drogue kept fouling up. To keep it to any degree functioning, John had to do his best to watch virtually nonstop and to "work like mad" on its behalf. But his effort was fruitless. It wasn't that the storm stopped *Britannia* from making progress; it was again pushing her back east—and fast.

The gale blew from the southwest all the next day and all the next night; the winds were Force 6–7 the entire time. For the next two days, February 19 and 20, the wind continued to blow almost nearly as strong, Force 4–5, also from the southwest. John logged: "Waves still very high despite the slight wind reduction. Impossible to row and, since the least three days have been overcast, I have no idea of our position. Are we ever going to get out of this trap? The gravity of this problem is increasing by the day. Unless we can get out of here within the next week or two, we will never beat the hurricane season to Florida. We had a month to spare when we left; now we have none."

He could just not understand how they could be stuck in such aberrant wind directions: "Since leaving we have had 85 percent southwesterly winds—this in an area where there is supposed to be almost nothing else but northeasterlies. . . . I shudder to think how far back we must have drifted. All those days of rowing like mad, all this wasted effort!"

John was not angry at the sea—its "thundering charge," its "plunging cascades of white fury," for he could "fight, hit, taste, spit at it." Rather he directed all of his anger at the damnable, deviant wind. The perverse wind coming from the southwest was "everywhere and nowhere." It "could not be seen, only heard, laughing, always laughing, the God-damned laugh of the wind . . . pressing, pushing, destroying in an hour the slavery of days." He hated the wind with every ounce of his being. In the middle of the four-day gale, he realized that his hate for the southwest wind was his only defense against it: "Hate—brutal, single-minded, animal hate, born of impotence and frustration."

Curiously, John also placed more than a bit of blame for the threatening situation he was in on *Britannia*. Even before they faced the early storms from the west, John had developed complaints about the boat—and, characteristically of John, his complaints were mired in a high level of misogyny. As good a boat as she was, "for all her graceful lines," reliability, self-sufficiency, and steadiness, *Britannia* also had "an obstinate mind all her own, a temperament to match that of a prima donna and, apparently, the virginal conceit of a debutante. There was no doubt that she considered herself a much better boat than I was a sailor—or at least a rower." John wanted to totally command her every move through the water, rough or otherwise, and did not like it when he couldn't: "*Britannia* would be alive only for as long as I manned the oars. The only line that separated her from being a brave, graceful, purposeful little boat and being a brightly colored bit of flotsam was my will to row." He was sure that she often ignored him: "Telling *Britannia* that somebody had obviously goofed would not improve matters. . . . With *Britannia*'s confidence in me stretched to the limit, my apologetic explanation that electrical and mechanical gadgets were the bane of my life would have done little to ease the tension. It is quite doubtful, anyway, that she would have bothered to listen. After lying to the drogue all day, with no indication from me as to whether I would ever man the oars again, she was clearly on nonspeaking terms with me."

The more extreme the trouble they got into on the ocean, the more John's opinion of *Britannia* deteriorated into a gendered mislike and distrust. When the boat was not responding to his oars as he would have liked, John kicked her "to see if she had anything to say about it." John was the boss, not *Britannia*, and "it was my prerogative to decide what to do. . . . That did not mean I could rest in peace—as *Britannia* retaliated by refusing absolutely to remain head-on to the waves." What particularly bothered John was *Britannia*'s "unwillingness to run on a straight course with the wind aft"; that was "her most infuriating fault."

It is clear from his log and his subsequent writings about his Atlantic crossing that Fairfax clearly understood the capacities of the rowboat were mostly good and that whatever "defects" ingrained into the boat were the result of design compromises made by its architect, Uffa Fox. Ideally, John wanted *Britannia* to behave "like a surfboard"—that she should be able to ride out a crest of a wave much better than she did, which was hardly at all. John understood well that the cause of that limitation fell to the boat designer, not the boat. When the self-righting chambers that Uffa Fox had incorporated into the boat were hit by a breeze, *Britannia*'s tendency to yaw got worse. Once the yaw increased, there wasn't sufficient rudder surface to counteract it; John knew that was innate to the design and did not like it.

The direct physical relationship between rower and rowboat, on the sea, in the moment, especially during times of crisis, was deeply personal and highly emotional. If the boat's performance fell short in some way on the sea, it was natural that the oarsman, in his frustration, made this an issue to take up with the boat. The only way for John to correct *Britannia*'s inclination to yaw was "to pull on one oar almost twice as hard as the other, unnecessarily expending my energy and continually interrupting the regular rhythm of my stroke." In other words, he had to be very quick on the ball. Unless he applied correct pressure at the very onset of the yaw, it would be too late, and John would lose control. *Britannia* would broach and, as John told it, "if the next wave happened to be a rotter—most were—we were in for a cold shower." This usually happened after John had managed to dry out from the previous dousing and was beginning to feel warm again. "The general effect on my nerves," John wrote, "was as repetitive as it is unprintable." More snotty remarks from John on February 18: "*Britannia*, a brightly colored little toy, hides in the troughs, reels on the crests, wallows in the slopes, gathers momentum; a vicious jerk from the drogue checks her, then releases her, and she staggers, crabwise, dazed."

"Pull yourself together, Britt!" John exhorted. "Don't just stare. Head-on to it."

No doubt, John Fairfax, in his own way, loved *Britannia*. But nothing Tom McClean said in his logbook or subsequent books and speeches about his Atlantic crossing was so unpleasant, offensive, and ultimately self-serving about his boat *Silver*.

Even after she helped him move on from the storms and adverse winds into calm water, John still had a nasty, smug anger and disrespect to express. On March 18: "I know, as sure as her deck was all my weary bones had to lie on, that the unspeakable bitch had engineered the whole thing. The unspeakable bitch either was jealous, or resented the implication of a mistrust of her seaworthiness. . . . That's the trouble with small boats: the moment you show a bit of affection they start thinking they own you. Give them a finger and they will take your arm. Next she will start saying she wants a new coat of paint, or maybe that her bottom could do with more scratching."

On February 21, after four days of hellish gale from the southwest, the weather turned blessedly in their favor: "A day of absolute calm," wrote John in his log. It had arrived just in time. At sunset the day before, their position had been 25°21'N, 16°35'W. Forty miles to the east of that and they would have entered the 50-fathom line of the African coast. Any further westerly wind would have landed them on the shore of the Western Spanish Sahara. A few more miles farther east and they would certainly have been dry.

At first the new weather seemed absolutely ideal for making up lost ground, but it quickly became insufferably hot, over 95°F. By midmorning, as John described it, "the sea, with not a ripple on it, had the appearance of a dead lake, and I felt as if I were cooking in my own steam. To go on would have robbed me of what little energy I had left, and if calm persisted into the night, I would lose the best rowing hours through sheer exhaustion." He spent most of the day sleeping, leaving *Britannia* to herself to bask in the sun, drifting untrammeled by the drogue.

Late in the afternoon, to cool off and clean himself up, John went for his first swim of the voyage. With flippers, mask, and snorkel, he dived into the pleasantly warm water. Grabbing his knife from within the boat, he maneuvered under *Britannia* and began scraping away the hundreds of barnacles that had managed to attached themselves to the bottom of the boat, as a hull free of the clinging shelled organisms would improve its speed through the water. Finishing the job on the port side he looked starboard . . . and stopped cold. One of the biggest sharks he had ever seen was coming straight at him. John's first impulse, of course, was to get out of the water and into the boat, but the shark was too near: "Any attempt I made to climb onto *Britannia* would leave my legs dangling for some time, a perfect target for those teeth." Gripping his knife in his teeth and flattening himself completely against the keel, he readied himself for whatever came. Spearfishing and skin-diving in the Caribbean during his years as a pirate had given John his share of encounters with all kinds of sharks: tigers, bulls, duskies, nurses, hammerheads, great blues. From his own experience with them, and hearing about them from other divers, John had it in his mind that 99 percent of sharks will not attack a person unless provoked.* But the particular shark threatening him now was a mako—one of the more unpredictable species that made fairly frequent attacks upon boats. Fully grown, a mako could get as big as 12 feet in length and weigh over 1,000 pounds.

The shark kept coming. There was no time to think, only to act, and John was exceedingly good at the latter. He was also expert at dramatizing his exploits in his logbook: "about a foot from me, and my hand was beginning to come down on him with the intention of slashing his nose when he swerved, as if to scratch himself against the boat with me in between. My knife hand was already about to hit him with all the strength I could muster. Because of his last-moment movement, I missed his nose but caught him right under the mouth, in the soft underbelly. About seven inches of razor-sharp blade went in—and the world exploded in front of me. In a sudden burst of energy, the shark pulled away from me and, with my knife stuck in his underbelly, ripped himself open from mouth to tail. As he turned to swim away, I saw all his entrails hanging out. He scraped me on the arm and gave me a terrific blow with his tail on my left upper arm and shoulder."

As the shark sped away, John climbed into *Britannia* in record time. Sore and battered but otherwise okay, John took an hour to rest and regain his composure. When he was sure that the mako was no longer around, he went back into the water to scrape the barnacles on the

---

*   In his logbook Fairfax initially stated that 99 percent of sharks will not attack a man unless provoked or otherwise tempted. Later in his log he called 80 percent "a slightly more realistic figure."

starboard side. It took him a long time, as he kept looking out for sharks every 15 seconds, but he finished.

The next day, February 22, the heat was just as oppressive, the wind and sea equally calm. Sore from where the shark's tail hit him, John rowed for only five hours. With no breeze and only a very slight westerly current to help, *Britannia* made little progress.

The wind picked up the next day, reaching Force 2–3, but was still not a trade. It blew from the north. This meant drifting more to the south than John wanted. It also meant difficult rowing because the waves, from four to six feet, came across the boat from abeam. John logged that *Britannia* was "rolling and pitching in a most violent and unusual manner" and had even "gone to the disrespectful extreme of tossing me overboard once or twice."

Feeling depressed, unlucky, frustrated, angry, and now wet and sore, John was even more vulnerable to temptation than he was ordinarily. He had not started his Atlantic crossing truly committed to it being a completely "unassisted" trip, but he had hoped that he and *Britannia* could fundamentally succeed in making their voyage mostly on their own. It did not take a shark attack to corrupt his motive. Already the purity of his motive had been sacrificed when, on February 8, his 19th day at sea, John had encountered a passing ship, the *Skauborg*, a Norwegian freighter. John had brought on the encounter himself. Having sighted the ship at 0930 GMT stopped three to four miles away, John made a special effort to row for the best part of hour and pull alongside. It turned out the *Skauborg* had sprung an oil leak and had stopped to repair it.

The master of the *Skauborg*, Captain Block, invited John on board. (When Tom McClean got such an invitation from a passing ship—and he would receive three of them—he always declined, asking just for a fix on his position.) John did not hesitate. He scrambled up the rope ladder and stepped on to the cargo ship's "rock-steady" deck. The first thing he was offered, and accepted, was a hot shower. Then he had a great big breakfast: four scrambled eggs; three rashers of bacon; strong coffee, as much as he could drink; and two bottles of beer finished off with a Cuban cigar. The way John described the meal in his log was "heavenly bliss."

Captain Black and his crew had treated him as a VIP. The radio officer, a former journalist, "insisted on taking all sorts of pictures and a detailed account of my experiences and feelings so far. . . . Not to be outdone, I took some pictures myself." As repairs in the engine room were taking longer than expected, the Captain invited John to stay for lunch. "How could I refuse?" John remarked, later adding "If my experiences at sea entitle me to a modest word of counsel, I would like to suggest to all future shipwrecked mariners that they try their very best, whenever possible, to be rescued by a Norwegian ship. It was a castaway's dream."

If the little relaxing, stomach-filling recess on board the *Skauborg* had been Fairfax's only holiday at sea, perhaps his crossing might still qualify as predominantly unassisted. But there would be a number of other helpful, invigorating recesses from the main action.

On February 12, the day the wind shifted from the west to the north-east, a Greek ship, the *Argonaftis*, stopped by at 1800 GMT. Besides giving John his position, the ship also gave him "some cabbages, lettuce, canned vegetables, and a loaf of bread." After all, it was suppertime.

On February 24, three days after John's tangle with the shark, a Russian ship, the *Talsy* stopped by. Again, John abandoned little *Britannia* and went aboard the big vessel. Its captain, Victor Nikitin, and crew proved to be as accommodating as that of the *Skauborg*. It was like a little party: "After a most pleasurable half hour spent swapping gossip in the captain's cabin, we parted in high spirits, greatly helped by half a bottle of excellent vodka, downed in a spree of toasts that included the Queen, Lenin, the Royal and Russian navies, Shakespeare, Tolstoy . . . even ourselves." Nor did John leave empty-handed. As he logged, "Got more cans of food and water," then added "I think this will be one of the last ships, as I am about to get away from the shipping lane. This is good, as all this time I have been afraid of being run down."

True enough, it was "one of the last ships" for a while. Before his voyage was over, John would meet up with and spend some time aboard seven more vessels—including a Russian freighter, US aircraft carrier, a Canadian Pacific liner, another Norwegian freighter, two fishing boats, and a large private yacht—making a total of ten such side trips, all of them very enjoyable and vivifying. One gets a clear impression from his logs that John would have liked to rendezvous with even more ships than he did.*

◆

In his Atlantic crossing Fairfax also benefited from regular communication with the outside world. To a significant degree, that regularity was determined by the publicity agreements John and his business agents—John Austin and his partner John Stevens—had negotiated with Independent Television News (ITN), the UK-based TV production company, and the *Daily Sketch* newspaper.† Both media outlets had made

---

*   For example, on April 20, Fairfax logged: "Off the Canary Islands it was like Piccadilly Circus, so much that I lived in fear of being run down. I didn't really need ships then. Now I do and they are not around." On May 7, he wrote: "A ship is passing, all lights ablaze and so near I could almost touch it. Makes me feel full of nostalgia, and the temptation to light a flare and to hell with everything is very strong. Instead I switched off my torch, lest they see it, and watched it disappear. I shall soon be in the shipping lane that goes to South America, east coast, if I'm not in it already. Maybe I will stop a ship then and ask them for some goodies and cigarettes."

†   Agent John Stevens, who Fairfax called "a free-lance do-it-all," took over the task of gathering the necessary equipment and stores for Fairfax's voyage and the training that would necessarily precede it, while John Austin arranged to sell the story of John's forthcoming journey to ITN TV and to a newspaper, which turned out to be the *Daily Sketch*, a politically conservative British national tabloid. The amount of money and property value involved in the deals is not known. Inferring from the few things John wrote about the advances he received from ITN and the *Daily Sketch*, a good guess would be that the two advances together amounted to around £500 (roughly £8,700 today, or $11,400). If the advance represented 10 percent of the total to be received at the end of the trip, John would have altogether received some £5,000 (roughly £87,000 today, or $114,000), minus the standard agent commission, which was likely to have been then, as now, 15 percent. John Stevens was also the one who got Yorkshire businessman Martin Cowling to finance the design and building of *Britannia*. In actuality, it took Fairfax himself to convince Cowling to provide the money. According to John, Cowling was willing to pay for the boat, "provided I was able to convince him not only of the feasibility of my venture but that I was capable of carrying it out. Or, to put it bluntly, he was not prepared to help a lunatic forfeit his life for a bit of cheap glory, at his expense."

it clear that the only way they would provide any money for the expedition was if John could "stay in touch with them in London throughout the journey." That meant a radio—not just a decent two-way radio but one that was capable of receiving and transmitting voice across a range of 3,000–5,000 miles. Sure, the vessel making the crossing was going to be sophisticated—Uffa Fox would make sure of that—but, damn it, it was an open rowboat! The radio would have to be compact, lightweight, rugged, and capable of operating on a 12-volt car battery that would have to be recharged with a small generator. Various components for such a radio already existed, but the portable marine radio system *as a system* that Fairfax needed essentially had to be invented, with every component mated and harmonized with every other. It wasn't going to be cheap to design and build—and, in routine operation on a rough sea in an open rowboat, maybe not even very reliable.

Fortunately, Fairfax's growing team of associates found an extraordinarily fine transceiver, which met all specifications, made by Marconi of Canada. Known as Model CH25, Marconi had designed the radio specially to operate from lorries and trucks (as lorries were known in the US and Canada) that made long-distance hauls. Its price was indeed hefty: £1,200. But Marconi's technicians assured "the Fairfax team" that they could "install the whole shebang and make it operational" for no additional cost. The *Daily Sketch*, which by this time was sold on the idea of exclusive rights to publish John's messages during the crossing, advanced enough additional money to cover the radio's cost. Good equipment for the rest of the communication system was also found and secured, including a small and simple-to-operate generator made by an English company, Conyers. Although unrelated to radio voice communication, a small SARBE (search and rescue beacon equipment) unit was acquired for use in an emergency. Battery-powered, it would automatically send a signal on two fixed international distress frequencies that could be picked by any airplane or ship within a 200-mile radius. Finding a small boat at sea that was disabled—or one with an incapacitated or unconscious oarsman—could be enormously difficult, and the SARBE beacon could zero in on a disabled boat quite precisely.

Fairfax appreciated the safety of his communication system, but during his ocean crossing he found the obligation of reporting in to ITN and the *Daily Sketch* to be quite a bother. His logs are full of complaints about having to do so.

According to the schedule worked out in England between ITN and the *Daily Sketch*, John was, in his words, "supposed to attempt to contact with them every four days at 0800 GMT." Failing that, he was to try to establish contact at the same time every day afterward. Specifically, he was to make his contact through Baldock Marine Radio Station (GBC 4), a receiving station in the town of Baldock in Hertfordshire (40 miles north of London) that was part of the United Kingdom's long-range radiotelephony service, which was operated via the International Telephone Exchange in London.*

It proved difficult to get through to Baldock. The crux of the problem lay in the antenna for the radio, which John was told by the radio engineers to raise to a height of 20 feet. During trials in the calm, secluded waters of Las Palmas, John had no trouble deploying the antenna. He simply attached the aerial to a hydraulic mast, clamped it against the boat's forward self-righting chamber, pumped it up to the required height, and it was ready to go. But doing this out in the ocean was a different cup of tea. Typically, John found a way to blame it on his boat: "*Britannia* simply hated the sight of a metallic rod gracelessly sticking out of her skin, and if there happened to be any sea about, she would go positively

---

* The radio receiving stations for the UK's long-range marine radiotelephony service were located in Baldock in North Hertfordshire and Bearley in the Stratford-on-Avon, with its transmitting stations at Rugby in northeast Warwickshire and Criggion in central Wales. Circuits from the International Telephone Exchange were routed to the transmitting and receiving stations via the radio terminal at Brent. Although a 24-hour service was available, there were no specific watch-keeping hours. Ships generally initiated communication by sending a message to the radio terminal indicating their request for communication on set frequencies at a particular time, which was arranged for Fairfax's expedition. Larger passenger ships that were frequent users of the service often arranged further contacts at the end of each session. It was also possible to alert the receiving station automatically by transmitting a carrier that operated an audible alarm.

mad. Pitching, rolling, shaking, she behaved with such excited frenzy that in a matter of minutes, she contrived to wrench the wildly whipping aerial from its bracket."

Truth be told, Fairfax simply hated dealing with the radio, especially having to meet the schedule of reports he was obliged to transmit back to England: "As the radio cubicle was aft, I had to make my calls crouching between the generator on one side and the gas stove and gimbals on the other, continually scrambling in and out every time the aerial snapped away." It is clear from his logs that he often ignored his obligation to send radio messages, finding excuses for not making them. On February 6, his 17th day at sea, he wrote: "For all my efforts, I have been able to get through only twice so far, and I am beginning to regard the whole business with distaste. If I could get through today, I wouldn't have to think about it for four days. Otherwise, I would have to try again tomorrow. Damn it! Why couldn't they hear me?"

When John did get through to GBC 4, he thought the radio operators were quite stupid about many of the questions they were asking him: "Naturally, the first thing they wanted to know was my position and how things were going. What could one say: that after 17 days at sea, one is probably still within spitting distance of the point of departure?!"

It wasn't just during the bad early stretch when the strong breezes out of the west were blowing back toward Africa that John was peevish about his radio experience. On March 24, his 63rd day, he complained: "ITN had the unbelievable cheek to ask, this morning, what do I do with my spare time! Spare time? By Jove don't they realize what it is like out here? I row 10 hours almost every day. When I don't it's because, like today, I'm too damn tired to grasp an oar, let alone pull it and move a ton of boat against the wind. I am navigator, cook, deckhand, engine, photographer, radioman: you name it, I got to do it—who else? Spare time?" John's indignation went on for another 292 words, one of his longest log entries of his entire trip, concluding with a final pointed thought directed at ITN, the *Daily Sketch*, and the Baldock radio operators who were trying to make the broadcast network and the newspaper happy: "Maybe that will give them an idea of what my days are like!"

Although John sometimes listened on a small transistor radio to the broadcast of the BBC World Service news on commercial AM radio stations, even that came to annoy him: "It may seem strange, but I loathe having my solitude shattered by the sound of the human voices chattering on matters and events happening so far away from my present world that I have lost all possible interest in them. All I crave, and even this only now and then, is a good concert. To listen to Beethoven's Fifth or Ninth symphony, for instance, would be marvelous. Unfortunately, all the world seems to be interested in listening to is bloody pop music, and rather than defile natural melodies of seas and winds with that, I would throw the transistor over the side."

◆

The one voice that Fairfax did not mind hearing over the ship-to-shore was Sylvia's.

Sylvia Cook was John's . . . well, girlfriend. She was a pretty brunette English girl, tall, thin, long hair and long legs, and fond of miniskirts. She was born on November 28, 1938, to a middle-class family. Her father was a teacher whose main subject was geography and who later became deputy head of a state school. Her mum was a clerk who worked at Garrard, the Crown jewelers on Regent Street. Sylvia excelled in grammar school but chose not to go to university. She was 29 years old when she met John in the summer of 1967, only 18 months younger than he. Everyone who knew her loved her witty intelligence and artistic flair. When she met John, Sylvia was coming off "a disastrous and sometimes violent marriage" that had ended just nine months earlier. Still feeling "rather unsettled," she was "on the lookout for something else" that she could find "fully absorbing and worthwhile." One thing that was a good match for John at that time was Sylvia's only serious hobby: competitive rowing of the shell racing variety. In addition, from her early teens, she had been "an armchair adventurer," inspired by the bestselling book *Kon Tiki*. After her divorce she shared a flat in Earl's Court with three other girls and took a job as a secretary in an art gallery. With little money, she found a way to dress fashionably, as best as she could afford. Raised Jewish, in 1967 Sylvia was debating with herself whether to go and help fight the Six-Day War that had erupted in June between Israel and the Arab states of Egypt, Syria, and Jordan. Most days she read the *Times* quite thoroughly, including the newspaper's Personal Column.

On Wednesday, June 7, 1967, Sylvia saw the following announcement in the paper: "I, John Fairfax, will row the Atlantic single-handed from East to West in a boat specially designed by Uffa Fox. If you wish to be associated in any way with this project, please telephone Brian Watkins at . . . or write . . ." (Watkins was one of John's few friends at that point in London. John was living in a small room he rented in a Kensington apartment building.)

In response to his advertisement John received six letters: three from "cranks," one from a student who was willing to help in building the boat, one a letter of encouragement with a check for £1, and one, in John's words, "from a girl who said she thought it was a magnificent thing for me to do and offered to help in all possible ways during her free time as a secretary."

Of course, that girl was Sylvia Cook.

"To my surprise," recalled Sylvia, "two days later John telephoned me from his friend's flatlet, a mere 200 yards from the flat I was sharing with three other girls, and said he'd be around in half an hour."

"Thrown into an instant panic" because her flat was such a mess, as was she, "I didn't know what to do first, made a whistle-tour with the Ewbank (carpet sweeper), bunged four girls' rubbish out of sight under anything, and even had time to powder my nose before the doorbell rang."

She opened the door to a "bronzed muscleman" not much taller than herself, with "sun-bleached brown hair flopping into his crinkly hazel eyes, who just "oozed vitality and enthusiasm." Bounding across the front room of her apartment, "Johnny"—as she came to call him—"installed himself" in an upright chair by the dining table overlooking the street. (It took her only a few minutes to realize that he chose the chair by the window to "better pursue his favorite hobby of 'birdwatching,'" meaning watching pretty girls go by. John's own first impression was that Sylvia was "a charming girl, a keen rower herself." (Sylvia was the stroke of the first eight of a ladies rowing club. Her crew traveled to regattas around the British Isles, competing often quite successfully. This involved pretty intensive training and took up a great deal of her spare time, especially when it came time for the European Championships.)

Interestingly, given their subsequent romantic involvement, John felt "I was definitely not her type, nor she mine, but in spite of all this we liked each other." Sylvia was more smitten than John. They talked of everything under the sun. John hardly mentioned his proposed trip at all. Rather, he "told the most outrageous stories," most of which she could not believe but later discovered from his mother and from several other people were true. Rake that he was, John kept asking for glasses of water, which Sylvia instantly understood gave him "the pleasure of looking me up and down as I crossed and re-crossed" the room. Bounding out of her flat an hour later, John planted a "quick kiss" on Sylvia's cheek and disappeared with the words "Now we are friends."

Two weeks passed before she heard another word from the bronzed muscleman—she was beginning to think that "perhaps I hadn't roused as much interest as I had hoped." Then, one day, Fairfax popped into the art gallery where she worked. Sylvia heard her boss's young son yelling "There's someone to see you!" She knew immediately who it was. John asked her to go for a coffee, which she did at her break. In the next weeks, they saw more and more of each other. "After a while, I forgot all others," said John, "and went out exclusively with her." (He had been dating five different women when he met Sylvia.) Looking back a few years later, John would remark, in his egotistical and unconsciously condescending way, "As far as 1967 was concerned, Sylvia was the only bright light in my life."

Where John had been for those two weeks was in the London casinos. Every night. No longer employed as a dishwasher—in fact, not employed at all—he had too few pounds in his pocket even to pay rent. The two Johns, Austin and Stevens, had agreed to represent him, but the deal-making had just begun. "No stranger to being broke, or to surviving on wits alone," as John later put it, he coaxed the pair of agents to advance him £250. After settling a few debts, that went down to £180-odd—and that was not likely to last long. Confident in his gaming abilities from his days in the Caribbean, he thought he could fix his predicament with a few evenings at the craps tables—better than that, he felt he might be able to win big enough to bankroll his entire Atlantic expedition.

For nearly a fortnight he watched the dice roll, determined to get "my own back(ing)." Allegedly, he "hated every minute of it, as it was a matter not of pleasure but of necessity." Everything inherent to his daredevil personality shouted at him that the only way to gamble was "big, or not at all." But he was in no position to do either. He had no choice but to "play very carefully, never allowing myself to lose more than a small set amount and always, always leaving when on a winning run." A good strategy, but it meant that even on the nights he won he took home little more than £5.

He had to up the stakes, bet bigger, take more chances. It didn't work. Over and over he crapped out, eventually losing every last shilling. "Have my own bank for the trip? Ha!" He didn't have money for rent, for meals, for training. Nada.

If John had won big at the casino tables, would he have gone back to Sylvia and to her flat? Perhaps not. But having lost everything, his best option was to begin a friendship, an employer-employee relationship, a love affair. Over the next few weeks, he did just that, quickly moving into her tiny bedroom with her, not in the least bothered, of course, by the fact that three other girls also lived in the apartment.

Truth was, young Sylvia Cook became one of John Fairfax's greatest assets. Without her, John's Atlantic expedition might not have materialized, at least not as effectively or expeditiously as it did. In the following months and throughout 1968, Sylvia "helped as much as I could" and learned that "half the success of an operation of this nature is due to careful and extensive planning and preparation," two qualities for success that were quite foreign to John's facilities. Besides serving as his secretary, assistant, and "Girl Friday," she also supported John financially as best as she could. The idea was that he could spend his days entirely in training for rowing the Atlantic if he didn't work a job. A couple of miles' running every morning. Two hours' weight lifting and swimming during midday in the YMCA. Three to four hours' rowing on the Serpentine in Hyde Park in the late afternoon.

"I was never sure whether I was in love with the man, or with his life story," Sylvia reflects today. "Or is this always the case with everybody? At least where Johnny was concerned. He said his heart had been broken and he could never fall in love again. A few times later on he did say he loved me and I suppose he did. I think his egoism overrode any feelings he had for anybody else."

It took many years before Sylvia developed a more analytical perspective on her relationship with John Fairfax, although she sensed something about him from the start that warned her to be careful. Being in love with him in whatever way she was at the time is surely what led her to make such a total commitment to Johnny and his Atlantic Ocean project. Looking back, it does seem that John loved Sylvia in his own selfish way. He later wrote: "During these months, Sylvia showed terrific understanding; and as it cannot have been easy to put up with my moods—which she did, apart from helping me in many other ways—I think she deserves all the praise as far as this part of my venture is concerned."

According to Sylvia, "Actually, Johnny was pretty cagey about most of the planning for his trip and used to arrange his own meetings and trot off mostly on his own." Still, she played a crucial role on the "Fairfax team" all the way through the enterprise. She dealt with agents Stevens and Austin. She helped arrange some meetings—and also attended some meetings herself—especially at first with Martin Cowling, the Yorkshire businessman who was putting up most of the financing for the trip. "Martin did not really want me in the picture," Sylvia remembers, "as he thought a debonair-free bachelor was a more salable article."

Once aware of this notion, Sylvia tried to stay away from Cowling as much as possible. At the same time, she recognized that John was not at all good with money or with paperwork. Thus, she took care of all the bills, invoices, and bank accounts, and made sure John signed all of the necessary contracts with ITN and the *Daily Sketch*. She also coordinated the planning for the trip's food rations with Horlicks's Archie de Jong and arranged for *Britannia* to be shipped as deck cargo on a freighter from London to Grand Canary Island. There was not much that Sylvia wasn't willing to do for her Johnny's trip.

Sylvia was right at John's side on Grand Canary for the start of his voyage. There she met his mother, now going by Mary, for the first time. (Especially around Americans, Mara had begun to use the English version of her given name.) The meeting transpired at the Las Palmas Airport, and it did not go as well as Sylvia hoped. John, on the other hand, hardly noticed their interaction, to the extent there was any: "My mother arrived, after an extremely long and tiring flight from Buenos Aires, at a most unearthly hour of the morning, to be met by what I was afraid would be an overpowering reception committee of four or five strangers, including Sylvia, John Stevens and his wife Margaret, as well as Noel Botham and Jeff White from the *Daily Sketch*, and myself. My mother was so overcome by our first meeting in over two years, intermingled with the thought that it would probably be our last for another year, that she seemed to have only the vaguest idea of what was going on. It was a wonderful reunion for the two of us, and in spite of feeling rather like the prodigal son, I was so happy to see her that I felt a huge lump in my own throat." No mention of Sylvia. No mention of introducing Sylvia or any of the others, for that matter, to Mara. Surely, if John was in love with Sylvia, and Sylvia had done so much for him, wouldn't he want his mother to meet her? Perhaps not, if the real Venus had just arrived on TWA from Argentina.

Whatever words were passed between the two women were virtually all about John—"what he liked, what he didn't like, thinly diluted by the usual women's chat, about clothes, food, scenery, et cetera. I never considered whether she approved of me or not and had no idea what sort of woman she wanted for Johnny. Mary and Johnny had an extraordinarily close relationship and Mary, at best, was very highly strung."

Mara stayed in Las Palmas for a few days but had to fly back to Argentina even before John launched in *Britannia* from San Agustín. To his surprise and disappointment, "My mother could not stay any longer: she had to rush to the airport or miss her plane. She could not see me off, after all." John was doing some work on *Britannia* in the water when somebody called out to him from the beach that his mother was leaving. "I swam ashore, bracing myself for what was to come. Sure enough, the moment I had her in my arms, my mum, who had been extraordinarily brave up till then, burst into tears, and I felt like a rotten fiend. What could I say that would make any difference? Mothers are mothers, and I was her only son! Finally, unable to prolong the agony, she almost ran away, still crying. Don Salvador Moret, the manager of our hotel in Las Palmas, with a protective arm across her shoulders, guided her through the crowd toward her taxi."

John already knew that Sylvia was flying back to London later that day, along with John and Margaret Stevens. All three of them were on an all-inclusive two-week package holiday, and that was the flight on which they were required to return. "Of course, we had all planned to see Johnny start his trip," Sylvia remembers. "But then his start got delayed a bit. We were all so broke we could not afford to buy new flights."

Having said goodbye to his mother, "a bitter taste in my mouth, fighting to keep my own tears back," he turned around and bumped into Sylvia, who was there also to say goodbye to John. "She was sobbing, her eyes streaming like waterfalls. It was too much! Grabbing her quickly, I smacked a rough kiss on her wet lips, then let her go. As she fell back into somebody else's arms, I sprinted for the sea, yelling that I would see her in Florida."*

---

*   On occasion over the next few years, the mother and the girlfriend would again be in the same place, together with Johnny, occasionally alone, but those meetings never went well. "Difficult!" exclaims Sylvia. "When Mary came to London after his Atlantic crossing, on the second day she announced in her broken English, 'You have kitchen two days. I have kitchen two days.' It was my flat, my rent, my kitchen, I felt like telling her. But I agreed to save the peace."

"Johnny left us in London and went to the U.S. for two weeks on a caper. One evening an old flame of mine—long extinguished—came round and stayed till 4 A.M., perfectly innocently but Mary was furious. When Johnny returned here a couple days later a gorgeous girl he'd met in Florida came with him. What did Mary say about that: 'Dere is noting wid dis girl, Sealvee.' I told her not to be ridiculous, a girl doesn't follow a man halfway round the world if there is nothing. Things got so bad between the three of us that it became a matter of one of us being in each room peering out to ensure the coast was clear before leaving any room."

"When Johnny took me to Argentina with him—once and only once—he gave me a one-way ticket to get there and I had to promise to leave in three weeks' time. But I was unable to get back before winter came, cold and wet. We were again without money, so I asked Johnny to buy me some wool so I could knit myself a warm cardigan. In the car Mary started ranting and accusing me of spending all of Johnny's money!"

"On another occasion Johnny went off to the States and treated Mary and I to a brief holiday in Italy. Every mealtime on that trip with her it was, 'John, he like this very much but I make it this away, better.' She brought a huge framed photograph of him on the trip and put it beside her bed every night and talked to it, 'Goodnight, John! I wonder what you are doing now?' It was like a shrine."

Author's email interview with Sylvia Cook, September 24, 2020.

7

The Big Gamble

ohn's first reference to Sylvia in his logbook did not come until March 13, the 52nd day of his voyage. It was one of the days that he was obligated to make contact with ITN in London through the Baldock Marine Radio Station. "Got through to London," he logged, "and had a word with Sylvia." Talking to her "cheered me up a bit," but he noted nothing more. John was mainly interested in having Noel Botham of the *Daily Sketch* to "get in touch with the American Coast Guard and see if they can offer any advice as to my chances of reaching Florida provided I can make it to 60° West Longitude by the end of May." John was "sure that their answer will be negative, but we shall see."

As much as John thought and fantasized about his beautiful goddess Venus, and about women, the erotic, and sex in general, one might think Sylvia would have shown up more often in what was his deeply contemplative stream of consciousness. But she didn't. On March 23, his 62nd day at sea, a thought about Sylvia did bubble up in an interesting context concerning the great difficulty of trying to ply the ocean in a rowboat all alone: "It is quite obvious to me now that, at least at this latitude, it is almost impossible for a single man to row a boat on his desired course. The drift to the south is too fast. Two men could, probably, by taking turns to keep the boat moving most of the time—20 hours out of 24, anyway. They would not stop drifting, but their westerly progress would be much faster. Even so, I guess they would have one hell of a job. Well, I am on my own and have no regrets whatsoever about that. *If anything, I would like a girl to be around, preferably Sylvia; but that's a wishful thinking* [author's emphasis]. I can only go on and row, row, row . . ."*

And row he did. Over the next month there were few days he rowed anything less than 10 hours and a few that he rowed 12. He rowed day and night. He had no choice. In the 27-day stretch between Wednesday, February 26, and Monday, March 24, the wind came from the north, northwest, or northeast on 18 of those days—two-thirds of the time. Four of the days it was very calm. Only on five days did the path of *Britannia* benefit from any breeze from the east.

When "for the first time in ages," a strong wind started blowing from the northeast (Force 4–5), John thought it was "beautiful," just "what I need." If it "keeps up like this for a week or two I should start making some decent progress." He soon changed his mind about that. The next day, he realized that "northeasterly winds are not so good after all." The dilemma John was facing was not just that he desperately needed to start going west, ever west, but that he needed to quit going south. Yet that was exactly where the prevailing northerlies—even from the northeast—were

---

* While crossing the Atlantic, Fairfax only mentioned Sylvia Cook in his log-book one other time. His entry criticized Sylvia for buying defective matches, which became a crisis when his Ronson lighter stopped working and he could not light his smokes (he alternately smoked cigarettes and cigars but mostly a pipe). It read: "Sylvia bought some supposedly special waterproof ones in Las Palmas—but she doesn't speak Spanish, and God knows that they understood she wanted. The first one exploded in my hand. The second one shot away all over *Britannia* in a shower of sparks and finished in the sea. The third simply went *pouff!* in a cloud of stinking smoke. They are little petards for fireworks displays, and they won't light the Calor gas (cooker)! Threw the lot away in disgust and sat down to repair the Ronson." Fortunately, John got his lighter to work, as it was the only means he had of making fire. Without it he could not cook and, more importantly, could not make drinking water. He only had seven gallons of water left (14 days' supply), the rest he would need to distill. After reading this entry in his log, Sylvia became "most indignant," strongly denying that it was she who purchased the matches.

blowing him. For every mile his boat moved south, John knew, he would
have to recover them the hard way: by endless hard rowing. He lamented:
"Another month has gone, and my progress so far is too ridiculous for
words." He issued himself a grave warning: "If, by the end of March, I
am not somewhere between 30° and 35° West Longitude, I will never
be able to reach Florida before the hurricane season. But I will never do
it at this rate."

He definitely wouldn't, not when his position at his last fix, three days
earlier, was 16°52'W and Grand Canary itself lay at 15°36'W. That was
barely 1 degree farther west than John had started! Ridiculous, indeed,
considering that February 27 was the 38th day of his trip and that a
straight line back to San Agustín was a distance of only 222 miles; he had
actually traversed more than three times that mileage. Taking his next
fix at sunset on March 1, John read his position to be 23°00'N, 18°54'W.
That pleased him; he had managed to get *Britannia* another degree west.
But he had not been able to stop its drift to the south, having lost another
degree and a half of latitude.

That trend—managing slow westward progress but constantly
drifting farther and farther south—was very high risk, given John's
objective. Gaining a degree, even two degrees, of longitude while
simultaneously losing a degree or more of latitude absolutely would not
do, not given John's absolute commitment to a predetermined, precise
destination.

If John had not cared where in the Americas he would arrive—if it
had been okay for him to land in Venezuela, Puerto Rico, or the Dominican Republic, for example—then it would not have mattered to him so
much how far south the northerlies were taking him. But he did. He
would accept nothing less. It had to be Florida, and it had to be nonstop:
"If I failed and arrived in the West Indies or, even worse, someplace in
South America, I might still claim, in the eyes of the world, to be the first
man to row across the Atlantic single-handed; but in my eyes, and that
was all I cared for, I would have failed miserably." The way John saw it,
"almost anyone with a good boat, know-how, and reasonable perseverance
could row across, if that was all he wanted." To him, the real challenge

was to take *Britannia* "to where I said I would": across the Atlantic and to Florida. "Anything short of that would not, could not, do."

He knew he was getting close to the point of no return. Considering his predicament, he logged on March 11: "Had the winds been northeasterlies from the beginning, as they were supposed to be, we would probably be halfway across the Atlantic by now. In theory we should have been able to complete the journey in three and a half months, and now, after 51 days at sea, our westerly progress was only 420 miles (an incredibly poor average of slightly over 8 miles per day), and we were 300 miles *south* of our intended course."

These figures were cold, stark, and realistic. No amount of wishful thinking could change them. What more could have been done that John did not do?

With great reluctance he considered terminating the trip: "Things look so bad that if I had any sense left, I should not only forget Florida, but steer *Britannia* to the Cape Verde Islands, some 240 miles south of our present position, and start afresh, if at all—now while the north and northeasterly winds still make it possible." A few more days and that escape route would be gone. There would be no turning back; ultimately, the trade winds would make sure of that. John and *Britannia* would be facing the tousled expanse of the Atlantic at its widest. "Shall we go on, regardless of the consequences," John asked, "or turn back?" It was an "agonizing decision," with "no margin of error," but he had to make it entirely on his own. And he had to make it that day.

Given John's wildly venturesome, audaciously headstrong personality, and extraordinarily intrepid life story up to this point, there was really no chance he would be turning *Britannia* toward Cape Verde. He would continue to fight the ocean, remembering the parting words of his favorite pirate of the Caribbean, Captain Z, to "never, never give up."

Fairfax figured that only some extremely dramatic act could give him a fighting chance. He couldn't count on that happening with the winds. It had to be something he could control and that could continue to be an advantage for the rest of the trip. Brainstorming, he focused on four elements he could largely control: his boat, his food rations, his rowing, and the relationship between the previous three.

Britannia weighed over 2,000 pounds. At John's best, without a tailwind or a strong push from the following sea, he could row the boat at a speed of up to some 1.65 miles per hour (1.5 knots). But he couldn't keep rowing like that—full-out—for 10–12 hours a day. He had to pace himself, resulting in more like one mile per hour without helping winds. Whatever the speed, rowing a one-ton boat took an incredible amount of energy. And up to this point in his trip, much of his rowing had been into serious headwind and crosswind.

He had to lighten the load.

On day 64, Tuesday, March 25, John, the inveterate craps player, rolled the dice again: "A gamble, yes, perhaps one of the greatest gambles of my life." Inside *Britannia* was stored enough food to sustain him for three and a half months. Clearly the trip to Florida was going to take him quite a bit longer than that. Notwithstanding, it took John only a matter of minutes to throw most of his food overboard: 300 pounds of it. That left him only enough food to last for 20 days. Actually, he had planned to keep enough food for 30 days, but he took so much "joy in dumping Archie's grub overboard" that he got carried away and tossed more of the special Horlicks rations into the sea than he had planned, later realizing that he had food for 10 fewer days.

What in the world was he thinking? Exactly how big of a gamble was this? What were the odds that once again the inveterate gambler would crap out?

It wasn't that John misunderstood how much food he would need to provide the 4,000 calories required daily to fuel all the rowing he would need to be doing. He realized he might not be able to get it from passing ships. The nearest shipping lane to him at this point—New York to the Cape of Good Hope—was slightly over 800 miles to the west. If he dropped all the "surplus food," might the increase in his rowing speed enable him to get there in three weeks or a month? Not without great favoring winds. And could he rely on being sighted by a ship even if got there? In that case, he reasoned, he would have to depend on catching and eating fish. "I might find enough to survive," he thought, "but not enough to go on rowing: I would soon become too weak for that." Still, if he could gain half a mile per hour by lightening *Britannia*, and row 12 hours instead of 10, and get favorable winds, his daily average could be increased by 10 to 15 miles. In the past couple weeks, he had been doing 20 to 25 miles, so that would bring it up to 30 to 35 miles. With a very good easterly, *Britannia* might even make 40 miles a day, which would be double the speed they had been making. Plus, "there were plenty of things I could do without." The big if, as John knew, was whether a 300–400 pounds lighter *Britannia* would respond to the oars and increase her speed as much as John calculated.

"There's only one way to find out," he noted in his log.

John came to look back on March 25 as the day "I crossed the Rubicon." It was a gutsy decision. But perhaps it was not as gutsy as he would make it out to be after his trip was over.

There was some science supporting Fairfax's gamble, and he knew it. John was a great admirer of the French physician and sportsman Dr. Alain Bombard, who, in 1952, had crossed the Atlantic in an inflatable life raft (with rigging for a sail), surviving off a diet only of fish, all of his catching. Bombard made his ocean crossing as a scientific experiment more than an adventure, as his objective was to prove that a human being could survive only on fish without any other food or fresh drinking water. Dr. Bombard's hope was to show a viable means of survival for the thousands or people who, over time, would be variously lost at sea. Fairfax knew that Dr. Bombard had reported very optimistically on the results of his trip, which was from Tangier to Barbados, taking 66 days. Using hooks, a harpoon, and a net that he assembled on his raft from simple miscellaneous materials, the Frenchman used only fish for food, and fish oil and fish blood for his liquid intake, though he did end up drinking a limited amount of seawater.

When John crossed the Rubicon on March 25, Bombard's theory went with him.

But his faith in Bombard's controversial theory was not absolute when John dumped 300 pounds of Archie de Jong's "horrible" rations over the side of his boat. For the first couple weeks out of Grand Canary, John hadn't seen a single fish. It was not until February 5 that he saw an edible sea creature of any kind. It was a turtle, a big one, over 100 pounds. An evasive prey, but a "perfect shot" with his spear gun through its neck, and an exhausting tug-of-war struggle to pull it on board, led to a supper of turtle stew: "I have never tasted a better one, before or since. My very own recipe, too, created on the spur of the moment." According to chef John, the meal was "one of those once-in-a-lifetime strokes of culinary genius." The dish was so tasty it was likely a factor in his tossing all the Horlicks food overboard.

Following turtle came dorado—or dolphinfish—but not into John's cooking pot until two weeks later. (Dolphinfish are unrelated to dolphins, which are mammals. Commercially, the meat of dolphinfish is labeled with its Hawaiian name, mahi-mahi, to reduce public confusion.) As remarkably beautiful as dorado were, with yellow tails and a long blue dorsal fin running the entire length of their body, and as enjoyable as it was for John to watch migrating schools of the fish swimming along, around, and under his boat (he came to call them "his boys"), what was paramount about the dorado to John was their abundance (once or twice, he saw groups of 40 to 50 or more), their large size (they can grow to six feet in length and to 60 to 80 pounds), and their delicious mild taste. One dorado provided enough food for several meals, with John often frying up the remains for breakfasts. If there was just one sort of fish that John was thinking about when he made the decision to cross the Rubicon (in the company of Dr. Bombard), it was the dorado.

The omnipresence of schools of dorado during different stretches of the ocean crossing brought other fish to Fairfax's plate. Swift-moving and agile, the dorado were highly effective predators. John witnessed them feeding during the day (and sometimes on a clear Moonlit night) on a variety of small fishes, including man-o-war, triggerfish, tuna, billfish, mackerel, and pufferfish. But the biggest treat, for John and likely the dorado, was watching them snare flying fish. Although flying fish did not actually fly—they possessed rigid wing-like fins, which did not flap—they could swim with terrific speed toward the surface and then, as John put it, "keep on going." When they left the water, they went into airborne glide, "sometimes for a surprising distance." Ichthyologists generally thought this ability to be an adaptation that allowed flying fish to escape predators, but it was not enough to stop a school of dorado from getting at them successfully. In cutting open the stomachs of many of the dorado that he caught, John found a number of flying fish, most of them still alive. On March 13, for example, he fried a few of them for himself "with my last onion—delicious!"

Shark meat also found its way into Fairfax's meal fare. Much riskier to catch and kill, of course, the occasional shark, as we have seen, came silently by, moving its body from side to side to propel itself through the water to check out *Britannia*. The first rendezvous with a shark had come on February 20. To catch it, John had made a loop with a half-inch-thick nylon rope that he weighed down at the sides with lead wire and a few bolts, baited the loop with a chunk of fish meat, threw it into the water, lassoed the shark around its snout and gills, and tightened the lasso with a hard pull. It was a brutal fight, with the shark generating tremendous power, but John was eventually able to haul him in. Cutting the big fish's stomach open, John found two dozen little sharks in her belly—a few of them wriggled away, but he grabbed the rest and put them into one of his plastic buckets. They, too, made for good eating. Another shark turned up on April 10, attracted to the water around *Britannia* by a dolphinfish that had arrived "so terribly mauled that he could hardly swim, so I put him out of his misery with my speargun and fed him to the others." As John tossed out the chunk, he noticed "a stranger partaking in the feast."

Bottom line: Fairfax had managed to catch and eat a lot of fish, justifying his decision to dump so much of Archie's rations overboard. In fact, he ate so much fish that he began to complain about it.

On April 1, he fretted about a passing ship that could have resupplied him: "The thought of missing out and eating nothing but fish for 600 miles makes me shudder. I have never liked fish so very much anyway."

On April 11: Going overboard with his speargun, John had the "battle of his life" killing and bringing into his boat a "beast" of a fish—"about six feet long and at least a hundred pounds in weight"—of "a species unknown to him." The same day he also killed two sharks. That night he ate a huge filet of the unknown fish, tossing the rest away: "I had never seen one like it, and I decided to find out what it tasted like. The meat seemed white and juicy, much better-looking than that of my dolphins. So, having run out of cayenne pepper, I decided to open a little bottle of Tabasco sauce since I kept it for occasions such as this. Well, I figured only a few drops at a time would come out of it and shook the bottle vigorously. When I stopped, I discovered, to my horror, that nearly half of my precious treasure had gone into a pound of fish and small fistful of rice. I was so hungry I ate it all, but for the life of me, I couldn't say what that fish tasted like. The trouble is, my stomach didn't seem to appreciate it and is now working overtime trying to get rid of it. I can just imagine, as I squat over the gunwale, what the big fish must be thinking as it looks up from the bottom, or wherever dead fish go: Well, well! Look at that, now. Ain't that bastard that went and done for me made a big ass of himself!" (The "beast" of a fish was likely some kind of sunfish or perhaps a sharptail mola.)

On April 17, he returned to his pet theme while also connecting it to his lack of tobacco: "Unless I stop a ship, it will be fish forever. Smoked my last cigar, too, and have tobacco for two pipes only, and the tobacco is not even pipe tobacco but cigar butts. I am not really sure which bothers me more: eating fish, or not smoking."

On April 19: "I smoked my last pipe, God damn it! And ate fish for breakfast, lunch, and dinner. Oh, I've had enough."

April 20: "Off the Canary Islands it was like Piccadilly Circus, so much that I lived in fear of being run down. I didn't really need ships then. Now I do and they are not around. Thought for the day: I hate fish!"

April 25: "Ate a lot of fish today—one of them was a barracuda. Don't like it, but ye gods, I'm hungry!"

May 27: "Fish! What a stinking word that is! I eat a hell of a lot of it—have to if I want to keep up my energy: 5, maybe 6 pounds a day. Boiled, raw, dried, it doesn't matter how I prepare it; the result is always the same: nauseating. I eat as much as I can, actually forcing myself to swallow more than my stomach can reasonably hold. Because if one fills one's belly to the point of bursting, one should not feel hungry all the time, as I do. Apparently there are simply not enough calories in six pounds of fish to replace what I burn. But if I try to eat more, and I have, I only succeed in vomiting, feeling sick and hungrier than before. It is getting so bad I find myself wishing I had some of Archie's stuff left. A turtle would make my day, but there aren't any to be seen."

In his confrontation with some of the Atlantic's biggest and most dangerous fish, Fairfax exhibited an exceptional level of aggression and ruthlessness partly called for under the circumstances and partly natural to his antipathetic personality:

Fighting to capture the sea turtle on February 5: "You bitch! I will follow you to the bottom of the sea before I let you go." Going after his first dolphinfish on February 20: "I am seeking satisfaction for my murderous mood. . . . Finding the sorry mess at my feet increasingly irritating, I got up again and wearily tossed the dorado spoils overboard." After catching a hammerhead shark on March 19: "Brought aboard, he proved a full 10 feet long. It took me over an hour to chop him up into pieces small enough for my boys (the school of dolphinfish then following along *Britannia*) to swallow; but to watch their zestful joy as they gorged themselves was more than worth it. The head and fins I kept for myself."

Contemplating his struggle for food and survival on the open sea on April 9: "Gradually but inexorably, the ceaseless struggle for survival, coupled with the backbreaking, soul-destroying task of manning the oars for hours on end, was subduing my vital energy. In order to survive I was returning to the primeval, shedding the veneer with which civilization had coated my animal instincts. I became a naked savage, a beast of prey which to feel alive was compelled to search for a means of escaping the tediousness that threatened to smother his urge to go on fighting. Because I was always desperately tired, every now and then I had to find a release from my self-imposed slavery. Somehow I could still laugh at myself—that, and bloody reckless sorties against the fish that *Britannia* lured to her, were my best outlets." Even when he incurred injuries himself, some rather serious, he enjoyed fighting the big fish as blood sport: "I was covered with blood—which, to my amazement, I discovered was my own. I had scratches all over, some of them quite big scratches, undoubtedly made by the dolphins as they swished by. In the frenzy of battle, I just hadn't noticed. I do now—they burn like hell! My hands are somewhat damaged too. All in all, I feel more bruised than after my scrap with the mako shark; but by Jupiter, such is the sport of kings—and as I relive it now, I can feel my blood run hot again."

Angry and wet from rain and high waves on April 19: "An hour later, an untimely shower of spray reduced me to unbelievable streams of madness, and during such periods, in my hate against the sea, I was capable of almost anything. . . . I started by catching a dorado. A monstrous newcomer, I speared it for the sole reason that it was so big. I usually choose smaller ones, easier to handle, but this time I had not been able to resist the temptation. . . . Wearily dragging the fast-stiffening carcass into the boat, I damned all fish to fry in hell forever."

In the delirium of a fever brought on by a sickness on June 1, he imagined an epic battle with a tiger shark: "I stared at it, an overpowering hate slowly began to boil up inside me and suddenly, screaming like a madman, I pulled out my knife and dived at it. . . . The white belly of the shark appeared and stood between me and *Britannia* and I plunged and slashed at it, cursing and yelling as I felt the blade go through, tearing, ripping, again and again. Then I regained my senses and saw I had been slashing at the white canvas of my rain catcher, and I just stared at it—then crawled into my rathole and lay down pounding the deck with my fists, until I finally cried myself to sleep. I can't remember doing that ever before in my life, and I hope it does not happen again."

For Fairfax, his necessary preoccupation with fish—slowly but surely—became a virtual mania, far less extreme that Captain Ahab's quest for Moby Dick but a haunting obsession nonetheless. Even his most pleasant association with the most familiar fish that had traveled with him and *Britannia*, for many hundreds of miles, off and on, ultimately turned tragic.

The dorado he came to know as Jerrycan first appeared along the boat on March 13.* This particular dolphinfish was easily identifiable because it had a scar on his back. Jerrycan came and went around *Britannia* for so long—nearly three months—that John thought the fish must have "adopted us." John regularly fed him scraps from the other fish he caught (he knew he was a male because male dorados had a blunt, almost square head, whereas the females "have more delicate lines"). Jerrycan, who was slightly over average size, about 4.5 feet long and around 40 pounds, was "spared the pot" because John had more than enough to eat with the female companion of Jerrycan that he had killed and brought aboard. Another reason John spared him was "that if I continue to feed him, his presence is likely to attract other dorados—who, if they get used to our company and follow us, will then be a real supply of fresh fish, always at hand."

The strategy worked very well. John enjoyed keeping an eye out for the large dorado with the scar on his back and fed him every day he saw him. The fish wasn't nearby every day, but whenever he was there he showed "no inclination to leave," staying as many as six days straight. Of all "his boys"—the nickname for whatever school of dolphinfish happened to be accompanying *Britannia* at the time, Jerrycan was hands down John's favorite.

But on June 4, 84 days after Jerrycan first appeared, the fish and his dolphinfish companions had what Fairfax called a "tragic encounter." It was such a stunning experience that it was the only thing that John wrote about in his log that day—he didn't even give the wind direction or report on how many hours he rowed, which was standard. John told the sad story, but with less the pathos and poignancy than one might expect: "We met a school of about 50 porpoises, the first I've seen since starting. They bore down on *Britannia* with high, squeaking noises and attacked my boys without a moment's hesitation. I'm sure that most of the bigger dolphins could have escaped, but they seemed to consider

---

*   A "jerry can" is British slang for a type of narrow, flat-sided metal fluid container having a capacity of 4.5 imperial gallons (or 5.4 US gallons).

Britannia as home, therefore a secure place. They all grouped around and under her, and the porpoises had a field day. When I dived to look at the battle from below there were only ten left out of at least a hundred. They were in a row, flat against *Britannia*'s bottom, and didn't dare to move as the porpoises circled around; and every now and then one charged the closely packed bunch, grabbing one and scattering the rest, although barely so, as they immediately regrouped in their position under *Britannia*.

"Eventually only three were left, and the porpoises stopped paying attention to them, turning their curiosity toward me. They circled me, squeaking and nudging one another, until, after 5 minutes, they swam away and soon disappeared. It was most interesting. Of the three surviving dolphins one looked a bit mangled, and I speared him for dinner tomorrow. All in all, a very bad day for them."

John expressed regret that "Jerrycan and my boys are no more." The dolphinfish had "kept us company for so long that I could hardly believe I would never see them again." Other such fish might come, "but my boys had a personality all their own." It would "never be the same without Jerrycan." He wondered what happened to him. He would never know, but it was "nice to think that today he had not been with the others." Having expressed what for John were some rather strong emotions, he concluded his entry by returning to clinical observation. In the awful event's aftermath, "I noticed that no shark whatever appeared in the vicinity. Considering the amount of blood and scattered flesh left by the carnage, one would have thought the sea would be alive with shark, but none came."

◆

Fairfax was not a devout man. However, if he had prayed on March 25, the day of his big gamble, it might have been for 40 days and 40 nights of favorable trade winds. For that was exactly what he got, a blessing whether he recognized it as such or not.

Starting late that very day and continuing through May 3—exactly 40 days and nights—the breeze blew from the east, helping propel

Britannia across the Atlantic at a speed and rate that John could have only dreamed of the day before. For 36 of those 40 days, the winds sustained speeds of 13 miles per hour (Force 4), for 24 days of 18 MPH or more (Force 5), and for nine days hitting 25 MPH and more (from Force 6 to as high as Force 9). His location moved during those 40 days from 19°N, 26°W to 22°N, 48°W. That was a movement westward of 22 degrees of longitude and a total distance traveled of 1,437 statute miles, for an average of 35.9 miles per day. As proud as John was of the endless hours of rowing he had put in (many of those days for 11–12 hours), he understood that "no amount of rowing would have allowed me to reach this longitude without the easterlies." He exhorted: "May they blow forever! I need them more than ever; I am not so strong anymore. Oh, Florida, where are you?" It was day 103.

The next morning John regretted making any reference in his logbook to those "beautiful easterly winds," because the wind overnight changed to a southerly. It stayed that way for three days and was a moderately strong breeze of Force 4. On the fourth day, May 7, an even worse change came in the form of westerly winds—only Force 2–3, but westerlies all the same. John wondered whether the Venti, the Roman gods of the winds, had turned against him. Perhaps Auster and Favonius, the gods of the south and west winds, had quarreled with Subsolanus, the god of the easterlies, and won a victory over him. If so, their victory was short-lived, because on May 8, Subsolanus and the trade winds again came in to prevail. Though the breezes were gentle, they came from the east, favoring John's course across the Atlantic for the next 18 days, until May 25. That got him to 22°55'N, 60°50'W, 12.5 more degrees of longitude westward and 821 miles closer to his destination. All told, over the past 62 days, *Britannia* had crossed 2,258 miles of Atlantic Ocean.

John recorded: "The West Indies are now only a few hundred miles to the south of us. If I wished, I could have stepped ashore by now on Antigua, Martinique, or Barbados; it would not have mattered. Who could have accused me of not having crossed the Atlantic?"

"But, instead, after 125 days at sea, because of a whim, I still have 1,200 miles to go! How many more days? Will I ever see land, any land, again? And if I did, and it was not Florida, would I have the fortitude, the determination, the madness to go on?

"That would be the final test. If I could resist the temptation to end my journey then and there, then surely, even if I never do reach Florida and the sea finally manages to destroy me, will I not, nevertheless, have won?"

8

Temptations

There were not many temptations in life in which Fairfax did not indulge. Even in the stretch of 40 days and 40 nights of racing along westward thanks to the favorable winds, John was not about to let a passing ship go by without trying to benefit from its bounty. And as always he credited the goddess Venus, his patron and protector, for making it possible.

"Would you believe it: she has done it again! At dawn, as my marvelous goddess blushingly disappeared behind the rising sun, a ship spotted us; and today's date is 27 (April)—my lucky number and obviously her favorite also. The *Rhine Ore*, a German freighter, after seeing my smoke flare, came straight at us: so straight that, as I saw the ponderous bows looming high above us—she was on ballast—I realized that her helmsman had miscalculated and we were about to be rammed. What a way to end!"

John rowed like mad and "by a miracle" managed to bring *Britannia* about the immense rusty bows of the German ship, passing a bare five yards from them. As the *Rhine Ore* sped by—"not fast, but enough to make me wish I had never seen her"—John breathlessly kept trying to steer away from her. The freighter sucked them in so close that John could not use his starboard oar without hitting her side. Hoping the props would miss them, he pulled in the oar, "cursing savagely at the stupidity of the gods and men alike." But he got lucky. The swirl from the props pushed *Britannia* away. They were okay, but it had been very close.

The *Rhine Ore* stopped half a mile upwind and up-current from John. He spent half an hour trying to get somewhere near the big ship before the German captain realized what the oarsman in the rowboat was trying to do and gently backed his engines. Drawing nearer, the crew passed down a rope. After that, according to John: "It was sheer bliss. Everybody was so kind. I had a breakfast of four eggs and bacon and two cold beers, and they also gave me everything I needed except a couple minor items that I forgot to ask for. Food and water for two weeks. By supplementing it with fish I can make it last for a month, and after that I will see. The captain promised to send some letters I had written, and also some film rolls for ITN. Now we are all set again. Thank you, Venus; with protection like yours I'll go through hell and come out unscathed."

Back on *Britannia* after his rest and relaxation on the *Rhine Ore*, John indulged, again, this time in a veneer of justification for not just accepting but actively seeking out such substantial favors from passing ships: "Leaving the *Rhine Ore* and watching her disappear over the horizon had been in no way as painful as, say, leaving the *Skauborg*. Meeting her and exchanging a few words with other human beings had been pleasant, but somehow I regarded them as intruders upon the privacy of my little world. Going on board, shaking hands, sitting at a table to eat—the whole episode struck me as odd and unreal. It was as if I had stepped onto another planet altogether. I very much needed the goods they could provide me; but once these had been supplied I craved for the solitude that had been my own for so long, and I watched them go without sorrow. Loneliness was no longer a specter to be feared, but more a cherished companion without whom I was at a loss."

One may sympathize with Fairfax for getting off his boat and accepting such generous assistance from the passing freighter. But it is hard to endorse John's after-the-fact dismissing of all the help he was given—and actively sought to receive—as an intrusion into "my little world," as the success of his entire ocean crossing was built on such a lenient approach. His voyage was just *not* "unassisted," it was greatly "assisted," almost the entire way. The manner of his expedition was nothing like what Tom McClean would venture in his North Atlantic by crossing in *Silver*, in which he took no supplies, once he started from Newfoundland, from any other ship—and certainly was never going to get out of his boat to have a bacon and eggs, cold beer, a sociable encounter with the ship's captain and his crew, and a general R&R. McClean was resolute that his crossing be absolutely unassisted. The contrast between McClean's crossing, to come, as it did not even start until May 17, and Fairfax's voyage could not be starker, in this respect—and in so many others.

On May 30 Fairfax received the benefits of meeting another vessel, a beautiful passenger ship, the *Empress of Canada*, with the Canadian Pacific Lines. Its veteran captain, a man with a distinguished career named Peter John Roberts, was "far from pleased" to be stopping for Fairfax and his rowboat. Captain Roberts did not invite John aboard and was peevish when John sent a hastily scribbled note up to the deck of the ocean liner at the end of a heaving line.

"So, this is your shopping list," the captain asked, a deep frown on his brow. "Shampoo!" he screamed. "What in the name of God do you want shampoo for?"

"To wash my hair, of course. What do you think?" John yelled back.

Shaking his head, Roberts told the chief steward to get everything on John's list: "On the double, do you hear? On the double." Then, leaning back to John: "Do you know, young fellow, that this ship is on charter. We have over 1,000 passengers. Every hour I lose will cost my company a thousand dollars. Who's going to pay for it? Hey?"

John heard his every word but said: "I didn't hear that, Captain. Would you mind repeating, please?"

"You are crazy!"

"Aye, aye captain. How about some water? I need some water, too. Think you could let me have some?"

"Water? To drink? Or to wash your hair with?"

"To drink, please."

"Anything else?"

"Well, yes. As a matter of fact, I could use some pipe tobacco and a carton or two of cigarettes—preferably tipped ones."

The captain nearly blew a fuse. John was disappointed that Roberts turned away before he could tell him the particular brand he liked.

Fairfax got everything on his shopping list and then some. Mainly he had asked for canned food, but the Canadians also gave him quite a supply of perishable stuff—cheese, butter, eggs, and bread. John was delighted to see those items because "I had such a terrible craving" for them and "I ate and ate and ate."

Captain Roberts moved the 27,000-ton, 650-foot-long *Empress of Canada* away so quickly that *Britannia* was nearly caught in the propellers' wash. Showing that he was a considerate and unselfish officer and gentleman, he blew his ship's horn three times in salute—perhaps to *Britannia*, the scrappy rowboat, more so than to John.

The next morning, whether it was from eating so much or not preparing his food properly, John became very ill, with nausea, vomiting, high temperature, and "feeling weak as a baby." It was during this bout with sickness that John had his recurring nightmare about taking on a tiger shark. "Feeling so frail I could hardly stand, my stomach quivering in relentless spasms of pain, I feelingly cursed myself for the dolt I was, having gorged myself with rich food" and "broken a cardinal rule of survival" by, in his case, "an unpardonable lack of willpower." John cursed, too, because the sea was "so calm, so frighteningly calm, that I felt, perhaps as never before, the awesome immensity of my solitude."

One might wonder how immense his solitude might have been if had not given in to the temptation, whenever he had the chance, to meet up with passing ships and receive their company.

He couldn't have felt too guilty about his lack of will because two days later, he crossed paths with another ship, went on board for a couple hours, and got an additional supply of canned goods. This time "the captain was most kind, and now I am more than all right with food and tobacco." However, John came away distressed from the encounter with the ship, the *Bay Ross*, a Norwegian liner, because he lost one of the prize "trophies" of his trip. After spearing and agonizing for five long minutes to bring the 10-foot-long hammerhead shark on board on March 19, he had saved its head and planned to have it mounted. Unfortunately, his "beautiful hammerhead trophy" bumped against the ladder of the *Bay Ross* and sank to the bottom of ocean. "After all the time I had spent working on it, I was really sorry to lose it."

On June 16, his 147th day at sea, John experienced his penultimate encounter with a passing ship when the American aircraft "supercarrier," the USS *Saratoga*, "stopped by this afternoon." Understandably, it was "quite amazing" for John, who was napping at the time, to scramble out of his rathole to see such a beautiful, gigantic ship—a 1,063-foot-long Forrestal-class "supercarrier" with some 5,500 sailors and some 70 to 90 aircraft on board—pass by. Although he had been treated generously, as a VIP, by almost all of the ships that met him, his experience with the *Saratoga* proved to be truly extraordinary.

It began with the US naval vessel lowering a lifeboat and coming all the way over to him, as *Britannia* was drifting downward. According to John, "None of us, neither the chap in charge of the lifeboat nor I suggested that I be towed back to the Saratoga and be given food there." Instead, the carrier sent a helicopter and dropped the food a few feet from John's boat. One can imagine how much John relished the scene: "Generous as usual, the Americans really overdid it a bit. In fact, the load was so heavy I could barely pull it inside *Britannia* and later on had to throw some overboard. But it was a very nice thing for the captain to do—I mean to stop the *Saratoga* for me!—and he also sent a personal gift: a carton of Sir Walter Raleigh cigarettes and a few other things and goodies."* The captain was Warren Harold O'Neill, a 1943 Naval

---

* In being given the carton of Raleigh cigarettes by Captain O'Neill of the USS *Saratoga*, Fairfax was sure that the captain was linking to him to Sir Walter Raleigh, the late 16th century English adventurer, ship captain, and writer, who Queen Elizabeth I knighted in 1585 but who was later put to death by Elizabeth's successor, James I, for treason. Perhaps Captain O'Neill had this connection of English maritime adventurers in mind when he gave Fairfax the Raleigh brand of cigarettes, but perhaps it was just a carton of available cigarettes. Certainly, Captain O'Neill would have been totally unaware of the many interesting parallels between Raleigh and Fairfax, as Raleigh, though the queen's favorite, was not

Academy graduate who had just become commander of the *Saratoga* on April 4, 1969.

Fairfax got to the point where he was discriminating in terms of what ships he would "receive." On June 28, his 159th day, a Russian ship, coming from Cuba, stopped by the *Britannia*, "obviously with the intention of coming to my 'rescue.'" John "waved madly" to indicate that he was all right and did not need anything. Yet the Russian ship came on and soon had a lifeboat in the water for him. John decided that since "they had gone through all that bother it would be just as well if I went."

The vessel was the *Krasnozavodsk*, a general cargo ship named after a Soviet-era town (located 60 miles northeast of Moscow) whose name translates as "red factory." Invited on board, John discovered the crew was "an extraordinarily nice bunch and kept insisting that I must surely need something." To make them happy, he accepted some water, cigarettes, pineapples, and canned fruit. The Russian sailors were "all surprised and amazed at what I was doing and asked me if I would mind having my picture taken with the whole crew around me." Of course, John was "delighted to oblige."

His eye, not surprisingly, was drawn to a "young, healthy-looking lass" who was part of the crew. Her name was Svetlana, and John, rascal that he was, pulled her to his side, in front of the flashing camera, and gave her a "from-England-with love" kiss. (John was referring here to the 1962 spy film *From Russia with Love*). According to John, Svetlana was "very happy about it" and, to make sure the picture would come out well, asked him to "repeat the performance" for the photographer. John was then offered the chance to take a hot shower—presumably

---

popular, but rather known for his hubris, extravagant spending, and unorthodox thought. Raleigh was also a bold talker with a vaulting imagination, interested in skeptical philosophy and atheism, as well as Greco-Roman mythology and history. Like Fairfax, Raleigh survives as an interesting and enigmatic personality rather than as a force in history—one who can be presented either as a hero or as a scoundrel. Both Raleigh and Fairfax possessed considerable practical abilities and a persuasive pen, but there were several discrepancies between their vision, their self-proclaimed narratives of their life story, and the actual facts.

without Svetlana joining him—which he accepted. When he finally left the *Krasnozavodsk*, "I was feeling very happy myself." "Russian ships, he thought, were "wonderful."

◆

On June 9, John heard on his radio that there was a tropical depression gathering strength in the Caribbean, with a good chance it would become a hurricane. "What the blighter on the radio didn't say," John logged, "is where and what course it is supposed to follow." Try as he did, he was unable to get any more information the rest of the day on the storm.

He had very vivid memories of being in a hurricane. When he was working for Captain Z in the Caribbean, the fishing boat on which he was serving as first mate got caught in Hurricane Anna, the first of the Atlantic's 1961 season. Initially a tropical storm, too, it moved across the Caribbean, reaching hurricane status on July 22 over the Windward Islands and intensifying to a Category 2 hurricane two days later. Anna peaked with maximum sustained winds of 105 MPH, then weakened slightly before hitting the coast of Honduras and making landfall in Belize (then known as British Honduras).

The center of the storm at its worst passed some 80 miles north of the boat that John was on. Called the *Orion*, a converted German mine-sweeper, the vessel did not stand a chance as she lay at anchor in the bay of one of the cays at Serranilla Bank, a partially submerged reef (with small uninhabited islets) about halfway between the southwest coast of Jamaica and the northeast coast of Nicaragua.

"It was at dawn, a dawn the like of which I had never seen before, that Anna made her presence felt. The air was hot, gray, oppressive. The cay, a barren patch of sand, grass, and rocks, half a mile long by 300 yards at its widest, maybe 10 feet above sea level at its highest point, had almost disappeared under a carpet of seabirds. There must have been thousands of them, and their frenzied cacophony had to be heard to be believed. Mountainous clouds hovered above, the blackness of the sky matching that of the sea. Yet not a whisper of wind, not a ripple stirred the waters.

"Then the first gusts of wind swept over us, accompanied by a thundering rumble, as ominous as it was distant. Within half an hour, pandemonium broke loose.

"The captain ordered everybody to abandon ship. Lashed by winds of up to 90 miles an hour, our little cay became a swirling mass of sand, birds, and water. Rain or sea, it was impossible to say. Everything that had not been solidly lashed or weighted down was swept away. We saved ourselves by huddling, with a few hundred birds, in a little gully behind an outcrop of rocks."

The *Orion* was wrecked in the first hour: "What could she do? The little lagoon became a boiling cauldron, and the sea pounced on her from all sides, mercilessly battering her into submission, all the time pushing her with relentless determination toward the reef that protruded mercilessly at the far end of the cay."

For a moment, John believed that the boat might be able to survive it all. But "the sea exploded under her keel—lifting her almost clear out of the water, then letting her go, with a sickening thump, right on top of the reef."

It was a terrible sight to see one's ship die like that. Terrible, yet magnificent. John, who often expressed himself poetically in his writing, wondered, "How can destruction be so grandiose in its beauty as to be obscene—and remain beautiful?"

Now hearing the report about the tropical storm developing in the Caribbean, as he was moving into it with *Britannia* in June 1969, John remembered the awesome power and beauty of Hurricane Anna.

He had no illusions as to what fate awaited them should their path cross with anything like that kind of formidable, magnificent storm.

The next morning John breathed a big sigh of relief when, according to the news on the radio, what was being called Tropical Depression Seven had hit Cuba and the south part of Florida, then dissipating shortly thereafter. *Britannia* was in the clear.

But John had a premonition that the Atlantic hurricane season of 1969 was going to be an active one, and that if he didn't get to his destination in the next four to six weeks, he would be in trouble. It was not a cheerful thought that he would soon be moving along the path followed by most hurricanes that form in the Caribbean. He was sure "I'm going to be hit by one, I can feel it in my bones." Unfortunately, the only way to prevent it was to relinquish Florida for the Bahamas. "Yet how can I do that," he admonished himself, "after so much fighting and struggling?" He was "not in the least suicide-minded" and "the barest common sense" suggested that he would "be asking for it" if he rowed on through the end of June into July. "After all, I have crossed the Atlantic, haven't I?" Why then be such a mule? The gods will surely be tempted if I go on." He ended his log entry for June 9: "I will think about it and decide tomorrow."

If on that night of decision Fairfax had known that the Atlantic hurricane season of 1969 would turn out to be the most active since 1933 and produce the highest number of systems to reach hurricane status—12—in a single season (only surpassed in 2005), he likely would have decided differently. One storm—ironically for John—was another Anna, reaching tropical storm status on July 27. Another depression, which began as a tropical wave moving off the west coast of Africa on August 5, developed into one of the monstrous, legendary storms of all time, Hurricane Camille. Peaking as a Category 5 hurricane on August 17, it devastated the US Gulf Coast, striking the states of Mississippi and Louisiana with ferocious winds and storm surge, killing 259 people, and producing severe flooding in the Appalachian regions of Virginia and West Virginia. Hurricane Camille caused $1.42 billion in damages, which in 2020 dollars was equivalent to $10 billion.

Opportunely, Fairfax did not know such storms would actually be coming, though clearly he feared something like it.

◆

Waking up the next morning, the weather was decidedly not of the type to encourage John to chance any encounter with a tropical storm or hurricane. As he had been for the past two days, he was in a drenching rain: "Everything is wet, and I'm beginning to think I should grow mushrooms." It was downright nasty, with "squall after squall" bringing sudden, gusty winds accompanied by slashing rain, some of them with thunder and lightning. Whether he could get to Florida or just to the Bahamas, there was "nothing I can do about it at present, as I cannot follow any other course than the one I am on."

That course was to take him to the Turks, the more northern of two groups of tropical islands—Turks and Caicos—in the Lucayan Archipelago of the northern West Indies. Located 100 miles due north of the island of Hispaniola (Haiti and the Dominican Republic) and 200 miles northeast of Cuba, the waters around Turks and Caicos provided the most direct entryways westward through the Caribbean. What Fairfax planned to do was use the trade winds to take him north of the Turks, move through the Caicos Passage, then navigate between Great Inagua and Mayaguana, the closest Bahamian islands, then keeping to the west of Andros, the largest Bahamian island, with the final leg of the trip being almost due north to Florida. The distance involved—from Grand Turk Island to Miami—was 645 miles. But the distance could turn out to be a great deal farther if the weather turned against him at any point, causing major redirections like what happened at the start of his trip back near the Canaries.

It was a mapped-out journey that gave him options. On June 15 he was still unsure, but only a little: "Still haven't made up my mind about Florida, but 100 to 1 I will go on. We'll see."

In the following days his endurance would be tested not by rain and wind but by sun and heat. "When it is not overcast, the heat is usually too great to allow me to row during the daytime." Often there was "not a whisper of wind" and it was "infernally hot," making rowing impossible. During the day the temperature would hover between 90°F and 100°F, so he slept by day and rowed at night. The only place John could hide from the sun was in his rathole, "a veritable oven," where "a few hours of sleeping would sap my strength almost as much, if not more than, if I had been rowing." When he couldn't sleep, he lay "in a state of torpidity, rivulets of sweat forming all over by body and trickling down to form a sticky puddle underneath." Most of the time he stayed totally naked, which he had been doing for some time anyway to prevent chafing of his legs and buttocks when he was rowing, from his clothes being wet most of the time. When the heat became unbearable, he would go out for a swim or simply hang on to *Britannia*'s gunwale until a prowling shark forced him to crawl back on board. "The hours would drag on forever," John noted, "as I softly cursed the day I had ever thought of rowing across the Atlantic."

Nights rowing on the Caribbean could be rather blissful and promote John's lyrical side: "For a few hours the whisper of the sea against *Britannia*'s hull as we doggedly plodded on, the rusty squeaks of the sliding seat, the regular, rhythmic *plump-thump* of the oars was a relief—a pleasure almost. Every now and then the sudden splash of a big fish somewhere in the distance would spark a living note in the otherwise cavernous expanse of the sea." But the quiet darkness also pushed out his subconscious: "Do I hear a voice singing, far away? Painful illusions stabbed at my solitude: someone was breathing hard at my back, almost touching me with barely suppressed gasps of burning passion, ready to change, as I knew too well, into sobs of anguish, or a derisive cackle, the moment I turned my head. The prelude of insanity?" Or the alter-ego of his goddess Venus? No. he didn't think so. He had just been at sea too long, that was all: "I was tired. Too God-damned tired."

By June 20, John managed to get himself into an excellent position to cross the Caicos Passage—his sextant reading showed his location to be 22°06'N, 72°67'W. He couldn't have been happier with his progress. "I wanted to go through it (the Caicos Passage) as far back as the end of April, and succeeding in doing so is no mean feat. I am now choosing an almost exact position and then trying to get there. In this way the challenge is still there and I'm out to shame the sea as thoroughly as I can, by going exactly where I want to go."

His boldly optimistic take on the status of his passage through the Caicos soon proved premature. On June 22 he found that he had been "pushed too far north by the southeast winds." Though "not unduly per-turbed," he did blame himself for "shoddy rowing" that did not make "enough allowance to offset the wind" while shaping his course. A big part of the problem, John thought, was how tired he became in the heat:

"I have to watch myself all the time or I suddenly find myself rowing 30 or 40 degrees off course." Nevertheless, he felt he was still in good position for the crossing, just southeast of Mayaguana Island (more east than south, really).

The Caicos Passage was about 20 miles wide, and it was John's intention to go through it without sighting land—"not trusting himself at this stage as to what my reactions might be if I physically saw land." For him it was "bad enough" to know that land was but a few miles either side of his course. "The temptation to row ashore might prove too great," he worried, "and I dedicated all my energies to rowing and navigation."

For this navigation to stay far enough away from Mayaguana that he didn't see its coastline, John relied entirely on dead reckoning. He knew that this was "far from satisfactory," but he hoped that after five months of judging winds and drifts, his skill would "prove equal to the task." As a matter of fact, if John's reckoning was correct, *Britannia* had already made its way through the Caicos Passage and was approaching the tip of the Acklins Island group, whose southwestern tip protruded far enough into John's potential course that he needed to be very aware of where it was if he meant to avoid it. He was conscious of the need to be quite careful, as he was "steering blindly through some of the most dangerous navigable waters in the world, with fierce-looking reefs, sandbars, and coral heads."

"I hope I am on course. Haven't seen any land, but it must be near."

He was especially wary about the Hogsty Reef, an uninhabited coral atoll, located between Acklins and Great Inagua (to the south), that rose up from 6,000-foot-deep surrounding waters and was five miles long by three miles wide. John's charts made it clear not only that good light would be needed to be certain about bypassing the nasty reef, but that a number of ships had failed to do so, as the charts showed the location of at least two impressive shipwrecks caused by it.

"Feeling a bit wary about Hogsty Reefs. Got a sixth sense for this sort of thing, and now something tells me I'm heading straight for them. It would be very bad luck indeed to have come so far only to pile up into a flipping reef. As I row I cannot see where I am going, and with rain and the noise I make with the oars, it would be almost impossible for me to sight or hear any breakers in time to avoid them. When riding a crest of a wave, *Britannia* goes at 3 knots and over; hitting a rock won't do her any good."

It was time to invoke his beloved goddess again: "Come, Venus, you ought at least to come out—let me have a peep at your lovely body."

"No chance. I just can't get a sight, not even a single position line."

"Well, let's trust luck."

◆

The next day, June 26, began with a portent of good fortune.

"Near dawn—ye gods! Saw her!—just as she was rising through a hole in the clouds. Horizon unbelievably black and low. How she managed to get through for me to see her I'll never know; but see her I did, for about two minutes, and all during that time she blinked and flashed at me like mad. Planets don't twinkle, so I knew right away there was something wrong and she was trying to warn me. Stopped rowing at once. Hit by a squall immediately after, and for two hours it was as if the sea and sky had gone mad. Lightning, thunder, rain, and the wind northeast, gusting up to Force 6–7. Magnificent spectacle of raw, naked fury! I felt as never before, as if I were part of it and, deliriously happy, cursed and sang throughout it all, at the top of my voice, while *Britannia*, frightened out of her wits, screamed bloody rape. I felt full of energy suddenly, and the strength and power of the gods burned like lava in my veins. And I positively itched to grab the oars and row, row, row. But I didn't. My beloved had warned me not to and I heeded her, which probably saved my life."

"The squall ended as suddenly as it had begun. And just at the last possible moment before the sun rose, I was able to shoot a couple stars and fix my position—which turned out to be only five miles northeast of the Hogsty Reef. Had I rowed, as I wanted to, I would have hit them square, right at the height of the storm. I'm sure *Britannia* would much have preferred to be raped by the sea rather than by them. As for myself, I'll just have to sacrifice a virgin to my goddess. It's been a long time since I last did, but surely she deserves it now. Trouble is, will I find one?"

Looking back on the near-fatal collision, Fairfax wrote in his log: "I simply felt, knew, that I had to stop rowing, no matter what, and that Venus—it was Venus, twinkles or no twinkles!—was trying to warn me of the proximity of danger. I heeded her and saved myself. What more is there to be said?"

The next day, June 27, it was not Venus he saw in the "fine weather" of the morning but rather the flashing beacon of the lighthouse off Acklins. Also known as the Remote Castle Lighthouse (or Castle Island Lighthouse), it was located (22°13'N, 74°31'W) on a small island off Acklin's southernmost tip and was famous, as John knew from his years in the Caribbean, for being a retreat used by pirates after attacking ships in in the Caicos Passage. He knew it meant land was very near. But he kept rowing right on by.

His first sighting of land since seeing the island of Hierro back in the Canaries came two days later, on June 19, his 160th day at sea: "Two points off my starboard bow the low shape of a very small cay was visible in the first light of dawn, maybe 3–4 miles away."

In a sense he gave way to the temptation. By the time he spotted what he later found to be Cay Verde, he had already passed it. Turning around, he rowed four hours, against the wind, to get back to it. John found it "lovely"—"green all over," with "a bit of white beach and dots of rocks all around." He anchored *Britannia* in two fathoms about 100 feet from the beach and went ashore, legs wobbly, barely able to walk. Seabirds all over the place, John spent the day "relaxing and trotting around, feeling great." In the afternoon he went spearfishing, determined to find a lobster for dinner. After three hours of searching he found one— "good size, too"—congratulating himself because he was "almost sure" it was "the only lobster in the surroundings."

He was content on the delightful, uninhabited cay that "I never wanted to leave the place." Having given in to the temptation of landing on it at all, now he considered spending "at least a few days in total relaxation." Luxuriating on the beach, he looked over at *Britannia* at anchor: "She looked so frail, so puny and dilapidated, that the idea of crossing the Atlantic in her, of actually living within her confines during the past 5 months, suddenly hit me as so unbelievable, so preposterous, that I almost cried. Surely it was not true; it could not have, it had not, happened. It was just another fantastic dream of mine, from which I would presumably wake up to find myself . . . where but on the sand of a barren patch of grass and rocks in the middle of nowhere!" If only in the "portion of my brain still capable of clear reasoning," John realized that he could not dally in paradise for long. If only a few hours on such heavenly dry land could throw him into "such a state of dejection" that, for a fleeting moment, he could even contemplate "the idea of sinking *Britannia* then and there" rather than go back to the oars, "what would 2 or 3 days do?"

Gradually, the joy of his first steps on terra firma turned into "a sour, frustrating bitterness" by the "inescapable need" to give up the notion that his gorgeous green cay was "paradise," in comparison to the "Hades" back in his rowboat.

So he left. Or, rather, he decided to leave. Hedonist that he was, he could not give up the chance of spending the brilliant afternoon skin-diving in the crystalline blue-green waters surrounding him.

Giving in to temptation after temptation, sometimes spurring guilt feelings and self-recriminations but more often leading to cunningly conceived rationalizations was essential to the workings of John Fair-fax's character. It was both a defect and a strength of his personality, depending on how one looks at it.

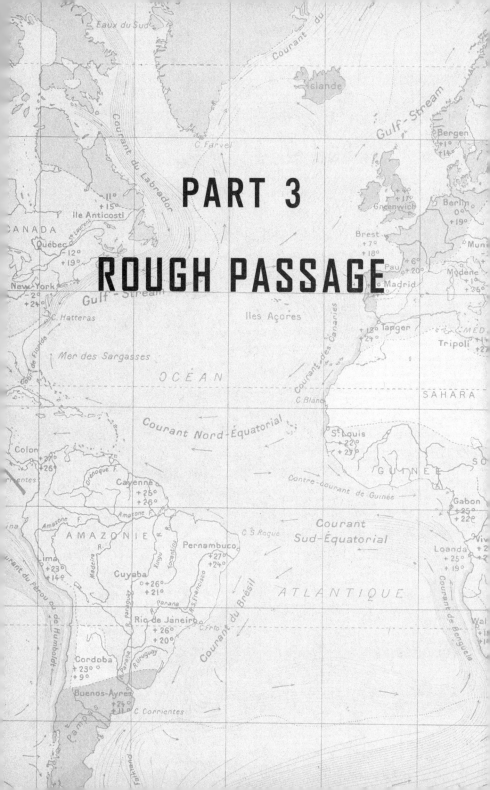

PART 3

ROUGH PASSAGE

9

Fegan's Orphanage

Tom suddenly realized he was shivering. He had not eaten for nearly 24 hours. He knew that no matter how difficult it proved, he had to get some hot food inside him soon. While it had been necessary to constantly pump water out of the boat, the cold had gone unnoticed. There was absolutely no way of keeping dry. He was damp right through to the skin, and there was nothing he could do about it except grin and bear it.

Starting with a mug of tea put new life into him. Propped up on one elbow in the bottom of *Silver*, and with the wind snuffing out match after match, it took nearly 15 minutes to get his camping cooker going. But the kettle finally boiled. Tom took off his mittens and wrapped his hands around the steaming mug and gulped at the thick dark brew, almost syrupy with sugar and condensed milk. But cooking a meal was out of the question right then. He settled for dry biscuits and curry paste spooned from the jar. It made a delicious meal.

Tom crawled into his shelter to nibble a piece of chocolate while he lay there looking up at a photograph he had pinned to the ceiling. It was of the man who had been his hero ever since, quite by accident, he read a book during his early army days (Tom had barely read a book as a boy) about the Antarctic explorer Sir Ernest Shackleton. Shackleton's epic adventures had captured his imagination as nobody had done before.* His refusal to give up, no matter how hard the going, his tremendous capabilities, his leadership and his tremendous strength of character, not only inspired Tom but "altered my whole way of life." Privately, to Tom, he was "the Boss."

He looked up at the salt-flecked photograph, wondering: "How long will I be out here?" The Boss had been in the Antarctic for 18 months, so his stint, even if it lasted 100 days, was "nothing more than a weekend by comparison." His mind drifted back over the years. Alone in the ocean he began to think more and more of his past life. Isolation was a marvelous state for being able to sort things out into some perspective.

◆

Thomas Colin McClean was born in Dublin, Ireland, on February 10, 1943, smack in the middle of World War II. Born out of wedlock, he didn't discover the names of his birth parents until many years later, when Tom was in his 60s.

His mother was Susan McClean of Castlefleming, raised on a farm in County Laois (Leix), southwest of Dublin. Early in the Second World War, the 38-year-old Miss McClean met and became romantically

---

* Shackleton (1874–1922) made three expeditions to the Antarctic. His first occurred in 1901 as a member of the National Antarctic Expedition led by Robert Falcon Scott, the famed British explorer; it made the deepest penetration of the continent at that time, to within 745 miles of the South Pole. In 1907 Shackleton led his own expedition; its goal was to get all the way to the pole. With three companions he almost made it, to within 97 miles. His third trip to the Antarctic, from 1914 to 1916, was his most famous—a true epic and nearly a fatal one. His plan was to cross the entire continent by way of the pole. However, ice in the Weddell Sea trapped his ship, the aptly named *Endurance*, which drifted for 10 months before being crushed by the ice. The 28 members of his expedition then lived on ice floes for five months before escaping in boats to Elephant Island in the South Shetland Islands. From there, Shackleton and five others sailed 800 miles to South Georgia Island, seeking aid. He and two of his men then made the first known crossing of that mountainous island. It took Shackleton four attempts before successfully rescuing his men from Elephant Island, but they were all miraculously saved. Shackleton died in January 1922, on South Georgia, at the start of what would have been his fourth Antarctic expedition.

involved with a man from a prosperous family in the nearby town of Ballybrophy. His name was William Sothern. Susan's involvement with Tommy, as William was called, led to her becoming pregnant. Unfortunately for Susan, Tommy Sothern had just joined the Royal Air Force and, irrespective of that, had no interest in marrying her, helping her out through the childbirth, or raising the child. This left Susan in a very difficult situation. An unmarried woman "with child" in a small Irish community created considerable scandal and often led to job loss, financial insecurity, and general personal hardship. Unable to cope with her circumstances alone, off she went to Bethany Home in Dublin, where arrangements had been made by Mrs. K. M. Glover, Bethany's matron, for the expectant mother to be cared for through the birth of her child.

Susan remained at Bethany Home for five weeks after giving birth to the boy. She must have loved the father or she wouldn't have named her son Thomas. But clearly Mr. Tommy Sothern did not love her, or he would not have forsaken her so completely. Distraught but feeling incapable of caring properly for her child, she gave up her maternal rights and left the baby in the care of the facility. She never saw her boy again, although she did make some inquiries about him while he was very young; she also pleaded with Tommy Sothern's mother to encourage her son to take some responsibility for the boy. But the father would have none of it. According to Bethany Home records, the father "takes no interest in him at all."

Little Tom remained at Bethany Home until he was almost five years old. There he received special care from the kind, loving Mrs. Glover, whom he came to know only as Auntie Kay. Officially, she was Bethany's matron, but, unofficially, she was closest thing to a foster mother little "Tommy," as she called him, would ever have. Auntie Kay had three sons—Carl, Stan, and Adrian—and Tommy interacted with them as if they were brothers. But as the boy approached his fifth birthday in early 1948, the authorities at the Bethany Home acknowledged Tommy was growing "too big for the Home (which) catered (to) younger boys." Reluctantly, Auntie Kay agreed, realizing that, with living circumstances so difficult in postwar Ireland, that the boy would have a better start on a good life if he were sent to a proper orphanage in England.

Auntie Kay applied for the boy's admission into Mr. Fegan's Homes, a well-known Protestant orphanage in Buckinghamshire, northwest of London. According to Fegan's synopsis of Tommy's condition at the time the application was being considered: "Thomas cannot read yet, and speaks little, mostly a mixed Irish English. His general appearance is clean and neat. He is a healthy looking little fellow and a credit to the Bethany Home, Dublin." Writing back to Auntie Kay, one of Fegan's directors, a man who identified himself only as Captain Martin, wrote on January 9, 1948: "I am particularly anxious to get hold of boys that are either orphans or who have no chance of ever having a home life of their own. It has been very difficult in so many cases when, after a year or so, the boy has been reclaimed. In this case, however, it looks as if we shall have Tom all his school days, and we hope that we shall be able to really influence him for the Lord. Please let me know when you will be able to make arrangements to send him. He will be going to the Small Boy's Home at Yardley Gobion, and I am sure he will be very happy there."

On a wet day in 1948, Auntie Kay put Tommy on a mail boat from Dun Laoghaire and sent him across the Irish Sea to England. Following the instructions sent from Fegan's, she pinned labels onto his coat and on his small tatty suitcase with the number 28 on them to identify the boy.

As young as he was, Tom remembers quite a bit about the trip: the docking of the boat in Liverpool; the train ride to London; the "stiff lady" who met him as "Number 28" at Euston Station and drove him to Fegan's; the large house—"dark gray and daunting"—that awaited him at Yardley Gobion. "They say an early shock or change stimulates the memory," Tom explains today. "For whereas some people can go no farther back than about their fourth birthday, I can recall my arrival at Fegan's with great clarity."

Looking back, being passed from person to person, that was for Tommy McClean the start of what was to be twelve years of a constant battle for survival. He arrived at the orphanage on February 11, 1948. The day before, when he got shipped over from Ireland, was his fifth birthday.

His mind racing back over the years, the thought of his "Mum"—the mother he never knew—brought unwanted tears to his eyes. He could barely see beyond the bow of *Silver* because of them. That made him angry. He wasn't on the ocean to dredge up old memories. But it seemed to be provoking just that.

In his early years at the orphanage he thought about his mother a lot. By the time he was eight he started asking questions about her, less so about his father, and when he didn't get answers, he got angry and very unruly. It got so bad by the time he was seven years old that the woman in charge of the boys at Yardley Gobion, a Miss Hayes, reported to her director, Captain Martin, that Tommy was getting "too hot for her to handle." The staff could no longer deal with the boy's "explosions." Captain Martin chose to send the boy "post haste" on to Fegan's other orphanage facility at nearby Stony Stratford—known colloquially as the "Big Boys Home"—even though Tommy was a year younger than the age minimum. There he would be under the supervision of a male super-intendent, Captain Flood.*

It took a while for the staff at Stony Stratford to figure out what was driving the boy into his severe disquiet, which had actually gotten worse when he entered the company of the older boys. On October 16, 1955, Captain Martin wrote to Auntie Kay (Mrs. Glover), soliciting her advice: "We have all felt for some time that Tommy is desperately anxious to trace his mother, and this is the reason for his unsocial behavior at times. He tells everybody about it. . . . I am sure that Tommy will eventually find out about his mother and until this happens he will continue to be

---

*   Fegan's Small Boys Home at Yardley Gobion kept boys up to the age of 11, at which time they were moved to Fegan's main orphanage in nearby Stony Stratford. The founder of the orphanage was James William Condell Fegan (1852–1925), an English Nonconformist evangelist who established a succession of orphanages for boys going back to 1872. The home was run mostly by women who, though they were not nuns (being Protestant), nonetheless dressed and acted like they were. Evangelical religious training at Fegan's was rigorous.

emotionally unstable. We have found it in so many cases that in spite of all that has been done to keep a boy from his mother on account of her bad influence, eventually he finds her. It is interesting also to note that the boy as a rule soon sums her up and leaves her, but having settled the matter. In his mind he becomes quite normal in this respect."

Aunt Kay agreed that Tommy's "acting out" likely stemmed from his obsession with knowing something about his mother. (Occasionally the boy got to spend the Christmas holiday with Auntie Kay and her family in Dublin, so she was aware of Tommy's moody preoccupation with mother.) She felt that the boy, only eight and a half years old, would be better off not knowing the truth. She proposed to Captain Flood that, on Tommy's next visit back to Ireland—if Tommy asked about his mother, which Auntie Kay was sure he would do—she would, as gently as possible, tell him "a convenient fiction." She would tell him that both his mother and father had been killed in a house fire soon after his birth. There was nothing else to find out about them, other than they had loved him deeply right up to the end.

It would be many years later, long after his Atlantic crossing, before Tom would learn there had been no fire: "It was a kindly tale thought up by Auntie Kay in my early life to stop me wondering about Mum and Dad."

The "loving lie" served its purpose. Back at Fegan's following his Irish Christmas in 1955, Tommy quit talking about his mother. More than that, he quit thinking about her or his father. They were dead. There was no point for the little boy to think about them any further.

But now Tom was a 26-year-old man, and he was so far into the Atlantic that he could not see land. In that burgeoning ocean the thoughts of a lonely orphan could not help but return.

Those thoughts were more nauseating than comforting.

◆

Whether induced by the bitterness of his childhood memories, the effect of fumes from his gas cooker, or not yet finding his sea legs, Tom was, in fact, seasick. For the second time.

Apart from the sheer misery of it, Tom knew from talking to Ridgway and Blyth that seasickness presented other problems. One was lethargy. When you are sick as a dog, it's hard to work and carry out even the simplest tasks, so there was a risk that Tom would neglect his boat. Two, he could lose strength due to the virtual impossibility of eating, digesting, and keeping food down. That, in turn, could lead to weakness and cold because there would be no fuel to provide body heat. The combination of all those things could reduce even a strong man like Tom to a useless weakling, incapable of looking after himself or his boat. If insufficiently strong-willed, he might experience a feeling of total hopelessness. There would be no escape from a horrid seasickness unless he managed to get ashore, drift into calm water, or be taken aboard a larger and more stable ship. And there was not much chance of that out in the western Atlantic on a dark night.

So, he forced himself to eat, attempted simple tasks, and, eventually, when he was sure it was safe to do so, lay down in a sodden heap. He slept fitfully, waking occasionally to be ill, eat some dry food, sip a little water, and keep an eye on the weather. For the first time he tried the radio. He picked up a station in St. John's. It was playing a record of the young Welsh singer Mary Hopkin performing "Goodbye." The DJ said the song was written by Paul McCartney and had risen to number two on the pop charts in the UK.

> *Please don't make me wait too late tomorrow comes*
> *And I will not be late*
> *Late today when it becomes tomorrow I will*
> *Leave to go a-way*
> *Goodbye . . . Goodbye . . .*
> *Goodbye, Goodbye, my love, Goodbye*

"Not yet, little lady," Tom muttered. "Not goodbye by a long chalk."

He felt miserable, no doubt. But he wasn't giving up. If that had been the pitifully weak sort of stuff his character had been made out of, he would never have survived his orphanage years or thrived as he did in the toughest units of the British Army.

◆

There had been nothing akin to family life at Fegan's. The staff could be kind but was always very strict about obedience: "It was a matter of 'them and us' as we marched around in our gray shorts, flannelette shirts, and lace-up black boots." Tom could at times make friends easily. His favorite was actually Mr. Gardener, a Scotsman, appropriately named because he was in fact the gardener for the orphanage; Tom enjoyed walking the grounds with him, learning about the vegetables, plants, and grass. Mealtime did nothing to encourage camaraderie. The food was poor, and the boys fought every meal to get enough to eat. If a boy put his knife down, another shouted "Overboard" and grabbed his food. The only way to survive was to never stop forking it in once the food arrived. How much grub a boy was given depended on how well he got on with the bigger boys serving it. Throughout the meal, an "orphan master" circled the tables, keeping order by striking the tables, and the boys, with canes.

Punishments were meted out for breaking any of the myriad rules. Offenders who got off easy were made to stand on a painted line for an hour never looking anywhere but straight ahead or they were assigned extra chores like digging up potatoes or weeding the lawn of the quadrangle on hands and knees. Otherwise it was a beating with a belt or a cane—six or more strokes. Tommy endured it all, many times. But he never gave in to any of it. During a whipping, he braced himself and looked tough. Or he hopped about laughing through it all, which brought on even more of a beating. The bigger the welts, the more he hopped and laughed.

Every day at Stony Stratford was very much same, regulated by a strict schedule and brain-numbing routine. Promptly at a minute before seven each morning the "orphan masters" hammered on the dormitory door. The boys leaped out of bed, knelt on the floor, and for five minutes, in Tom's words, "pretended to pray." Gathering up their coarse towels from the end of the beds, they ran down a staircase and across the quadrangle to the cold washrooms for a strip wash. Their cleanliness was inspected in front of large lamps by a particularly strident orphan master—known to the boys as "The Jailer"—who ticked off names against assigned numbers. Tom was 82, and his number was on many occasions atop the "punishment list."

As if being timed in a race, the boys ran back to the dormitory, quickly made their beds, folded blankets and sheets in a bed block army style, and put on their working clothes. Then off again across the quadrangle to the assembly hall to be inspected again and ticked off another list. A duty boy rang a brass bell, signaling an orderly rush into one of four assigned dining rooms. Of course, every meal began with grace. Breakfast was simple: a bowl of porridge, a cup of tea, and a slice of bread thinly spread with drippings. It was also quick—within 25 minutes the orphans were back in the dorm, sweeping and tidying their rooms. Donning their best uniforms, they lined for a march across orphanage grounds and off to the school in town. Before the gate was opened, they were again inspected and ticked off a list. Tom remembers especially hating to be seen by the townsfolk: "Can you imagine, 50 boys, some as old as 15, in boots, shorts, gray shirts and jackets, marching along the street holding hands. Holding hands! It always raised catcalls from the town kids." But the orphans got their revenge on the kids who teased them. Inside the school, the Fegan boys sized them up for pocket money and candy. If the townies had not brought anything good with them that day, they were "given a thumping" and told to bring something good the next day or they would be thumped again. "That was how we dealt with any boy who had jeered us on our way to school." The girls were treated differently. They would be tied up in the lavatories where they were kissed, or teased, or both.

Tom found most of his school classes boring. He enjoyed history and geography, but much of what he was taught was uninteresting and taught by adults who did not seem to care whether the boys learned or not. Mostly he enjoyed practical subjects such as wood- and metalworking. One year he made a wooden stool for Auntie Kay, which he gave to her as a Christmas gift.

The school day over, the Stony Stratford boys were marched back to their dormitory where, locked in, they changed back into their work clothes, washed and brushed up, and were checked against yet another list, followed by an inspection before tea. Once more a battle for food ensued, with good manners ignored in the interests of survival. After tea, the boys were free for an hour unless they had a red star against their name, which could have been earned for swearing, fighting, untidiness, or any one of a hundred violations. Tommy got into a lot of fights, mostly over stolen pennies.

Following an early evening hour for "recreation," the boys assembled in the main hall again for prayers and a reading from the Bible. More inspections, washing, and being checked off lists, then back upstairs to undress for bed. A half an hour was allowed for reading in bed before the masters came round to put the lights out. Usually a boy would serve as lookout. Occasionally after the masters had left the building, all hell broke loose: pillow fights, fistfights, struggles for sweets, lighting up dog-ends of cigarettes that boys had picked up on the road to and from school.

Though Sundays were different from the rest of the week, Tom disliked them the most. Three times that day the boys went to church: morning, afternoon, and evening. For him, doctrinal religious belief never took. Not a bit.

The orphans got few good glimpses of the outside world—in fact, the administration at Fegan's constantly warned them, and virtually sheltered them, from that world, for reputedly being wicked and full of sin and crime. Occasionally, the boys were sent to a summer camp in Dorset, where they lived in tents and had a freedom they never experienced at the orphanage. Over Christmas holiday a few of the boys who still had some connection with family got the chance to leave Fegan's and go on visits over the Christmas holiday. Tommy himself was sometimes sent back to Ireland to stay with Auntie Kay and her family. But in all such cases the orphanage always made sure those boys who were "on leave" were placed in the hands of Protestant guardians.

Not surprisingly, what Tommy and most of his chums most craved was a chance to go out and experience "the real world."

Ironically, without realizing it at the time, the tough love the orphans received at Fegan's proved, in Tom's view, to be "exactly what we boys needed to face whatever lay ahead." Not that he liked being an orphan. He hated it. But it made him into the strong-minded and determined man that he was.

The impulse to row a boat solo across the ocean would likely never have come to him if he had been a generally happy boy. One with a mother and father.

10

The Paratrooper

I t was another sleepless night by the pumps, with the morning ushering in even stronger winds. They were buffeting *Silver* at a rate of between 60 and 70 miles an hour. Tom blessed the sturdy craftsmanship of those Yorkshire boatbuilders who had designed his dory. Flimsy she may have looked, but flimsy she most certainly was not. Not even when it came to standing up to the Atlantic. "I am sure that *Silver*'s superb performance under such stern conditions helped to build my self-confidence," relates Tom. It was also creating a relationship between man and boat which was to grow into an unbreakable bond. In past days, they say, ships were made of wood and men of iron. "If I was not to fail *Silver*," Tom declares, "I would have to try to give a twentieth-century twist to that old adage."

It was to be yet another day of pumping, with little chance of snatching even a short doze. Lack of sleep in itself was no real hardship for Tom. After six years in the paratroopers and three years in the Special Air Service, roughing it came as second nature. He was grateful for his army training, especially that in the SAS. It was probably the most rigorously trained army unit in the world at that time. An SAS commando was trained to fight on his own, to live on his own, and to survive on his own. In Tom's words, "each man becomes what must be the most physically self-reliant human package known to any walk of life." Part of the secret to it was "knowing, and believing, you can cope with practically anything and everything."

Luck, however, has a part to play in most things. Because of the cold and the water, Tom had muffled himself up in two thick woolly undervests, a thick flannel shirt, a pullover, a seaman's heavy roll-collar sweater, and two sets of waterproof clothing. A bit cumbersome, to say the least, but they turned out to be a godsend. During the turmoil of the past two days and nights he had been flung about the tiny open space which made up the cockpit of *Silver*. He had been thudded into the gunwales, the cooker, the edge of the shelter roof, and the compass itself, which jutted out from the roof like a knobby-headed battering ram. By rights he should have been black and blue from head to toe. Thanks to the mass of clothing, he had been cushioned against the most severe effects of such a battering and merely felt a little sore.

Tom learned another lesson in double-quick time. There was no sense in trying to stand up or move about while *Silver* was bucketing about: "I had tried to stand, to move about as much as possible simply to give myself the sense of doing something." Rowing had been out of the question for hours. And for hours Tom lay on his side, half in and half out of the shelter. His back was wedged against the pack that was his RAF inflatable dinghy and his feet jammed tight against the supplies that filled up the rest of *Silver*. During the morning he managed to cook up some of his dehydrated curry and had left some in the pressure cooker ready to eat, hot or cold, "for I had no idea when this damnable storm would ease off long enough for me to prepare a reasonable meal."

Lying there, wedged in, while *Silver* lurched, rolled, rocked, and trembled, Tom became very conscious of his utter helplessness to do anything constructive. It was not a mood of despair. It was a feeling of complete frustration that swept over him. The only thing to do was to take stock of the situation that faced him if the storm continued for much longer: first, the water that was continuing to come inboard. His main comfort was that not nearly so much water was breaking over him as during the first few hours. He had become fully aware, however, of the Atlantic's ferocious talent for sudden change. A shift of wind, a breaking roller, and *Silver* could be swamped. Tom had by this time become fully confident of the efficiency of the pumps. They had been working splendidly.

By his rough calculations the pumps were capable of moving out about 10 gallons of water a minute. So far that had been generously adequate. One huge doubt nagged at Tom's mind. What if *Silver* took such a dunking that she filled up beyond the emptying rate the pumps were capable of? There was only one way to cope with such a situation.

Tom would have to go to his five-gallon bucket, lashed at the back of his seat. With it he would be able to get rid of about 60 gallons a minute. But how long could he maintain such a backbreaking pace? Not very long. And what if the flooding of *Silver* was so great that not even 60 gallons a minute could cope? Tom shrugged and decided to quit thinking about it until it happened.

Just before twilight he got his stove lit after 10 minutes of effort and nearly a half a box of matches. He managed to keep the matches reasonably dry by wrapping them in two bags of heavy-duty polyethylene and buttoning them down in the breast pocket of his shirt beneath the outer covering of sweaters and oilskins.

The leftover curry came quickly to the boil in the pressure cooker. There were just 10 spoonful, but they were every bit as good as a full-scale banquet. Tom had no doubt that regular hot food and drink was vital. Without it he feared he could become a victim of exposure and even more helpless—although that did not seem possible—than ever. It was just another problem to add to his mental preoccupations that saved him from worrying too much about his enforced inactivity and the bitter realization that he was still drifting south.

The screaming wind stayed with him right through another night. By this time, he was not bothering to creep into his sleeping bag in case he had to move in a hurry. It left him free to grab the pumps within a split second. He just wrapped his rubberized army poncho around him and catnapped in between the never-ending pumping sessions.

He suddenly realized that the blisters on his hands must be hardening up, or else he had become so used to them he did not feel them any longer. When he grabbed the pump handles he no longer felt the burning sensation slashing straight across the palms. It was small enough consolation, but to Tom it seemed like the boon of a lifetime. Hardly had he congratulated himself on that spot of luck, however, when he realized he had more serious troubles to deal with. With the morning, the Arctic wind was still rushing in from the north.

Tom had been aware for the past 24 hours of peculiar twinges of pain in his feet. As the time passed, the twinges became more severe. But they had lasted no more than a few seconds and, in any case, he had other things to think about. But now they were giving real trouble. They ached constantly with a dull, nagging pain. He could sense they were swollen so much that his seaboots felt drum-tight. The cold was getting at them. Soon, very soon, he knew, he would have to take off his boots and do something about his feet: "Perhaps I would have tended to them there and then—and saved myself a lot of misery—if the wind had not, at long last, shown signs of dropping."

"I can't waste time on my feet now," he told himself. "Any minute I shall be able to row again."

At that moment rowing was the most important thing in the whole world. War could have broken out somewhere, travel agencies could have been running pleasure trips to the Moon, or an unknown relative could have left him £1,000,000 and Tom would have turned his back on it all for the greatest privilege open to him—conditions that would allow him to row.

The "McClean luck" held good. By about 2 P.M. the storm died away and the winds became a whisper at a mere 15 MPH. Tom would now row as if he'd never row again. A grin spread across his entire face as his fingers scrabbled away at the sea-soaked lashings holding the oars along *Silver*'s gunwales. Then the blades were in the water, and he was bending his back. "I was truly happy for the first time in two and a half days," remembers Tom. "Except for a lunch break of really piping-hot curry and a couple of tea breaks, I rowed right through that wonderful day, through the evening, past twilight, and into the night." He did not ship the oars until 9 P.M.

He felt great, absolutely on top of the world. What did it matter that he had had to row south as the wind was still from the north? What did it matter that he had not seen the sun since the first day out? What did it matter that he had not seen a single ship apart from a Canadian frigate on that first day? Tom ventured: "I would not give a damn if I did not see either the sun or a ship until I got home."

It was only a matter of time. Weakness or strength, whatever happens, it was all in the mind. He had enough food and water to last more than four months. He had found his sea legs. He didn't care how long it took to get home. "I just knew, beyond all possible doubt, that I would get home."

But could he beat that blasted John Fairfax? Did he stand any chance at all of getting across the ocean first, when that playboy adventurer had started his trip five months before him?

◆

Like the Atlantic itself, Tom's moods were capable of dramatic change within seconds. Although he never lost sight of his main objective, never let go of his long-term plan, there were times when he, like most people, just lived for the brief moment of elation. Nothing else seemed to matter.

His spirits were soaring as he crawled into his sleeping bag and dropped off like a log. He didn't know what time it was when he woke. Nor did he have any idea of what disturbed his sleep. But automatically he lifted the side of the shelter's canvas cover for a precautionary look outside.

Away on the starboard side Tom spotted a light flashing on and off. His high spirits dropped like a stone—his immediate fear being that he had drifted back toward Newfoundland and that the flashing signal was the warning of a lightship or even a lighthouse.

Scrambling to his feet, Tom leaned on the starboard gunwale and stared hard and long, almost without blinking, at that depressing light. Sheer blessed relief flooded through him as he realized he was looking at the lights of a ship. The flashing effect was caused by the movement of the waves momentarily cutting it off from his sight every few seconds or so.

He did not sleep peacefully that night. Most disturbing was being roused by a sound he could not make out at all. With eyes wide open he lay there trying to figure it out. With a start he realized that it sounded for all the world like the heavy breathing of a large animal: "For one stupid moment I imagined a sea serpent coiled up on the roof of my shelter." Tom kept dead still, listening hard. Finally, he crept out to investigate.

The explanation was so simple that he burst out laughing. The rudder ropes that stretched across the shelter and down to cleats on each gunwale had worked a little loose. Although the movement this gave to the rudder was extremely slight, it was, nevertheless, enough to set those ropes rubbing with regular persistence across the shelter roof. Tom tightened the ropes and took his third stab at sleep.

As often happened, his mind drifted back to a pleasanter period of his youth when he finally got free of Fegan's.

◆

When a boy turned 15, Fegan's turned him out to the world. The orphanage didn't just kick him out and say "Get on your way!" The superintendent did what he could to help the boy make a proper transition into a productive life in the outside world. In February 1958 it was time for Tom to leave the orphanage after living there for 10 years. He was a little apprehensive but excited to go.

For years the orphanage had sent its "graduates" on to work on a farm that it owned in Sussex. But by the time Tom left, Fegan's no longer owned it. Arrangements were made for Tom to go to Uckfield, a small town in East Sussex, south of London, where he would live with a family named Brett and begin work as an apprentice carpenter at a neighborhood workshop. Tom was given a carpenter's tool kit worth about £50, a great deal of money in those days when a good wage was £10 a week: "My digs were fine. Mr. Brett was a retired butcher and Mrs. Brett was a gentle and sensitive woman who seemed to understand that I needed to stretch my wings a little. They never worried me or worried about me. It was a whole new world for me and I enjoyed it."

The minor tasks he was assigned in the carpentry shop didn't excite him, however. So, without informing Fegan's, he left the job, sold the £50 tool kit, and pocketed the money. He kept living with the Bretts but got a job in a nearby village with the Buxted Chicken Company. Every day Tom cut off the feet of 11,000 dead chickens as they came past on a conveyor belt: "It might seem like the sort of thing that would drive a person mad, but I liked the company of my coworkers—a number of them girls—and I had fun in the evenings at the pub drinking Stingo and Merrydown cider." Underage though he was, Tom never had trouble getting served in pubs. He also found that he was "a bit of a lad with the girls."

A report that Tom had defected from his carpentry apprenticeship to the "wicked atmosphere" of pubs frequented by chicken factory workers—a considerable number of them Catholic—was not well received at Fegan's. The orphanage authorities, still legally responsible for him, removed him from Sussex. His new posting was with the Venn family farm at Hartwell Hill near Aylesbury in Buckinghamshire. Tom liked the hard work at the Venn farm: "Up at dawn to clean out calf stalls, hump milk, many different physical jobs: it toughened me up and filled me out. Farming was good for me, that was certain." Mr. John Venn took him to the cattle market. Mrs. Pauline Venn taught him to save money, providing him with a bank book. Their three young children—Hilary, Cliff, and Greg—liked him and treated him like a big brother: "I was beginning to grow up and understand more about the civilized way to live, but after about ten months I began to get itchy feet."

Tom left the Venns, found digs in Uckfield, and got himself a job as a hod carrier (or "hoddie"), a day laborer who carried loads of bricks up scaffolding to bricklayers. "With a few quid in my pocket," recalls Tom, "I felt I was grown up—a man." In fact, "I was nothing more than a cocksure kid. I wanted to be on my own—to do exactly as I liked."

He fell into bad company and joined the Teddy Boys. The Teds were a rebellious group of British youth, most of them working class, which had emerged in the early 1950s. They distinguished themselves from the crowd by wearing snazzy fashions adapted from the Edwardian era: drape jackets with wide lapels (some with razor blades tucked under the collar), brocade waistcoats, Western bolo ties, high-waist drainpipe trousers, and thick-soled black suede creepers for shoes. Teddy Boys cultivated a sharp, tough-guy, even delinquent image—a look and reputation that appealed to Tom McClean, as it did to thousands of British teenagers during the era. In his fancy duds, Tom headed to the beach at Brighton for weekends on the "prom," where the cool thing was to brandish one's style and masculinity up and down the promenade, flirting with the pretty "birds."

Some Teds created gangs and engaged in aggressive and violent activities, gaining widespread notoriety in the UK for violent clashes with rival youth gangs and unprovoked attacks on immigrants. Tom remained apart from the most dangerous element of the Teds, not indulging in minor criminal behavior like stealing lead from church roofs, which was popular with some Teds. He did like excitement, however, but his pursuit of thrills one day landed him in London's infamous Bow Street Magistrates' Court: "With an equally rebellious chum I had gone to London for a few days. We spent most of the time stealing motor bikes and seeing how far we could travel before they ran out of petrol. We were caught and I was bound over for a year. That didn't bother me at the time. I was still my own boss, and riding high, wide, and handsome. The thought that I was leading an utterly useless life never entered my empty head."

Then came a chance meeting with an old friend from the boys' home. He was in the uniform of a British paratrooper. His friend told him that the Parachute Regiment was a "tough mob," the elite airborne infantry of the British Army. Tom liked the sound of that. In a flash he knew he wanted to be a paratrooper, too.

The day he became 17½—the minimum age for the Paras—Tom enlisted. It was July 1960.

He took to the army like a duck to water.

◆

Inside *Silver*, Tom slept until dawn and woke feeling fresh and anxious to row. He made tea and wolfed a tin of sardines for breakfast. The tea was more than welcome, for this was the coldest day yet. The temperature was at freezing point, and snow was thickly falling. It was not, however, settling on *Silver*. It brought to mind the troubling image of the pack ice lying just over 100 miles to the north. A sudden storm, such as Tom just had been through, with southerly winds could send him into the ice. That would be the end of him.

Tom was grateful when the winds dropped, but they were still against him. The day began with a 15 MPH southeasterly, which slowly edged around until it was due east. He was being blown back toward Newfoundland, and it was useless trying to row. He left the sea anchor out all day in a bid to stem that drift back to land. Luckily the east wind soon dropped to just 5 MPH.

Luckily? Tom had a lot of luck already. He wondered if he could legitimately ask for more: "I was sure I had got the hang of things out there. In just three days I'd learned more about survival in the Atlantic than I would ever have picked up in a year of practice rowing. One of the arts of survival is 'cheek' . . . the cheek to look for, and expect, far more than one deserves. And tomorrow I would be looking for a steady west wind. That would be real luck."

All the luck he needed for now, at least.

11

Into the Labrador Current

When planning his trip Tom had meticulously studied the current and prevailing winds of the North Atlantic. On paper it all seemed comparatively straightforward. Broadly speaking, the charts he had procured from the British Admiralty showed that his northern route was largely covered by predominant westerly winds and the eastward-flowing Gulf Stream. That stream, giving life-giving warmth from the Gulf of Florida to the shores of Britain, was the master key to Tom's plan. Once in it, he would be getting some help from the sea instead of having to fight it all the way.

However, there were two calculated risks that Tom had to weigh carefully before making up his mind on his route. First, the iceberg zone could still spread well to the south of Newfoundland late in the month of May. So, the chance of hitting an iceberg was a real hazard, instantly challenging and constantly worrisome. The threat of those glacial monsters and how the slightest bump could strip the bottom out of *Silver* was not one Tom could lightly dismiss. At night it would be like a ghoulish game of Russian roulette. Miss one, miss two . . . but how long could one go on missing and for how many nights? A collision while he was asleep would be the end of the adventure before it had really begun.

Second, Tom could expect, with practically 100 percent certainty, that he would experience raging gales that could last for days and nights without let-up. Winds of anything between 40 and 70 MPH, perhaps more, swept parts of the North Atlantic on more than 10 days a month. What if his journey coincided with those wind-torn days? Would he, with his inexperience, be able to handle *Silver* in such conditions before he had a chance to become accustomed to the temper of the sea?

Two grave risks, indeed. But Tom considered them both well worth taking for the benefit he would gain by taking the shortest route across the ocean, from Newfoundland to the British Isles. Taking that shortest route was the only way he could possibly ever catch up to, and get ahead of, John Fairfax in his rowboat *Britannia*, already months into his journey, taking the much warmer but longer route.

The first gamble paid off handsomely for Tom. He did not see a single iceberg. But the winds? That was another matter. They blew as predicted, all right—but in the wrong direction.

◆

The biggest obstacle that Tom knew he would have to face was the Labrador Current, also known as the Arctic Current. This stream of very icy water flows south along the coasts of Labrador and Newfoundland. Originating in Baffin Bay and the west coast of Greenland, it often carries icebergs as far south as the Grand Banks, the submerged plateau that extends 500 miles into the Atlantic Ocean from the southern tip of Newfoundland.

Could he stand the intense cold of that 200-mile-wide icy strip? Would he be able to row strongly enough to offset the southward drag of the current? Tom figured the answer to both questions was yes—or at minimum, yes, probably. He had calculated that it would take him roughly two weeks to fight off the clutch of the Labrador Current and slip into the blessed Gulf Stream.

By Saturday, May 24—one week into his odyssey—Tom wasn't nearly so sure. He awoke on the morning of his eighth day out with this problem eating into his brain. He had been blown well off course, and the wind, although light, was still from the east. He knew he had been steadily heading south for the last five days. But he had absolutely no way of telling how much vital mileage he had made—although perhaps *lost* would be the more appropriate word—to the east. He had made no attempt to plot his position. His only guide was the compass needle remorselessly showing his southward course.

The temptation to start rowing in a bid to swing *Silver* in the right direction just for the satisfaction of seeing that tantalizing needle pointing east was "almost too great to bear." Three times Tom unlashed the oars. And three times he lashed them back into place without even dipping them into the water. The realization that he would lose more ground by trying to row than by just sitting it out "won me around to the commonsense point of view."

Four days without a single stroke being pulled stretched into six days. Through Saturday and Sunday, in temperatures averaging no more than 35°F, Tom allowed the Atlantic to take *Silver* wherever it willed.

Try as he would, he could not draw much comfort from the thought that he was being sensible. The continual dull weather of the past seven days showed no signs of lifting. Cheerless clouds and humorless gray seas had become a depressing sight. For the first time, the immensity of the water around him began to strike home. He shuddered at the idea of being a professional sailor. The thought of those thousands of men who earned a living from the sea roused his admiration for them.

"Strange that I had never thought of them like this before," Tom reflected. "Sailors had been, well, just sailors." There must be many people whose main idea of a sailor conjured up a figure with a rolling gait—a happy-go-lucky guy whose main preoccupations were getting drunk and plunging into shore brawls, an irresponsible fool who threw his money away on women and gambling. "All I can say is if any sailor wants to live that way, good luck to him. But I do not think many do choose that as a permanent way of life."

"Do they ever think of what lies beneath their ships?" Tom wondered. He tapped the floorboards of *Silver* and thought of the flimsy wooden planking that was all that lay between him and the dark icy depths beneath. If something major ever struck the bottom of his dory, those wooden planks would continue floating, but he would not. Only he would sink to the "immemorial ooze."* Perhaps the sea would be kind enough to wash his remains onto a tropical beach in the Caribbean, Tom fantasized. In a rare moment of bravado, he told himself, "Even if I have to hold *Silver* together with my bare hands I'll keep going to the end or bust." An extravagant boast, perhaps. It really boiled down to a vow never to give up.

"Crikey," he thought, "I'm getting morbid." It was a condition of mind that had to be broken. The enforced inactivity had allowed his body to get thoroughly chilled. "And your brain!" he told himself, conscious of the fact that, despite sweaters and oilskins, he was literally shivering. His clothing had been continually damp for days—and the dampness had penetrated right through to his skin. It felt as if he was encased in a skintight suit of ice. As he breathed he watched his breath hang in many clouds for a fraction of a second before being snatched by that frustrating northeasterly wind.

Like millions of people around the world who sought to relieve the tensions of their day with a cup of tea, he got his cooker going, filled the kettle, and huddled around the gas jets. It took gulping down two pints of scalding tea before he began to thaw out a little. "It is impossible to tell just how much warmth I drew from the gas jets of my cooker," Tom declares. "But psychologically they were a perfect tonic. The mere sight of those flickering bluish-yellow flames gave me the same feeling of well-being that one gets from a log fire at Christmas. I did not want to turn that cooker off." Although it was only 11 in the morning, Tom

---

* The words "immemorial ooze" comes from a passage in a 1955 book by novelist C. S. Forester, *The Good Shepherd*. The passage reads: "And the big ships, to insignificant man so huge and so solid, sank to the sea bottom, to the *immemorial ooze* in the darkness and cold, with no more ado or stir than would be caused comparatively by specks of dust falling on a ballroom floor." *The Good Shepherd* was a nautically oriented novel about the Atlantic War early in World War II. Recently, the story has been adapted for the first time into feature film, titled *Greyhound*, written by and starring Tom Hanks. The film premiered during the summer of 2020. Tom McClean remembers reading Forester's book only after he made his Atlantic crossing in 1969.

decided on an early lunch. He boiled up a block of dehydrated army curry and took as long as he possibly could. To make it last and to make every mouthful as hot as possible, he kept the cooker simmering and ate his meal from the pot without once taking it off the flames.

There was a certain amount of dreary satisfaction in knowing that he had been right in thinking the Labrador Current would be his biggest obstacle. Tom was in its grip with a vengeance. An extraordinary feeling of being trapped in a cage of liquid ice ran through him. He had to find a way to beat it. But how?

Tom hammered himself with that question. The answer was always the same. There was nothing to do but stick it out until that damned eternal northeasterly blew itself out. Then perhaps he would be able to get a move on toward that almost mythical Gulf Stream, which by now had developed into the only thing that mattered in Tom's life.

Mentally he prodded himself into action. The effects of the tea and the curry would soon wear off. Burning the cooker continually was out of the question. At all costs Tom had to conserve his supply of gas cylinders. Although he planned on making the journey in 100 days at most, he had to look ahead. Foreseeing emergencies was an essential part of the art of survival. There was no way of telling exactly how long he would be out there. And if he overran those 100 days by any length of time, he would still have to eat and would still need hot food. The risk of wasting his gas just could not be taken. Within an hour the knife-thrust of the frigid Labrador air would be needling through to his bones yet again: "I had to fight it before I became a quivering jelly with no more thought than to lie down and bury myself as deep as possible in my sleeping bag."

Sitting on the seat, Tom flapped his arms across his body hard and fast for one or two minutes. With hands on hips, he went through a series of trunk-bending and rolling gyrations from his sitting position. He alternated the two exercises with two-minute sessions of basic arms forward and outward stretching. Everything was carried out with as much speed and energy as possible. Throughout it all, Tom held his breath until his eyes bulged in his head, then sucked in more air and held his breath again. He kept it up until he could feel the blood rushing through him like a mini Niagara Falls. He didn't stop until he was panting and sucking in air like a man who had just run a mile at full tilt all the way.

He had planned to exercise himself in this way, at a more leisurely pace, of course, simply to keep fit. He had not counted on it as a means of climbing out of the deep freeze he now found himself in.

With a heaving chest he crawled into his sleeping bag in a bid to preserve his new sense of warmth as long as possible. As there was nothing he could do until he felt the next attack of warning chills, he turned the radio to St. John's. He waited for the news broadcast. The first story was about the US Moonshot, something that interested him a lot. The Apollo 10 mission with astronauts Tom Stafford, John Young, and Gene Cernan was due to head back to Earth that day after spending the previous three days in lunar orbit. America's next lunar mission, Apollo 11, the broadcaster said, would try to make the first landing.

Tom looked upward. It was not easy to find the Moon in the morning sky, as it was in the phase known as a waxing crescent, merely the slimmest of slices seen from Earth. In comparison to his trip across the Atlantic, a voyage to the Moon and back was stupendous, he reckoned. In a span of just three days a spacecraft rocketed nearly a quarter million miles to get there and in three more days flew all the way back. Six days total, a million miles. That worked out by Tom's quick calculation to 166,666 miles per day, 6,944 miles per hour. Quite a bit farther than he would go with *Silver* across the Atlantic, that's for sure. The rowboat would only be traveling some 2,000 miles. If it took 100 days to make the crossing—hopefully no more than that!—that figured out to 20 miles per day, eight-tenths of a mile per hour. Quite a difference between one man rowing a little wooden boat in the ocean and the most advanced nation in the world assembling hundreds of thousands of its best scientists, engineers, and technicians into a vast and highly expert team focused on the singular national goal of shooting a crew of astronauts through the vacuum of space, landing them on the Moon, and bringing them back safely.

He was still pondering what was happening in the vicinity of the waxing crescent when he was startled to hear the radio broadcaster mention his name: "Tom McClean." "Nobody," the voice said, "has reported seeing Atlantic rower McClean since he left St. John's on May 17. And nobody has heard from him. The coastguards have been maintaining a daily radio watch but have heard nothing."

"I'm here! I'm here!" Tom shouted, half standing and still looking skyward, as if the astronauts in lunar orbit might even be able to see him. It was a "strange experience," he recalls, "listening to someone he didn't know saying that he had been at sea for a week." The thought that a watch was being kept for him was comforting.

Tom dickered with the idea of having a go at getting a radio message through to the land. But it would have meant unlashing the watertight box containing the radio. A simple enough job, yet he decided against it. He was determined to stick to his original intention of not using the radio for anything except emergencies. Tom was intent on making the crossing without help, without stopping, without asking passing ships for a single thing except, perhaps, a check on his position. "Let's see if that rascal Fairfax does his crossing so unassisted!"

Tom considered himself "a fairly gabby sort of person by nature." A "good natter"—English slang for a "healthy conversation"—was something he truly enjoyed. Very early in his army career he had been nicknamed Moby by his pals, because, they said, he "spouted like a whale." For anything up to 100 days and more he would be alone. Nobody to talk to. Nobody to get fed up with his gossip. There was more than a little doubt in his mind that if he once got into contact with somebody by radio he would be tempted to try it again and again just for the sake of a chat. That did not fit with his idea of a single-handed Atlantic row.

As for stopping? Well, there were no islands anywhere on his route that might lure him in with visions of hot baths, comfortable beds, fresh food, and girls in bikinis. He wouldn't be able to stop even if he wanted to do so. He had not seen a single ship apart from the Canadian frigate on the first day. He figured if he was going to do it at all, that was the way it would have to be. Having braced up his spirits with this redeclaration of his plans, he settled down to waiting out the icy hours that lay ahead.

By this time, he was aware that he had a pretty regular case of the sniffles. His nose was running and his eyes were watering. This was no time to go down with the flu. Popping the kettle on, he dug out his medicine chest—a plastic food container with a self-sealing lid packed with codeine tablets, glucose pills, morphine tablets, antiseptic creams, Vaseline, bandages, and emergency surgical kit. Half-filling a pint mug with neat black currant cordial, Tom topped it off with boiling water and washed down four codeine tablets as fast as he could. It seemed to work. By the next morning there was barely a sniff left in him.

Long before the next morning, however, he had to come to grips with yet another problem. He had begun to show the first signs of exposure. His face was raw with the cold. Every time he blew his nose it felt as if he was grabbing an open wound. It was tender, swollen, and peeling. Too sore to even blow his nose.

Having stowed away his medicine chest and lashed it back into position, Tom didn't want to bother getting it out again. Wedged in a corner by the cooker was an opened sardine tin with a couple of fish he had been keeping for his tea. The oil was frozen almost solid, but he managed to thaw it out a little by holding the tin close to a steaming kettle. He dipped a finger in the oil and gently smeared it over his face and nose, rubbing the remainder into his hands, which were also red and swollen.

The stench of sardines must have been pretty powerful, but Tom didn't notice. His nose was so swollen and sore he couldn't smell a thing. The oil was both soothing and warming. He reckoned if he didn't get out of Labrador's grip before long, he would have to mask his face as much as possible to shield it against the bitter, cutting temperature and wind.

Tom wound a towel around his head, covering his exposed forehead, and wrapped a scarf covering his face to just below his eyes. Digging back into his medicine chest, he applied a thick coating of Vaseline. While working this plan out it suddenly struck him that his water bags, located below *Silver*'s floorboards, had not frozen. These plastic containers, each carrying two gallons of water, showed no signs of being affected by the weather.

It was impossible to check them all. Most of them were well stowed away, acting as ballast until needed. It would have meant shifting a lot of the supplies to get at them and then would come the business of re-stowing and lashing everything down again. Tom couldn't take that chance. In the few days he had been out he had used practically nothing of *Silver*'s stores. It had taken enough trouble to get them arranged so that *Silver*'s trim was just right. To alter that delicate balance now could well be fatal. Too much weight at the head or at the stern or a slight list to either side and the next storm could well capsize the dory. Tom decided that even if they did freeze, he would just have to rip them open and chip off pieces of ice small enough to slip into the kettle.

So far the wind had been driving him south and was still doing so. Eternally south. But at least, if that kept up, he *must* eventually end up in warmer waters. Perhaps it would not be where he wanted to be, but it would be preferable to being blown north.

Counting that small—if frustrating—blessing, Tom felt a little better, a little more human. In the meantime, he had to get on with the task of preventing himself from freezing solid. He ran through his exercises for a few minutes once again. This time, after his body had warmed up, he rose to his feet and, without thinking, started to stamp them slowly and deliberately. Agonizing stabs of pain that ran through his feet from the toes to just above the ankles reminded him that he still had a problem, which, psychologically, he had been refusing to face.

Gingerly lowering himself on to his sleeping bag, he lifted both feet in the air. Right then it seemed as if he could not allow them to be in contact with anything. The dull, slow throbbing had the effect of shaking his body from head to toe. He held his legs high as long as he could, then slid toward the bows until he could rest the backs of his thighs on the edge of his rowing seat, leaving his feet still levered in midair.

He thought the throbbing would never stop. Each pulsating beat seemed to blow up his feet to such a size he felt sure they would burst his rubber seaboots. Gradually, it seemed like hours, the throbbing died away, leaving a dull ache. This too gradually faded until once again his feet were so numb that they might just as well have dropped off for all the feeling that was left in them.

The danger signals were now loud and clear. The problem was, in Tom's words, "Should I treat them now or could I hang on a little longer? I desperately wanted to hang on as long as I could. For if the wind changed in my favor I would have to be ready to row, and row like the blazes, in a bid to scramble out of this icebox. To be with my pants down, or rather with my boots off, would waste valuable time."

How long would they take to get off? Maybe Tom would have to cut them off? No matter what he did to protect them, could he withstand the pressure that would be applied once he started rowing without the thick rubber soles of his boots to offer what little shield they could?

The questions drummed through Tom's brain time and time again and all without an adequate answer. The most important question was, while still in these freezing temperatures, did the boots actually offer more protection than anything he could devise by wrapping his feet in socks, jerseys, towels, or anything else he had in the boat? Tom finally voted to keep them on. He felt he could hold out for a little longer. He had to.

That Sunday, May 25, became one of the longest days in Tom's life. Frantically seeking ways of keeping himself occupied and warm, he made a brew and burrowed into his kit bag for a box of letters his recently hired agent Paul Sargent had sent to him in St. John's.* The instructions in the accompanying note had been explicit: "I was to open one each Sunday." They turned out to be letters written by buddies back at the SAS headquarters as well as a few other friends. Paul Sargent's idea was for Tom to break the loneliness of his row with a weekly reminder that quite a few people were thinking of him.

The first letter was from Paul himself: "He told me not to get tight on the run—I had some bottles of Navy Neaters on board†—as I could still

---

*   While preparing for his ocean crossing Tom took on Paul Sargent, a former Fleet Street journalist, as an agent; this is discussed in chapter 16.

†   Navy Neaters was a brand of undiluted rum (95.5 proof) served to the petty officers on board British ships.

be 'done' for being drunk in charge of a rowing boat." As a matter of fact, Tom had not (yet) touched a drop of it. That rum was for emergencies or to celebrate seeing a boat. At this point, "I certainly had nothing to celebrate, and I refused to regard my feet as an emergency. It was ridiculous. If I started tippling at every little setback I wouldn't have anything for the time I hit real trouble. After all any number of emergencies could be ahead of me. I had been out only one week."

One week!?

Tom found himself drifting into temptation as steadily as *Silver* was drifting south. The thought of a shot of that rum was tantalizing. He thought of the "bite of the spirit" as it swilled over his tongue, down his throat, and the spreading warmth as it settled in his stomach.

Just one shot, just one, would solve all his problems.

But he quashed the urgent temptation and made a cup of instant coffee instead. As it went down he realized that he had been sitting idle for far too long. He glanced at his watch. It was barely four o'clock. Would this day never end? Never had Tom known time to drag by so painfully.

Suddenly he felt a change in the wind. It had swung around slightly—at long last—and was not coming from the northwest. It was still driving him mainly to the south, but at least he could pick up a fraction of that lost distance to the east. Like a fretting child, he wondered how long ago it had changed. How much of it had he missed while so preoccupied with himself?

Feverishly he hauled in the sea anchor and found himself marveling how the smallest slice of luck could change his whole outlook. Only a minute before he had been feeling miserable, angry, frustrated. Now he couldn't have felt better if the sun had been shining and the temperature had been 80°F. Even his feet began to feel better.

From then on he rowed solidly. Steady strokes and fairly long. *Silver* skipped before the wind like a racing yacht. In, out, in, out. On and on, hour after hour. Tom's back bending forward and backward with hardly a halt. He felt as if he could go on forever.

And just as steadily the wind blew for him. It gradually increased from about 5 MPH to 10, through 15, until it reached a constant 20 MPH.

And Tom was sweating. In this deep freeze that had been eating into his bones for so long, he was sweating. He grinned with joy to himself. As he shipped the oars, he could feel the sweat running down his swollen face, rivulets of it sliding under his collar.

He wrapped a towel around his neck and with another dabbed gently at his face and finally crawled into his sleeping bag. He fell asleep as soon as his eyes closed.

12

How Thick the Fog

Tom didn't know how long he'd slept, but when he woke it was still dark. He lay there trying to drop off again and was prevented from doing so by wondering what it was that roused him. Through the fog of sleep that was still tugging at him, he realized that it was the chugging of a ship's diesel engines. The steady throb seemed to be coming from a long way off. But it was getting louder. Still he did not move. He just lay there listening to the sound moving toward him.

Forcing himself out of the sleeping bag, he groped his way out of his little shelter. He blinked out over the starboard gunwale . . . nothing but darkness filled by that engine throb. Bleary-eyed, he switched his sight to port and was instantly awake. Just 800 yards away was a ship. Her lights carved a hole in the darkness, and she was heading toward him.

Tom got a radar flare out of the watertight container and grabbed his flashlight to take a good look at whether the flare was dry. When these flares exploded they let off metal particles that in theory should be picked up on the approaching ship's radar—that was, if a radar watch was being maintained. That depended on the size of the ship and if she had sufficient crew to set up a round-the-clock radar lookout.

The ship came on, filling the night with light and noise. *Silver* would be so much matchwood if it got a swipe from that monster. The ship was about 200 yards away when, as Tom was preparing to trigger off his flare, he suddenly realized that he had misjudged her direction. She was going to pass by *Silver* with plenty of room to spare. She swept by about 200 yards astern, and *Silver* rocked in the wake. It was obvious that nobody on that ship was aware of the dory's existence. It had been a scary moment, and now the danger had passed. It dawned on Tom that he could have flipped his flashlight on and off as a first line of defense. He could only suppose that he had been too intent on ensuring that his radar flare was dry and picking the right moment to fire it.

There can be times when one can pay too much attention to detail, if that were indeed the case. On the other hand, it was equally, if not more so, apparent that he had not been thinking quickly enough. It was plain that the question of whether or not the flashlight should have been used was now unimportant. What had infuriated Tom was that he had not even thought of using the flashlight so that he would have been able to make the decision of whether or not to use it. That decision should have been his to make in that moment, and it wasn't. It should not have been a matter of chance.

For how many chances will the Atlantic allow one man?

While mentally kicking himself, he watched the ship's lights fading away, and it occurred to him, judging from the diesel note of the engine, that it could well have been a fishing vessel. If it was, then it would be just possible that he was as far south as the Grand Banks. There the depth of water varied between 80 and 100 fathoms, and the shallowness allowed the sunlight to penetrate the water and develop a vast crop of marine life. It was there that the great schools of herring and cod gathered for feeding. It was easy to understand how this area became one of the world's greatest fishing grounds. That ship was the clue. But Tom wanted to be sure.

If he could pick up the ship on his two-way radio, the crew would be able to give him his exact position . . . the first time he would have known it in eight days. Making a brief mental note of relief that his brain appeared to be ticking over properly once again, Tom unlashed the radio and tried to get it working. He tuned in and started rapping out the message that would have startled any ship's radio operator—if he had heard it.

"Rowboat *Super Silver* calling, rowboat *Super Silver* calling . . . Come in, please; come in please."

Nobody heard him. Tom heard the Canadian coast guard receiving positions of ships at sea. Again, he sent his message. Again, no answer. Again, those ships reporting to the coast guard. All that activity somewhere out there in the darkness, and nothing he could do about it.

But there was just "one more shot in my locker." Perhaps the ship that had passed so close was also giving her position to the coast guard. Maybe, if Tom could pick her out, because her call would be stronger than the rest, he could gauge his own position from the information she sent to the coast.

Once again Tom tuned in. He picked up three more messages, but there was no distinctive difference in the strength of the messages. There was, however, one common denominator. The positions they gave were all roughly with 50 miles or so of each other. Tom concluded that he must be somewhere near the fishing grounds.

Making rough and ready calculations, he figured he had traveled some 200 miles and mainly on a southerly course. On that reckoning, his movement to the east could not have been much more than 100 miles. It was a depressing thought. He still had 100 miles of this icebox to cross before he came to its meeting point with the Gulf Stream, where usually the mixture of cool and warm waters produced a fog that was known as "Arctic smoke." No matter how thick the fog, Tom knew he would not be really happy until he saw it.

By Tuesday morning, May 27, Tom was still making crushingly slow progress. He had awoken early. As he boiled the kettle an unreal brightness gathered all around him. The categorical grayness that had dogged him for so many days was lifting. Up in the sky to the east, a pale, watery sun was peeping at him, through a chink in the usual spread of heavy cloud. The chink opened to a crack, and the sun seemed to hang there as if it had stopped. Wispy clouds raced across it like the ends of a chiffon scarf blowing over a lady's face. Then it vanished for good, the clouds once again taking over the entire world in their shroud of lowering gray.

But it was a different day. A wonderful day. A look at the thermometer showed Tom just how hard that sun was trying. The temperature was 50°F, the first time it had been so high since the voyage began. From the northwest a 25 MPH wind was helping *Silver*, at least in part, toward the east. He hauled in the sea anchor and let her have her head.

◆

Given that Tom McClean had spent his whole life up to this point fighting authority, it may seem odd that he would voluntarily sign up for military service, but that's exactly what he did. Perhaps because it was finally his own choice—and he didn't much like the alternatives.

From the moment his train reached the army base at Aldershot station in 1960, Tom's feet never touched the ground. He fell in love instantly with the Parachute Regiment and the extraordinarily intense training that went along with it. After Fegan's, it was "like a kids' tea party," although he "could not make some of my fellow trainees believe that."

Joining the elite Parachute Regiment of the British Army at age 17½ was the critical turning point in Tom McClean's life. None of the adventures that he would later undertake are imaginable without his first having not just survived but happily experienced, valued, even relished, his highly unique and rigorous military career.

More than a few of the young men who started the training course for the Parachute Regiment at Aldershot were beaten into quitting or were drummed out. Tom thrived on it. As he was accustomed, he was the youngest and smallest in the platoon and more than ready for the extra effort to race ahead of the rest. On one training run over a tank training area rutted with tank tracks, he exerted himself so hard that he collapsed at the finish. But he finished first.

Parachute training happened at Abingdon, just below Oxford. There, in a big hangar, the troops learned how to fall, use the harness, pack chutes, and carry out the emergency drills in case their main parachute did not open. The first jump was made from a barrage balloon sent up on a wire from a trailer, the basket containing two nervous trainees and a jumpmaster suspended underneath. According to Tom, "Anyone who says he is not nervous during those early jumps is a liar, but the long training had prepared us for the moment." When Tom's turn came, he dropped down through the trap in the floor of the basket "quite pleased to be away" from the swaying box. Before he had time to take it all in, he was on the ground.

"My first jump, cheers! This was the life for me."

Another jump from the basket was followed by five jumps from a transport aircraft. Then came the great day when Tom and his mates were presented with their maroon berets and regimental brevets (wings). Tom could not have worn his more proudly.

His assignment was to the 3rd Battalion, 3 Para as it was called. He graduated ("passed out") with very good marks for shooting, appearance, running, and general physical fitness. His only "mediocre" fell "on the schooling side." His main problem was reading—not that he couldn't read. But he hadn't read a single book cover to cover the entire time he had been at the orphanage. Magazines, comics, that sort of thing, but never a book. Noticing his lack of academic preparation, a couple of his fellow paratroopers encouraged him to use the base library. Significantly, he took out two books that would greatly inspire him and ultimately spur him on to make his great ocean adventure. The books were *The Voyage of Discovery* (1905), Robert Falcon Scott's account of the British national expedition of 1901–1904 that launched the "heroic age of Antarctic exploration," and *South: Sir Ernest Shackleton's Glorious Epic of the Antarctic* (1919), the story of the fateful trip of 1914–1917 in which Shackleton's ship *Endurance* and its crew of 28 became trapped in pack ice short of their destination but miraculously found a way for all to survive. "These two books became a source of great happiness to me," Tom maintains, "as well as setting a challenge, and later, an example."

In what turned out to be six years with the 3rd Battalion (airborne infantry) of the Parachute Regiment, Tom first saw action in the Middle East—in Bahrain and later in Aden. In both cases the Paras were deployed—in combination with other units of the British Army—to combat insurgents, either nationalist or communist, and generally defend

British strategic, economic, and political interests from aggressive moves against the Commonwealth and its allies.

His first deployment, in the summer of 1961, came as part of Operation Vantage. This was a combined land, sea, and air campaign in support of the newly independent, oil-rich Persian Gulf state of Kuwait against territorial claims by its neighbor, Iraq. With the 3 Para, Tom, then 19 years old, was placed on the island of Bahrain to the south. The paratroopers bivouacked there, ready to jump into action in support of a half brigade of British troops put into Kuwait, two groups of commandos situated at the Kuwait-Iraq border, and Kuwait's own troops—all ready to go if Iraq moved against Kuwait, which it did not do. British forces stayed there until late October, when the Arab League (Egypt, Jordan, Lebanon, Saudi Arabia, Syria, and Yemen) took over the protection of Kuwait.*

Two memories of Bahrain stayed with Tom. One was the backbreaking work of laying concrete and building a camp of aluminum huts, made to reflect the blazing heat of the Persian Gulf; "Silver City," the Paras dubbed it. The other memory, a much more enjoyable one, was his first experience with building a boat—rebuilding actually, as it involved renovating an old dhow that the battalion padre had found deserted on a beach—and taking it out some distance onto the open water, some 300 miles across the Gulf from Bahrain to Dubai.† The crew was a motley bunch with no sailing experience to speak of. One man had a broken leg. Together they were fearful enough of the possibility of encountering pirates that the crew members all carried automatic weapons. In the

---

*   Britain continued to monitor the Kuwait situation and kept naval, ground, and air forces available to protect the country until 1971. The majority of the available land and air forces to the United Kingdom were based in Kenya and Cyprus, which even today are part of the British Commonwealth.

†   Actually, before getting involved with the restoration of the dhow, Tom, on his own, had constructed a simple little sailboat from materials he picked up at the base supply store. Tom used the boat, a wood frame covered with canvas, to make short expeditions up and down the coast of Bahrain, never going more than 10 miles one way or 10 miles the other.

middle of their voyage, a vicious storm hit. A plank flew out of the hull. Water flooded into the engine compartment, which promptly filled with steam. The crew pumped for their lives. They signaled a mayday call for help. An RAF plane flew overhead. It took three hours for a rescue boat to arrive. But the water was too rough for her to come right alongside. She could only come within leaping distance—and barely that. One at a time the men on the dhow did their athletic best to jump aboard, including the chap with the broken leg. When it was Tom's turn, the rescue boat suddenly dropped away. Tom jumped so hard that he cleared the boat and landed in the sea. The crew had to haul him on board. Wet, cold, and seasick, they were taken back to Bahrain.

It was Tom's first encounter with the open sea, and he figured he would never make a sailor.

Tom' second deployment came in 1963 when his battalion of paratroopers were dispatched to Aden, the major port city at the southern tip of the Arabian peninsula. The capital of what was then the Federation of South Arabia, a protectorate of the British Empire (subsequently made part of Yemen), Aden was important for its role in protecting British shipping routes through the Suez Canal to India and the Far East. Anti-British guerrilla groups in South Arabia had coalesced into two militant organizations: the National Liberation Front (NLF), supported by Egypt, and the Front for the Liberation of Occupied South Yemen (FLOSY), a Marxist paramilitary organization. The Aden Emergency, also known as the Radfan Uprising, began on December 14, 1963, when a pan-Arab nationalist threw a grenade at a gathering of British officials at the Aden airport, killing two and injuring 50. The emergency worsened with additional grenade attacks largely focused on British officers and policemen but incidentally killing and wounding a number of children. The 3 Para was based in tents at the military airfield at Kormaksar (Khur Maksar), a large installation a few miles north of Aden that had been greatly expanded after World War II to serve the soldiers and air divisions stationed in the British military base of East Suez. Much of the violence instigated by the NLF and FLOSY was happening in the town of Crater, the old Arab quarter of Aden. It was the task of SAS commandos as well as Tom's paratrooper brigade to intercept weapons being smuggled into Crater by the desert rebels.

It was a bloody business in which Tom experienced his first direct combat action, and he relished it. Under the command of Colonel Anthony Farrar-Hockley—known to his men as Farrar the Para—the 3 Paras were dispatched 60 miles north of Aden into the Radfan Mountains, where the SAS had been operating against tribesmen who had mined and ambushed the road running along the Yemen coast. According to Tom, "One of the SAS patrols had been outnumbered by about 25 to 1. They had put up a good fight, but one SAS man had been captured. He was decapitated and his head displayed on a pole over the main gate of Sana, a large mountain town high in the Radfans. We were sent there, along with a company of Royal Marines, to sort things out." Together, they moved into the Wadi Dhubsan, a sheltered valley in the Radfan Mountains. The enemy, as Tom and his mates soon learned, were "very able fighters who knew the land and even with antiquated weapons were good shots." Tom's platoon was given the job of scouting the ridgeline above the valley. Leading them was a tenacious regimental sergeant major, Herbert D. Arnold. Nicknamed Nobby, RSM Arnold was a "great character—tough, hard, and fair."

Moving slowly to their position on the ridge, Tom and his mates suddenly came under fire from rifles 1,000 yards across the wadi. Tom's reaction was typical of his cavalier approach to extreme situations: "It was great fun, our first taste of being under fire. At nineteen it was a real adventure, a great game. We felt invincible." Tom wielded the general-purpose machine gun, or GPMG, an air-cooled, fully automatic weapon featuring a quick-change barrel that fired full-powered rifle cartridges. Tom considered it "a very good weapon." Assessing the situation, RSM Nobby Arnold spotted the source of the enemy fire and directed Tom and his partner on the GPMG, Brendan Merrifield, to move up into a position on the ridge where they could "pepper-pot" the rebels' position. "Hard going, but exciting," in Tom's view. The enemy was firing from within some small buildings, but with Tom and Brendan firing at them, they were keeping their heads down. It was midday and very hot—about 120°F.

When the platoon was near enough to attack, Arnold raised his handkerchief signaling his men to hold fire while his riflemen all fixed bayonets. They charged, killing several tribesmen, wounding others, passing right through the enemy position like a knife through butter, and forming up on the far side.

It was one of the very few bayonet charges carried out by any army, British or otherwise, since World War II, and Tom and Brendan had a great view of it all below them. The two men were about to start down the side of the ridge to join their mates when Tom saw a cow moving slowly out from the huts to his left. There was nothing odd about that except that instead of four legs, the creature had eight. Tom fired a long burst, killing the animal as well as two rebels hiding behind it trying to escape.

The skirmish at Wadi Dhubsan became fairly well known in the annals of the British paratroopers, primarily because of the bayonet charge led by Nobby Arnold. (The Paras came to call it Arnold's Ridge.) Upon their return to England, every member of Tom's battalion received a General Service Medal. Although not well known to the British public today, the Aden Emergency took quite a toll on British forces—some 92 killed and 510 wounded. The death toll among the insurgents was far higher—382 killed and 1,714 wounded—in part due to interfactional fighting among the different rebel groups.

Tom prefers not to discuss some of his experiences in combat, saying only: "War is war, and if you are in a situation where others are out to kill you, for whatever reason, then the answer is to kill them first. It is a sad fact of life that has existed since time began. Kill or be killed."

Tom saw a lot of death and injury, but he himself never suffered a wound. However, he was nearly killed in a freak accident that occurred not long after he became a paratrooper.

The accident happened in 1961 during a NATO operation in Greece called Exercise Fabulous. The biggest airborne drop since World War II, the exercise involved soldiers of 16 Parachute Brigade, with the Greek Parachute Regiment acting as the enemy.

The exercise itself went well enough, though a number of paratroopers came out of it with broken arms and legs—but nothing too serious. It was after the day was over that the accident happened, as Tom relates: "One of our people suggested that I ought to walk up the hill to the big tent where the Greeks stored their weapons and ammunition. So off I went." Another British trooper was already there, and he was looking at a Colt 45. Tom asked if he could see the revolver, which was a classic. "He turned round, pointed the gun at me as if to hand it over, when it went off, two feet away from me. As the bullet hit me I felt nothing. All I thought was, 'Bloody hell! What's happening?'"

The bullet hit Tom in the lower part of his stomach. It went through his bladder and pelvis, missing the bone, the veins, the nerves, the arteries—everything. It blew off the left cheek of his buttocks, hit another bloke in the leg, and buried itself in the ground. Fortunately, a medic was nearby, as blood was pouring from Tom. He was told later that he would have lasted less than 15 minutes if help had not been swift. "The pain in my backside was terrible, as if the whole of my bum was on fire." Someone found a field dressing while someone else rolled Tom over onto his stomach and pulled his shorts down. An emergency dressing was crammed into the vast wound to stanch the bleeding. Another chum gave Tom a piece of wood to bite on, which stopped him from grinding his teeth until they broke. Another trooper dashed a half mile down the hill to get help and bring transport. On the way he was met by his regimental sergeant, who was coming up the hill. "Soldier, where's your beret?" the RSM screamed. "Someone's been shot, badly wounded, sir. I'm off to get transport. He's probably dying." "I don't bloody care if World War III has started or the Queen's been shot," roared the RSM. "You don't go rushing around bloody Greece without your beret. Go and get it!" The trooper returned to get his beret then ran again for help. Tom remembers passing out just as a Land Rover arrived for him.

In a flimsy building used as medic's station, an army doctor, Captain Kenneth Hedges, MD, operated on Tom. Three pints were needed—nearly half of all the blood there is in a person. The surgery took three hours. Dr. Hedges later told Tom that, during the surgery on his buttocks, he could see right through him. In retrospect, there are other amazing facts about the emergency. Tom was a rare blood type: B negative. Rare and not carried in field supplies. A call had to put out for anyone with B negative blood. It turned out Tom's best pal, Trooper Brendan Merrifield, was the only man in the whole battalion of 800 men who had B negative, the same Brendan Merrifield who would be Tom's mate on the same GPMG machine gun during the Aden Emergency battle at Wadi Dhubsan. The other striking coincidence was that the same Dr. Hedges who saved Tom's life would be a vital member of the four-man British Trans-Arctic Expedition of 1968–1969—led by famed Arctic explorer Wally Herbert—that was the first to cross the surface of the Arctic Ocean and successfully cross over the top of the North Pole on dogsled. In conditions of extreme severity, the trek covered 3,800 miles, crossed 11 times zones, and lasted 470 days.*

As soon as he was out of imminent danger, Tom was flown by RAF transport to Malta, where the nearest British hospital was located. As he recalls, he almost died on the flight: "I was strapped to my stretcher, arms tied by my side. I became airsick so a nurse brought me a mask, tied it to my face and left. I got sick again, choking with the vomit inside my mask. I could do nothing. I was drowning in vomit with the mask over my nose and face. I lay helpless, rolling my head from side to side. I wasn't even able to shout for the fear of choking further." At last a horrified nurse returned and saved him.

In Malta it took six days before he was off the critical list. Transported home by the RAF, he stayed in the military hospital in Aldershot for ten weeks. The nursing staff jokingly called him "the Waterworks" because of all the bottles and tubes hanging out of him. It was then three more months before he was able to go back to active duty.

---

*   In 2020 Dr. Hedges was the only surviving member of the four-man team, living a quiet life in northern Ontario, Canada. He is a member of the Royal Geographical Society, a commander in the Order of St. John, and a Polar Medal recipient from Queen Elizabeth II. Like Tom McClean, he also moved from the Parachute Regiment to the British Special Air Service (SAS). The other two men who were part of the British Trans-Arctic Expedition of 1968–1969 were Allan Gill and Fritz Koerner.

◆

Crossing the Atlantic, whenever Tom started worrying too much about his aches and pains and blisters, Tom thought back on how bad the pain had been when he was shot through his stomach. It had truly been beyond horrible. More than that, he felt lucky not to have been "ruined for life," sexually and otherwise. As for his left butt cheek, it took months of recovery before he could sit down properly. Sure, the hard bench seat on *Silver* was none too comfortable, but all that was left of the bullet damage to his butt to see was "a neat dimple."

Much more of a concern in the Labrador Current was the condition of his damned feet.

The time, the situation, the weather: everything was right to deal at last with the problem of his feet. Tom knew he might not get another chance for days. Tomorrow the Labrador Current could turn nasty again, plummeting the temperature to the freezing point. Now that he had allowed himself to think of his feet again, Tom realized they were so numb he would not have felt a dagger thrust into them. A holy mess, they were so swollen it took about 20 minutes to ease his boots off. The skin was grayish white and wrinkled like pickled pork that had been left far too long in the brine tub. The skin, in places, peeled off his soles and heels. They were numb to the ankles and so swollen that he thought they never would be the right shape again. They looked useless, and they *were* useless. What the hell was he going to do?

He doubled over on the bottom of *Silver* and started trying to squeeze some life back into them. He couldn't even feel the touch of his own hands up to a point just below the ankles. As he applied the pressure a little higher, coming into the area where the blood was still trying to circulate, the pain was so intense that he snatched his hands away as if he had burned them.

Carefully he dried his feet thoroughly, put on a pair of woolen socks and then wrapped them around with a thick woolen sweater. One thing he knew for sure: "I couldn't mess about with a roughshod treatment this time. It would take a lot more than a few drops of oil from a sardine tin to get these ugly clumps of dead flesh into shape." He needed help. And there was only one place to which he could turn. That was to one of the few books that he had brought on the trip: *A Traveller's Guide to Health*. The book, written by Lieutenant Colonel James M. Adam of the Royal Army Medical Corps, provided a compact directory to prevention, diagnosis, and cures for travelers and explorers. Tom knew it had helped many an adventurer through sticky patches and saved them from too much severe discomfort.

Reading the entry on frostbite he had to chuckle. It said: "The test of a true friend is to put feet in danger of frostbite on his abdomen to warm them." Tom seriously doubted that any chum of his, had he been with him, would have allowed his feet within a mile. He also looked up "trench foot." That entry read, more ominously: "First brought to the attention of the medical profession in World War I, trench foot, or immersion foot, is a disease that largely attacks the toes, though in many cases the leg also becomes swollen up to the knee. In severe cases, large blisters, filled with clear, gangrenous smelling fluid, is present."

Tom wasn't sure which of the two conditions was tormenting him—hopefully, just some frostbite, as serious as that too could be. In either case, massage seemed to be out. If that pain had not shot through his ankles a few minutes before he would have been rubbing the daylight out of them. He couldn't lie down in a warm place and couldn't go indoors, as advised by Lieutenant Colonel Adam, who, naturally, had not had lone Atlantic rowers in mind when he wrote his book. There was one conclusion applicable to either complaint: keep the feet dry and keep them warm.

Uncovering them, Tom again dried them and then dug out three pairs of thick oiled wool seaman's stockings—he had brought about 20 pairs with him—and pulled them on one after the other. That, he thought, should handle the problem of keeping them warm. But how to keep them dry?

He couldn't get his boots on again. He was stumped for a while. It was while he was wondering how to keep his boots dry until he could use them again that he hit on the way to solve both problems. The heavy-duty plastic bags in which his rations were packed would be the perfect answer. They measured about one foot by two feet, and he had a few spare ones on hand.

The boots were separately wrapped up, one to a bag, and then sealed with masking tape. Tom put the toes of his right foot into one corner of a bag and meticulously wrapped the remainder of the bag around his leg up to the knee. This he held in place with strong elastic bands—he had seen those stout bands in a shop back in St. John's and bought a bundle, thinking vaguely that they were bound to be useful for something—which stopped above the ankle, giving the lower part of the bag a balloon effect around his foot. They looked as if they were floating in two huge air bubbles.

They looked utterly ridiculous. He held them up, examined them, waggled them, and laughed his head off.

"Here I was wondering what I looked like and there was nobody to share the joke. I looked around. The wind was still from the northwest. It was still blowing for me. I felt great."

"Gulf Stream here I come."

13

Who Dares Wins

Tom was rolled up into a tight ball, like a cat trying to bury its paws and nose in its own coat. During the night he must have slid down inside his sleeping bag until his head was entirely covered. His knees were drawn up as high as he could get them, with his elbows tucked into his groin and his forearms pressed against his chest. His hands were cupped around his face with the little fingers meeting across his nose.

Each breath was a luxury. The warm air from his nostrils, trapped by his hands, momentarily rolled over his face before escaping. As he came to—that is the only way to describe it, for waking up had become more like breaking through a bout of unconsciousness—Tom kept his eyes shut and breathed harder and faster into his hands. The warmth was like a drug. For a few minutes he lay there without moving, thinking of nothing but the warm air on his face.

He slowly stretched until his head poked out of the top of his sleeping bag. Gingerly he opened his cupped hands without taking them from his face. The cold sliced across his raw flesh like a knife. He discovered later that his guess that the temperature was at about freezing was only four degrees off. Hurriedly he recupped his hands back into position and lay there opening and shutting them to acclimate himself to the chill dawn.

Even through the thickness of his Portuguese mittens Tom could feel the bristles of his beard rustling with each movement. He had not shaved, or washed, since leaving St. John's. He was still wearing the same shirt and the same underclothing, and he had the residue of old sardine oil on his face. All he had managed to do in pursuit of cleanliness was to brush his teeth.

Salt crystals had begun to form in every corner of his flesh. They rubbed against his neck, rustled under his armpits, and gleefully crackled away in far more uncomfortable spots. Tom promised himself a thorough bath and change of clothing at the very first alteration in the weather.

To look at the new day he reached forward to pull aside a corner of the canvas hanging in front of his shelter. A new day? Once again there was no change. Overhanging cloud, slate-colored seas, the horizon hidden in mist, and only the seagulls for company. How maddening, those birds! They sat in the icy water, bobbing about like corks and looking as if they were reveling in a warm bath.

It was full daylight, if the eternal grayness could be described as such. But there was something different about this morning. The tangy smell of the sea was not nearly so strong. In fact, there was a completely different fragrance in the air. It was the smell of curry—strong, spicy, and, even at 7 A.M., mouthwatering. Tom sniffed at it like a hungry tramp. At first he thought his imagination was playing tricks. It was, he figured, a sort of olfactory mirage. Yet it did not fade. The more he sniffed, the stronger the smell became. He couldn't rest until he tracked it down.

Down on his knees in the shelter he rummaged around. Out went his sleeping bag. Out went the air mattress—which he no longer bothered to blow up. Out went practically everything.

Then he found it . . . a broken jar of curry paste. When it was broken, how it was broken, he had no idea. But it was a minor tragedy. Tom's near-obsessive liking for curry was born when he was serving with the Parachute Regiment in Malaya. He ate curry in one form or another nearly every day when he was ashore. He had chosen it as his staple diet for his Atlantic trip.

He was carrying 100 days of SAS field rations. Each day's pack had been scientifically selected by army diet specialists and contained enough calories to keep a hardworking man going for a whole day. One pack contained three brews of tea, complete with sugar and powdered milk. There was a porridge block that could be eaten as a biscuit or rolled up to a normal breakfast consistency by adding boiled water. There were plain biscuits and a tube of margarine, a tin of cheese, a tin of sardines, two Mars bars, and a slab of chocolate. There were matches and salt, toilet paper, vitamin tablets, and a can opener.

And, of course, the most important item of all . . . the main course . . . a large block of dehydrated curry plus a little rice and a few raisins. Each pack weighed about one and a half pounds. With so much curry on board little *Silver*, most people would wonder why Tom would worry about one broken jar of curry paste. After all, there were three more jars among his supplies.

To say he was dismayed would perhaps be overestimating the drama. But Tom was certainly upset. He cleaned up the mess and dumped the broken jar overboard. Then he set about repacking the remaining three jars as if they were thin-shelled eggs. Each one he wrapped tightly in two or three inches of clothing and then wedged them tightly into a plastic box, which he then lashed against the boat's side in the far corner of his shelter. He shook it, tugged at it, and was not satisfied until there was absolutely no sign of movement either inside or outside the box.

As time passed he began to realize that no matter what happened, there was usually some compensatory factor. Even the episode of the lost curry paste had its good point. The mental concentration used in tracing the smell, the first moments of slight panic, the feeling of frustration, and, finally, the steps taken to ensure there were no repeats. All this had completely driven from Tom's mind thoughts of the weather, his bastard feet, and *Silver*'s certain misplaced position in the ocean. If only he could keep busy enough—difficult in such a small space—there might be no time left for self-pity.

He followed up his homespun philosophy with immediate action: a cup of tea, a bit of cheese, and a couple biscuits for breakfast. By 7:45 A.M. he had the oars out and was rowing.

At least the wind was with him. He was heading southeast with a following wind of about 15 MPH. He rowed for three or four hours. Perhaps more, perhaps less. He had no idea exactly how long he rowed, and didn't care, just so long as he did row.

There was a tremendous satisfaction in getting the oars into the water again. In, out. Body forward, then back. Stretching, pulling, bending like a man possessed. It was almost as if he was driven by the wild thought that he could reach the shore of the British Isles that very day. *Silver* behaved like a dream, sliding through the water, calm and steady. She seemed to be urging him on, telling him, "If only you will row, I will get you out of this Labrador icebox."

Tom was only too anxious to comply. The sound of the water rippling along *Silver*'s sides was like music. The sense of movement was exciting. The feel of the wind blowing into his face stimulated and refreshed him. As he bent and pulled, he was filled with a new determination: "It could be done and I will do it." Frozen feet, blistered hands, aching bones, soaked to the skin, and without the slightest clue to his position—none of those hampering circumstances was going to hold him up any longer.

Whether it was competing in a running race or taking on any other army trial, Tom's philosophy was simple but effective: "Win or bust." As he heaved at the oars, "I ran that race again and vividly saw every step like a cine film in my brain." The effect was almost hypnotic. Like a slave master standing in the stern of a galley, he began pacing his rowing time. With each stroke of the oars he breathed: "Win . . . or bust . . . Win . . . or bust . . . Win . . . or bust."

"Beat John Fairfax or bust"?

Painted on the bow of *Silver* was the SAS badge and motto: "Who Dares Wins." Tom could see the blue outline sometimes as *Silver*'s nose rose to the swell. He told himself, "Well, you've dared, now start winning," mentally thrusting himself along for hours. "I don't know how long I rowed that day. Time held no meaning at all. Only distance, and plenty of it, counted."

Not until the late afternoon did Tom notice that *Silver* was beginning to toss and turn again. The wind had built up and was slapping her at about 40 MPH and growing stronger all the time. But it did not matter too much. For it was holding steady from the northwest and kept *Silver* moving in roughly the right direction: east.

Not until he lashed the oars inboard and set about making a meal did he remember that after sorting out the broken curry jar in the morning he had slipped and fallen against the cooker. In his fall he broke off the door of the cylindrical windshield. He figured he would be able to mend it all right, but not right then. Crouching in front of the opening left by the broken door, Tom shielded the gas jets with his body. It did the trick, but he knew that he could not continue in that way for long. The door would have to be repaired as soon as possible.

There was a last decision to make before bedding down. Should the sea anchor go out or not? The wind had shown signs of swinging around and there was a chance that during the night it would come right around until it was blowing him back over the precious distance he had covered. Yet if it did not change, the sea anchor would slow down whatever advantage the wind provided. It was time for a gamble, and Tom decided to take a chance. He kept the sea anchor inboard.

Thursday, May 29. After a rather uncomfortable night he woke to find the wind had made a fool of him. It was blowing strongly from completely the other—the wrong—direction. Luckily for his peace of mind, he would never know whether or not he had lost his gamble. He would never know whether the change had been so recent that it had made virtually no difference to his progress. Mooning over a question to which he would never find an answer was a complete waste of time. He cut it out of his mind and did the only thing possible—put out the sea anchor.

Checking the temperature later, he found it had risen to 38°F. "Maybe I am fooling myself," Tom thought, "I don't know," but he "drew great consolation from that reading." He reckoned it was evidence that his gamble had paid off, after all—that he had made good distance and was actually edging into a warmer area.

Patting *Silver*'s gunwale as if it were a pet dog, he grinned with delight: "Good girl, you're a good girl."

Maybe *Silver* felt her oarsman was becoming a little too sure of himself and needed to be shown a lesson. Whatever the reason, when Tom stepped over the seat to reach for a fresh pack of rations, he did not step far enough. In failing to do so, he was committing the cardinal sin of a lone sailor when moving about his small craft: to be caught without both feet firmly planted on the deck.

Stretching toward the ration pack, he judged that he could reach it by leaning forward just another six inches. To manage this, he should have put both feet over the seat. Instead, he allowed the back foot to rise above the deck as he bent outward and downward. As his hand grasped the top of the pack, *Silver*, caught by an awkward wave, heeled over. Tom fought for his balance. His raised foot instinctively stabbed down toward the deck as he tried to straighten up. "Idiotically, I still retained my grip on the ration pack," he recalls. As his foot went down, the force of it meeting the deck jarred his ultra-sensitive ankle. "There was no sense of feeling in the foot itself, but the pain just above the ankle was murderous. It felt as if I had snapped my foot off."

Straddled across the seat as he was, there was nothing he could do. His eyes watered with the pain and he cursed at the top of his voice. But *Silver* was still heeling over; still moving in one direction; and that was tipping the deck until it was angled at about 45 degrees.

Once again Tom's back foot jabbed down toward the deck. This time he forced himself to keep it there as he struggled to lean in the opposite direction to *Silver*.

She went over.

With a sudden rush Tom felt himself falling for the water, helpless and utterly out of control.

Although the whole event could not have taken more than a few seconds, everything was as clear to Tom as a sharp photograph. As the water seemed to rise to meet him, he let go of the ration pack and watched it splash into the sea. *Silver* was still moving over, and just one inch would have had Tom's feet completely off the deck. But he couldn't be sure, for his feet were still numb. He judged his precarious position solely by his body angle and the feeling of tension in his calves, thighs, and hips.

As he fell he grabbed madly for the gunwale. In that split second he knew he had misjudged his timing. His right hand slid right over the gunwale, missing it by a hair. He felt the pain of his left hand slap hard against a firm object. It was the handle of the water pump. What incredible luck! But for that he would have been straight over the side. His reflexes, sharpened by his years in the military, were working overtime. At the moment of the touch, his fingers locked around that handle so tightly that nothing but a knife would have loosened them, and his arm stiffened into a desperate bar of straining muscle.

At the same instant his right hand scrabbled back inboard and clamped itself over the edge of the gunwale. As he checked his headlong rush, the jerk half-slung him over the side, leaving him hanging out as far as his waistline over the water. His face was just a couple of inches above the water, and *Silver*'s gunwale had heeled over so far that Tom could feel the water splashing over his right hand. As he hung there, his head was dunked by a passing wave, leaving him spluttering and dripping. Then, with maddening slowness, *Silver* gradually righted herself.

Panic over.

Sitting on the floorboards to regain his breath, he found himself quivering from head to toe. Admittedly, he was wearing his safety harness, and if he had gone over, he should have been able to pull himself back aboard. But a full-body soaking in that icy Labrador Current was the last thing he needed. The thought of having to strip down to the buff did not strike him as very amusing. He tested the water temperature. It was 32°F—freezing point. How could he have lasted in that?

Yet fate stalked him that day. He was destined to get a soaking, and nothing was going to prevent it.

This time it was, well, humorous. The Atlantic caught him "bending." Performing one's natural bodily functions was a tricky affair at the best of times. A plastic bucket and a peaceful moment were the most one could hope for. This time Tom had only one of them, the plastic bucket.

There he was with his pants down, and along came another freak wave. He had his back to it and therefore had no warning as it curled up and rose to splash down right over him. It is difficult to say which was the greater shock, the sudden wave of cold that swept over his entire body or the unexpected impact of several gallons of water hitting him in the backside so hard it knocked him off his feet: "Believe me, that water was brass-monkey cold and gave me an instant teeth-chatter."

So it was a strip to the buff, after all. If a ship had come along then, the crew would have seen a naked, unshaven, and apparently wild man asking if they would be kind enough to direct him to the nearest beach in the British Isles: "I must have looked like a refugee from the cast of *Hair*."*

Tom dried and changed in record time. Nevertheless, his body was a mass of goose pimples long before he had finished dressing. By then he was trembling as violently as a leaf being battered by a rainstorm. Racing through an exercise session, he unlashed the oars and fell into a couple of hours' rowing.

Another bitterly cold night had to be faced—and an uncomfortable one. Winds, swinging steadily around to the east, built up throughout the night to more than 50 MPH. *Silver* bounced and quivered and shipped water by the hundredweight. Standing by the pumps all night caused a great loss of sleep, but at least it kept him warm. By the morning the wind had shifted completely and was blowing directly from the east at about 60 MPH.

Yet again Tom was being blown backward on his course. Yet again he was losing precious distance yard by hard-won yard. He groaned with angry frustration: "Will this bloody shuttlecock existence never finish?" He felt as if he had been chasing up and down the same stretch

---

*   *Hair* was a landmark American rock musical that premiered off-Broadway in 1967 and on Broadway in 1968. It tells the story of the "tribe," a group of politically active, long-haired hippies of the Age of Aquarius living a Bohemian life in New York City and fighting the draft (conscription) into the Vietnam War. The musical's profanity, depiction of the use of illegal drugs, treatment of free love and sexuality, irreverence for the American flag, racially integrated cast, and nude scene caused a great deal of comment and controversy.

of ocean for days. And each blankly gray day was frustratingly so much like the other. The only change was the size of the waves and the ever-changing wind.

Once again he was lying down in the bottom of *Silver* with his back jammed against one side but within reaching distance of the pumps. St. John's radio could still be heard loud and clear, and that added to the depressing impression that he was making little headway. Listening to the newscast, it seemed to Tom that they thought he was a goner.

The report was short: "Lone Atlantic rower Tom McClean has not been sighted since setting out from St. John's two weeks ago. It is most likely that he has met some severe weather conditions, but so far he has apparently not used his radio. Neither the coastguards nor ships in the general area have reported hearing from him. Shipping experts believe it likely that he is between the normal shipping lanes and this would explain why he has not been seen."

"Maybe I was a little oversensitive, but I couldn't help feeling that what those shipping experts were really saying was: 'McClean is a bloody nuisance as well as a bloody fool.' To worry about what other people thought of me right then wasn't going to help my morale." Tom shrugged his shoulders "Not to worry," he told himself, "just keep going."

The last thing in the world Tom wanted was for anybody to get concerned about him, but "I must confess I yearned to see a ship just to find out what progress I had made." Having been without sun, he had been unable to take a sighting, and during the rough weather it had been impossible to use his plotting board, first because he couldn't keep it steady enough and second because he did not want it to get soaked.

Navigation had really become quite a problem. Tom's rough calculations were unsatisfactory but were the best he could do. He must have made between 50 and 100 miles in a more or less easterly direction before those maddening winds turned him on to what he was sure was a due south course. Deciding how far he had traveled south was pure guesswork. It could have been anything between 100 and 200 miles—but no good to Tom and *Silver*.

Although he didn't like to be too sure in case of later bitter disappointment, he felt that at some point in the last couple of days or so he had been heading in an easterly direction, thus completing the last leg of a zigzag pattern.

◆

The break he had been needing came the next morning. He woke at 4:30 A.M. to find a steady 10 MPH wind breezing along from the northwest. Beautiful. In fact, almost perfect. Tom celebrated with a breakfast of biscuits and Marmite, followed by biscuits and strawberry jam and tea. Then he placed a bar of chocolate within easy reach and got cracking with his rowing.

What a day! What an absolutely marvelous day!

Tom started rowing just before 5 A.M. and went right through until 9 P.M. Sixteen beautiful hours of heading east with that wonderful northwest wind never rising above 15 MPH. He stopped only for lunch and several cups of coffee. So important was it to take every possible advantage of the best conditions he had so far encountered that he decided he couldn't waste such vital minutes, even for coffee. He worked out a scheme whereby he did not need to stop rowing completely while he drank.

Shipping the oars inboard, Tom left them in the rowlocks and then leaned forward to put the kettle on. Then he grabbed the oars and got in a few more strokes while waiting for the kettle to boil. Inboard with the oars again, make the coffee, take a few sips, and jam the cup in a tight corner while continuing to row. Then he repeated the process until the cup was empty.

Maybe the coffee got cold, but that didn't matter. Maybe the plan sounded cockeyed, but that didn't matter, either. What did matter was that, true or false, it gave Tom the great feeling that not a single moment was being thrown away. He felt happier than at any time since the trip began. The army had a phrase that described perfectly how Tom felt: "I was chuffed, oh boy, was I chuffed."* Just a few more days like this would make all the difference.

Tom's wishes came true the next morning, Sunday, June 1.

It was almost too good to be believe. That 10 to 15 MPH wind from the northwest was still behind him.

He woke at about 6:30. That surprised him a little, as he had planned on making another start before daylight. But yesterday's effort had taken more out of him than he expected. His hands were certainly feeling the effect. They ached from wrist to fingertips and were almost too stiff to bend. He could hear them crack as he massaged them, trying to restore them to some state of suppleness. It was vital that his hands did not pack it in now, so he decided to start rowing a little later to give them a chance to regain some strength.

In the meantime, he pulled out one of his Sunday letters. It was from Val and June, the girls on the switchboard at the SAS base in Hereford. He could picture them clearly in his mind's eye: "Both pretty, both with gorgeous smiles, and both kind and considerate. Pretty girls have always been quite a weakness of mine and it struck me that this was the first time I had thought of a girl since setting out. Frankly I was astonished. I hadn't even glanced at the girlie magazine the guy had thrown into the boat at St. John's. Lone rowing can certainly keep a man's mind well occupied. It was just as well, for it would be a long time before I would be dating anybody again."

Tom's thoughts reminded him of a small mystery that he had forgotten in the rush of getting ready for the row. Just before leaving England he had received a postcard picturing a "lucky black cat" and bearing the message: "You won't remember me, but I met you on a train traveling

---

*   The word *chuffed* predominantly means "very pleased" though in most dictionaries one will find its number one definition to be simply "pleased." Curiously, the number two definition of the word is "displeased." In other words, *chuffed* belongs to the unique class of words that can be their own antonyms—sometimes referred to as auto-antonyms, self-antonyms, contranyms, or amphibolous words. Examples of such words in formal English are *cleave*, which can mean "to cling" or "to split apart," and *fast*, which can mean "fixed in place" or "move quickly."

from London to Hereford and you told me all about your boat. Good luck, Paula." There was no address.

Who was Paula? What did she look like? "What drivel had I been spouting?" Tom mused. He tried going back over every train journey he had made in the past few months. But he could not remember Paula. "I felt a little sad and a little guilty," as he felt that he should be able to remember someone kind enough to think of him. Hopefully, there were quite a lot of people thinking of him.

Suddenly he felt quite lonely under the moody gray clouds and surrounded by the slate-colored sea. Going back to his days in the orphanage and strengthening through his years in the army, he had been determined not to be tangled up by being involved emotionally with anybody. He had been dedicated to being a loner. But maybe that was not such a good plan for him. He thought of the words of the song: "People who need people . . . are the luckiest people in the world." Perhaps that was right. Maybe one cannot be a loner all through life.

Right then that letter from Val and June was the best company in the world. It began with a little prayer: "May the Good Lord keep you safe." The Almighty had certainly been doing a fine job of that so far: "I had come through some pretty bad patches and was still all in one piece."

Val and June reminded him that a pal at Hereford had given him a small plastic pink elephant for luck. Tom had forgotten about that, too. It was packed away somewhere aboard *Silver*. He took a quick look but without success. Pinky the elephant and his accompanying luck suddenly became quite important. Tom really wanted to find it. Torn between superstition—for he really thought of it now as a lucky mascot—and the need to start rowing, he plumped for the rowing. That wind was too good to waste any longer.

"To be perfectly honest, I was also a trifle apprehensive of allowing myself to get maudlin," Tom admits. Deliberately sarcastic, he told himself: "Hell, you'll be crying in your beer before you know where you are!"

The pain of rowing was a perfect antidote. Yesterday's burst of action had eaten deep into his hands. Each pull on the oars stretched his fingers until the very joints seemed to be coming apart. Giving in would have been so easy. The temptation to kid himself that he needed rest was hard to resist. But he couldn't, he wouldn't, allow himself to just sit through such perfect conditions. For nearly half an hour he rowed with his eyes screwed up with the effort and his teeth gritting into each other. It took about that long for the pain to wear away . . . or was it just a case of getting used to it?

At times he would swear that he was only partly conscious. But at last the pain began to fade. Sweat poured down Tom's face and into his now open eyes. Stopping to wipe it away would be a big mistake. He was sure he would never have the guts to start again. "Row, you stupid bastard!" he snarled. Blinking, he shook his head to get rid of the surplus perspiration and by the end of another half hour felt somewhere near normal once again. He chanced a short pause to wipe his face and wrap a towel around his neck and started again.

Monday, June 2, began as another perfect day. A concerted search for Pinky located him tucked away in a plastic container together with his fishing gear. Would there ever be a day when he would be able to use that gear? The idea had been to provide himself with a little fresh food now and again. Tom tied Pinky firmly to the side of the compass with nylon parachute chord. It was quite extraordinary how much better he felt for that simple exercise. Luck, he felt, was with him now, but he couldn't leave it as Pinky's sole responsibility.

Tom had nailed a St. Christopher medal to the roof of his shelter, and alongside it went a Canadian one-cent piece given to him by a well-wishing Newfoundlander. He could see that array of lucky charms from his rowing position. He chuckled to himself. "What a superstitious idiot you've turned out to be." But, after all, it was legendary that most sailors are inclined to be superstitious, so Tom felt he was in good company.

Perhaps lucky charms take some time to become effective, for no sooner were they all in position than the winds began building up again. Tom managed to keep rowing for a bit, but eventually it proved too dangerous to remain sitting up. His comfortable days were over for the time being. That was obvious.

◆

By midday a savage northwester was lashing the seas into mountainous waves. Before packing in the day's rowing stint Tom just sat there, watching the beginnings of the storm racing toward *Silver's* stern like white-topped walls of gray slate. Each wall grew larger, higher, and faster as he watched. From Tom's "safety" position on the floorboards he hurriedly boiled up a curry lunch and a mug of tea. "This blow," he told himself, "is no short-term job." Tom figured he could be stuck on the floorboards of *Silver* for three or four days. It seemed to be set for a hurricane.

The wind came howling over the side of the dory, tearing at anything that was loose, rattling Tom's cooking pans like a BBC sound-effects studio man trying to simulate the sound of a huge kitchen. The canvas draped over the front of his shelter was snatched into the air and cracked like an angry stock-whip. Crawling around on his hands and knees, he checked all lashings and tied down everything that showed the least sign of movement. There was nothing to do after that except crawl back to his position by the pumps, wedge himself in, and stand by to pump when needed.

It was a nightmare of a night. *Silver* pitched and rolled as if deliberately trying to throw Tom overboard. She seemed to have developed a sudden frenzied personal hate for her oarsman. There was no sleep at all for him. *Silver* shipped water all through the night. Tom pumped, he bailed, and he clung to the boat like a limpet. There were moments, Tom was sure, when *Silver* was completely out of the water. He could feel the waves carry her high into the air as if trying to throw them up into the black void overhead.

Suddenly a wave would chop itself away from under *Silver*, leaving her hanging in midair. Then she would drop. The sense of falling was terrific. It was probably no more than a few inches, but it seemed like yards. When *Silver* hit the water, Tom literally bounced on the floorboards. The sickening thuds seemed to be threatening to split *Silver* apart at every seam. Every time Tom clung to whatever he could get hold of, and every time it seemed that he would be torn loose and thrown into the teeth of that screeching wind and swirled away into the darkness like a helpless leaf.

Within the first five minutes of the storm Tom was soaked through to the skin. Throughout the night there was a constant level of water in *Silver*, which Tom never managed to get below a foot deep. He just had to lie in it and fight for survival in a world that had gone stark raving mad.

His arms ached, his body was bruised and sore, and his head rang with the din of the storm. Experts who had experienced the Atlantic in all her moods had warned Tom it would be rough at times. He knew it would be rough. He had already experienced an angry Atlantic. But neither his experience nor his imagination ever stretched to the vicious savagery of this punishing night.

Looking back now, Tom tries to tell himself he was not afraid. But he wonders. He does not recall being afraid at the time. Scared, yes. But the fear that lurks in the pit of your stomach? Fear of dying? Fear that paralyzes the brain and the muscles? No, he doesn't think so. On the other hand, a man can be afraid of being afraid.

Tom does know that he started talking, or rather yelling, to himself during those murderously tormenting hours. He screamed it out against the fury of the storm: "You'll be all right. You'll get there. Stick it out . . . for Christ's sake, just stick it out."

Stick it out he did. But not entirely by himself. He had never been a great churchgoer—except when forced to as a boy in the orphanage—but that night he prayed. It was simple and straightforward: "Help me see this through, please help me fight."

That's all. A few words which he addressed in the general direction of the sky. "When you are alone under these conditions," Tom realized, "it gives strength to think there is someone greater watching over you."

14

Unassisted

He had been wrong. The storm did not last three or four days. By Tuesday morning, June 3, it had begun to blow itself out. Tom had never before been so thankful to be so utterly wrong. He was still sitting by the pumps as dawn rose. He had not shut his eyes all night. Exhaustion, sheer complete exhaustion, seemed only a breath away. The mere thought of moving was a monumental effort in itself. But move he had to.

Tom forced himself to his knees to light the cooker and brew some tea. The hot tea almost scalded his throat as he swallowed. He blanched as his throat burned. It was the first quick movement he'd made in the last 10 minutes since turning the cooker on. He drank deeply again, stinging himself into action with the smarting pain of the hot liquid. Slowly he felt himself coming back to life.

Miserable he might be. Cold, wet, and battered he might be. But he was a long way from finished. Tom started singing—it was more of a croak, actually. The song was "A Scottish Soldier":

> *There was a soldier, a Scottish soldier,*
> *Who wandered far away . . .*

After the first two lines, the words dried up. How had he forgotten the words of one of his favorite songs? Not that the words mattered right then. Tom hummed his way through the rest of the song in a tuneless, rasping mumble. Once he had finished he started again. Four times he hummed his way through the song.

With his hands clasped around a second mug of tea, he sat on the seat, waiting for his breakfast to cook. Until this morning, no matter what happened, the all-important thing to Tom had been to row for as long as he could at every opportunity, even if it meant going without proper food. But last night's storm had changed all that. Food had become absolutely vital. He boiled up two of his dried porridge cakes and added a liberal helping of condensed milk. This was followed by a half-pound of dry biscuits heavily smeared with strawberry jam. It was the first time during the trip that he had eaten until he felt utterly full.

As he ate, he contemplated the eternal grayness of the sea and sky, which had dogged him practically every yard of the way. Even the wildlife seemed to be giving this depressing stretch of the Atlantic the cold shoulder. He had seen very few birds during the past 17 days, and he had not seen a single fish, shark, or porpoise. He had seen only the one ship. At the thought of another ship he peered long and carefully around the horizon, going through every point of the compass until his eyes were back where they had started, staring over *Silver*'s bow. Nothing. He knew there would be nothing. He knew there would be nothing when he looked again. But it did not stop him. His eyes scraped every yard of the sea between *Silver* and the horizon once more. Far to the east and high in the sky he spotted four birds. They were heading east. Tom wondered if they were heading for Ireland and how long the journey would take. All he could think of was that if they were heading for the Emerald Isle, they would be there a long, long time ahead of him. Loneliness began to hit him again.

"Should I have made this a double-handed trip?" Tom wondered. "Would a companion have eased the situation?" But the whole purpose of his adventure was to do it alone. To do it any other way would have no purpose at all. Ridgway and Blyth had already pulled off the double in great style. Tom's job was the singled-handed voyage, and he had to get on with it. At least he had only himself to worry about.

And yet not quite only himself. There was that confounded John Fairfax somewhere out in the Atlantic, no doubt well ahead of him in terms of making the crossing.

There was also *Silver*. Perhaps she couldn't get concerned about his welfare, but he could worry about her, and right then she looked a mess. After the hell of the night's storm, all Tom had done was to indulge himself in a sort of self-pity. He had not given a thought to the tough little dory, which had so gallantly carried him through hours of ocean fury.

About six inches of water swilled around on the boat's floorboards. Dirty water, which had developed a sort of frothy scum as the force of the storm sloshed it around in the bottom of *Silver*. Everything that would absorb moisture was dripping wet. Those items of Tom's supplies that were covered with heavy-duty plastic seemed to be okay. Drops of water covered every plastic package but, when he opened two or three to check, everything inside was still perfectly dry.

His sleeping bag, air mattress, and a sweater he had thoughtlessly left lying in his shelter were sopping. Tom lashed all three across the roof of the shelter, leaving just enough looseness for the wind to get underneath them, in an effort to dry them out. He pumped out the last six inches of water and threw out a bit of seaweed. That was about all he could do for *Silver* right then, but she looked a lot better.

The wind had dropped to a steady 15 MPH, and Tom started rowing to the southeast. But not for long. By the early afternoon the wind and sea started building up again. He shipped the oars, lashed them down, and sat there looking at the empty scene once again.

All at once it wasn't empty any more. In the distance to the northeast he spotted the outline of a ship. It was miles away and looked no larger than a toy, but to Tom it was like a block of flats—apartment buildings—filling that wide-open space. "After days of absolutely nothing it was a strange feeling to think that there were actually people over there," he marveled. "Talking, laughing, singing people." No doubt those people would be only too willing to take him aboard and give him the run of all the comforts that were on board. A bath with piping-hot water. Soft towels for his feet. What a luxury, a superb, blissful luxury to wallow and soak in that bath and let all his aches and pains ooze away. Perhaps those folks would offer him hot food, with crisp vegetables. They might have fresh fruit and cream—tinned cream, no doubt, but still cream. Then to bed with a mattress, to lie between clean white sheets in a warm cabin protected on all four sides from the piercing fingers of the Atlantic winds. There would surely be a doctor onboard, with pills, lotions, and ointments to treat his feet, his blisters, his salt sores. Maybe even a pretty nurse.

Such a dream!

The ship was not heading anywhere near him, and there was absolutely no chance at all of them spotting him from that distance. And just as well. Tom wondered if he could have withstood the temptation of such an invitation. Could he? There was no telling. He told himself that he would be able to do so. That he would decline all offers with thanks and simply ask for a check on his position. "To be perfectly honest, I had my doubts," Tom confesses today.

The real test was just three or four hours away.

◆

The afternoon started as a complete waste of time. The wind was too strong for him to think of rowing, yet not strong enough for *Silver* to ship water in dangerous quantities. Tom supposed that if he really wanted to do anything he could find a dozen small chores to tackle. Most important, he should have looked at his feet. But he was tired—and probably a little idle also—and he told himself it would do him good to rest, maybe even to snatch a doze while his anchor was down.

Certainly, once that ship had passed out of sight, Tom became weary of looking at nothing but the empty sea. Propped up against his folded inflatable airbed, he watched the thin steel rod of *Silver*'s radio mast tracing a constant rolling pattern against the white-gray clouds as they rolled and pitched.

He watched the tip of the mast for ages, trying to judge how many inches each pattern would be out of line with the next. For a while he was far away from the Atlantic. Far away from this ever-moving water. Far, far away among green fields, listening to the soothing sounds of the English countryside in the summertime. He was back in Buckinghamshire on the Venn farm, walking the fields of barley and wheat, patting the cattle, chasing a broody group of hens. It was the time of the year for mowing. The sweet smell of newly cut hay lingered in his Atlantic daydream. Tom walked miles, across fields, over hills, through woods, into the surrounding villages, and back to the farmhouse for the sort of tea that only Mrs. Venn knew how to set before a hungry young man.

The craving for human company returned. Tom switched on the radio, tuned into St. John's, and lit the cooker. This time there was no mention of him on the news broadcast. "Well," he figured, "that is better than hearing them say that they were losing hope of seeing me again."

He hunched up in front of the cooker, squatting on his haunches, listening to the music, when it happened. It was the sound of a bell, loud and distinct, right behind him. For a few seconds he didn't move a muscle. He just perched there, frozen into that one position, absolutely unable to believe the message his ears were pounding through to his brain.

Tom turned around and there was a fishing vessel almost on top of him. She was about 25 yards off his port side, so close he could read her name printed on the bow: *Rio Alfusqueiro*. He just stood and stared, hypnotized by his first sight of moving, waving human beings since . . . how long was it? A hundred years? Not quite three weeks, and yet it was as if he had stepped into another world. For the first time in his life Tom got some idea of how Alice in Wonderland must have felt as she walked through that crazy looking glass.

They were lined along the rails, shouting and waving. They too must have been away from home for some time. They were unshaven and salt-crusted. Tough, sturdy, swarthy Portuguese fishermen looking like a bunch of pirates. But jolly ones! Some wore the traditional Portuguese stocking caps of wool, the tassel dangling rakishly down the right-hand side of the face. Tom almost glanced at their masthead to see if the skull and crossbones was flying there.

They were a wonderful, wonderful sight. As the *Rio*'s bridge drew level with *Silver*, Tom heard the skipper yelling at him in broken English: "Hey! You all right, eh? You want anything, eh? Help maybe? You in trouble, eh?"

Grabbing his chart, Tom waved at the skipper then crossed his two forearms into an *X* to indicate that he wanted to know his position. At the same time Tom yelled: "My position, Captain! Can you give me my position? Where . . . are . . . we?"

The captain waved as if he understood, but the *Rio* just steamed slowly past him. At first Tom thought he was ignoring him, that the fishermen had called out to him just for a spot of fun. "Blimey," Tom spluttered aloud, "the bastards don't care. The lousy, rotten, stinking pigs!"

Tom soon realized that his ire was misplaced when he spotted that the trawl was still out on the Portuguese boat. The captain had steamed off to pull it onboard. Once that was done, he turned and steamed back on Tom's port side, once again protecting *Silver* from the swell. The two vessels rolled there together no more than 20 yards apart, Tom with a hand cupped around his ear trying to catch what the *Rio*'s skipper was bawling through his cupped hands.

The captain got it. "Poseeshun is 46 degrees 54 minutes north, 47 degrees 24 minutes west," he yelled. Then he asked again: "Maybe you want food or water, eh?"

"No thanks," Tom shouted back.

"Then you want something else, maybe," he bellowed.

"No thanks," Tom replied. "Nothing but my position. And thanks a lot, Captain!"

Silver and the *Rio* parted with the gap between them slowly widening. The Portuguese crew still lined the rails. They had been grinning spectators of that little interchange between Tom and their skipper. In respect to the oarsman in the dory clearly being British, they saluted Tom with the *V* made so famous by Winston Churchill.

Tom waved back with both arms way above his head. But it didn't seem enough to express the tremendous elation he was feeling. He had an inspiration. Diving into his shelter, he dug out a bottle of rum.

Gesturing toward them to wish them good luck, Tom took a great swig from the neck of the bottle. The roar of approval from the Portuguese came rolling across the water.

It was a strange little ceremony, but what a difference it made to Tom. His weariness vanished. He was once again "as full of battle as a fighting cock." Now it was over he realized that he had passed the test without even thinking about it. He had refused all help, and he had not had to force himself to do it. In fact, the refusal had come as naturally as asking a chum to have a drink. He had done it without a single shaky doubt rearing its ugly head.

To cap it off, Tom at last knew exactly where he was: 46°54'N, 47°24'W. Just about 350 miles southeast of St. John's. Oh brother! "I was really chuffed." He had beaten what he thought to be the worst part of the trip, and he and *Silver* must be—had to be, impossible not to be—on the edge of that Holy Grail that was the Gulf Stream.

His luck had changed—he was sure of it. Now all he asked was two or three easygoing days with friendly breezes to give him a chance to sort himself out. And he got it! Was anybody, anywhere, ever quite so lucky? Those days—long, long days when the air temperature never rose above 40°F and the water never above 35°F—were over. Tom had won the first round.

◆

For four solid days and nights, the wind became his ally. From the west it came with hardly a change of course. Nursing him, coaxing him, coddling him in one great swooping surge to the east, and never rising much above 25 MPH or falling below 10 MPH. In the air there was warmth so distinct that his ice-capped brain actually imagined it could be touched. There was no doubt about it—it could be felt. Tom was escaping from the freezing embrace of the Labrador Current, and he swore he would never set eyes on that area of natural savagery ever again.

The yards, the miles, were spinning away with the water rippling and creaming away from *Silver*'s bows in the shape of a huge arrowhead. As the little dory ate up the distance, so the temperature rose degree by degree, climbing gradually all the time, day by day, until it hit the all-time high so far: a balmy 48°F.

Everything was so perfect, so intoxicating. By comparison with what he had experienced, the four days were like booking into a five-star hotel on the Côte d'Azur. Tom had learned something during the past three weeks. It was a vital lesson, and hardship and danger had been his tutors. No matter how perfect the conditions and weather, no matter how calm the sea, he must never relax completely. He had said he would learn the hard way. And he had.

Despite the discomfort that he had endured, Tom was truly glad that the opening stage of the journey had not been easy enough to tempt him into thinking the whole thing was going to be a cakewalk. Neither was he going to be tempted into kidding himself that he had taken everything the Atlantic could throw at him. He deeply suspected that it had an abundant supply of dirty tricks still to play.

When Tom had talked with John Ridgway and Chay Blyth, both men spoke at length about the hazards he would ultimately face crossing the ocean. He now knew that nobody could put into words the full measure of what lay in store out in the North Atlantic. It had to be experienced for oneself.

◆

Tom was quite a sight. His beard was matted with dried saltwater, his eyes were red-rimmed and sore, and his face felt as raw as a piece of beef. Salt sores had begun to erupt at the edges of his mouth. A rash of them had begun to build up at the corners of his neck, wrists, armpits, and, most uncomfortable of all, his backside.

Wherever saltwater had managed to penetrate between skin and clothing—and that was everywhere—it had crystallized, rubbed, and chafed away at the skin with every movement Tom made. And every movement made them burn, as if acid were being slowly but regularly dropped into the heart of each individual sore.

He looked lousy and felt lousy. But his luck of the last few days was still holding good right into the morning of June 5. The temperature climbed to 48°F. After what he had been through, that was virtually a heatwave. Near midday the sun actually poked through the cool gray lining overhead.

The clouds split apart, showing a large patch of blue, blue sky. The sun, blazing, almost blinding, poured its healing warmth into every aching bone, every smarting sore, and every throbbing bruise on his body. Tom hurriedly stripped off every stitch of clothing and sat there stark naked, arms outstretched, head flung back, trying to make sure every inch of skin, including his still blue-looking feet, got its quota of life-giving warmth.

The water in the kettle was still warmish from his morning tea. There was about a pint of it. Using it with care, he bathed and washed until most of the salt crystals disappeared from his skin. A change into clean clothing, and he felt like a new man.

He spread out on the seat, basically the only really dry spot on *Silver*, and basked in the sunshine. The wind was from the west, and it was light. Perfect rowing conditions. Tom should have been bending his back, not sunbathing. However, he would have defied anyone to resist the temptation to lie in that sun. The lazy, luxurious warmth drove home the truth of how truly lucky he had been to survive the Labrador Current.

For the first time Tom begrudgingly admitted to himself that there had been times when he wondered if he would make it. As soon as the admission was out he forced it out of his mind with all the willpower at his command. To admit that was to admit the possibility of defeat and he had convinced himself that once he allowed even the slightest doubt to shadow his mind that his resolve would weaken and it could be the first step toward failure.

Failure? Just failure? That sounded like no more than giving up rowing and just walking ashore somewhere. Like a boat on the Serpentine that headed for the boathouse when its hour was up. Let Fairfax head for the boathouse! "Out here in the Atlantic," Tom told himself, "a man has to face up to the inescapable fact that failure means one thing only . . .

death." He felt he could face up to it. It would be "no disgrace to die as long as I had fought every inch of the way."

Closing his eyes to shut out the sun's brightness, Tom was pleased to discover that he could so calmly think of death. Amazingly, he had never thought of it before, not even in the jungles of Borneo. There, of course, "I had had companions to share the hardships, to joke at the discomforts, and to dismiss any spot of trouble, no matter how severe, as just part of a normal way of life."

Tom dozed off in the sun. In a half-dream he was back in the jungle, looking for terrorists, waiting for a Royal Marine helicopter to swoop down and pick him up.

◆

In 1965 Tom was deployed with the Paras to the Malaysian-Indonesian border, where they were joined by units of the SAS and Royal Marines. The emergency deployment of British military forces was directed at Indonesia's active and ongoing opposition to the new state of Malaysia, which had been established in September 1963 as an amalgamation of the Federation of Malaya, Singapore, and the British protectorates ("Crown colonies") of North Borneo and Sarawak. British soldiers were sent in to stop Indonesia's campaign to infiltrate into Borneo and exploit ethnic and religious diversity in the region by attacking native villages and generally destabilizing the society, with the intent of unraveling the new nation. Essentially, Indonesia and Malaysia were at war, though an undeclared war, with the British naturally supporting the latter because of its connections to the Commonwealth.

Tom's battalion was based in Brunei, a small country semi-independent from Britain situated on the north coast of the island of Borneo. Given that the terrain of Borneo was mainly jungle and that the contentious Malaysia-Indonesia border lacked roads, the military action was characterized by isolated ground combat conducted by company- or platoon-sized operations. For everyone, including Tom and his mates, that meant dozens of long foot patrols into the jungle.

Introduced to the special character and subtleties of jungle fighting—basic survival, tracking, ambushing in dense vegetation—21-year-old Tom McClean quickly found that he loved the challenges, especially the premium on working in the very small four-man fighting patrols: a patrol leader, a radio operator, which was Tom's duty, a lead scout, and a medic. "Living off the land in that sort of country was my idea of heaven," Tom recalls. Taken into the jungle across the border by helicopter and abseiling to the ground down a rope, a patrol would track the enemy a month at a stretch, then be picked by chopper, and brought back to Brunei.

In the jungle Tom was virtually fearless. He felt that the Paras held a significant advantage over the enemy: "It was one thing for four trained men to be in the jungle quietly listening and watching, quite another matter for large enemy groups to try to cross the border and avoid us hearing or seeing them. . . . There were many tricks to remember in order to survive, do our job, and return to base safely. We never walked along riverbeds. The easiest way of trekking in the jungle was always the most dangerous. We used the thickest undergrowth and most difficult climbs and descents. At night, to avoid insects and snakes, we slept in hammocks slung between trees, putting repellant around the base of each tree to deter 'trouble' from climbing up after us. No one ever seemed to give much thought to insects and snakes coming down the trees at us, but none ever did. No smoking was allowed—before getting into the helicopter we were searched for cigarettes—because the smell of tobacco smoke in the jungle traveled up to half a mile. We were also checked for metal mess tins. The sound of one clanking against another piece of equipment carried up to three miles on a still humid night. We took no soap or washing kit. We smelled like jungle animals when we eventually returned home. Our weapons were different from those normally carried by the army. The lead scout had a Remington shotgun with a magazine of six cartridges. If he ever saw anything whatever, he would fire all six shots."

Jungle fighting was made for Tom's personality. At dawn the patrol "stood to," quietly taking positions facing the four corners of the compass, each of the four men with his quarter to watch. For up to two hours they just waited, watched, and listened. No talking, no smoking, no brew of tea. Just silence, broken by the noises of the jungle waking. If there was any combat, it would happen during the day, because movement in the jungle in total darkness was virtually impossible. Even in daylight the umbrella of foliage made everything quite dark.

"We set out slowly, cautiously, silently into the jungle. We seldom spoke, but used some 70 hand signals to communicate with one another." The patrol's lead man carried the lightest pack, whereas Tom, as signaler, bore the heaviest, with the radio as well as all his personal kit. Progress through the jungle was tediously slow, not more than half a mile an hour. A few slowly and carefully made paces, a few more paces, then stop again. The squad moved like that for an hour, then rested. Whenever they stopped they crouched in a firing position, watching and listening to the many sounds of birds and occasional animals. Monkeys were a giveaway for anyone on the move, as were the elephants, which Tom and his mates could hear crashing through the thick brush miles away.

Tom never worried about being killed or even getting wounded, so cocky was he about the superior techniques of his special training. One might imagine that the enemy, native to the region, was better than the British troopers in the art of jungle warfare. "Not true," asserts Tom. "The enemy Indonesians were hopeless, moving about talking, whistling, and even playing transistor radios. They would stick to the tracks in groups of about 80, and we could hear them miles away." On one recce, Tom's squad hid a few yards off a path and counted 112 men as they passed by. "There was no point taking on a gang like that, but we reported their position, their direction, and other details back to base at Brunei. We were the watchers." In making camp for the night, the patrol never prepared a space: "We never, ever, cut anything in the jungle. It would have been the quickest way of being found by the enemy. We cooked in the dark on a platform of sticks so as not to leave signs of our cookers. We didn't even cut notches in trees to support our hammocks, which we made from our parachute panels and shroud lines. Each morning we rubbed earth into the places on the tree where the lines had been attached to cover up any bruising."

The Paras' weapons were always ready and within reach, even when they were taking a crap, making tea, or sleeping. Remembers Tom: "Loaded, one bullet up the spout and the safety catch on."

Day after day, night after night, on patrol in Borneo—always the same routine. After a few days of it they lost sense of days and weeks. Jungle fighting became an almost timeless experience.

"For me this was real soldiering. I enjoyed the close comradeship of the small group where everyone was responsible for the safety of everyone else."

Tom also loved facing life-and-death challenges . . . and facing them all on his own. No help from anyone. That made him feel more alive than anything he could do with other people.

His favorite story from his time in Borneo was the time a contingent of some 30 enemy insurgents forced Tom's four-man patrol to scatter, each to find his own way back through the jungle to the previous night's camp, as was standard procedure. Tom arrived back at camp to find no one else was there. When the other three troopers still had not made it back by the next morning, Tom headed to the prescribed landing zone where they were to be picked up by helicopter. It took a few days to get there, and even then he had to watch the area for a couple of days to make sure it had not been found and made into an ambush, not just for him—and his three mates (who trickled back to the landing zone and subsequently rescued)—but also for the Royal Marine chopper pilots who were to come haul them out.

Rather than feeling alone and in need of assistance through it all, Tom relates, "I was in my element." It was not just that his jungle survival training and previous patrols prepared him for the experience; he loved facing the challenge solo. It also didn't hurt that Tom, while off duty, had spent a great deal of time visiting the local *kampong* (village) and getting to know the people of the Punan and Dayak tribes. To one of the native boys Tom gave a wristwatch. In return the fascinated teenager gave Tom a blowpipe complete with poisoned darts, then made sure that

Tom was taken along on a hunt for monkeys, which the tribe killed for food. Divided into groups of five men, the hunters wore nothing but a loincloth—no protection from leeches or insects as the British soldiers all had. Each hunter carried a bag for the game killed and a bamboo holder for the deadly darts. Tom got into the spirit of the hunt by stripping down to his briefs. He didn't hit a monkey with any of his darts but his ability to talk, shoot, and maneuver in the jungle impressed his new friends.[*]

"The tribesmen were a happy people with few cares in the world—no money, just barter, and living a day-to-day existence. I liked them and appreciated their interest in me."

Back at the village after the monkey hunt, Tom tried their local brew, a kind of rice wine to which the tribesmen added "strange things" to sweeten it. The Malay cocktail had the appearance of gooey milk porridge and was drunk out of a straw made from bamboo. "It was very strong and could knock you out," Tom remembers, with eyes wide open.

Becoming friendly with the native people was another way Tom acted as his own man, doing things his own way. When some senior army officers saw Tom in a sarong, native sandals, and almost every other native fashion except plaited hair and a pierced nose, "They were a little concerned to find that Signaler McClean had gone native—the wild man of Borneo." Getting to know the locals was one thing, but the brass "must have felt I had taken things a bit far." But Tom was exactly the type of man that pushed the cork a bit farther than most.

---

[*]   According to Tom, "To kill a monkey the tribesmen would surround a tree where one or two monkeys would be sitting or scampering about and fire several of the poisoned darts at one of them. The first dart had little effect but after three or four the monkey began to sway about on the bough. After a few minutes it dropped to the ground, to be grabbed and cut through in several places, with blood flowing rapidly everywhere. The loss of blood freed the body from the darts' poison, which, it seemed, simply stopped the heart by paralyzing it" (McClean, *Rough Passage*, 29).

15

The Sunday Letter

Nestled down in the dory, Tom woke up cold, so cold his body began shaking. The blanket of fog and cloud overhead had knitted together again, blotting out the sun. A glance at his watch showed that his nap had lasted between 20 minutes and half an hour. He shook his head, chuckled at the memory of his blowpipe, and looked around at the customary salt-glaze gray.

The wind was still light and from the west. There was nothing to do except get out the oars. He kept *Silver*'s stern to the wind and maintained a steady rowing action. Under these conditions one had to fight off the temptation to pull like mad. It would serve very little purpose. Tom would be exhausted in a couple of hours and in no condition to cope with any wind that threatened to shortchange him on any progress he made.

His inexperience had already tempted him into that sort of error earlier in the trip. Now he knew better. In any case, he figured that he must conserve his strength. Every day, every hour in the Atlantic, must, to some small degree, eat away at his reserves of energy. He had to guard against any reckless use of his powers of endurance.

Once again his army training came in useful. Training for the Paras had been hard, mentally and physically, with two solid months of running, marching, assault courses, and long forced marches with full equipment. During the Aden Emergency, he had made several very long

(24-mile) night marches through the Yemeni desert, carting a jerry can of water weighing 50 pounds strapped to his back; on one occasion, he had carried two full cans the last nine miles when his mate sprained an ankle and could not go on. When as a 21-year-old he joined the elite SAS commandos, the first test for selection was a forced march of 40 miles carrying a pack of bricks weighing 66 pounds. "Fitness was important, the training taught me," Tom realized, appreciatively. But, for him, "endurance was more a question of attitude."

"Strange," thought Tom, "how so much of a soldier's training can be adapted to survival at sea." Tom had learned how to doze while stepping it out on a forced march, when a certain amount of distance had to be covered in a certain amount of time no matter if he had not slept properly for days. He had come to accept this "marching doze" as a state of mind—a situation where he could shut off about 25 percent of his active self, mentally and physically, and yet automatically keep putting one step in front of the other. Perhaps his capacity for that even went back to all those days of disciplined marching in line back at Fegan's orphanage.

Tom found he could comfortably adapt himself to doing much the same while rowing. The oars dipped in and out. He bent backward and forward. It became as automatic as placing one foot in front of the other. He was sure that his catnapping while on the move helped tremendously to conserve his strength, which would otherwise have probably been frittered away in bouts of walloping physical effort.

But the catnapping brought with it an attendant danger: mental indifference. Tom had been warned about it. He knew it would likely happen. He knew it was happening to him right then. With the few days of quieter weather, the blissful peacefulness of a calm ocean, and the coziness of a gradually warming temperature, part of his mind was slowly, almost imperceptibly, becoming dulled and lethargic.

He noted with surprise how much slower his reactions had become. Yet, at first, he did nothing to counteract the danger. It was almost as if he had somehow managed to step outside of himself and observe his body taking part in a weird slow-motion film that had no ending. The hours had slipped away, yet he had no sense of speed or time. Nothing at all seemed to matter anymore.

That was the danger sign, and luckily Tom managed to recognize it in time. He knew if he ever got to the stage where he failed to spot the danger signals, then he, *Silver*, and the entire adventure were headed for disaster sooner or later.

Silver rocked gently in the westerly breeze, lulling Tom deeper and deeper into his waking sleep. He struggled to whip his mind into a state of activity. It was a strange and eerie process. Telling himself he must find something to do, he looked slowly around *Silver*, trying to decide what it should be. Before he ever hit on anything, the reason for looking had been forgotten, and once again Tom would have to flog himself into mental awareness.

It was impossible to judge just how long he dithered about in his half-conscious state. It seemed to last for days, and yet Tom was aware that he continued to row. Just how effective his rowing was, he would never know. He suspected strongly that it was basically nothing more than lifting the oars in and out without bothering too much about pulling, steering, or even reading the compass. He was sure of one thing. It was too long. Half an hour in that fuddled state was too long.

A stray thought, which came out of nowhere, broke Tom out of his trance. He pictured the "proper" Englishman of colonial times who, even in the most barren of deserts or darkest jungle, dressed formally for dinner. Tom had always laughed at that absurd level of civility. Not this time. In his attenuated state of mind Tom thought he had come to a profound realization: that dressing for dinner in such situations was a creditable form of self-discipline. And a judicious bit of wisdom imposed on oneself never did a person any harm.

The struggle of grappling with a mosaic of so many variegated thoughts almost proved too much. Tom had reached the state where he was telling himself that no matter what he was thinking, one thing he couldn't do was slip into a dinner jacket and bow tie and head into a formal dining room. He was about to give up again, and quite willingly, when he realized that he was tugging fiercely at his scruffy weeks-old beard. Maybe he couldn't dress, but he could shave. So, he would shave. He shaved with hot water, scented shaving soap, and a brand-new blade.

It worked. Tom was jerked out of his psychic muddle. Whether it was the actual act of shaving or the agony of scraping a blade across weather-beaten skin and salt sores that opened up until the blood ran down in rivulets, he'd never know. But he preferred to think it was the act of shaving.

By the time Tom stanched the flow of blood on his face, it was 11 A.M. on Friday, June 6. He could only vaguely recall creeping into his shelter to sleep, but he could not be absolutely certain that his memory was not of the night before. He had drifted through nearly 24 hours without knowing much about it. And he didn't like it.

The temperature had dropped again. It was down to 44°F. He remembered the sunbathing of the morning before, when it had been a wonderful 48°F even before the sun broke through. The temperature had obviously risen above that while the sun shined. For a wild moment he feared that *Silver* had drifted back toward the icy clutches of the Labrador. That savage stretch of current would prey on Tom's mind until he was so far away from it that he knew that it would be impossible to return.

Flicking a glance at the still-leaden sky, he wondered if the sun would break through again. Perversely, he also hoped it would not, as he blamed the lulling warmth of yesterday for accelerating the dangerous state of mental indifference into which he had glided. The wind, still from the west and dead astern, had dropped to between 5 and 10 MPH. *Silver* was steady and heading due east. She was nipping along beautifully.

A few days like this would have been the perfect situation to lure Tom into dropping all thought of doing anything else except row. Admittedly he could have pushed her speed up a little by getting the oars out, but while she was heading in the right direction there was a far more important chore to do. He checked the lashings on the rudder, slightly adjusted them to keep *Silver*'s bow pointing east, and then retightened them.

With that out of the way, Tom set about sorting out *Silver*'s trim. At that point there was not actually anything to worry about. She was sitting nicely in the water. But Tom had used eight gallons of drinking water. In terms of water supplies, this was nothing to worry about—a mere half-gallon a day was a rough average for the rate of usage. But it meant four empty spaces that had each been filled with two-gallon plastic containers of water, each one a vital factor in maintaining *Silver* on an even keel. Those containers had to be filled with sea water, the caps marked to distinguish them from the drinking water, and then replaced beneath the floorboards.

All his water supplies were stowed away in this fashion and thus acted as ballast for *Silver*. Tom was not taking any chances on upsetting the little dory's balance. In October 1966 two British journalists, David Johnstone and John Hoare, had drowned when their rowboat *Puffin* overturned during an Atlantic attempt. Tom had been told that overlooking this very precaution was the cause of their disaster.*

These days were some of the easiest Tom spent in the Atlantic. And it was just as well. For though nothing went wrong while he was handling the water containers, he was well aware that he was doing everything at a very much slower speed than was normal for him. The effects of "mental indifference" were taking longer to wear off than he thought. But at least he was able to congratulate himself on the fact that, despite the slowness, his mind was able to beam in on whatever he was doing and remain concentrated on that without wandering or forgetting.

But by Sunday, June 8, he had something else to keep his mind occupied. The wind still light, still no more than 15 MPH, had swung right around until it was hitting him from due south. Luckily it was not too

---

*   Johnstone and Hoare disappeared with *Puffin* after 106 days at sea. The duo's goal was to cross the Atlantic from Virginia Beach, Virginia, to England. Their trip was sponsored by *The People*, a London Sunday newspaper. Frogmen eventually found *Puffin* deep on the bottom of the mid-Atlantic. Today, the rowboat is on display at the River and Rowing Museum in Henley-on-Thames, England. Even more important than the boat, the divers found a 35,000-word journal in Johnstone's handwriting that gives a day-by-day account of the vicissitudes he and Hoare suffered. Graphically written, Johnstone's journal depicts heroism of a high order. Without question, it is one of the most moving and vivid documents of personal maritime experience and ocean high endeavor ever written.

strong to row. From 5 A.M. until 8:30 A.M. he rowed to the northeast, trying desperately to conserve as much of his hard-earned ground as possible. He judged that he had made fairly good headway and, deciding not to wear himself out, heaved out the sea anchor while he breakfasted and read his Sunday letter.

It was from Major F. H. Woods, Tom's SAS unit's education officer at Hereford. "By sheer chance," Tom relates, "I had picked up the very letter that could set my brain ticking over, help to get it speeded up a little and thinking positive." The letter spoke of the power of strong motivation, the need to believe in oneself, and why many people may start a great endeavor but few complete it. The SAS way was to be 100 percent positive, not a whisker less. Luck and good fortune came to the daring. Not to shirkers.

◆

Tom had originally signed on with the British Army for a term of six years. When that period of service ended in 1966, he decided to try what he called "civvy street." He took jobs on different building sites, but was not happy doing it. Craving a life of action, he thought he should join the Special Air Service, the cryptically named special forces unit of the British Army. Several Paras that Tom knew had talked about it and a few had joined. One morning, instead of going to work, he decided to try for the SAS, no easy group to get into. Becoming an SAS commando made more sense to him than anything else he could do with his life at this point. After all, the SAS motto was "Who Dares Wins." And that's what Tom wanted to do with his life.

Normally a solider transferred into the SAS while still on active duty with the British Army; for Tom, that would have meant rejoining the Parachute Regiment and qualifying for a move over to special forces from there. He could not be bothered with all that involved, so he climbed into an old Bedford van he now owned and drove down to the SAS depot at Hereford. Arriving at the main gate, he identified himself and told the guard he wanted to see the commanding officer. "Sir, you can't see the

CO without an appointment," the guard told him. Tom was insistent, so the guard brought in the officer in charge of the gate. When they realized that Tom was not going to leave, they began making phone calls around the base. To their surprise—and Tom's relief—the CO, Captain Colonel John Douglas Slim, commanding officer of 22 SAS, said he would see Tom that evening.

Colonel Slim exercised quite a bit of clout at the base. He was the son of Field Marshall William Slim, a distinguished veteran of World War I and one of Britain's leading soldiers in World War II as commander of the 14th Army in the Burma campaign. After the war, William Slim became the first British officer who had served in the Indian Army to be appointed chief of the Imperial General Staff. He rose to the rank of Field Marshall in 1949 at age 58. His son, John Slim, born in British India in 1927, fought with the 6th Gurkha Rifles (later to become Queen Elizabeth's Own 6th Gurkha Rifles) during the last of World War II and exercised command of the 22 SAS Regiment through various actions during the 1950s and 1960s, including the Indonesian-Malaysian Confrontation, in which Tom had seen jungle combat.* Retiring as a lieutenant colonel in 1972, John Slim then began a political career in the House of Lords as the 1st Viscount Slim.

Colonel Slim told Tom that by regulation no one could join the regiment straight from civilian life; however, as Tom had managed to get into the depot and had an outstanding service record with the Paras, an exception could be made. Tom could attend the next SAS selection course, two months away. "As happy as a kid with credit at the sweetshop," Tom

---

*   The Gurkhas are special units of Nepalese soldiers whose service in the British Army goes back to the early 19th century. In 1814–1816 the British East India Company fought a war against the powerful city-state of Gorkha, in what is now western Nepal. Although victorious, the British were greatly impressed by the fighting qualities of their Gurkha enemies. Under the terms of the subsequent peace treaty, large numbers of Gurkhas were permitted to volunteer for service in the army of the East India Company. In the years that followed, the Gurkhas proved to be among the finest soldiers in what became the Indian Army; in fact, the brigade of Gurkhas in the modern British army has the well-earned reputation for being comprised by "the toughest soldiers in the world." Tom McClean, during his time in Malaya, often served as scouts for units of Gurkhas. The 6th Gurkha Rifles was a rifle regiment of the British Indian Army, before being transferred to the British Army following India's independence in 1947.

went home to get himself ready for one of the most steeled units in the British Army.*

The SAS was perfect for Tom: "It required a real behind-the-lines man, able to parachute, have imagination, be very fit, and have an inbuilt will to survive."

Tom arrived at the SAS base Hereford with 105 men to take the SAS selection course. Only three passed—one officer and two soldiers, Tom being one of them. From the start, the whole SAS selection course was an individual business, which was perfect for Tom: "You were on your own, no one to team up with, share decisions or share the load, whatever load, mental or physical." What the SAS was looking for were fit, keen young men intent on being "real soldiers, determined to survive, able to evade and escape, not to be broken by pressure, and, most important, able to do all of it entirely on their own."

Given that SAS commandos often went on highly dangerous and secretive missions behind enemy lines, a vital part of the selection process concerned a candidate's capacity for holding up to enemy interrogation. In SAS selection, that meant four days of torment and not-so-restrained torture. Tom never forgot the horrid experience: "I was put in a dark hole, pitch-black, in fact, wearing just my underpants, and sprayed with a cold hose. There was only artificial light and I had no idea whether it was night or day. The guards wore foreign uniforms. They dragged us into

---

*   The Special Air Service, or SAS, first formed in North Africa in July 1941, during World War II. Its founder, Colonel David Stirling, saw the potential for an elite commando strike force that could operate independently deep behind enemy lines, attacking airfields and other select targets. By the end of the war, the SAS had expanded into a brigade and had seen action in Italy, France, the Netherlands, and Germany, on occasion taking very heavy casualties. After the war, it became a permanent part of the United Kingdom Special Forces, which, along with the SAS, included a Special Boat Service, Special Reconnaissance Regiment, Special Forces Support Group, an integral signals regiment, and an air wing. Essentially, the SAS selected, organized, and trained elite commandos for special operations, surveillance, and counterterrorism. Staffed with the toughest and most resourceful enlisted and commissioned soldiers the United Kingdom had to offer, the SAS only accepted the cream of the crop. Of all the candidates who tried to earn the coveted beige beret and title of Blade, only the very best made it through.

the interrogation room, and they were really rough. They would thump you with a pick handle, physically hit you, trying to provoke a reaction. The questioning was severe. Interrogators would ask about family, school, girlfriends, anything. They seemed to know everything about us. They would suggest that your girlfriend or wife, whom they knew by name, was carrying on with a pal. They would give his name and a whole load of accurate details. After more than an hour of questioning, with me sitting on a stool in wet underpants, they would say, 'Okay, McClean, off you go for a hot shower and we'll chat again in an hour.'"

Whew. Relax.

But no sooner was Tom out of the door, thinking of that shower, that three guards grabbed him and gave him a real hammering, blacking an eye, bruising his ribs, and kicking him in the crotch. Then they sprayed him with more cold water and put him in a 40-gallon oil drum with airholes halfway up the side and the bottom covered with rotten animal offal. The lid was slammed shut and Tom was left there for what seemed to be about a day and a half. His only distraction was a piercing whistle that blew every so often for long periods. It destroyed all thought and concentration and made Tom's head sing with almost physical pain.

Apart from the mental and physical discomfort, there was the added element of degradation. During one interrogation period when Tom was at a fairly low ebb, he was again promised a hot shower, a dry towel, and clean clothes. Having answered their questions, he headed for the door indicated by one of the interrogators. Tom walked through into a dark space and through a further door. Opening it, he found that he was in a plain white windowless room where another guard ordered him to strip. The guard then left. A few moments later three women came in, according to Tom, "large and none too pretty." They stood looking at Tom. "Look what we've got here!" said one, with a teasing grin. "That wouldn't be much fun for a girl like me on a Saturday night after a party." It was one of the few times during the four days of interrogation that Tom lost his control. "If it was you I had to spend a Saturday night with, I wouldn't be bothered trying," he said. The women left, but not without after a few insults at Tom.

Instead of being released after this trial, the SAS interrogators again placed Tom in the large oil drum. This time the bottom of the drum was some nine inches deep with odd bits of liver, lungs of pigs and sheep, sweetbreads, and slime. Every so often, the barrel was turned upside down, resulting in a putrid shower. Bits of the stinking slime clung to Tom's hair, filled his nose and ears, and found its way into his mouth as he fought for breath. These sessions of torture were interspersed with more rugged interrogations, more nasty surprises and letdowns, but Tom battled on, determined to pass the selection procedure. He often spoke to himself out loud, carefully choosing his words in case his surroundings were bugged by hidden microphones, as he was almost certain was the case: "Come on, Moby, don't react. Keep calm, think, It's only a game!"

Similar to what had been the case during punishments back in the orphanage, physical reaction to the beatings only brought more beatings: "The answer was to hang on as long as you could. Give nothing away. The idea was to try to find out if you could keep your mouth shut. This might mean that in action, if captured, you would be able to hold out until any information wanted by a real enemy was out of date if and when you eventually cracked."

Finally, the days of interrogation, torture, and degradation were over. Tom was bruised, battered, damp, but unbowed. Days later he was awarded the famous khaki brown SAS beret with the winged dagger badge and was posted to D Squadron, 17 Boat Troop.

For the next three years he served with the SAS. In 1967 Tom was deployed briefly to Guyana, on the northeast coast of South America, where the job amid jungle training was to discourage Venezuela from moving to seize a region of Guyana (formerly British Guiana) that was rich in gold and oil. The worst thing to happen to Tom there was a venomous snake bite to the back of his neck. Coincidentally the doctor who treated Tom was Captain Kenneth Hedges, the same doctor who had performed his emergency surgery in Greece after Tom was accidentally shot in the stomach.

D Squadron of 17 Boat Troop went on many exercises and worked alongside the Special Boat Service. The three-part role of the SBS was to provide special reconnaissance, which included information reporting and target acquisition; offensive action, mainly direction of air strikes, artillery and naval gunfire, precision guided munitions, use of integral weapons, and demolitions; and support and influence, including overseas training tasks. The SBS also provided immediate response teams for counterterrorism. Special skills of SBS troopers involved boating, climbing, freefall parachuting, and wireless communication. Several exercises in 1967 and 1968 took place in the Brecon Beacons mountain range in Wales. Typically, Tom excelled in individual performance. In one exercise in the Welsh hills, he was hunted by "captors" from whom he had "escaped." Tom remembers: "It was snowing hard and getting dark, I found some fertilizer bags, big plastic ones, and made trousers and a waistcoat out of them, covered myself with some more, and lay down. By morning a good two feet of snow had fallen and I was completely buried. I was about to start moving but first I listened out for sounds. Someone was coming so I lay quite still. A whole patrol of searching soldiers went right by without seeing me, only five yards away."

In another exercise the Boat Troop joined the Royal Marines for a surprise "assault" on a "target" along coastal Norway. Dropped in the sea about 15 miles out, they got in their rigid-hulled inflatable craft (16 feet long and six feet wide) and made a fast, silent raid on their target.* "It was a very rough night landing," Tom recalls, "and my first time at sea in a small boat."

Was he scared? "Of course not, I loved it."

◆

---

*   The SAS's rigid inflatable assault craft were designed and built by Gemini Marine, a South African company. It was a lightweight but high-performance, high-capacity, and virtually unsinkable boat constructed with a rigid hull bottom that was joined to side-forming air tubes that were inflated with air to a high pressure so as to give the sides resilient rigidity along the boat's topsides. The design was stable, light, fast, and highly seaworthy. The boat's inflated collar acted as a life jacket, ensuring that the vessel retained its buoyancy even when the boat was taking on water. The boat had a rubberized fabric bottom that was stiffened with flat boards within the collar to form its deck.

The letter from Major Woods brought his entire SAS experience back to him very vividly. He read the letter twice, thrice, stopping each time on its most compelling lines: "You are doing what many people, particularly members of the Regiment, would like to do but have just not got up to that extra bit of self-effort to get started and make the journey. For this reason, our admiration for someone who has the guts and drive to actually get moving and make the effort is therefore tenfold.

"Ambition, motivated in any direction (preferably for good), is the driving force that keeps man going and striving toward betterment.

"I know that as long as you feel and accept in your mind and thoughts that you will succeed, then no force of nature will prevent you from reaching your destination.

"By continually keeping the mind full of success images, confidently expecting and accepting that all is OK and that you will reach your expected landing place, then you will.

"Try to see yourself at your journey's end, form a mental image of yourself sighting the land, rowing forward, and stepping ashore."

Tom folded the letter and put it back in the plastic box. Looking up, his eyes brightened as he saw the evidence of his ambition, positive thinking, and, yes, even luck. A mist was rolling in . . . a beautiful, wonderful, delightful mist. It was the Arctic smoke—shallow, wispy, smoke-like steam fog created when very cold air from the Arctic encountered warmer waters. It was the surefire visible evidence Tom was waiting for, that he and *Silver* were finally leaving the waters of the Labrador Current and shooting into the warm embrace of the Gulf Stream.

Vaporously delicate and white, the sea smoke curled around *Silver* until Tom could barely see her bow. He could not in fact still see what his mates had painted in blue letters on the prow of the dory, as a finishing touch, before the dory left the carpenter's hut at Hereford. But Tom knew very well it was there: the proud SAS emblem—the winged dagger—and the regimental motto: "Who Dares Wins."

16

Why?

In the months leading up to Tom's departure for his Atlantic crossing, most people had wanted to know: "Why?" To many of them the idea of crossing the ocean in a rowboat, let alone doing it alone, seemed beyond stupid. Some told him straight out, "You're either stark raving mad or a self-serving showoff, because what you're planning is a completely insane and aimless adventure!"

Tom didn't think he was either. "I wanted to achieve something. I wanted to amount to something. I wasn't trying to be a hero. I just wanted to make my mark." Very early in life he had "faced up to the indisputable fact that I just didn't have what it takes to be a Prime Minister, an industrial tycoon, or a Nobel Prize winner." He accepted that he was woefully short on glitter when it came to any sort of stardom. Come to that, for most of his early years, he recognized that he was also "short on common sense."

Tom had first gotten the idea of rowing the Atlantic solo in the summer of 1966 while serving in Malaysia with the Parachute Regiment. In a British newspaper brought in on a resupply trip, he had read that Captain John "Ridge" Ridgway, a 28-year-old Englishman, and Sergeant Charles "Chay" Blyth, a 26-year-old Scot, were planning to row across the Atlantic Ocean as a two-man team. Tom jumped straight up out of his seat. He knew Ridge and Chay quite well. They were his officer and sergeant in the anti-tank platoon, 3 Para.

"Blimey," Tom thought, "what a great caper!" He couldn't get them out of his head. "I thought about them all morning." He was still thinking about them as he swung off on jungle patrol. "If they can pull that off," he judged, "they will really have done something worthwhile."

Tom was back in England by the time Ridgway and Blyth pushed off in their 20-foot open dory, *English Rose III*, from a beach near Cape Cod, Massachusetts, on June 4, 1966. He followed their progress across the Atlantic "almost inch by inch." He read and reread every news flash, starting with the report of "a rapturous sendoff by a crowd of some thousands" and continuing through his two friends "braving two hurricanes, vicious storms, huge waves, whales bigger than their boat, massive fatigue, and near-complete lack of rations." Tom remembers well the day Ridgway and Blyth reached the Aran Islands off the Irish coast. They arrived at the small fishing village of Inishmore "in gale force conditions" on September 4, after 92 days at sea and some 3,000 miles in the water. For the next several days Tom scoured every newspaper he could find. Not only did the two intrepid paratroopers-turned-mariners receive "a rousing welcome" wherever they went in Ireland; they received a "euphoric chaotic welcome home" upon their arrival back in Great Britain. Tom himself came to Heathrow Airport to congratulate them upon their arrival in London. Both men were presented the British Empire Medal personally from Queen Elizabeth II.

"A few months later a bunch of us were chatting about Ridgway and Blyth in the barrack room at the Special Air Service HQ in Hereford." Impulsively, Tom said, "I reckon one person alone could do it."

Even now Tom doesn't really know what prompted him to say it. He hadn't made any sort of study of a lone row. He hadn't thought about it in any detail at all. "I don't think I had even thought of myself attempting it." But, suddenly, impulsively, he felt "positive it could be done."

"Belt up, Moby," said one of Tom's chums.

"You're bats!" another said. "It took Blyth and Ridgway all their time to do it together and, as they have told the world, it was no picnic."

A third mate chimed in: "And those two British journalists just went missing in the middle of the Atlantic. They're goners. If you want to make headlines around the world like them, Moby, go ahead. Give it a try!"

Tom didn't argue. He didn't say he would, or could, row the Atlantic alone. He just repeated: "I think one person could do it."

From that day on Tom "began the long preparation without having any clear idea of what to do, how to do it, or even that I would do it." He sent off to the Office of the Admiralty and Marine Affairs for charts of the Atlantic Ocean and the Irish and British coasts. He burned up the telephone wires with inquiry calls to boatbuilders.

The firm supplying the charts for the Admiralty could not understand why an SAS man would want such detailed information about the Atlantic: "I don't know what they thought about it. They never told me and I never had a chance to ask. To say the least, they must have thought it damned odd. At the most serious they probably believed that some breach of security was involved. Or maybe they figured I was planning to desert." Whatever their reasons, the office reported the matter to SAS authorities.

The report aroused concern at Hereford. Tom got a "sharp summons" to appear before Major Dodds, his squadron commander.

"Now then, McClean," his commander barked. "What's all this business with charts?"

Tom made up his mind in a flash: "At last I really knew what had been pushing me, urging me for the past months. I knew what I wanted to do." His brain raced with all of his old orphanage dreams of "making good," "amounting to something," "achieving something which would make my life worthwhile." He heard himself reply:

"I want to row the Atlantic, sir."

"Alone?" Major Dodds asked cynically.

"Yes, sir."

Tom didn't say he wanted to be the *first* man to do it alone—but there was no question that's what he meant. Ridgway and Blyth had already done it together. Two others, Johnstone and Hoare, the journalists, had perished in a two-man attempt. Anybody who made the first lone

Atlantic row would be establishing an all-world record, for the truth was that it was not just about the Atlantic. No person alone had ever rowed across any ocean. At this point, Tom knew nothing about John Fairfax. He figured he might have "a clear run."

"You're mad, McClean," Major Dodds declared. "Are you absolutely sure? Do you realize just what such a project would entail?"

"Yes, sir. I think so," answered Tom.

"You think so?! Are you daft, man?

"I know I can do it, sir."

"All right," Dodds relented, provisionally. "I'll get you an interview with the CO."

A few weeks later—it was now 1968—Tom was escorted into the office of Colonel Slim, his second visit there. "The colonel was great," Tom remembers. "He didn't preach. He didn't enthuse. He just asked, with great deliberation: 'Are you absolutely sure that you want to tackle this?'"

"Yes, sir," was Tom's straightforward reply.

"Do you have a boat? Do you have a great deal of experience rowing?"

"No, sir."

"No to what?"

"No to both of your questions, sir."

"Riiiight," said Colonel Slim, slowly, then pausing to think a bit. "First, I want you to find out exactly what sort of boat you want. Then have a shot at rowing a boat for a few hours. Then have a talk with Ridgway and Blyth and get their firm opinions on your chances."

Colonel Slim asked him a few more questions, testing to see if Tom truly had any common sense of what he was taking on.

"Fair enough," concluded the colonel. "But keep this on the QT. Let's see how this works out. We don't want the newspapers hearing anything about an SAS trooper taking on something like this. Not before we see how serious you get about this. And probably not even then."

"Yes, sir. Understood."

"For the present, do all you need to do only when you are off duty. We'll see how that goes before you do any of this on SAS time."

"Absolutely, Colonel. Yes, sir. Thank you, sir."

◆

The very next weekend Tom took a train down to the Isle of Wight, where he hired a rowboat and immediately put in a stint of eight hours. Apart from an odd splash on the Serpentine, the 40-acre recreational lake in London's Hyde Park, it was the most rowing he had ever done in his life. "I knew nothing about rowing, but that was something I had to keep to myself. If that had been made public, people really would have thought me utterly crazy."

The Isle of Wight practice was nothing like rowing the Atlantic, of course. It gave Tom no inkling at all of what lay ahead. Later he was glad that it didn't. But at least it confirmed what Tom already knew: "My muscles were capable of standing long hours of severe physical effort without any serious effect."

His next step was to visit John Ridgway. Ridge, who for a time had been Tom's platoon commander in the Paras, was running an adventure school based at his croft in the Scottish Highlands. "I found him somewhat dubious about my chances. John did not want to discourage me, yet, at the same time, he did not want to feel himself responsible in any way for urging me into a foolhardy venture which might end in my death. That was one of the difficulties of having officer training—he felt responsible for the well-being of one of his men. You cannot shake off that sense of duty after being in the army for several years."

Cautiously Ridgway advised: "Quite honestly, Tom, I don't think one man could do it. There were times when Chay and I did not think we would be able to make it together. There is really no way of describing briefly the incredible number of emergencies which can suddenly overtake you out there. And there is no way of advising how to cope with them except to say you just have to stick it out."

Despite his reluctance, Ridgway was enormously helpful to Tom. The two soldiers chatted for well over an hour on Atlantic seamanship. Ridge pointed out some "very valid details" that Tom had only vaguely contemplated. His last words to Tom were "I would estimate that you will need about three years to get ready if you decide to go ahead."

Three years to prepare? On the train back to London, Tom knew that he couldn't accept that prolonged of a period for preparation. Ridge had really "laid it on the line," and Tom was more than grateful for it. But three years?! "Phooey!" he spouted out loud, looking out the train window. "Three years be blowed. That's far too long. I'll find ways to cut down the time."

His next stop was Chay Blyth's home near Portsmouth. Blyth was much more enthusiastic about Tom's plan than Ridgway had been, but he was also absolutely blunt. "It's a great idea," Chay told Tom. "But I want to make it quite clear to you that you are taking on a hell of a handful. I won't beat about the bush. I reckon you have an 80/20 chance of success." Tom nodded sternly. Studiously, Chay paused, then grinned and said, "Okay, let's get down to cases and see how we can really help you."

The two troopers talked for hours. Tom took a lot of notes. One of the notes underscored the need for a canopy over part of the boat. Ridge and Chay had possessed no shelter at all on their boat; their main protection against the weather had been rubberized army poncho capes, and they had suffered. Tom figured his boat would definitely need some sort of shelter.

Blyth's pretty wife, Maureen, was in the room for part of the conversation. Tom shot her a glance and couldn't help thinking, "Here is the girl who waited without a murmur while Chay was thirteen weeks in the Atlantic. She's got a lot of guts, but I wonder how she really felt about it all." As Tom left their home, Maureen kissed him lightly on the cheek and said, "Goodbye, Tom, and good luck." At that moment he realized how lucky he was to be a loner. He wondered how much his determination would have been affected if he had been married: "With no wife, not even a steady girlfriend, I thanked my lucky stars I was completely free of any chance of emotional upsets."

It was time to go back to Hereford and give Colonel Slim a report on his preliminary plans for the trip. There were no more questions. Satisfied with Tom's progress, the colonel wrote to the War Office asking permission for Tom to make the row. It was granted. "The army was magnificent," Tom proudly remembers. "I was told I would be given paid leave

while I made my preparations and unpaid leave to make the row itself."
The army was also prepared to help Tom "in any way possible within the
terms of its own commitments to the British taxpayers."

It was approaching Christmas 1968. By this time, Tom knew from
newspaper accounts that another man, named John Fairfax, also intended
to row solo across the Atlantic Ocean. He knew that the renowned
naval architect, Uffa Fox, England's leading designer of small boats,
was building Fairfax's rowboat. That meant that Fairfax's boat would be
a superior vessel, the best money could buy. Tom had no idea when this
John Fairfax would be leaving for his crossing, but figured it wouldn't
be until the spring, as crossing the North Atlantic in the winter months
was way beyond foolhardy. What Tom didn't know was that Fairfax was
about to cross the Atlantic in the other direction, from east to west, from
the Canary Islands to Florida, a southerly route that would allow him
to put his boat into the Atlantic much sooner—in fact, the very next
month, January 1969.

If Tom had known—and he would learn about Fairfax's alternative
approach soon enough—it wouldn't have changed his plans one iota. Tom
was crossing the North Atlantic. To blazes with anyone else trying to do
it. A lot of things could stop Fairfax from making the trip successfully.
Tom wished the man no ill will, but if circumstances got in Fairfax's way
to finishing first, Tom wouldn't be the reason. The paratrooper only took
the responsibility of daring to be first. Nothing would stop him.

That was, after he had a boat of his own.

Deciding on what sort of boat to use was simple. What had served
Ridgway and Blyth so well, Tom thought. "could surely not be bettered."
Both men had spoken highly to Tom of their little Yorkshire Dory, no
matter how flimsy it looked. Tom ordered one from the same Bradford
Boat Services that was three feet shorter than the *English Rose III*.

How to pay for it? The price was £200—£3,500 today, or nearly
$4,400. Tom could cover that sum, just barely, from his savings. But
the basic dory needed a number of modifications. At a reasonable price
Tom found a company to put the nylon sheathing on the hull. But the
rest of the alterations he would have to manage to make himself, as

inexperienced as he was when it came to building boats. Fortunately, SAS headquarters in Hereford gave him a space in a carpenter's hut to work on the boat. There, and with the occasional help of carpenters ("chippies") working at the military base, Tom raised the deck by 10 inches, beefed up the wood around the gunwales with oak, built buoyancy compartments fore and aft, stuffed those compartments with blocks of polystyrene, put in the turtle decking on the top, and built a shelter.

It was not just the price of the boat and its modifications but also the cost of all the ancillary equipment and necessary supplies that Tom had to cover, including special clothing, food, navigational instruments, oars, pumps, and a radio. The full price for everything was a little over £3,000 (£52,000 today, or roughly $65,000). To Tom, it seemed like "a never-ending list." An ordinary soldier just did not have that sort of loot.

But an ordinary soldier intent on doing something as extraordinary as solo rowing the Atlantic found that there were a lot of people who wanted to come on board to help—"kind-hearted people" who had heard of Tom's ambition and "began rallying round." One of them was Den Colam, a Herefordshire businessman, who not only contributed three sets of special oars but also had workmen in his factory manufacture a cylindrical metal shield to protect Tom's camping-style cooker from the ocean winds and also make a watertight metal box to guard Tom's radio from the salt air. Then there was Tesco, the UK's leading supermarket chain, which donated tins of jam, fruit, pots of curry, chocolate, and other goodies. Not to be left out, Whitbread, a historic brewery based in Bedfordshire, threw in six dozen cans of beer, to which the distillery at Kinloch added a few bottles of rum. Nor did the SAS let him down. It supplied him with the 100 SAS field ration packs, each one containing enough calories, mostly in dehydrated form, to keep a hardworking man going all day.

Though reluctant to do so, Tom, on the advice of Chay Blyth, took on publicity agent Paul Sargent, a former Fleet Street journalist. The arrangement worked out well, with Sargent finding sponsors resulting in waterproof watches, a chronometer, a two-way radio, a life jacket with an emergency radio attached, and miscellaneous other items. Some items were on loan, but most were given free of charge. With most of them, Tom made an advertising agreement that would kick in after his voyage if it was successful.

Tom was not making the trip for financial gain, but he did hope it could pay for itself with a little chunk left over. His term of service with the SAS was over in 1969, and he felt he would be "better equipped to face civilian life" if he had "a stake," perhaps enough to start some sort of small business. He didn't want a nine-to-five job back in building construction. After the excitement of six years in the troopers, that would be "a drudge."

For their enterprise Ridgway and Blyth had benefited from the sponsorship of a national newspaper. Tom was pretty sure that wouldn't work: "Most newspapers don't like encouraging somebody to do something which at first sight seems thoroughly foolhardy. Quite understandably, no newspaper wants to finance what could turn out to be a disaster." Tom and Paul Sargent considered a different tack. Instead of asking for outright support, they would offer exclusive coverage to a newspaper, but payment from them to Tom would be made only if the trip was successful. Sargent's approach was to the *Sunday Express*, a daily middle-market paper with a traditionally strong interest in adventure stories. Sargent arranged for Tom to meet with Peter Vane, the chief reporter and a former Royal Navy man: "I think Vane was frankly horrified when I told him I had practically no rowing experience, had never handled a rowboat in heavy seas, knew nothing at all about seamanship, and that my navigational talents were limited to my army experiences operating on land." Not once during their conversation did Vane reveal what he really thought—nor did Tom ever discover what the journalist reported back to his bosses. But subsequent meetings did develop with Vane and the newspaper's feature editors. Eventually a contract was drawn up on the basis of the *Sunday Express* buying Tom's log of the trip and any photographs Tom took. Sargent managed to get the paper to agree to a two-part contract. The first part assured a payment to Tom if he made it to "the halfway stage" of his voyage but then, for whatever reason, had to give up. The second part brought full payment if Tom made it all the way.

By April 1969 Tom was ready to go. So was his boat, *Super Silver*, a name suggested by its cosponsor Gillette, which in the late 1960s was promoting its new Super Stainless razor blades, known in Europe as Super Silver (made from an improved steel alloy).

What wasn't ready was the weather over the North Atlantic. Winter was still very much around. Large Arctic air masses covered the area. Cold fronts came and went. Nighttime temperatures dropped below freezing. Winds from the north frequently blew at 15 to 30 MPH or more. Those winds could push icebergs further south. Small pieces of icebergs, known as growlers or bergy bits, could be numerous. The seas would likely at times be extremely rough. And it was not lost on anyone considering an Atlantic crossing that it was on April 12, 1912, that the RMS *Titanic* sank after hitting an iceberg in the North Atlantic, killing 1,500 of an estimated 2,224 passengers onboard. The "unsinkable" British luxury liner was on its maiden voyage, from Southampton, England, to New York City. Its disastrous loss was met with worldwide shock and outrage. No one ever after—not even Tom McClean, the SAS trooper—could cross the North Atlantic without thinking about the *Titanic*'s deep, watery grave on the bottom of the ocean.*

Tom would wait until the month of May.

---

*   The closest Tom McClean would get to the location of *Titanic*'s sinking was just after he left Newfoundland. *Titanic*'s location when it sank was 41°43.5'N, 49°56.8'W. Tom's closest relative position was 44°42'N, 49°48'W. The distance between them was thus 205 miles, the site of the *Titanic* wreck (on the compass) being 178° to Tom's south. For further reference, when the *Titanic* wreck sank, it was 1,084 nautical miles from New York City and 325 nautical miles from the tip of Newfoundland.

17

Over You Go

The silence was uncanny. It came rolling in with the fog, dissipating the wind and flattening the water. Tom and *Silver* were trapped in a cell of dripping condensation. Huge glistening drops settled everywhere like quivering blobs of quicksilver as the dory softly tilted on the gentle swell.

Curling fingers of mist undulated around Tom as he tried in vain to see farther than 15 yards. Clammy, dense, and impenetrable, it lay over the surface of the sea and literally ruled the waves. There was not a whisper of wind to disturb it, and Tom looked in wonder over the side of *Silver* at the suddenly still waters, calm, black, and glassy. The silence was shattering. The incredible experience of not hearing a sound except that of his own breathing came almost as a shock after days of having his ears filled with the roar of the sea and the screaming wind.

After a breakfast of hot porridge and instant coffee, Tom unshipped the oars. If ever there had been a pure chance to row, this was it. *Silver* slid through the brume, setting up a steady hissing sound and spreading ripples across the glassy black water. As time passed, the oarsman became obsessed with the notion that there may be a ship close by, unseen, unheard, lurking in the fog, just waiting to smash his boat to splinters.

Tom started counting his strokes, and at every 20th he would stop rowing to listen and look. Cupping his right ear with his right hand, he turned his head slowly, sweeping the area on the starboard side of *Silver* from stem to stern. Then, changing hands and ears, he would do the same on the port side. Not a sound. "Rather idiotically I had overlooked taking basic precautions as soon as that fog surrounded me," recalls Tom. "I had failed to test the miniature foghorn bolted to my shelter roof alongside the compass, and I had not hoisted my metal radar reflector on the radio mast." Shipping the oars, he did not waste any more time before putting those ordinary safety measures into operation.

Back in the carpenter's hut at the SAS base in Hereford when *Silver* was being readied for the trip, Tom had tested the klaxon, and it sounded fine—strident enough to be heard clearly, at a distance, on the ocean. But in the muffling fog it seemed to produce no more than a rusty squeak. It sounded so pathetic that he just sat down and laughed. He could shout louder than that! To prove it he cupped his hands around his mouth and bellowed: "Ahoy there. Atlantic rowboat *Super Silver* here and bound for Blighty."

The resonance of his voice bouncing around on the foggy walls surrounding him startled and delighted him. It was almost as good as having company. So good, in fact, he shouted it out several times, pitching his voice at differing levels to see what effect the fog would have. Then he hoisted the radar reflector. There was no more he could do to protect himself except trust that if a ship did cross his path, it would be equipped with radar and an operator alert enough to pick up the infinitesimal speck of light that his reflector would throw on his screen.

The fog stuck with him through the day. By midafternoon there were no signs of its dispersing, and he began to worry about the night. Should he chance sleeping? Or should he sit up all night listening for the sounds of imminent danger—a bell, a foghorn, the throb of slowly turning engines?

Tom opted for sleep. He had seen so few ships that it was hardly likely that one would run into him just because it was foggy. In any case, he had originally planned always to sleep whenever the weather allowed him to do so. A blunder made in an emergency because of lack of sleep could prove every bit as fatal as a crash in the fog. Having made up his mind, he stopped worrying about it.

At nightfall there was still no sign of a lift in the fog. But Tom rowed on for a couple of hours, determined to grab as many miles as possible. It was like moving through a ball of black cotton wool. When he crawled into his sleeping bag, it was a few minutes after 10 P.M., and he was fast asleep within seconds.

A huge shuddering bump, shaking every timber in *Silver*, sent the boat lurching forward as if hit by a hammer. From his sound sleep Tom jerked upright. Had he been hit? By what? He shot out of his shelter so fast he forgot all about first getting clear of his sleeping bag. It slithered to his ankles, trapped his forward step, and laid him in a breathless heap across the seat. As he lay there trying to kick his way out of the bag and wondering what the hell had happened, something rumbled and rasped down the full length of *Silver*'s port side.

Finally kicking himself free of the sleeping bag, he scrambled to his feet and turned his head rapidly in all directions, straining to pierce the thick blackness in which he and his boat were still wrapped. There was nothing to be seen, nothing to be heard: no lights, no bells, no sounds of ship's engines.

"Then what in the hell was it?" he asked himself aloud. By what? A floating log? A large piece of driftwood? An empty oil drum? Some ungainly piece of flotsam from a ship? Maybe even a whale? Fear gripped him, not for the first time in that extraordinary loneliness, exaggerated by the oppressive mist.

Had *Silver* been damaged? Was she leaking?

Adrenaline running at 100 MPH, Tom dived back into the shelter, grabbed his flashlight, and examined every inch of *Silver* inboard from end to end and side to side. Not a sign of damage, not a scratch.

But what about the bottom side? Was the hull damaged? Maybe she had been damaged below the waterline?

On all fours Tom crouched in the darkest of darkness to shine the flashlight over the floorboards, at least as much of them as were not covered with his supplies. There was no sign of water flooding in. He hoisted the little trapdoor that led to the compartment beneath the boards where his freshwater supplies were stored. Still nothing to raise alarm. All seemed well.

Yet he could not turn off his concern. Maybe *Silver* had not been holed, but suppose—just suppose—she had been weakened by that thump just below the waterline? How long would she hold out? How long before the pressure of the sea, especially in rough weather, forced its way through the weakness and flooded *Silver*?

These unanswerable questions nagged and tormented him. There was only one thing he could do. He would have to go over the side and find out for himself. And it had to be *then*. He did not dare wait for daylight. For the morning might bring winds, making the sea far too rough for him to risk taking a dip.

He stripped in the pitch blackness of that foggy night, leaving only the plastic-bag protection on his still numb feet. He strapped a lifeline around his waist and lashed the free end to the samson post near the bow. As the world's self-confessed worst swimmer, he had to pull himself together. "Coward McClean!" he shouted to the fog. "Okay . . . over you go." He took three deep breaths and went headfirst over the side into the ocean, "Shit, it was cold!" he remembers with a shiver.

The underside of *Silver* loomed green and ghostly in the light of his waterproof flashlight. Strings of sea grass that had collected on her hull snaked out in the current, grass sliding across his hands, arms, and face. Slowly, painstakingly, he worked his way along the entire port side, prodding with his fingers, gently stroking with his hands, feeling for the telltale crack or dangerous splinters. Then he repeated the performance along her starboard side. Again, not a scratch as far as he could find.

His delight at finding *Silver* as sound as a bell knew no bounds. He hauled himself inboard, teeth chattering, limbs trembling, but grinning with sheer joy. He toweled himself off until his skin tingled with the rush of blood through his veins. Once he had dressed and changed socks and plastic bags—he had to keep his feet dry—he made a massive cup of cocoa and sat there drinking it and giving *Silver* the odd loving pat and telling her, "You're a real beauty." He had grown fond of the little dory during the trip, and now he had fallen totally in love with her.

It was difficult trying to get to sleep again. Tom lay there staring out into the darkness with his eyes open and thought, "It's great to be alive."

And he prayed. It was a prayer of thanks, really. The previous day he had listened on his radio to a Sunday church service from St. John's, which had left quite a mark on him. He had actually listened and enjoyed it. Out on that dark quiet ocean at dawn, in the little boat that was serving him so well, he marveled at the thought of himself actually wanting to listen to a church service. What a fantastic change.

◆

As a youngster at the orphanage, Tom had had to go to church three times every Sunday. He hated it. He grinned in the dark as his mind went drifting back to those the years. The orphans were given three pence per week. One of the three pennies was banked for them. One penny had to be put into the church collection each Sunday. The third penny was usually spent on sweets by mobs of boys in the school tuck shop, which was open only on Friday evenings. Tommy figured that one of the three pennies he got weekly was the same one he put into the collection plate on Sunday.

It all seemed years and years ago. Inside *Silver*, as his eyes closed at last, Tom reflected: "No matter what I thought of Fegan's at the time, it didn't do me any harm." Maybe it had even done him some good.

By morning the fog had cleared. The unplanned dip in the Atlantic must have knocked some of the stuffing out of him. He slept until 9 A.M. "I figured it must have been more like a bout of unconsciousness than a night's sleep," Tom reflects back. The wind from due south had swept away the ghostly mists and was building up steadily. By 10 o'clock it was howling in at gale force.

Silver was being driven north, and once again Tom was helpless to do anything about it. He threw out the sea anchor and hoped he would not drift too far off course.

But he needn't have been so gloomy. For the next five days the winds were generally from the west and never above 25 MPH. The temperature dropped below 50°F only once, and then by only a degree or two, and once it actually soared to 60°F.

And all the time *Silver* was eating up valuable mileage to the east. "I suppose I should have been feeling chuffed under such almost perfect conditions," Tom says, "but it allowed me to get my rowing organized on a fairly civilized basis. I should have sensed nearing home with every stroke, yet those days dragged by, long, slow, ponderous hours."

At first he could not fathom what was wrong with him. "I supposed it was just a generally a feeling of anticlimax after the sustained punishment from the Atlantic." He kept telling himself that, though the actual truth was not too long in the dawning.

It was simple: "I was pretty crocked, groggy, punch-drunk, call it what you will. I realized I was feeling absolutely battered." Tom ached all over, as if he had taken a thorough pounding in a rugby match that had been played nonstop for several days. It was no longer the ache of stiffened muscles that could be ironed out with a session on the oars. This was deep-seated pain. Putting it simply: "I must have been bruised from head to toe. And now it was beginning to tell on me. I was beginning to learn the deeper meaning of endurance." And endure it he would, even if he had to row with one hand.

To talk himself into taking things easy while he had the chance would have been too simple. The temptation to lie down for a few hours in the belief—a mistaken belief—that he would be resting himself was fairly strong. Just how long are a few hours? His suspicion was that a few hours would almost certainly stretch into yet another few hours, perhaps even a couple of days, if the weather lasted that long, hours or days that would be utterly wasted. There was absolutely no doubt in his mind that the temptation had to be resisted.

In a deliberate attempt to be methodical Tom jotted down on paper a plan of action. He mapped out a program that keep him steadily busy. Perhaps the most important was working out his new rowing schedule of three hours on and one off. In those off-duty hours, apart from mealtimes, he slotted a number of items all of which had a vital bearing, if not immediately, at least in the future, on his safety and the success of the trip.

For example, he had been eating mostly from the supplies stowed at the stern. This had naturally resulted in *Silver* settling her bow deeper in the water as the days passed by. Admittedly, at that stage, Tom and his boat were not in any sense facing imminent danger, but he knew it would not be wise to allow the margin of risk to widen any further.

To his delight he discovered that, despite his low-ebb physical condition, his brain was ticking over sharply enough: "For even as I was thinking of *Silver*'s trim it struck me that I had been unable to check the condition of the rudder since setting out. And it would obviously be sensible to check the rudder while it was just a little higher in the water." Trimming *Silver* would be the second job.

Tom had determined not to rush things: to pace himself and just take everything as steadily as possible. He could not have rushed the rudder inspection even if he had wanted to do so. He had to climb on to the top of his shelter and then, lying as flat on his stomach as possible, slide over to one side of the five-foot stretch of turtle decking that covered the aft buoyancy compartment. Being absolutely smooth, the turtle decking had nothing to offer in the way of handgrips.

He managed to hang on by wrapping the fingers of his left hand over the edge of the bow and hooking his left foot round the wooden samson post set between the turtle decking and the shelter roof. He slid his right foot over the edge of *Silver*'s other side and pressed inward with both feet, just as a horseman gripped the flanks of his mount. The plastic bags on his feet made it difficult to maintain a firm grip, but luckily *Silver* was fairly steady, and Tom managed the job in reasonable comfort. His lack of height helped considerably. A taller man would never have been able to flatten himself out as he did.

From that spread-eagled position Tom had a pretty good view of the rudder. Apart from sea grass, which was beginning to gather on the lower half, it was in perfect condition. The eye-bolt hinges showed no signs of weakening, and there were no signs of strain on the wood. Laboriously he slid backward to the roof of his shelter, crouched there for a few seconds to regain his breath, and then set about sprawling himself out again in order to examine the other side of the rudder. That too was okay.

Back in his cockpit he broke open a can of beer—his fourth at that stage of the trip—and downed it in almost one gulp. Another can would have been more than welcome, but, although he had another 32 cans on board, he decided against a second drink. His plan was to save them for the hot weather that he was sure was due to come his way before too long. As things turned out, he could have drunk the lot then and there, for there was to be no blazing summer the entire trip.

The rudder inspection took up nearly three-quarters of his non-rowing hour. He sat on the seat for the last 15 minutes, mentally sorting out where the stores would be redistributed when he set about retrimming *Silver*. That job took nearly the entirety of another hour. It was not so much a matter of the amount of work involved, for he had only to shift 24 days' provisions from forward to aft. It was the extreme care with which he had to ensure that each item was stowed in exactly the right position. He felt that he just could not risk even the slightest list to either side.

Tom clucked away at this job "like a fussy old broody hen." After moving every two or three packages, he squatted as low as he could to measure, as far as possible, the alignment of *Silver*'s bows with an imaginary line in the sky. Then he raised himself until his eyes were on a level with the horizon and tried to line up the bow with that. As a third check he stood on the seat with legs fairly well spread apart in an attempt to "feel" if *Silver* was level or not.

It occurred to him at the time that he was probably being overly elaborate with his precautions. But not being an experienced sailor, he could not leave it all to instinct. In any case, the concern shown for *Silver*'s trim by those hardy seafarers so scrupulously observant of his handling of his dory back in St. John's had indelibly impressed itself on his mind.

Perhaps the most cheering point of all was that his program was working out so well. Slowly the list of ticks against the items he had penciled down grew and nothing went wrong.

Even his plans for an emergency water supply came through with flying colors. During a hard downpour of rain one night, Tom spread out his army-issue rubberized canvas poncho between *Silver*'s gunwales. When the rain stopped he found about two and a half gallons trapped in his makeshift gadget. He filled up one of his empty water containers and poured the rest into his spare kettles and pressure cooker. Even if he had to stay on the Atlantic longer than he anticipated, at least he would not run out of drinking water too quickly.

Thursday, June 12, turned out to be Tom's first—and only—day of brilliant summer weather, with light westerly winds and a 60°F temperature, and he decided to enjoy it. Off came the plastic bags and socks. He rolled up his jeans as far as possible and stuck his seriously abused feet into the warm sunshine. To accommodate his greater leisure, he also altered his rowing schedule to two hours on and two hours off. It was a good thing he took advantage of the gorgeous day, because the weather would change much for the worse the next day.

His feet continued to be a major issue. They were still too swollen to wear his seaboots. Although he had tried to ignore them, his frostbitten feet had been causing him more anxiety than he cared to admit. They certainly did not seem to be improving rapidly enough for his liking. It alarmed him a little when he discovered that he could not really feel the sun on them. There was one consolation: they had started stinging a couple days back. The blood must have begun running through them once again. And now they were stinging like the blazes. There was nothing more he could do, so he told himself, "They'll be okay in the end," and tried to forget them.

Still fighting off worry about his feet, Tom forced himself to stand up. He grabbed every bit of damp clothing he had and spread it out to dry. He laid it over the seat, over the shelter roof—anywhere, in fact, where the sun could get at it. *Silver* looked like a floating laundry.

He chuckled as he thought how handy it would be to have a woman's touch around the boat. Naturally, he thought, she would have to be pretty and shapely. In his mind's eye he checked over all the girls he had ever known, wondering if any woman would accompany a man on a trip like this. Tom didn't think so. Women were too smart, too practical. Anyway, there was nobody back home so deeply attached they would ever consider it. In fact, there was no one back home even to worry about him—so why in the hell was he worrying about *himself*? His feet could drop off, just so long as he managed to do what he set out to achieve—get *Silver* to the other side of the Atlantic.

At that moment he asked himself, "Where am I exactly? Am I too far north or too far south?" Having relied for navigation almost entirely on getting his compass needle to point east as often as wind and weather would permit, his position in the ocean was mainly guesswork—and he guessed he was a little farther north than he would have liked. The last, and only, fix given to him had come from the Portuguese skippier whose ship had passed by him just a couple hundred miles off Newfoundland. Certainly, that fix was no longer of any real use in trying to estimate his position.

Tom had to face it. Basically, he was lost. If weather and drift carried him too far to the north, there was every chance he could miss the Irish coast altogether. Scotland too, perhaps, and then be swept on up to the icy waters off Greenland and the Barents Sea. He found himself searching the waters ahead of *Silver*—looking far, far ahead. Looking for what? It was almost as if Tom was hoping to see a signpost or a policeman he could ask for directions.

Some fish that had been following him all day were still alongside his dory. Small, platinum-gray shapes just a few inches below the surface, sometimes almost motionless except for a flick of their tails, then darting forward or sideways in a flurry of action to gulp down some tasty morsel that Tom could not even see, most likely a small fish, squid, or crustacean. They looked happy enough. At least they knew where they were. And if they didn't, then they were certainly not worried about it.

Tom had hoped to use the plotting board from his army service to work out his fixed-line position. But the board had to be used every day to be of any real use, and that had been absolutely impossible. A plotting-board route depended on being able to draw straight lines and accurate angles. It was okay in the classroom back at camp, but not here. The thought of trying to draw straight lines in the roaring weather *Silver* had been through brought only a rueful smile to Tom's face.

Yet there was another way to figure out his position. "I figured I could not have drifted far enough to take me right off roughly the same latitude as Greenwich. That could be used to advantage." The nautical almanac that he brought with him could give him the time of sunup at

Greenwich. All Tom had to do was wait for an unclouded sunup out here, then divide by four, the difference between the two times, to find the degrees west of Greenwich. That would be accurate to within 15 miles. Maybe it would not suit the *Queen Elizabeth II* ocean liner, but it would be more than good enough for *Silver*. All Tom had to do was wait for the first clear unclouded morning.

The next morning—Friday, June 13—dawned as dark as Davy's gray, and there was no change in that situation throughout the day. No chance to try out his system for making a fix. The wind, too, decided it had neglected Tom McClean too long. Not only was it building up in strength, but it was coming from the north. The previous night a cargo ship had passed about a half mile from him. Quite obviously it had not spotted him. Now, he felt that he should have put what had been a half thought into action: fire a flare to attract that ship's attention. Then he could have asked for his position.

That afternoon was a comedy of minor irritations. As Tom was sitting down to a late lunch, a freak wave broke right over him, filling his pressure cooker and ruining his curry. He made do with a tin of fruit. Then he discovered that the water was not draining through the floorboards quickly enough to get to the suction outlets of the pumps. With ax and sheath knife Tom hacked a hole roughly three inches by three inches in the boards to help it on its way. "Rough and ready maybe," recalls Tom, "but it worked."

Adding to his agony he found that his chronometer had been flooded and its batteries ruined. Some of the spare batteries for his transistor radio had also been made useless by the sea. Anxiously he examined his deep-sea diver's wristwatch—at least that was still going strong.

The next three days passed at a plodding pace, so slow that Tom can hardly remember them at all. The entries in his log were mainly confined to wind and temperature. "I think the rowing and my bruised body were really getting through to me at last." One entry for June 14 certainly seems to indicate that he was in a pretty hazy state. It simply read: "Gas cooker blew up." According to Tom, "It is impossible to recall exactly what happened, but I am sure that I turned it on and then found the matches were damp. Foolishly I left the gas running while I hunted for more matches. One touch of the lighted match and a sudden blaze of gas singed my eyebrows and the backs of my hands. I think I was so soaked with seawater by that time that nothing short of a forest fire would have made any impression on me."

The days passed in snatches of memory. Tom remembers wishing that he'd kept a count of how many hours' rowing he had done each day. He thought, "How perverse this business of rowing turned out to be! Sometimes it drives you mad with pain. Sometimes you don't notice it at all, it becomes almost automatic. What an astonishing amount of useless trivia the memory bank stores up!"

The only interesting item was a St. John's radio program commemorating the 50th anniversary of the first nonstop transatlantic flight by John Alcock and Arthur Brown in June 1919, whose route took the pioneering British aviators also from Newfoundland to Ireland. The announcer said that they took 16 hours 12 minutes. "The next time I want to cross this bloody ocean," declared Tom, "it will be by plane."

Finally, the danger signals hammered through his thick head. He needed sleep, and to hell with his bright ideas of keeping busy. Self-discipline was the only way that Tom knew of dealing with difficult situations, whether they were mental or physical. It was, in Tom's view, a damned good substitute for courage. He had never regarded himself as a particularly brave person. Courage could not be weighed, balanced, or measured. It could not be doled out to those who needed it or taken from those who had it in excess. It could not be switched off and on as and when needed. One did not even know if one possessed it in enough quantity, or even any at all. No, all that anyone could rely on in tight spots was self-discipline.

But, in this case, Tom had overdone the self-discipline bit. Thankfully, he crawled into his sleeping bag. After swallowing a large shot of rum, he was deep in the land of z's. He slept almost solidly for over 12 hours. The only disturbance was a sort of instinctive clock that made him wake three times just to check that all was okay, and that he did without getting out of the sleeping bag.

Tom woke around before dawn on Monday, June 16, and by comparison with the last three days was a completely new man. He sat up breathing in the air and watching the sky lightening. What a wonderful morning! The sky was blue and getting bluer by the minute. At last he would be able to use his sextant to take a sight.

With the aid of his nautical almanac, Tom went to work on his little mathematical problem. It was a perfect sunup at 6:22 by Greenwich time. His calculations put him at 48°N, 38°W. He made that 840 miles in a straight line east of St. John's. He reckoned that he had actually covered something like 1,200 miles in all. "That has to be coming close to reaching the halfway mark" in his crossing of the ocean.

One other thing he felt even more certainly—and it was self-revelation that surprised him: "Nobody can really come through an adventure like this alone."

Unless God was in the boat with him, that was—a thought that once or twice came to mind.

18

First Six Months Are the Worst

Seabirds, black-headed, billowy gray, white, and yellow-beaked hovered just a few feet above him. The outstretched wings of petrels, shearwaters, terns, skua, boobies, and gannets were braced and slightly quivering as they thrust their snowy chests into the wind. Dipping, soaring, banking, they effortlessly kept pace with *Silver* with no more than an occasional flutter of their wings. They had been around for several days. *Silver*'s turtle decking and some of the stores bore the evidence. It was decorated with seemingly well-aimed drops of lime.

Tom shook his head with mock anger and dared them to aim at him. Every now and then one would dip his head sideways and a single beady black eye would fix him with a knowing stare. So far not a single albatross, with its yellow nose. A good omen? Or just not a bad one?

The seabirds were his only companions, and Tom was glad to have them. It seemed as if the birds had accepted him into the exclusive circle of strange beings who made the Atlantic their home. Tom felt honored. He saved food scraps and fed them each day. There was a never-fading fascination in watching the extraordinary grace of those long sudden swoops to the water. Finishing up with the most expert dip of the beak to scoop up the scraps before they sank too low for recovery.

He tried to tempt them closer by placing scraps on *Silver*'s turtle decking. It was days before one of them overcame his suspicions to risk landing there. It was a white-faced storm petrel that came fluttering in to perch himself on the very tip of *Silver*'s stern, as far from Tom as possible. His arrival was the signal for an outbreak of harsh cawing cries from his companions still circling overhead. It was as if the petrel had been ordered in as some sort of advance scout and was now being asked for an immediate report. He squawked just once, and there was silence from above.

Tom was sure that every bird there was watching the petrel's every move as he perched there on the stern, head flicking left and right and his body continually bobbing as if ready for instant takeoff at the slightest alarm. But at first the bird, about eight inches tall, did not move toward the food.

Sitting stock still, Tom scarcely dared to breathe for fear of scaring him away. After a few moments the bird took two or three hoppity steps toward the food, stretching his neck full length and recoiling in short bursts of reconnaissance. Then he stopped and, with a lightning twist of his head, flashed an unwinking wary eye at Tom. A few more jerky steps forward, another stop, and then he inched forward again.

As soon as the petrel started to move, it signaled a continuous and strident outcry from his friends in the air. It was for all the world as if they were trying to divert Tom's attention away from the little drama on *Silver*'s forward turtle decking.

Finally, the petrel's straining beak closed over a delectable middle cut of a two-day-old sardine. At that identical moment, the raider, with a flourish of wings, was back in the air, almost giving a victory roll as he swooped upward to accept the screeching plaudits of his envious chums. Before long one or two of the braver—Tom preferred to think of them as the friendlier—birds were eating regularly from the turtle deck café. Tom watched them and nurtured his friendship with them with great care. It was not difficult to believe that the stories of long-term prisoners making pets of rats in their cells had more than a ring of truth about them.

Isolation, exposure, and hardship play havoc with a man's proud supposition that he can face anything alone. Tom had been at sea one month and spoken only to the crew of the Portuguese trawler, to *Silver*, and to the birds—and most frequently to himself.

Yearning for the sound of a human voice, he tuned in the radio to St. John's. They were broadcasting a documentary-type program about the Battle of Waterloo. The fact that stuck in Tom's mind was that the Duke of Wellington's bounty for that battle had been £60,000 compared to £1 6s 8d for a private soldier. But the radio had nothing to say about the private soldier who, at that moment, was figuring that a chat with the birds was bounty enough in his personal battle with the Atlantic. "There was, of course, no reason, why I should have been mentioned in that broadcast," despite the fact that he himself had had an extraordinary military career and was now rowing solo across the North Atlantic.

◆

Silver was coasting along in a nice 15 MPH westerly. It was just before midnight on June 17. Tom had rowed steadily and was more than happy with the day's progress. As he shipped the oars, the blade of the port-side oar was awkwardly struck by a wave while it was balanced precariously on the gunwale and, of course, out of rowlock. The oar spun out of his hand, slid rapidly over *Silver*'s side, and disappeared into the darkness. It was sheer carelessness on Tom's part: "I should have made sure the oar was hoisted well clear of the water and balanced in such a way that if I did lose my grip, then it would have slid inboard instead of out."

He was in a foul temper and practically grinding his teeth with rage as he turned in for the night. Something like two hours later he had a bumper crisis on his hands. The lost oar was completely forgotten.

Silver was tossing and turning, bucketing and shuddering in a gale that came screeching out of the night. The wind was 50, 60, perhaps 70 MPH. There was no time to try gauging it accurately. It didn't matter: "We were getting our worst battering of the trip, that I knew." In the darkness the rushing waves looked like skyscrapers. Water was pouring into *Silver*.

Tom had found, some time before, that when alone in moments of stress and anxiety such as this, it helped to shout orders at himself, and as he grabbed for the pumps he was shouting: "The pumps, you fool, get to the bloody pumps!"

"Looking back now," says Tom, "I think that this business of ordering myself about gave me such a sense of urgency that I was under the impression that I was moving and reacting faster than normal. And that impression was very comforting."

Silver was being thrown around so much that there was absolutely no use trying to kneel at the pumps or even lie down between them. Tom tried to jam himself in there with the aid of his folded life raft and the stores and "then pump, pump, and bloody well pump again." There was no let-up at all. The pumping sessions lasted throughout the night and into the next day while the wind tried to blow *Silver* from the face of the Atlantic.

"I didn't kid myself that night. I was literally fighting for my life, and I knew it."

There were moments when Tom thought *Silver* would be pounded to kindling, moments when the sudden lift of a wave shot the dory up and up into the night, leaving his stomach several feet below him, while he wondered if he was going to be thrown out of the boat.

This was the fifth storm Tom had had to ride—and the fifth occasion when he marveled at the secret strength of his little Yorkshire dory. Wave after wave thumped into it with teeth-rattling impact. He would not have been the least surprised if it had shaken apart, board by board, around him as he lay there.

When trying to describe the violence of the sea, its anger and hunger, there is always the danger of being overdramatic. Yet unquestionably a turbulent ocean provides stark high drama. Such ferocity unleashed over such a wide area for so long a time crushes a mere man back to size—puny, helpless, and crazy to think that he could defy such mighty power. "Looking back, the issue was a simple one," relates Tom. "I was going to either live or die."

That night, however, there was no time for Tom to think about living or dying. There was no time to allow fear to wind its sticky fingers around his heart. That night the Atlantic was so frightening that to be afraid would have meant that the game was up.

The incredible savagery of movement, wind, water, and noise totaled up to a degree of violence that could drive even a balanced mind to the edge of insanity. It battered the body, dared the brain, drained the lungs, and assaulted the ears for hour after hour until it seemed there was no escape. And if, by fluke, death did not arrive, then the Atlantic had a gibbering fool at its mercy.

"I don't think there is anybody who can truly advise how to live through that sort of torment alone in a storm-tossed flimsy shell of wood. I can only offer what I think I did."

Seas breaking over *Silver* constantly flooded Tom's nose, eyes, and mouth, which fell open more often than not to suck in vital breath. With hands almost constantly at the pumps, there was no opportunity to use a towel or handkerchief. In any case they would have been sopping wet within seconds. Tom gained spasmodic momentary relief by spitting to clear his mouth and by snorting and blowing to clear his nostrils.

As far as his eyes were concerned, the easiest thing was to keep them closed most of the time. By shutting out the sight of the fury around him, Tom built a barrier against fear. In some extraordinary way he was able to close his mind to danger and ignore the excessive punishment of the cruel, cruel sea. All that was left to do after that was to hang on until he either sank or survived.

Tom found himself blinking at various streaks of dawn when trying to shake some of the water from his eyes. Streaks of sullen dirty yellow changed shape and size constantly as low-lying clouds of black malice charged across the sky, hurrying to wreck their malevolence on whomever and whatever they could find. And still *Silver* was being twisted, thumped, and shaken until the sky seemed to be rocking and twirling. Tom was sure the entire world was about to "throw up dolphins and sea turtles." Conversely, he would not have been surprised if he had suddenly found *Silver* and himself riding through the clouds and looking down at the ocean.

The fury lasted all morning. Tom could not eat. He could not even pause for a cup of tea. It would not have been possible to boil a kettle even if he had dared to leave the pumps.

At noon the nightmarish storm began to run out of steam. At first slowly, and then with a suddenness that was uncanny, the wind dropped and faded to a 10 mph caress. The waves fell away as if weary and snuggling down to rest. Tom stared in wonder at this instant peace and continued to pump until *Silver* was clear. He felt as if he had been to hell and back.

The clouds became a champagne white, and behind them the yellow haze of a hidden sun began to dry them up. This diffused sunshine glistened on the still wet floorboards of *Silver*. Strewn all over the boards and tucked in between the stores was the storm's debris. Bits of seaweed, an odd shell, grains of sand, a couple of jellified creatures, and a strange little pink fish no longer than three inches. The fish was dead, but Tom threw it back, along with the weeds and jellies, as if he could appease the Atlantic by returning its lost property.

Yet Tom could not shake off the thought that this calm was nothing more than the Atlantic having a fit of sulks while it worked out a new plan for getting at the property it really wanted: Tom and *Silver*.

He was so hungry that he had little time to brood. A curry was soon bubbling away in his pressure cooker. As he lifted the lid, he sniffed at the life-giving aroma "like a Bisto Kid in seventh heaven."* Beer, sardines, biscuits, and cheese rounded off the meal. But Tom was still hungry. A tin of fruit and two spoonsful of honey stopped the gap. Then he permitted himself the luxury of a shot of rum.

He rolled the liquor around his tongue, swilling it from one cheek to the other until the inside of his mouth was stinging. He swallowed it, trying to jolt it into the pit of his stomach in the hope that the impact would fire him with new life. He took another drink in the same way, and gradually the fumes began to rise, pricking the back of his nostrils and seeping into his head. "I was slightly tipsy, and it felt good."

◆

---

*   Bisto Kid is a reference only Brits will likely understand. It refers to a popular brand of gravy and other food products in the United Kingdom and Ireland.

After two hours' sleep Tom decided to get some rowing done, with a new pair of oars.* The wind had remained steady at between 10 and 15 MPH and was still from the west. It had been from the west all night. That had been the only consolation. *Silver's* head was pointing due east as she slid along on her homeward course. To Tom it was "the sound of music."

As if to cheer Tom and make sure he was still okay, shoals of flying fish appeared, throwing themselves through the air for a few feet before flopping back into the sea. There were about a couple of hundred of them, never more than a few feet from the boat. Tom had heard that they made a great fried delicacy. None landed on *Silver*. "In truth, I am sure that if they had I would have thrown them back. After the previous night, I felt that everything had a right to live for as long as possible."

But he was not to be left in peace for long. By late evening the dreaded wind, still from the west, began building up in new fury. The frenzy began all over again. For two days it blew, never falling below about 30 MPH and reaching into the 70s in wild bursts of angry temper. Tom had thought that he had gotten used to Atlantic weather, but he was wrong. He would *never* get used to it. There were times during those 48 hours when he thought he could actually hear the prayers of his friends back home. He too prayed. "And it does not stretch my imagination to think that God heard me," Tom said. "For I am still alive. And while I live I shall never forget those terrible days."

By the morning of Friday, June 20, Tom was a mess. His hands were so sore from the continual pumping duty, and the joints so stiff, that they stayed cupped as if still round the pump handles. Blisters had been giving him constant trouble. Because his hands had been wet for three days, the skin of dead blisters peeled off and then yet another blister formed as he got cracking at the pumps. In between the really heavy winds he managed to smear them with lanolin and Vaseline. Maybe it was imagination, but

---

* McClean took three pairs of oars with him on the journey. Each one was made from a single piece of ash. They had been supplied free of charge by Den Colam of the Denco engineering company in Hereford after Colam heard of Tom's forthcoming row.

it seemed to ease them quite a bit. In any case, he had to ignore the pain, for he dared not stop pumping.

His old salt wounds itched like mad, and the new ones burned as if cigarette ends were being stubbed out on his skin. After catnapping for two days and two nights, he felt as if he was going to drop off wherever he happened to be standing, sitting, or crouching. He felt so filthy he would have given anything for a hot bath.

While clearing up, he found that his thermometer had been broken sometime during the vicious storm. The last reading had shown a temperature of 54°F. Not overwarm, but at least there was the satisfaction of knowing the danger of freezing was long gone. But Tom was in no condition to worry overmuch about anything less than an emergency. As the winds had lessened to some 30 MPH for a couple of hours, he decided to chance taking a much-needed nap.

He woke three hours later, at about 11 A.M. Weather conditions were roughly unchanged, except that now it was a little foggy. Tom thought it must be low cloud, for it was more than a thick drizzle. Visibility was down to between 250 and 300 yards.

Making a rough calculation of his position he reckoned he should be nearing 30° West. It was a depressing piece of mathematics, for during his trip planning he had figured what came next would be the hardest part of the whole journey emotionally. Ridgway and Blyth had warned him: If anything was going to go wrong mentally with him, it would happen after the point he had now reached, roughly halfway across. Yet Tom had already struggled through "a dangerous mental stage" while stuck in the Labrador Current. "How could it be worse than that?" he asked himself. He had no answer for that. He had to be ready for whatever came next. It was just something more to stop worrying about until it caught up with him.

Tom figured he should soon be coming within range of the RAF *Shackleton* aircraft on their Atlantic patrols. He checked over his Motorola Saber radio with great care, for the thought of having a chat with someone was overwhelmingly cheering. He would be able to ask the RAF to pass on a message to the folks back home. Perhaps the newspapers would be interested enough to run a small story. He wondered what sort of headline he would write if he was sitting in a newspaper office when the news came in: "Moby McClean, safe."

Not very bright, perhaps, but, to Tom, being safe was the most important thing in his life right then. And in a funny sort of way, if the radio broadcasts occasionally said something about him, he could reassure himself that he was really okay and heading home. That he had yet to hear his name mentioned in a news report was dispiriting.

The thought of getting a message through to the outside world drove him once again to try the two-way radio on the off chance of picking up a ship. He had tried about a dozen times since he left St. John's but had not had any success. This time, he hoped, would be lucky.*

Out went his hopeful message, searching for a friendly ear:

"Atlantic rowboat *Super Silver* calling. This is Moby McClean . . . come in, please."

But it was a no-go. There wasn't a ship within range of the radio, its full scope being 200 miles. In all directions around *Silver* for those 200 miles, no one was there. "How lonely can you get?" Tom muttered.

It was a depressing thought, but there was nothing he could do about it—except shrug and tell himself: "Oh, you'll get used to it."

---

*   Months after his voyage McClean discovered that, because he did not figure in many news items, there were many people, both in the United Kingdom and in Newfoundland, who feared the worst.

19

23,000 Oar Strokes a Day

Tom was lost for hours in the pages of one of the three books he brought with him. The pages were swollen and warped from the damp but were still readable. *Sailing to Freedom* was the true story of a Finnish family who escaped when the Russians invaded Finland during World War II. It was an account of their journey to the United States in an old sailing boat. They were at sea for 130 days.

Reading of the dangers faced and survived by the Finnish family helped Tom to forget those that now surrounded him. To a degree, the book was sheer escapism for him, but he grew to regard it more as a kind of shock treatment—like getting straight back on a horse that had just thrown you. The effect of the book on Tom was transformational. It strengthened his determination to succeed. His feeling that he would not fail was deepened by the simple formula of telling himself, "If they could do it, so can I."

Although his food supplies had in no way been damaged and, all things being equal, could be made to last another 60 to 70 days, Tom was taking no chances. Whatever he did not eat from each day's ration he stowed away in plastic bags. For days he tucked the stuff away like a squirrel hoarding its winter nuts. He had gotten to the stage where he couldn't bear to dump anything edible overboard. If he had to stay out there for more than 100 days, even a few stale crumbs would prove valuable.

At 5 P.M. the moan of a ship's foghorn interrupted his reading. He looked up and heard it a second time away to the west. He saw nothing. The fog of the morning was still writhing and swirling, covering the sea in a cloak of secrecy. The horn sounded again and again, bellowing through the thick walls of mist. Tom became so frustrated with continually trying to see through the fog that at one point he was momentarily convinced that a plane was circling overhead.

The sound closed in on him. It could not be coming from anything but a ship. Tom became very excited at the thought that other humans were nearby. His attempts to pierce the fog became quite frantic. The very thought that a ship might slide past, unseen and unspoken to, was utterly unbearable. He shouted a couple of times: "I'm over here, over here." Yet each time he opened his mouth, he knew it was useless. So, he just stood there, leaning on *Silver*'s gunwale, straining to see through the dank curtain that was cutting him off from his fellow human beings.

He stood like that for a little over a half an hour as the ship drew closer. Suddenly he spotted her just 300 yards away. She looked like a huge monster feeling its way through the murk. The excitement than ran through him was suddenly chilled by the realization that the men aboard the ship would probably never spot him in this half-light.

The ship was heading straight for him! Excitement fled, leaving only an aching anxiety in the pit of his stomach: "I was sure she was going to hit me." The very human companionship that he had been craving would prove his end.

The titan edged closer and closer. *Silver*'s radar reflector was not rigged up. Yet again, despite all Tom's good intentions, he had been caught unprepared. As he tried desperately to think of some way of alerting those aboard the approaching ship, he still found time to feel an unsettling flash of concern about his mental condition. Was his mind slowing down? How much slower might it get? How many more chances would the mighty Atlantic give him?

As the alarm signals clattered through his brain, Tom tried to hoist the radar reflector into place. But it was impossible. The palms of his hands had become studded with nothing but tucked in and stunted thumbs. Finally, he compromised by holding part of the reflector above his head in the wild hope that it might work. He tried to put a spot of his old jungle training into effect. That training had dinned into him that it was shape, shine, silhouette, and movement that caught the eye. Tom turned the reflector above his head and waved it slowly from side to side, hoping that would do the trick. But it did not catch the eye of anyone on the ship.

With the behemoth bearing down on *Silver*, Tom felt utterly trapped. The sea anchor was out and he knew he could never get it onboard before the ship hit him. And it was absolutely impossible to row while that anchor was out. He just stood there looking for a way out, trying to get his mind churning, trying to think of something—anything.

The only thought he came up with was "to get the hell out" of his dory. The thought of deserting *Silver* made him "as miserable as sin." It was "like planning to leave a friend to the enemy." Tom dragged out his inflatable life raft and stood ready to snap the seal that would automatically blow it into shape. A few more seconds, he thought, and "it would be over the side."

Then "my incredible stupidity dawned on me like a kick in the pants." The flares! "Why had I not thought of the flares? What a fool! What an abysmal idiot I am!" Even as he cursed himself and reached for the flares, the villainous ship changed course and passed by him between 150 to 200 yards off his starboard side.

As she disappeared in the fog, her blasted horn still sounding its terrifying warning, Tom realized he was trembling all over. It was not from fear. "I was literally shaking with anger at myself. I had allowed myself to drift into a state of mental lethargy which had nearly killed me. And all the time I had been kidding myself that I was okay. That no matter how tired, how bruised my physical condition, I was at least mentally alert. But when the crunch came I had turned out to be a hopeless idiot of a failure."

LEFT: Young Tom McClean (to the left), with a friend, during his years at Fegan's orphanage. RIGHT: Tom's lodgings as a teenager at Uckfield, where he became an apprentice carpenter.

McClean in the Paras.

Tom "tabbing" (loaded marching to prepare a soldier for carrying heavy kit and equipment over long distances within a certain time frame) with a 60-pound backpack.

ABOVE: Prior to leaving from Newfoundland, McClean got advice from local sailors about the operation of a dory. BELOW: Tom McClean and his boat *Super Silver*.

ABOVE: McClean needed all the warmth he could get from his "featherlight," a special military blanket that retained 80 percent of his body heat. BELOW LEFT: Sometimes the sea could be beautiful, as here when *Super Silver* left a silver wake. But the waves could also be imposing. BELOW RIGHT: A pair of polythene bags provided some helpful waterproofing for McClean's frostbitten feet.

McClean keeping his log.

Even in the middle of the Atlantic, McClean found a good shave to be a morale booster.

McClean inspects his emergency fishing tackle.

Tom's cooking stove provided him with his favorite meal: curry.

Loneliness for McClean was broken occasionally by visits from porpoises.

TOP: A closeup of Bluey, the shark.
CENTER: Rowing was arduous, with as many as 20,000 row-strokes per day.
BOTTOM: Though Tom never boarded a ship, seeing the SS *Hansa*, the last of three ships that gave him his position, was still a cheering sight.

ABOVE: McClean watches over his adventure center at Ardintigh in northwest Scotland. RIGHT: Tom with his wife Jill and sons James and Ryan.

In 1982 McClean sailed across the Atlantic in his self-built *Giltspur*, the smallest boat to accomplish that crossing.

In 1985 McClean lived on Rockall from 26 May to 4 July, with the idea of reaffirming United Kingdom's claim to the tiny Atlantic island.

In 1990 McClean completed a west-east crossing of the Atlantic in a 37-foot bottle-shaped vessel, an endeavor sponsored by a British tea company.

McClean's most recent feat was the construction, in 1996, of a boat shaped like a giant whale and named the *Moby, Prince of Whales*. Standing 25 feet high and 65 feet long, the unusual vessel, with a spout that could launch water as high as 20 feet, completed a 2,000-mile circumnavigation of Britain.

The man who designed *Britannia* was famed English boatbuilder Uffa Fox (right), seen here in 1968 discussing the design and construction of the rowboat with John Fairfax (left) at the historic Clare Lallow boatyard (established 1867) in the seaport town of Cowes on the Isle of Wight. Fairfax called Uffa Fox, then 69 years old, "a lover of life, a lover of the sea" with "the fire and vigor of a man of only half his years." Eccentric though he was, Fox (1898–1972) was responsible for producing several key innovations in boat design. He was also a longtime friend of fellow sailing enthusiast Prince Philip, Duke of Edinburgh.

ABOVE: Right up to the last minute before starting his row across the Atlantic on January 20, 1969, Fairfax and his girlfriend, Sylvia Cook, brought supplies to *Britannia* as it awaited departure from the beach at San Agustín on Gran Canaria. Having met Sylvia in London in 1967, John knew that he was "definitely not her type, nor she mine," but "in spite of this we liked each other." Quite a rower herself, Cook joined Fairfax in 1971 on a 363-day mad adventure by rowboat from San Francisco to Australia, the tandem becoming the first persons to ever row across the Pacific Ocean, and Sylvia becoming the first woman to row any ocean. RIGHT: Sylvia Cook on board the *Britannia II* during her year-long Pacific voyage with John Fairfax in 1971–72.

Fairfax posed beside his 22-foot rowboat at King George V Dock in London in mid-January 1969 prior to traveling with his boat to the Canary Islands from where he rowed to Florida. *Britannia* was towed to Gran Canaria free of charge by a large American sailboat, a ketch named *Camelot*, with Fairfax as its guest passenger.

Prior to departure from Gran Canaria, Fairfax demonstrated for a photographer his method of spearfishing for food.

Fairfax setting out from San Agustín on January 20, 1969.

ABOVE: A great deal of unexpected rough weather made Fairfax's rowing much more difficult than he expected. BELOW: In an era long before "selfies," Fairfax managed to take a "pocket Kodak" snapshot of himself at sea.

RIGHT: Fairfax lassoed and held to the side of his boat a huge hammerhead shark, which he killed and feasted upon for several meals. BELOW: Proud of his victory over the shark, Fairfax posed for a self-portrait with the desiccated head of the hammerhead, which he kept as a trophy.

ABOVE: On July 9, off the Great Bahama Bank, a seaplane carrying two photographers landed, took pictures, and conversed with Fairfax. Earlier that afternoon, a different plane chartered by ITN flew over *Britannia* but did not land because the sea was too rough. ITN did drop some supplies to John, including a large pack of his favorite pipe tobacco. BELOW LEFT: On July 10, the yacht *Costa Grande*, chartered out of Miami by ITN, found *Britannia* at anchor and snuggled close enough to *Britannia* for Fairfax to swim over for a leisurely stay, food, drinks, and a pleasant night's sleep in a bed. During John's time on the yacht, an ITN journalist conducted a lengthy taped interview, soon to be broadcast across the UK on Channel 4, a British free-to-air public broadcast television channel operated by the state-owned Channel Four Television Corporation. BELOW RIGHT: A pipe-smoking Fairfax posing for a photograph on the *Britannia*.

TOP: With boats swarming around him, Fairfax arrived in Florida at 1:45 P.M. on July 19, his 180th day at sea. CENTER: Fairfax in *Britannia* upon arrival off Hollywood Beach in Florida. In his log that night John wrote: "Our reception was magnificent, and—oh, I love America, love everybody today, but mere words cannot express my feeling, and I will not try." BOTTOM: Swimmers and jubilant spectators greeting a victorious Fairfax. The next day several of the onlookers, as well as Fairfax himself, would be among the millions watching, at a distance, the historic launch of Apollo 11 to the Moon.

Fairfax showing the blisters on his hands from the thousands of hours of rowing.

The only time that Fairfax and McClean were ever together was at the Earl's Court boat show in London in January 1970. Under a large banner reading ATLANTIC ROWERS: WEST TO EAST ▶◀ EAST TO WEST, the prows of *Britannia* and *Super Silver* faced each other almost nose to nose, as did the two rowers. Tom manned the stand for ten long days whereas John only stayed for two, which was long enough for him to meet those he considered to be "the most important people," including Princess Margaret, the sister of Queen Elizabeth II, and her husband Lord Snowden. McClean stands to the far left, Fairfax second from the right.

In the early 2000s, Fairfax, seen here sitting in the Top of the World restaurant at the Stratosphere, became a well-known personality on the Las Vegas Strip. John died at his home in Henderson, Nevada, on February 8, 2012, at the age of 74.

That was what he had feared and tried to guard against. He crawled into his "dog kennel" to try to forget it. He sat there, his arms circled tightly around his knees and his head pressed down hard, trying to control his shaking body. And, more importantly, fighting to dominate a brain that had become dulled and a dangerous liability.

He had been sitting there a few minutes when he heard the foghorn once again growing nearer. "Oh, my God," he thought. "Not again!" He grabbed some flares and scrambled out of his shelter: "Somebody must have seen me, after all." The monster was about 200 yards off his stern and heading toward him at a creeping pace. He could see people along the rails waiving and shouting at him.

The ship crept closer and closer until she was no more than 20 or 30 yards away. Her bow loomed high above him, and he was able to make out the name *Regina Oldendorff* before she edged along until he was staring up at the bridge. She was a West German freighter, and as she had closed in, Tom heard someone shouting, "What you want? What you want?"

"My position, please," Tom bawled back. But the German sailors did not seem to understand. Tom waved his chart above his head and then overlapped his arms to make an X to indicate that he wanted a fix. His sign language worked. By the time the bridge was abeam of *Silver*, a dozen shouts told Tom: "49 degrees, 45 minutes north, 36 degrees 5 minutes west." He was in the vicinity of the halfway point of his voyage, after all.

From the bridge the German captain shouted through a battery-powered megaphone: "Are you all right?" With tongue in cheek Tom told him, "I am in perfect shape!" While other people were watching, Tom found it quite easy to put on a bold front, even though he knew how abject he would feel once they had gone.

The captain shrugged, waved, and turned away to get his ship under way again. As that huge steel wall of riveted plates slid past, the crew on the rails continued to wave and shout: "Du bist verrückt, Mann! Raus aud dem Dingy und mach mit! Wir geben Ihnen alle Wurst und Kartoffeln, die Sie essen können! Und all das kaltes Bier, das du trinken kannst! Wie auch immer—Viel Gluck!" Tom knew almost no German, but he did make out the word for beer and later found out that *Gluck* was German for *luck*. But he didn't need to understand a great deal of the foreign language to understand its essential meaning. There were times when Tom wondered if he had completely run out of luck; he didn't worry so much about running out of beer. He knew he had more of that.

Tom waved back to the German sailors with gratitude. The *Regina Oldendorff* slowly gathered speed and steamed off into the fog. The paratrooper listened to her foghorn until she was out of hearing range and he was alone again.

He slept all night. Nine solid hours without waking once. His dreams were about friends, old and new.

◆

He woke up refreshed. The fog had cleared and a cozy 20 MPH wind from the west had *Silver*'s bow pointing happily eastward, toward Ireland.

Now a little more than halfway home, it was difficult for Tom to think clearly about how hard his journey had become. Physically he had taken a battering, but he was pretty sure he could take more. It was the slowing of his mental processes that worried him. He had suspected it for some time. The incident with the *Regina Oldendorff* and his inability to remember his flares confirmed his suspicions.

For a week the winds remained light enough to save him great discomfort but not strong enough to constantly require the engagement of his mind. Tom had to force himself into a rigidly applied routine: to do certain things at certain times and whip his sluggish brain back into a state of active readiness.

In a way, his fright over the *Regina Oldendorff* coming at him from out of the fog had been a fortunate scare. It had been an object lesson in what he was still going have to face. The true danger of his mental weariness was that, although a person might know it was eating away at him, it can still catch you off guard. He did not intend for it to happen again.

But little slip-ups continued to happen. That very next morning he draped his sleeping bag over the roof of his shelter in an effort to dry it out. But he promptly forgot all about it until just before dusk. When he looked, the sleeping bag was gone. Tom had failed to tie it down. He had to wonder just how many more little mishaps he would be allowed without him doing something really stupid. Fortunately, in the case of his sleeping bag, it must have fallen overboard just a few minutes before he looked for it, for there it was floating in the water about 50 yards astern. He rowed over to pick it up, wondering how he was going to drill "this brain of mine into precise activity" once again.

He committed himself to a more rigorous daily routine. He would be sure to rise between 5:30 and 6:00 A.M., rinse his face with seawater, then check over every corner of *Silver*. He would then very deliberately make a breakfast lasting at least 20 minutes, to force himself to maintain a keen watch on the time.

After that it was row. Not the sort of rowing that followed a more casual schedule of roughly three hours on and one hour off but rowing for exactly one hour by his watch then carefully shipping the oars inboard and spending exactly 10 minutes going through a regimen of deep breathing and knee bends—exercises also necessitated by the fact that the cramped space of *Silver* was getting to his knees and thighs, stiffening them into a state of creakiness that could almost be heard as he moved.

Then it was back to rowing for another hour, followed by 10 minutes of checking the stores and counting the number of days of rations he had left. Tom sometimes arrived at two or three different tallies: "But that didn't matter; at least I had carried out the counting routine at the right time."

Row again for two hours and break for lunch, which, Tom decided, would last exactly half an hour. Then row again for one hour exactly, then stop to count the food stocks again, this time for 15 minutes. And so on until 6:00 to 6:30 P.M., when he would force himself to stop rowing for the day. The evening was similarly broken up with exact periods for eating, a cup of tea, writing in his log, and then putting his head down by 11 P.M. at the latest.

Tom was not overly concerned with how well he performed all his self-set tasks. His main object was the timekeeping. He wanted everything to run on the dot—like clockwork. He felt that if he could discipline his mind to follow and accept a rigid timetable, it would prevent it from drifting off into any never-never land. That did not prove easy: "I found myself forgetting to look at my watch for time checks and consequently would quite often overrun the laid-down time."

Sometimes he found himself wanting to alter the timetable to suit his mood of the moment. For example, when the deadline to stop rowing arrived at the end of the day, he would tell himself it "wouldn't matter if I kept on for a bit." In fact, he felt he would "benefit by stretching a few more miles toward home." A couple of other times, when he was scheduled to count the food stocks, "I almost did not bother," thinking in a "fuddled sort of way" that it had already been done.

These were "strange days." They passed in a weird slow-motion style. Tom found that, although it was comparatively easy to plan the timetable and abide by it for a while, it was entirely another matter to carry it out always and long term. "Perhaps the most uncomfortable sensation of all," Tom relates, was "knowing that part of me was doing its darnedest not to cooperate."

It was a peculiar struggle, but he stuck to it and gradually got on top. By the start of the second week with his schedule, the most he was off on any one of his timed periods was a couple of minutes. Such success prompted him to claim victory: "The temptation to tell myself that I had the situation well under control and to relax was almost suffocating." Indeed, the temptation was so strong that for nearly a full day Tom allowed the time schedule to go by the board. "But I snapped to the danger just in time and forced myself to apply it with even more rigid discipline than before."

At one point, Tom even tried estimating the number of rowing strokes he made in a day. He got to 23,000 and packed it in: "It had been a bad idea and I dropped it." Far from relaxing him, counting the strokes made him quite tense. Over tea that evening, Tom hit on what turned out to be the perfect answer. It was so simple he kicked himself for not thinking of it before.

Tom's counting of the food supply left him with the undeniable conclusion that he had enough food for another 100 days, so unless something really dramatic happened, he was not going to starve for a long time. Even so, he decided he had been wrongly using his tea and sugar supplies: "I had been making a pint of tea at a go. This meant I could have only three brews a day, and more often than not I would be drinking at least half of it when it had turned cold. From then on I made half-pint brews, thus giving me six tea breaks during the day." He adjusted his timetable accordingly. He also decided to step up his daily vitamin intake from two to four pills a day.

Maybe it was purely psychological but, by the start of the second week of his regimen, Tom felt as sharp as he would ever be on his timetable. His slow and ponderous brain was once again beginning to prod him into action at more or less the right time, place, and speed. "I doubt if anybody would have called me a ball of fire, but at least I was beginning to smolder."

It was at that stage when Tom hit on a solution to a problem that had been bothering him for some time but he kept shelving because he could not think of an answer: "I had forgotten to bring a can of oil with me. It was needed for many things—squeaky rowlock sleeves, squeaky rudder pivots, and to protect *Silver*'s metal fittings against the corrosive rust of the Atlantic." The answer had been staring him in the face for days: use the surplus oil from his daily can of sardines. "It worked well, and I began storing it in an empty honey jar."

It was like coming to after a bout of drifting in and out of consciousness. For the first time in the last several days he was fully aware of what day it was: Thursday, June 26. Tom had groped his way through several days in a mental fog. Part of that time he could remember, for the notes were right there in his log. The rest would be a mystery forever: "I was by no means 100 percent mentally alert yet, but I had improved enough for the true dangers of the past few days to come crowding in on me and to be able to consider them calmly."

How close to giving in had the incident with the *Regina Oldenforff* driven him? He would never know the answer exactly. One hazard, however, was crystal clear: "It was possible to stand on the very edge of failure entirely against my will." Tom was convinced that his self-imposed timetable had a lot to do with bringing him around, and he determined to employ it whenever possible. Storms created their own timetables, no doubt. It was another long bout of fairly calm weather that he had to guard against.

The treachery of the Atlantic had no limits: "Even when at peace it is waiting to grab you." Day and night chased each other until the sheer automatic monotony created a state of hypnosis in a wearied brain that had been working overtime to spur on an exhausted body. Just how much had the days on end of being alone altered his mental state, Tom wondered? He couldn't be sure, but he did give considerable thought as to how he could measure, and regulate, it.

To his daily timetable Tom added a fixed routine of listening to the morning and evening news. He was far enough eastward that he had started to pick up the BBC. His idea was to switch on at the exact moment the broadcast commenced and to switch off precisely at the end. That would promote self-discipline. No matter how much he may want to hear a music program, he would follow his own orders to the letter.

On the evening of Friday, June 27, Tom switched on the BBC as usual. He heard the program introduced and then a couple of loud crackles came from the transmitter and then silence. He jiggled with the knobs, shook the set, and changed the batteries. Nothing. He tapped it, first softly then moderately hard. He hoisted the telescopic aerial and pushed it up and down several times.

The set was dead. Tom sat looking at it, hardly able to believe what had happened and absolutely unable to believe such bloody awful luck. A sense of utter loneliness pressed in on him until he felt as if he had been cut off from the rest of the world forever.

His feelings of utter despondency seemed to last for hours. He faced the risk of plunging into a pool of self-pity, which, after he completed his voyage and looked back on it, he considered to be one of the biggest dangers in this sort of extreme adventure. Even at the time it was happening Tom knew he somehow had to cast off this feeling of being sorry for himself.

What could do that for him? Immediately what seized Tom's consciousness was his innate sense of competition. For the third or fourth time since he left St. John's, the name John Fairfax popped up like a jack-in-the-box. Fairfax was the man he had sworn to hate—the man he had sworn to beat. How long ago was that? "It didn't matter how long," Tom told himself: "A good hate session would put me in a solid competitive mood."

Fairfax must have made land by now, Tom figured. He had left the Canary Islands in January, more than six months ago. Thinking of his rival's tremendous head start was more than enough to get a good dose of hate going. Yet somehow it didn't seem enough. Tom switched to a mixture of envy and hate. Fairfax, he told himself, was likely wallowing in hot baths and comfortable beds and drinking long pints of cool beer, and he probably had a beautiful girl sitting at his side. Tom's efforts at imagining the worst about Fairfax still didn't work. It made Tom envious all right, but his hate wasn't strong enough. In fact, it wasn't really strong at all.

"Good luck to him," Tom whispered. "My turn is coming."

He found out a few weeks later that John Fairfax, the playboy adventurer, had still been at sea at the time.

Truth be known, McClean still had an outside chance of winning the race of the solo rowers across the Atlantic.

20

Bluey

On Monday, June 30, Tom reluctantly wrote in his logbook 13 words that he hated to read: "I must confess that, at last, I am beginning to feel worn down." To even admit it was like wringing a confession by torture from him. But the facts had to be faced and dealt with.

The winds were still light—little more than breezes, in fact. But for the last three days they had been switching back and forth like a yo-yo. Northerly one day, from the south the next, and that morning he had woken to a southeasterly. Not to be able to proceed in the one vital direction had become sheer frustration. He knew he had passed the halfway mark, and yet he could not convince himself that he had.

Tom's mental condition was still patchy, and although he stuck to his timetable like a drowning man clutching at a straw, it was difficult to shake off the tormenting idea that he was actually heading back to Newfoundland. He could not have been blamed if he had begun wondering whether or not he should consider seeking help if things became too bad. That if things got to that pitch, he would have to ask for aid from the next ship he spotted or call up assistance on the radio. But judging from the number of ships he had seen, that could have been days or weeks before another came along. But the truth was Tom never once thought of asking a ship for help.

As *Silver* slid through the overcast gray waters, Tom totaled up the for-and-against scorecard: "The side for giving up totted up in rapid-fire style. I had been at continuous full stretch now for just on six weeks. Every muscle, every nerve, every sinew, and every tiny brain cell had been strained without let-up with the single object of keeping myself alive. I was a mass of aches, bruises, blisters, salt sores, and a couple of agonizing boils had begun to erupt on the back of my neck. I was filthy and itchy to such a degree that I felt as scabrous as a mangy cat."

The rowing was becoming more difficult, and sleep, even during those calm nights, had degraded into fitful restlessness. And he was going off his food. The only thing he really fancied the previous two or three days was canned fruit.

And the salt! The ever-present salt. He was caked with the stuff. Practically everything in the boat was covered in a thin white crust. It was in his hair, in his nose, in his eyes, and under his clothes, and he could not get rid of the taste.

Tom had to ask himself, could it get worse? The only answer was not only that it could, but it would.

Despite his discomfort, there was a voice inside his head telling him he was not beaten yet. He had to be sure that he could hang on and would. If it was possible to be granted one wish, he wondered, what would he ask for? He decided that it would be a pair of "braces"—what Americans called suspenders. His oilskin trousers kept slipping down in Chaplinesque style because the elastic waistband had disintegrated. He tried tying them up with a piece of string, but it did not work at all well.

It was not a very imaginative wish. Even a little crazy. But it served to help Tom resist wishing for the impossible—the feel of land under his feet.

His feet were not yet really ready for the land. Although by this time he was able to pull his seaboots over a couple pairs of socks, they were still too tight. The swelling had decreased until his feet looked almost normal size once again. But that was about the only normal thing about them. They still had that pickled look, and they were still stinging and painful. They were quite obviously on the mend, however, and that was all that mattered.

The hours slipped by, virtually unaccounted and unheeded. They merely acted as markers for the vital timetable that Tom hoped would help him nurse his mind and body back to strength.

On Tuesday, July 1, he managed to work out a rough position. He had made it to 50°30'N, 28°43'W. Maybe it was not pinpoint accurate, but it was as near as possible under the circumstances. Without a doubt, he was over the halfway mark at last and truly on the way home. There could be no thought of giving up now.

Tom was surprised with himself that the discovery that he was definitely past the halfway mark caused such little excitement. If it had happened a week or 10 days earlier, he would have felt like throwing a party. His elation would have known no bounds, and it would have been a moment of congratulations to both *Silver* and himself.

He had been looking forward to the moment ever since he left St. John's. It had been the big goal, the massive target that had kept him going through the most severe experience of his life. Yet when it came, it brought only a slight sense of relief. "I am only thankful that it was enough to bolster my determination with the sort of cynical resignation used by most servicemen to describe the early period of their military careers: 'Cheer up! The first three years are the worst!'"

◆

It has been said that sharks, like vultures, can sense the dying and travel many miles to attend the feast at the wake.

At 2 P.M. on Wednesday, July 2, Tom saw his first shark. It slid alongside silently and without warning. Tom was emptying his after-lunch tea leaves over the side when he saw the sinister dark gray shape keeping pace with *Silver*. He had, of course, expected to see a shark or two. But this first meeting was so sudden Tom nearly dropped his tea mug over the side: "He was so close; I swear I could have reached over and touched him."

Once Tom had got over the shock of the shark's sudden appearance, he watched him for a few minutes swimming alongside. All Tom could think was "My God, he looks bloody ominous, with his evil pig-like eyes and mean long jaw." He appeared to be about 15 feet long. Not just dangerous. Voracious.

Tom looked around on all sides of *Silver*, expecting to see other triangular fins cutting through the water. "God knows what I really expected to see, but in that first wild moment I thought the sea would be littered with them and all heading for *Silver* like U-boats zooming in for the kill." To Tom's surprise, and great relief, there was not another shark to be seen.

One shark, however, was more than enough. "This one kept me company for seven hours. First he would appear on one side of *Silver*, then on the other. At times he would disappear from view for five or 10 minutes, but then suddenly swim back into sight again." The shark swam alongside *Silver*, ahead, astern, and underneath. There were times when he came so close that Tom could hear him scraping the boat.

When the unholy fish first appeared on the scene, Tom sensed a chill of apprehension such as he had never quite felt before. And it did not begin to wear off until at least an hour had passed: "I supposed that one can get used to practically anything in time, even a shark."

"What does one do about a shark which appears bent on much more than just a passing acquaintanceship?" Tom asked himself. He tried chucking old tins over the side, hoping the villain might choke on them, but the shark would have none of it. "Should I perhaps try throwing so much food over the side that he would eventually become so full that he would swim away?" thought Tom. "How much food would it take to fill up a shark?" Probably more than Tom had—and which Tom would need for himself anyway. The shark might be able to eat Tom, even eat *Silver* if that was possible, and still be hungry for more. And if more sharks came around, he couldn't possibly feed them all!

The shark shook Tom more than he thought possible. But he had nothing else to do but let his mind churn over the different scenarios. The winds were still light, and Tom figured that trying to think of ways to get rid of his unwanted companion was as good mental exercise as anything else. Wild ideas, some just plain stupid, were examined and gone through step by step. It did not matter how unworkable they were so long as they kept Tom thinking.

Tom toyed with the notion of making a hook out of one of the row-locks, baiting it with a paste of biscuits and porridge cake, and trying to "catch the blighter." The fact that Tom didn't have a file with which to fashion the hook did not stop him from working out the best way of shaping a rowlock for the purpose. He even went to the extent of planning how to shape it into a barbed hook.

Tom planned an ambush. The plan was to tempt the shark close to *Silver*'s side with tidbits of food and then spear him with one of the oars after sharpening the shaft end into a point with his bowie knife. Recalling a Tarzan film he had once seen in which actor Lex Barker had wrestled with an alligator before stabbing it to death, Tom thought in a fit of flamboyance of jumping over the side and tackling the shark with his knife: "Needless to say, I didn't bother to work that one out." Nor did Tom act on his memory of the scene from one of his favorite books, *Moby Dick*, when the obsessed Captain Ahab, "possessed by all the fallen angels," planted his harpoon in the flank of the great white whale, only to have Moby Dick smite the whaleboat, toss all of its men into the sea, and ultimately snare Ahab around the neck in his own harpoon line, "smiting him" and taking him with him under the sea to his death. Tom knew the story of Moby Dick too well to try anything like that. All it would take from his shark was one good shove upon *Silver* and its five-foot six-inch Irish oarsman would be gone in a couple bites. (The nearest thing to "attacking" the shark came when Tom had to pee. He took the pail of urine and tossed its contents overboard. Of course, it made no difference.)

Finally, Tom ran out of ideas. The last one was to give the shark a name. At least it would make the situation seem "a little chummier." Tom dubbed him Bluey and started talking to him like he was a long-lost friend. The shark stayed until dusk before suddenly flipping over and speeding off to the west. Tom watched him until his fin was out of sight. "Cheerio, Bluey," Tom called out to him with a sigh of relief. "Don't bother to call again."

But he did. Bluey returned the next day. He slid on the scene just as before, silent and sinister. It was about midday, and Tom had been rowing for several hours. "I don't know how long he had been keeping an eye on me, but as I was shipping the oars to prepare my lunch I spotted him about two yards off *Silver*'s port side and just about a foot beneath the water, stiletto gray, vicious, and apparently ravenously hungry." Again, the shark kept pace as *Silver* drifted before a 15 to 20 MPH wind. Tom scanned the water to see if Bluey had brought any of his friends along this time, but again he was alone. "Maybe he figured I was big enough for a meal for one." Tom watched him nosing along as he ate his lunch of curry, "not too heartily, I must admit."

With a pathetic dash of bravado Tom waved his spoon at the shark and said, "That's right, Bluey, just hang around until you think I'm fattened enough for your liking." Even as Tom spoke he shuddered as his imagination vividly presented him with a picture of Bluey grabbing him by an arm with his jaws. "I was brooding far too much on Bluey," Tom realized. "If it went on like that, I really would begin believing that I was about to end up as a shark snack."

In an effort to forget the cursed fish he tried his Lifeline radio again.* He made his call without too much enthusiasm, because he hadn't had any success in picking up a ship's operator for days—they were either too far away or not listening. He mouthed the brief message: "Atlantic rowboat *Super Silver* here. Come in, please."

---

*   Clearly, Tom saw the shark as an evil, dreaded omen. But, of course, the shark was just being a shark. Humans above the water are not prey sharks would understand. Humans in the water in the middle of the ocean would be unusual. Neither Bluey nor any other shark is actually evil. It's a sea creature with no apparent intent to attack Tom. Fish of all kinds will often follow along with a boat or a larger fish. Things moving in the water provide cover and opportunity, and sometimes following along just satisfies curiosity. Sharks, like wolves, snakes, and bats, get a lot of bad press. Most of it is based on movies such as *Jaws* and is simply not true. Therefore, whenever the author of this book suggests that the shark is evil or sinister, the intent is to show how Tom *felt* about the shark—not that the shark was *actually* evil. I wish to thank my colleague and friend Francis French of San Diego, California, for suggesting that I make this clarification for the reader.

Tom repeated it several times, then he heard a faint voice: "Sailing ship 50 miles to your north."

Almost jumping with excitement, Tom shouted at the top of his voice: "Hello, hello there! Atlantic rowboat *Super Silver* here. Come in, please!"

Again, that faint voice. And again, the same message: "Sailing ship 50 miles to your north." He repeated it several times. Tom cut in with "*Super Silver* here. Are you mistaking me for a sailing ship? This is rowboat *Super Silver* . . . row . . . boat . . . *Super Silver.* Do you read me, please?"

He obviously did not read Tom, for all Tom heard was another message about a sailing ship. He gave up trying to tell him differently and switched off. Looking over the side, he saw that Bluey was still with him. The sheer persistence of the brute was unnerving. He did not disappear until dark. Even then Tom could imagine him slipping quietly alongside *Silver* and just waiting, waiting, waiting . . . for Tom. Needless to say, the only sleep Tom got that night was fitful.

Next day, July 5, the wind swept in from the east. It built up to 40 MPH and, although it was from the east and causing him to lose precious distance, Tom blessed it, for Bluey did not appear. The shark had no doubt headed for the calm of deeper water. The wind lasted all day, and there was nothing for Tom to do except heave out the sea anchor. Tom stayed in his shelter all morning, trying to build up his strength. He dozed off and on most of the day, turning and twisting on the hard floorboards.

Tom's discomfort, as he tried to rest on those boards, was a result of the clinging inertia that had possessed him with increasing danger over the past two weeks. His air mattress was no longer inflated, the result of constant chafing and continual soaking in gritty salt as *Silver* rolled and pitched her way through the sea, which had worn a hole right through the side. Having forgotten to bring a puncture repair kit with him ("One cannot remember or foresee everything"), he tried mending it, but his desultory attempt to patch it with adhesive bandages (known as Bostik and Elastoplast) lasted a few hours only. "An insignificant mishap," Tom thought, "and certainly of no importance in terms of my safety." But it was yet another illustration of the risk, lurking like a submerged iceberg, that could rip the bottom out of his undertaking simply by allowing himself to drift into "a stupid state of not caring." These little incidents drummed home again and again the inescapable fact that if anything went wrong in a lone adventure of this sort, there was "nobody to blame but yourself."

Tom had reminded himself of this before but had to keep reminding himself. There had been moments when the temptation to lie back and say "Well, I've done all I can. Now it's up to luck, or fate, or God" had been almost unbearable. "Yet I had been able to pat myself on the back and say that I had fought against that—and fought well."

By lunchtime it came to Tom with "a knock-out impact" that for the first time he had given up the fight without knowing that he had done so. He had been lying in his shelter all morning bemoaning his luck, "kidding myself that I was not giving in and wallowing in self-congratulations" for having fought the good fight so well. The whole morning had gone without Tom once remembering his timetable, without his once making the conscious effort of prodding himself into even the most ineffective action, and without his once remembering what he had to do simply to stay alive.

The dawning realization of the chilling truth jolted him psychologically as nothing else had done so far on the trip. He was literally panting with anxiety as he scrambled out of the shelter. Doing his best to stand, he took great heaving breaths of that rich Atlantic air.

But he could not stand. Whether from the effort or shock, Tom's knees trembled so much he just could not keep his feet. It was not just a quivering type of tremble. Seized by rapid shakes that seemed to be moving his kneecaps at least two or three inches and sending shuddering jerks along the muscles of his calves and thighs, he found that his legs were completely uncontrollable.

He sat down on his rowing seat, legs outstretched as far as possible, and clamped a hand over each knee. He sat there with his eyes shut, rocking slightly backward and forward until the fit of shakes died away.

One thing was crystal clear to Tom. He had to get into action, and quickly. His mind, however, was not so clear: "I have a distinct recollection of not wanting to move from that seat. My thinking mechanism was hampered by a haze of such improbabilities, impossibilities, and wishful dreaming that I think I was like the amateur mountain climber who, having got so far, made the mistake of looking down. I just wanted to stay put. To cling on to the one spot which seemed to be safe."

"If I moved, would I fall?" Tom worried. "If I moved, would those damned knees start jerking about again? If I moved . . ." He had to move. Slowly he opened his eyes and looked at his hands. Even more slowly he eased their grip on his knees. Nothing happened. He shook each leg in turn. Again, nothing happened. The trembling had stopped. Gingerly, he got to his feet, expecting the whole ghastly business to start again. It did not.

He didn't feel like eating any more than he felt like jumping over the side of *Silver* into the ocean. He went about his preparation for lunch in such a deliberate fashion that it was almost like moving in slow motion. "God Almighty," he told himself, "if you get into a state like this again, it is you who will be cooked."

The aroma of cooking curry that day, usually so mouthwatering for Tom, became a repellent odor: "I had been off my food for a couple of days, but I never dreamt I would see the day when the smell of curry would actually make me feel sick." The more he thought about it, the more it affected him. It swirled around his head in great choking waves until he thought it would actually stick in his hair. The first spoonful produced such a bout of nausea that "I had to force myself to swallow it." Food was vitally important to him at that stage. He knew that he had to eat that dish of curry even if it took the rest of the day to get it down.

Without a doubt it was the worst meal of the trip. As Tom sat there literally willing himself to spoon, swallow, spoon, swallow, that damn Bluey popped up again. He knew it was Bluey because he had been snapping photographs of the shark ever since his first appearance, mapping the shark from a standing position, from a sitting position, from the stern, from the bow. The markings on the creature's head were easy to recognize—they were nasty and threatening, and reminded Tom of a seaman "plaiting his own cat o' nine tails before being flogged." He also recognized Bluey's length and the shape of his head.

Mealtimes were like a magnet to the shark. There he was suddenly along *Silver* again, just a few inches below the surface with that evil fin cutting its own narrow wake in the water. In an almost mesmerized state, Tom sat watching him until his curry grew cold: "I started eating again, stuffing the cold mess into my mouth with haste. All I wanted to do was finish it." And all the time he watched the shark.

Thinking that the hot bite of a dehydrated curry block might give the blasted fish "a bit of gyp in his belly" and drive him off, Tom threw one over the side. Bluey did not even give it a glance. As if to demonstrate his contempt of that feeble effort, the nasty fish changed course, sliding head-on toward *Silver*'s beam. Something—his fin or tail—rasped along her bottom as he passed underneath to take up his shadowing position on the other side.

Suddenly Tom realized that Bluey had not come alone. He counted five fins. *Only* five?! Five or 55, what did it matter?

To blazes with him and his buddies. "I'm on my way home, and I'm going to get there, Bluey or no Bluey—and with or without his companions."

Tom shouted at the whole shiver of sharks: "I'll make it even if you follow me all the way to Ireland."

21

It Can't Last Forever

Under the beam of his flashlight Tom took a look at the compass before turning in. Sure enough, he was heading west. Not at all the direction he was supposed to be heading. Nothing during this torturous journey was so morale-sapping as those times when the wind had him heading willy-nilly in the wrong direction.

He groaned and cut himself short. He had been doing too much groaning. Severely, he told himself that the first step was for him to "give up the ghost." Giving himself a mental shake, Tom placed himself under two strict orders as he bedded down:

One: "Snap out of the lethargy that is clogging you both mentally and physically."

Two: "Get *Silver* heading in the right direction and get as much distance under your belt as soon as possible."

He tried to introduce a military crispness and urgency into those orders. Stretching his aching bones out on the hard boards of *Silver*, he kept repeating them until he dropped off into a troubled sleep.

◆

Like a lot of dreams, it started pleasantly and turned into a wicked ordeal. As plain as day, he saw a handful of buddies that had been with him when his SAS Boat Troop launched a practice assault onto the Norwegian coast. They were all there—Horse, Nick, Lofty—all grinning, all shouting. His mates were buzzing around *Silver* in their rubber Gemini assault craft. They all came aboard the dory, each man carrying a large crate of beer.

Strange how little *Silver* could take so much extra weight without apparently showing any ill effects. In his dream, as he was lifting a bottle of beer to his mouth, he puzzled about it. It wasn't natural. He looked over each side of *Silver* to make sure she was okay and found she was riding perfectly. He stopped puzzling. But as he took his last look over the side he saw that the SAS craft had drifted away. Horse, Nick, Lofty, and the rest were bobbing away, drifting farther and farther from *Silver*, but staying parallel with her course. "We will be with you all the way to Ireland, Moby!" the boat troopers shouted.

Puzzlement turned into panic. All of Tom's effort so far had been for nothing. Instead of making his landing, having rowed the Atlantic alone, he would be stepping ashore in Ireland in the company of a crowd of chums. The whole adventure would be a nonevent. He would have to start all over again. Back to St. John's. My God, back through the Labrador Current!

◆

Thunder woke him around 3 A.M. It cracked right overhead and nearly blasted him out of the boat. There had not been much in the way of fair weather on this trip, but this was the first major thunderstorm he had run into.

There was no more sleep that night. The storm lasted nearly four hours: "I do not think I have ever known anything quite so fantastically fierce." *Silver* rattled with every clap of thunder. The noise from the heavens filled the entire space between sea and sky, rolling and echoing in the blackness as if some monster was hurtling toward them at breakneck speed. In between the thunder Tom could hear the swishing and surfing as the sea built itself up in a fury to match the rage overhead. The wind came whistling in, developing itself into a continuous savage scream, almost with glee. And it came from the east, pushing Tom yet farther and farther away from home.

Every now and then the thick, choking, booming blackness was split by great streaks of forked lightning. It cleaved its way from sky to sea in vast electric sparks like the side-effects of some monumental scientific experiment being carried out by crazed gods and going hopelessly wrong.

As frightening as it was, the lightning was also the most comforting part of the storm. Comforting because each streak lit up the sea for split seconds and it was a blessing to find even fractional relief from the blindness of the night. But it was indeed frightening, as each fork of electricity seemed to be working its way closer and closer to *Silver*. Each streak of power was so hostile that Tom felt it must surely sizzle and steam as it dug its way down into the dark waters. Little *Silver* wouldn't stand a chance if she was struck . . . just a puff of smoke and a few black ashes as epitaph.

The dory began to buck and pitch with growing violence. There was something almost supernatural about that alien night as Tom clung to the seat and listened to the boiling savagery around him.

Then the rain began. A biblical tempest. It fell in sheets, from start to finish. Pouring down, it drummed on *Silver's* turtle decking and rapped with throbbing persistence at Tom's head and shoulders as if they were surfaces of a snare drum.

Tom was wearing two sets of waterproof clothing, and he pulled both hoods tightly over his ears to cut out the noise. But there was no escape: 'I realized that if I sat out in the open much longer, I ran the chance of becoming scared." There was only one remedy: "a spot of the old ostrich treatment." He dived into his shelter and tucked himself as far up in one corner as he could get. He had only one consoling thought—he was 100 percent certain that Bluey would "no longer be in attendance."

He was right. By daybreak the storm began to fade, but the rain continued to lash down, and there was not a sign of Bluey or any of his chums. Tom had not felt so satisfied for days. The wind dwindled to a mere 25 MPH, but it was still from the east. Monday, July 7, was the third day on the trot of easterlies. For a moment Tom felt the lethargic depression of the previous day creeping in. Then he remembered his orders of the night before.

That easterly wind had to be beaten somehow. Tom hauled in the sea anchor and started rowing head-on to the wind. The sheer uselessness of the effort was not lost on him. But he stuck at it, driven on by a perverse fit of cussedness that he hoped to substitute for the spirit of lethargy. He rowed for three hours, knowing full well that he was getting nowhere. Every time he began wondering how long the easterlies would last, he chased the thought out of his mind by the simple formula of saying "It can't last forever."

By midafternoon he had to give up. The sea was running high again, and *Silver* was shipping water in dangerous quantities. Tom had to stand by the pumps at least twice in every hour: "But I was glad to be there. I was being forced to fight again." The pumping session made him realize just how much punishment he had taken. His muscles were stretched to torture point, but the pain was a blessing as it stung him into a sharp awareness for the first time in over two weeks.

His concern about the easterlies was banished the next morning when he woke to a 20 MPH west wind. By 10 o'clock it had risen to about 40 MPH and *Silver* was zipping along so beautifully in the right direction that Tom was so overjoyed he could have cried if he were a crying man. After lunch the wind dropped, but he didn't care; it was still from the west. Feeling that he could not afford to waste even a second, he began another crushing session of rowing. He kept at it until dark without even stopping for tea.

Tom clawed his way through the first two hours of rowing, ignoring the pain as his back creaked with each movement and his arms felt as if they would drop off. For most of the time his eyes were tight shut and his teeth so tightly clenched that his jaws ached. Then suddenly he was through the curtain of agony and rowing automatically, insensitive to the demands he was making on his physical strength. "What was driving me?" he wondered. "I wish I had known the answer." With almost clinical detachment he examined himself as he bent backward, forward, backward, forward, plodding on and on and not daring to stop.

One thing was clear: "I was out not out there striving for anyone or anything. Success or failure meant nothing to anyone but myself. Strangely, I had to remind myself that I had decided this was the only way for me to make something of myself; to make the world notice me, even if only for a short time; and to make a place for the name of McClean on the lists of those who have dared and won. But how ever I wrapped it up there was no getting away from the fact that I was doing it for myself." For money, too? Tom had to admit that money had also come some way into his calculations. What about pride? Yes, that drove Tom even more than money.

Whichever way he looked at it, Tom kept coming up with the same question: "Am I just being bloody selfish?" And there was always the same answer: "Yes, you are. But you're stuck with it now." There was no doubt that this habit of handing out self-lectures every now and then was a real lifeline: "I daresay the lads back at camp would have had a chuckle if they had known. They would have said it was a foregone conclusion that Moby would talk to himself if there was nobody else around."

Tom's worries about being delayed by easterlies completely vanished on Wednesday, July 9. That morning marked the beginning of 12 days of westerly winds almost without a break. He didn't know it at the time, but it was really the start of the last lap.

It was also a great day for a very different reason. An examination of his feet showed that they had almost fully recovered from the rigors of the Labrador Current. Those frozen days seemed such a long way off, yet Tom remembered every minute of them: "I resolved that never again would I go through anything like that, and as if to seal the vow, my seaboots slipped over my feet with ease."

The rash of salt sores on his neck, wrists, and backside, however, showed no signs of lessening. The blisters on his hands still built up one on another. His muscles ached so much that if he moved to relieve the pain in one point it cropped up somewhere else. The boils on the back of his neck felt like mountains. And trying to sleep had become a nightmare. His shoulders had started to give him so much pain at night that it was impossible to lie on his side for more than a few seconds. After rowing or pumping sessions, his hands felt as if they would never open fully again. There were times when there seemed to be no power at all in his fingers.

There had been moments when he wondered just how far the limits of human endurance could take him. Yet once those seaboots were on his feet, none of the agony, the pain, or the worry seemed to matter anymore. If his feet were on the mend, then the rest of his body would catch up before long. The seaboots and the westerly wind were exactly the ingredients for the tonic he needed. "Maybe I looked a mess, maybe I was a mess," Tom reflects. "But I was on top once more, and I didn't intend to fall off again."

But how far? How long? How many more storms? How many more hours of rowing? And, more important, how many more chances would the Atlantic grant him?

This, however, was not the moment for cares or for thinking of what might be. This was a moment to think of other things, and there was plenty to think about—a walk in the hills, a beer with the lads, the things Tom had done, the things he hoped to do. All the good things, all the happy times. All the things that add up to a sailor's dream of home. "I knew for sure that the fire was back in my belly at last," declares Tom. "Nothing except final disaster could lick me now."

It occurred to him that up to now all his prayers on his trip had been a plea for help in moments of trouble. Surely now was the moment for a prayer of thanks, heartfelt and humble thanks for the help that had reached him without being requested.

At 5:30 A.M. on Thursday, July 10, he was awakened by the drone of an airplane overhead. To Tom it was the sound of *land*. By the end of the day he realized that he was in an area where he would hear planes several times during the day and night. But two days passed without him being able to sight even a wingtip. The shutter-gray cloudy skies had dogged him almost all the way whenever he heard a plane, trying to follow the direction of the sound until it was out of earshot.

The days were passing with unflagging monotony. Wake up, eat, row, eat, row, tidy up *Silver*, pump, row, pump, sleep: over and over again the same routine, one day following another almost without change except for the speed of the wind. But his buoyant mood was still with him. It was going to take more than a spot of boredom to get him down from here on. He had worked out an estimated position on Saturday, July 12. It was 52°06′N, 20°W. Tom made that just 720 miles from Ireland: "The whiff of home was well and truly in my nostrils."

Sleep was out of the question. Tom was too excited for that. Whatever had happened, whatever could happen, he was sure he was going to make it: "I had to do something, and the only real exertion open to me was to row. I had rowed steadily through most of the day. Admittedly, I had been looking forward to supper and getting my head down. Now I could not bear the thought of missing a single valuable minute."

Throughout the night he stayed at the oars, rowing as if he would reach land by the morning. He stopped only for tea and a shot of rum at about 2 A.M. About an hour later he saw the lights of a ship heading east. Almost at the same moment he became aware of a shining ghost-like shape darting about in the water. He watched it from side to side of *Silver*. Apart from his tea breaks this was the only time he shipped his oars: "I don't know how long I watched, but I think I was mesmerized for a while."

It was a large fish glowing with the phosphorous that sparkled like tinsel glitter over the surface. Tom had no idea of exactly what it was. Maybe Bluey had returned to haunt him. But whatever it was, it was both beautiful and spooky. It hung around for about 10 minutes and then suddenly vanished. One minute it was there bursting through the water like a shooting star, leaving dancing fire in its wake. The next second, nothing. "It must have dived," Tom supposed, "having tired of its game with *Silver*.

By dawn Tom was bone weary, but he was happy. So happy, in fact, that his appetite returned in a rush. He breakfasted on porridge, tea, biscuits, and marmalade and then crawled into his shelter for a couple of hours of sleep.

A couple of hours was a complete underestimation. The night row had taken far more out of him than he had thought. He did not wake until three o'clock in the afternoon. Strangely enough, he couldn't have picked a better day to sleep if he could have forecast the weather ahead with pinpoint accuracy.

It was a completely calm day. The Atlantic was barely ruffled by the mildest breeze. Yet even the term *breeze* was too strong to describe that peaceful day. Contrary to what many people believe the word to mean, the perfect word for the wind that day was *zephyr*, which the *Oxford Dictionary* defines as a "gentle, mild breeze" and even "the west wind personified." How true, how true. Throughout the day it never blew harder than between two and three miles per hour, and Tom took full advantage of it. After a hurried meal he rowed through the afternoon until about 5:30 in the most perfect rowing conditions he had yet encountered. *Silver* fairly floated along.

And there was to be a perfect end to a perfect day. Just before 6 P.M. Tom spotted a ship that he thought might be the weather ship *Juliet*, which was on station somewhere in the area. But she was steaming eastward and was, Tom was sure, too far away to spot him. But this time he was taking no chances on being overlooked. It was the first ship he'd had a chance to stop, and Tom was anxious to get a message to his friends back home.

He lit a flare and, standing on the seat, waved it above his head. The ship showed no sign of seeing him. Tom tied a red hooded jacket to the telescopic radio mast and raised it as far as it would go. Again, there were no signs of recognition.

Tom fired one of his radar flares. It rose to 2,000 feet and exploded, shooting out a shower of fine metallic dust which could—and should—be picked up by a ship's radar. It worked. She changed course and bore down on him. As she steamed slowly past on his port side, there was a shout from the deck: "Are you all right?" Tom yelled back, "Yes, I'm okay. All I want is my position and to ask your skipper to radio a message back to Lloyd's in London."

It was the SS *Hansa*, a German steamship, on her way to Deptford, London, with a cargo of newsprint for Express Newspapers. Tom waved his chart above his head as she inched past him. Then the *Hansa* stopped and Tom rowed alongside. The captain climbed down from the bridge to the midships deck and shouted down: "Your position is 52 degrees 24 minutes north, 20 degrees 26 minutes west."

Tom scribbled it on a blank page in his logbook and then passed up his message and several rolls of film, which he asked the captain to pass on to the *Sunday Express* when he got to Deptford. Then the captain asked if Tom wanted to come aboard, have a bath, or just have a drink. Tom refused them all with thanks.

"How about food and water?" the *Hansa* captain shouted. "Are you okay for supplies?"

"I am absolutely fine, thanks," Tom shouted. "I don't need a thing now I've got my position."

The captain answered, "Okay. Keep clear of my propellers."

He gave Tom time to row off before starting his engines and heading for England. Tom watched her for a few minutes, feeling a little wistful. But it did not last for long. When he checked the position that the captain had given him he found he was only 10 degrees from the Irish coast. Tom made that no more than 600 miles.

"The smell of the land was with me with a vengeance."

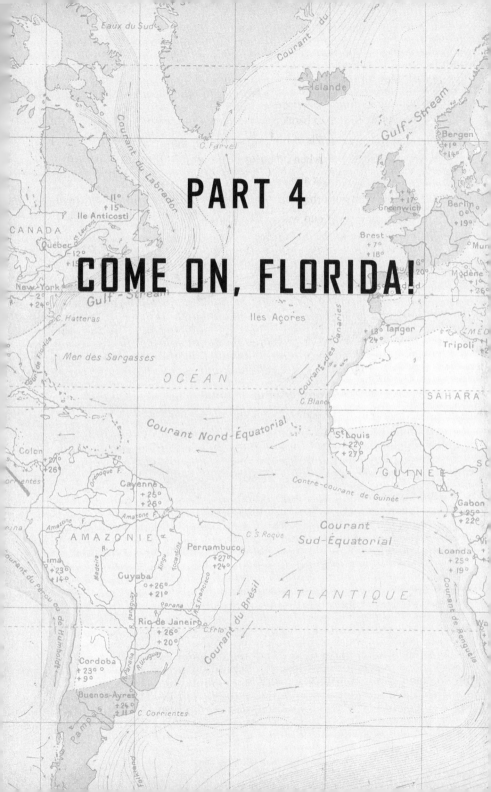

PART 4

COME ON, FLORIDA!

22

Interview on a Yacht

From Cay Verde it had been John Fairfax's intention to go northwest, enabling him, with luck, to pass north of Andros, the biggest of the Bahama islands, and then move from there into the western end of the Bahamas and on rather directly—at about the same latitude as the tip of Florida—to the Miami area. But wind and currents from June 30 to July 2 prevented the plan. John could only manage to make good along an easterly course. He found himself approaching the Cay Lobos light-house, atop a 156-feet-tall cast-iron tower painted white at the southern fringe of the Great Bahama Bank, an enormous expanse of shallow water averaging a depth of only four fathoms. To the south of Cay Lobos only some 30 miles lay Cuba. John wanted to give the land of Fidel Castro wide berth, given what Cuban patrol boats might make of *Britannia*. That left almost no other option. There was only one navigable passage toward South Florida from his position near Cay Lobos, and that ran right along the Cuban north coast. It was called the Old Bahama Channel, a narrow strait in which ship captains historically had to pick their way through numerous low-lying cays and shoals on the southern Bank.

It looked to John as if, in spite of all of his efforts, "the fortunes of my landfall were now entirely at the mercy of a whimsical breeze." Rather than Miami, his arrival could be in Havana. There was one other option. If the winds did change, as long as he stayed in the shallow waters of the

Bank, he could always anchor *Britannia* and wait for better luck. But that posed a danger. If at night *Britannia* strayed into the deep water of the Old Bahama Channel, and the wind changed before he realized what was happening, he was in trouble.

Never averse to receiving help, the next day, July 3, John saw a couple of fishing boats, rowed over to them, and "had a chat with the guys." The fisherman told him that as long as he stayed on the Bank, he had little to fear from Cuban patrols. That's what John did. For the next two days, with light winds from the southeast, he rowed due north. His progress was painfully slow, but he finally saw the Cay Lobos lighthouse disappear to the south.

July 5: "Come on, Florida, move a bit toward me or I feel as if I'll never make it! These last days are the worst. I get tired so easily now. I'm definitely not fit anymore."

Fairfax wanted to speed things along as best as he could. He wanted to leave the Bank and get across the Florida Straits "without being swept past Miami" by the two to three knot current generated by the Gulf Stream. "At least I will be drifting north," he told himself, "whereas now I have easterly winds and it is very hard to row north, as I'm doing."

So why didn't he just proceed? Who or what was stopping him?

The answer lay in his contract with ITN and the *Daily Sketch*. Under the terms of his contract, John had promised them an exclusive interview to be held at sea. The only possible place and time that John thought that would work was if he stayed on the Bank, got as close to its western edge as he could, then radioed his position to his sponsors waiting in Miami, and have them get themselves down in a boat—all of it done as soon as possible. John Austin, his agent, and Martin Cowling, his main financial backer, had already flown to Florida a few days earlier and were organizing his reception. With them from England came a number of interviewers, photographers, and reporters. "In principle I had nothing against all this," John noted, "but I wanted to get it over as soon as I could."

John had been in radio contact with London almost daily for the past week, but the process of doing so was not easy. Everyone involved in the enterprise was "getting anxious." On July 6, John told London that he wanted to be met by Austin, Cowling, and company on the morning of July 8. "I hope they can do it," he told them. "I am finding it very hard going to keep on the Bank. I spent the whole day at anchor. Naturally I want to get going, and the current is favorable. Once in the Florida Strait I ought to be able to go like a shot, and fooling around with this anchor business to stay on the Bank is time-consuming and does nothing to improve my temper."

London's reply did nothing to distemper him. Apparently there had been some trouble in chartering a suitable boat.

That afternoon an airplane with a group of photographers flew over *Britannia* for about 20 minutes. John did not know the plane was coming. He was listening regularly to a radio station out of Fort Lauderdale and had heard nothing about anyone expecting his arrival.

John grew increasingly angry about the situation. What made it worse was that, due to technical problems with his transmitter (he had the right crystals but the wrong aerial), he could communicate to Miami only by relaying his messages through London. Though not especially difficult, the relay process was "time-consuming and open to confusion." It turned out that the plane John had seen flying overhead was not even an airplane that was looking for him—none of his associates now in Miami knew who chartered the plane he had seen or how anyone who was on that plane knew who he was.

The next morning, July 7, John again reported his position to Miami via London. The word back was good—that the *Daily Sketch* and ITN would meet him the next day. John was not confident: "I hope everything goes O.K.," he wrote in his log. "I'm fed up. Hopefully, all will be over soon, but now the hours seem to drag forever."

Once again he spent the entire day at anchor. He was mad at himself for not getting his position right that morning when he reported it through to Miami. "No knowing where I am," he muttered out loud, "I dare not drift." All he could do was sit tight, hoping the ITN yacht would find him the following day. "Once the blasted interview was over and done with," John intoned, "nothing can stop me." In the Gulf Stream,

"I hope to average 60 miles a day." Two days and "I will be there. Two God-damned days is all!"

Whatever good feelings that anticipation of finishing the job brought to John were strongly soured by the misinformation he heard that day coming from a Miami radio station: "John Fairfax, the Englishman rowing a boat solo across the Atlantic Ocean, could arrive any day now. The Coast Guard has reported that it has seen his rowboat, the *Britannia*, some 150 miles *northeast* of Miami. That position is consistent with sightings made by several other ships. So that crazy heroic man who has been rowing his boat since January should soon grace our shores. Maybe he will get here in time to go with the three intrepid NASA astronauts who are blasting off from Cape Kennedy on July 16 for the Moon!"

He soon had an even better reason to be fuming. London radioed and told John that the boat that ITN and the *Daily Sketch* had chartered had broken down at sea and they wouldn't be coming today: "To stop short of my goal when I am practically there—for a television interview in the middle of nowhere!—is lunacy. After all I have gone through, the task of rowing *Britannia* across the Gulf Stream may appear deceptively easy; but until I actually beach her on Florida's sands, I am not done. A hundred things could still happen: a sudden storm; a collision; a stupid accident, like breaking an arm or a leg at the last moment—anything could happen, anything!!

"I have promised, and I will wait, but only for another day. No more."

The next day, July 9, he was still at anchor waiting: "This is terrible, to be so near and to sit on my arse like this instead of going on. I'm not there yet and I'm allowing myself to relax—swimming and fishing—as if my journey is at an end. This is wrong, wrong! I still have a dangerous, difficult stretch to cover, 140 miles, and I am just asking for trouble by not pushing on. Why the hell don't they come?"

The chartered boat from Miami was still being repaired, but a seaplane flew over *Britannia* during the afternoon. It dropped a package containing pipe tobacco and a note saying they could not land because the sea was too rough—"this when there is not a whisper of wind and the sea is like a mirror." Never very generous to other people,

John wrote, "That pilot must be out of his mind, and a lousy navigator to boot." In the note, ITN asked John to wait for them until the next day at sunset, as they would do their best to find him. "Against all better judgement, I'll wait," John logged, "but I'm definitely not staying around here a moment longer than that. Look after me, please, Venus—don't let me relax too much, please."

By midafternoon the next day, he was beginning to give up hope, when they finally got to John, in a beautiful yacht, the *Costa Grande*. John, darkly tan, tussled hair, no shoes, and in a white tight-fitting swim shorts only, bounded on board, shouted "Hello there!" to everyone on deck, crashed onto a deep-cushioned divan sofa under a canopy on the main deck, said "I'm going to sit here," drained a large glass of icy lemonade in virtually one gulp and then another, and spoke a few minutes with Martin Cowling before the television interview began.

ITN INTERVIEWER: Thank you for coming aboard. We would like obviously to hear the story from yourself. But first of all, what is the one thing that was running through your mind as you stepped out that boat knowing that Miami is so very near? Are you proud of this? Are you relieved?

JOHN: *(smoking a cigarette)* Well, I had no idea that Miami was so very near. For three days I have waiting for you guys to arrive here. Obviously, very pleased. I think what I have done is not easy and it took about everything I could give to do it. I am pleased with myself. Well, I have never been a very modest guy. I am bloody proud of myself for doing it.

ITN INTERVIEWER: You said it took everything you got. You've strained a whole lot. You've really put everything you had into this, haven't you?

JOHN: I had to put everything I had into it and a bit more.

ITN INTERVIEWER: Did you ever get lonely?

JOHN: Not really. I am a lone wolf by inclination. I was very busy all the same. I never had the opportunity, really,

of feeling lonely. I usually enjoy myself, with my own company. I am a person who is completely self-confident. I am very happy with myself, with what I am, what I am doing. I have no complex of inferiority or anything. I am just a happy guy and therefore I just have don't any problems. That's all.

ITN INTERVIEWER: Was there any point where you thought you might not make it?

JOHN: I never felt that I might not make it. I mean, I thought it could be very difficult, I knew it was going to be very difficult. It was a lot harder than I thought, I must confess. But the main thing about me is that I never give up. I know that and knew when I started either I would make it or I would kill myself.

ITN INTERVIEWER: Right at the beginning, when it looked very much to us like the whole thing was going completely haywire, because you appeared to be going totally in the wrong direction. You were going due south when you should have been going west.

JOHN: I was going in the wrong direction because I had, from the very beginning, very strong westerly winds. I was going west and I was rowing, I was not sailing. Anybody who has, in his life, rowed a boat, knows what it is like to row against a contrary wind. If you can imagine a contrary wind of about 30–35 miles per hour against you, in the open ocean, rowing on your own, a boat that at the time, weighed more than a ton. You just can't imagine what it was like to fight against it. It was all I could do just to prevent myself from being swept onto the coast of Africa. I think that was really the hardest part as far as rowing was concerned because I did an average of about five miles a day—sometimes I did five miles backward, sometimes more. I knew I was going wrong and I can tell you one thing, after a whole month of rowing my guts out, and I looked at a chart and I saw that I was about 200 miles from the Canary Islands—*south* of the Canary Islands. That means I still had to go the whole way, to go west.

ITN INTERVIEWER: About those early setbacks when it seemed you didn't seem to making the right way . . . There was one moment when we thought things were going even worse and that was when you apparently threw overboard most of your food. Why did you do that?

JOHN: That was another turning point on the trip. It was a hell of a decision to make and I made it because I was going very slowly and to make Miami I had to be here before the hurricane season. As it is I just about made it. . . . I was doing about 20 miles per day—this is considering drifting. *Britannia* was just too heavy for me to row. I just had to make up my mind. Either I lightened her and was therefore able to arrive at Miami or I had to satisfy myself with just crossing the Atlantic and that meant getting anywhere—South America, Barbados, anywhere. But I wanted to get to Miami, by God. *(Slamming his hand on the sofa seat.)* Florida was my obsession! Therefore, I took the chance of my life, you might say, and I threw away everything.

ITN INTERVIEWER: You saw some ships, got some help from some ships?

JOHN: A couple ships, yes. One was a Russian ship . . .

ITN INTERVIEWER: Can we perhaps at this stage, turning away from the actual routine of how you got across and think of some sort of typical day, about the sort of things that could happen to you in a day. Now, for example, May the 21st, you had your 32nd birthday, was it?

JOHN: Yes, my 32nd birthday. I was at the time uncorking the only brandy bottle I had on board, to toast myself. I was in a very strong gale; in fact, that same gale almost overtook the Virgin Islands and surrounding islands and they declared a state of emergency around there. Well, it was stronger than a gale; it was a strong wind force of 8–9. I was laying broadside to the waves. On rough water, the boat, she was like a submarine. Just as I uncorked the bottle and was about to drink, I saw this wave coming at me about 15 feet high. *Britannia* usually just went up in a wave like a cork. But this wave, I saw it breaking right on top of me. I just stood there looking at it. There was nothing I could do about it and it broke right on top of me. If you have ever been on a beach and have been hit by a wave, a breaking wave, you can have an idea of what it was like, for a 15-foot wave. Just the crest breaking right on top of you. It smashed around the boat, I hurt my feet and legs. The next thing I knew I was in the sea, still clinging to the brandy bottle for dear life, with my thumb on the top to prevent any sea water getting into it. But it did get sea water into it and I couldn't drink that brandy. I tried but it was positively undrinkable.

ITN INTERVIEWER: The image we get of you, based on all that you've told us, is one of a professional "tough guy." You seem to be quite extraordinary in that you have been able to survive all this. For example, what about this incident with the shark. This seems to typify just how tough you got to be.

JOHN: It was not really toughness. I was surprised by it. There wasn't much else I could do about it. I was scraping the bottom of *Britannia*. Do you mind if I relax now? *(Lying down on the sofa seat and propping up his head with his right hand.)*

ITN INTERVIEWER: For heaven's sake, of course not.

John then took roughly five minutes to tell the story of his encounter with the mako shark on February 22, which occurred when he was scraping barnacles off the bottom of *Britannia*. One thing he said during his story was that he did not pray for the killer shark to stay away from him, because he was not a praying man.

ITN INTERVIEWER:	"One thing that you just said that seems very revealing to me: you said you were not a very religious person. There must have been something, some sort of belief.
JOHN:	I've never been a religious person. Mind you, I was baptized in St. Peter's Cathedral in Rome, as a Catholic, a Roman Catholic. I went to nun's college when I was a boy; later I went to a Jesuit college.
ITN INTERVIEWER:	So, you are not a Roman Catholic, but there must have something that kept you going?
JOHN:	No, I don't believe there is a God. I don't believe there isn't a God. I just couldn't care less.

John spent the rest of the afternoon and part of the evening on the ITN yacht. In his log he wrote: "Had a ball and got sloshed. Tremendous meal, with big juicy steak. Marvelous!"

But, as he often did after what he felt was succumbing to lack of discipline, he regretted his night of partying: "What I feared has happened. I have let my defenses down. I was so happy to see them that I could not resist the temptation and committed the unpardonable stupidity of getting drunk. My self-discipline is gone, and I don't know how I am going to make it now."

At the end of the evening, the skipper of the *Costa Grande*, undoubtedly aware of John's inebriated state, had offered to tow him as far as he liked, even back to Miami. Returning to *Britannia*, as terrible as he felt, John started to think, "I should have accepted." But "how could I, after struggling so much, for so long, to get here on my own?"

He got into *Britannia* and did his best to row for a few hours. During the overnight, he "kept falling overboard . . . still under the effects of the whiskey and euphoria of the meeting."

The former pirate who truly had, in fact, technically, rowed the Atlantic Ocean had to admit: "I am really a fool."

◆

To get to Miami, however, he still had 150 more miles of ocean to traverse.

The *Costa Grande* skipper had suggested to Fairfax that, instead of going northwest as he planned, John should row due north. If he went much more west, said the skipper, the Gulf Stream might very well push *Britannia* on past Miami.

At first John was reluctant to take his advice. He had made a meticulously careful study of his charts and had a very good idea where the current of the Gulf Stream would be at its strongest. He figured that point of strongest current would not come for a full 100 miles west off his present position at 23°47'N, on the edge of the Great Western Bank. Once he pushed off the bank, he would not enter the Florida Strait proper but rather the Santaren Channel, which ran between Great Bahama and another bank known as Cay Sal. In John's opinion, especially because the day had no wind, the influence of tides clashing with the Gulf Stream over the Cay Sal Bank might produce a strong countercurrent running south along the Santaren Channel. On the other hand, the skipper of the *Costa Grande* knew these waters much better than he; John concluded that he had better listen to him.

He rowed west, with "the hope of making good a northwesterly course." But it did not work out. By the evening of July 11, the 172nd day, he found himself at the edge of the Cay Sal Bank, slightly south of the position he had been at in the Great Bahama Bank. "So, either there was no current whatsoever," he noted in his log, "or something went wrong." If so, what was it?

Not able to sleep, and given that his position was south of where he had been anchored for the past three days, John decided to row through the night due north.

In the morning, July 12, when he took a star sighting, he "couldn't believe my eyes" when he fixed his position at 23°22'N, 79°72'W, which was even farther south than where he had been anchored on the Bank for days, this after rowing north for most of the night. "Where is the current that was supposed to take me past Miami if I wasn't careful?" John asked in extreme frustration.

In the Canary Islands, John had gone backward, made curlicues, and gotten blown in various directions by the breezes, but what was happening here off the Great Bahama Bank was truly dumbfounding: "I don't understand at all what's going on in these waters. As it is, I have traveled in a circle. What next?" Three days earlier on the ITN yacht, everyone including John was certain that he would reach Miami in a couple of days. "How could anyone guess that on the morning of the 13th I would be just 10 miles from my position on the 10th? I would dearly like to know the answer to that myself."

It could have been stress or bad food, but for all three of those days when *Britannia* was wandering the southwestern fringe of the bank and into the Santaren Channel, making no less than five hairpin turns, John was so sick to his stomach that if he was not squatting over the side with diarrhea, he was vomiting; a few times he had to find a way to do both at once. He was miserable. Each day was unbearably hot—95°F with no wind. He was baking in the torrid sun, becoming dangerously dehydrated. "I could shoot myself," he managed to write in his log, "if only I had the energy. My fault, of course, and no one is to blame but myself. If only I could get some sleep! It's like a desert out here. If there were sand around me instead of water it would make no difference."

John found rowing for more than one hour impossible, and this was at night. He questioned whether he had any willpower left. "By Jupiter, am I going to throw in the towel now, when I am practically there? I cried victory too soon and now must pay the price of my own foolishness."

If there was ever a Kafkaesque experience in a rowboat, Fairfax was having it. Like the character Josef K. in Kafka's classic novel *The Trial*, John F. was being confronted day after day with what looked by all appearances to be an irrational and absurd ocean. Whatever he did to take rational action for navigating toward Miami, it seemed to make his situation worse. His predicament was nonsensical, his effort to understand and control his world seriously futile. He had come away from his ITN interview feeling he was "the greatest man ever to go to sea," only to be thrown back into his cramped little world "bewildering, sick, and now thoroughly dejected at the way things were going." To make matters worse, he was incommunicado, having run out of petrol for his transmitter's generator after the long call he made the day before his rendezvous with the *Costa Grande*.

The nightmare continued. Soon after dawn on July 14, he wrote: "Again today I have gotten the surprise of my life. During the daylight hours of the 13th, I seem to have drifted 40 miles south. How could that be possible? There was no wind, and the water seemed absolutely dead. Am I going nuts? I can't believe it, but after checking and rechecking, I have to admit the facts. What the hell—am I going to circle round all over again?"

With continuing diarrhea he was feeling extremely weak. His morale had never been lower. "The only thing that keeps me going," John logged, "is a shred of willpower left over from somewhere. I must get to Miami under my own steam. I'll bloody well sink *Britannia* and go down with her before submitting to the indignity of a tow. So help me, I'm going to make it."

John knew he was also getting dangerously near to Cuba again— "far too near for comfort." Today, in 2023, his fear of Cuba may seem overblown. But in the 1960s, relations between Castro's communist, Soviet-supported Cuba and the United States, Britain, and their allies were extremely tense: complete trade embargoes, cutting off all diplomatic relations, the Bay of Pigs invasion, the Cuban missile crisis. Plus, Fairfax had some experience with Cubans back during his days in the Caribbean as a smuggler. "I sure had no inclination to present myself as target practice for some trigger-happy zealot," John was thinking. "I might be wrong, but it had been my sad experience that when my South American friends turned Communist, their personalities suffered from loss of even the most elementary sense of humor."

There was no doubt in John's mind that *Britannia* had fallen into the grip of an uncharted southerly current, whose strength "fluctuated wildly" but that was, nevertheless, "unmistakably real." The fact that they had drifted 40 miles in 12 hours, in no wind and calm waters, was just not something John could get himself to believe: "Far more credible was that on the morning of the 13th I had made a navigational error," perhaps because he had made only a 2-star fix, which was "the absolute minimum under the best circumstances" when taking a sextant reading from rowboat level and looking for the horizon. Thinking through that possible error, however, he concluded he just could not have made that big of an error: "If I made a mistake, how gross could it be? Ten, 15 miles—surely not more than 20? Even so, to make me drift 20 miles in 12 hours, it has to be some current!"

The next day, July 15, John did 30 miles, but without gaining latitude. His fix that evening showed him to be only 20 miles off Cuba, smack on the 80° west longitude line, directly north of the coastal village of Isabel de Sagua. *Britannia* could be "kissing Cuban soil" sometime in the next day and a half: "If the drift south doesn't stop, Fidel will be hearing from us."

It was a stunning, disheartening turn of events. Navigation around islands and coastlines was proving so much more complicated, could be so much more perverse, than moving across the open ocean, as counterintuitive as that might sound to the non-mariner. "This looks like the Canary Islands all over again, only in reverse," John snorted. "But if we beat that, we're bloody well going to beat this one." At least his diarrhea had stopped—"about time."

23

A Victory, After All

W here is John Fairfax? What in the world has happened to him?" In Florida, from Kay Largo to Palm Beach, speculation in newspapers and on radio and television was that Fairfax had likely been captured by Cuban patrols and was either in some dismal jail or sitting at Punto Cero, Castro's summer estate outside Havana, smoking a cigar. The men from ITN or the *Daily Sketch* could not tell them differently, nor could the few members of John's inner circle, which included Sylvia Cook, who had already arrived in Miami to greet him upon *Britannia*'s arrival.

Where John was and what he was doing on July 15, his 176th day, was somewhere in the Nicolas Channel, doing "backbreaking, truly hellish" rowing, going—he hoped—in the general direction of Cay Sal Bank, a large atoll between Cuba and the Florida Straits.

Not just his trip, but John himself—along with *Britannia*—almost came to an end shortly after nightfall. A big ship nearly ran them down—something he had feared might happen from the very start of his passage, back in the shipping lane off the coast of Africa.

"Unaccountably, I was deaf to the rumble of her engines and props until suddenly when I did hear it, it sounded as if an express train were bearing down on us, making me jump out of my seat, panic-stricken and dumbfounded." It is likely he was suffering from the same brain fog that had plagued Tom.

There was no time for him to do anything. He just grabbed on to the side of *Britannia* and held on like his life depended on it, which it might have.

It was pure luck—or the divine protection of Venus—that saved them. *Britannia* was lying not broadside to the oncoming ship, but head-on and a shade off center of the big ship's starboard bow. An instant before the freighter would have hit the rowboat, its bow displaced a huge mass of water, which pushed *Britannia* aside "like a matchstick." According to John, *Britannia* "reared as if she were about to jump out of the water, then rode down the slope, swirling, swamped—but safe." Only the extraordinary stability of Uffa Fox's design stopped *Britannia* from capsizing. A disaster—surely a mortal one—was averted. John did, in fact, credit his goddess for their salvation: "The sky seldom looked so beautiful, or the stars so bright, as they did when I blew a fervent kiss to Venus."

He also had reason to thank Venus the next day when apparently, with the help of overnight southeasterly winds lasting into the day, "we have finally managed to pull out of the trap." Morning found him off the southwest tip of Elbow Cay, a four-mile-long barrier island located in the northeastern Bahamas off the larger Abaco islands. From there John estimated it was only 120 miles to Miami.* "All we have to do is cross the Gulf Stream," cheered John, "and I think our position for doing so is about as good as any I could wish for."

As he was about to cross between the rocky shores of Elbow Cay and a smaller island and go out into the Gulf Stream, a Coast Guard seaplane flew over very low. As it waggled its wingtips, John raised his oars above his head and crossed them in the sign of victory, "mainly to show I was all right and needed no help."

A few hours later, the early afternoon, another plane buzzed *Britannia*. A beautiful Aero Commander 500S was carrying Martin Cowling, who

---

* On September 1, 2019, Elbow Cay took a direct hit from Category 5 Hurricane Dorian, with sustained winds of 185 MPH.

dropped five or six packages of "goodies," including some petrol for John's radio transmitter. Unfortunately, all but one of the packages burst open when hitting the sea, spilling their contents. John managed to grab a few items, most importantly some petrol, but most of the spilled stuff sank or floated way.

One thing John did retrieve was a polyethylene bag that had been packed by Sylvia; he knew that because it had a letter from her to him. Inside there was a bunch of bananas. Sylvia's letter said, among other things, that she hoped John would enjoy them. "It was terribly sweet of her," said John nicely, and then in his typically chauvinist manner added, "but only a woman could think of putting ripe bananas in a pack to be dropped at sea from an airplane! Everything, and I mean everything, in the polyethylene bag I recovered had to be extricated from a whitish, gluey mess of banana, condensed milk, pipe tobacco, broken bits of glass and—God almighty! Suntan oil!"

Its batteries halfway charged, his radio sparked to life again. But John was almost immediately sorry that it had. His associates in Miami (via London) told him to make for the lighthouse at Fowey Rocks. Its location was on Key Biscayne, an island south of Miami Beach that was connected to Miami by a causeway.

John was not about to accept such specific direction. His intention had become, by that point, to "land anywhere in Florida." He had had "my fill of fooling around" and told them so. However, they insisted, and John, riding the axis of the Gulf Stream at what was for *Britannia* an "exhilarating speed," was "too happy to argue" and eventually agreed. They also asked him to listen on his transistor to the news bulletins of Miami station WGBS. If there were any important messages for John, the station had agreed to relay them.

By the late evening of July 17, John could see a glow on the horizon that he knew had to be the reflection of Miami. But nature had one last punch to deliver. Sometime after midnight on July 18, the 179th day, a squall hit: "Rain poured down as it used to in the old times, and the wind came from the northwest, Force 5–6, for nearly two hours before going back to the southeast. . . . Of all places, from the northwest! What in the name of a thousand gods have I done to deserve this? Are they trying to push me back into the middle of the Florida Straits to ride the Gulf Stream forever? Defeat me when I am but hours from victory?" At one point, in his futility to keep good control of *Britannia*, "I closed my eyes and cried."

There was also the old peril of getting hit by a passing ship: "A big tanker—at least 50,000 tons of it—passed a few yards from us without seeing my flashlight signals." John mused: "The sea seems determined to pull a few dirty tricks out of her sleeve as a final attempt to beat us."

If so, it was one of the sea's weaker attempts for, after two hours, the squall ended as abruptly as it started. The sky cleared and the glow—it had to be the glow of Miami—was still there, in fact, considerably brighter than before.

It was going to be victory, after all.

There would be no premature celebration this time. But there also would be no more rowing. John was too exhausted to do anything but lash his flashlight to the gunwale with the beam pointed at the aft blister and crawl into his rathole, where he passed out as soon as his head touched the deck.

It was a few minutes after midnight, local time, July 19, a Saturday. Fairfax's 180th day—and his last day.

◆

John's first welcome to Florida and the USA was not exactly the illustrious tribute he had been imagining for the past two years. Waking him up at dawn from a deep sleep with shouts of "John! Hey, John, where are you" were two middle-aged pot-bellied men in a rusting fishing boat powered by an outboard motor, "with the strongest American accents I had ever heard in my life." Their boat, bound for Bimini, was even smaller than *Britannia*. Rousing from his sleep, John saw a jagged cluster of tall buildings dotting the skyline, which he figured to be about three miles away. Pointing in that direction, he asked his new friends if that was downtown Miami. "That's right, chum—that's Miami, all right! You've made it!"

John stared at their pitiful vessel and then moved his look back to *Britannia*. As much verbal vitriol as he had launched at his rowboat during the crossing, he knew she was magnificent. By seeing what those two Americans were up to and how they headed off so carelessly for their day of ocean fishing in such a ramshackle craft, he also got a fresh new perspective on the overall *sanity* of his own experience: "The sea was in a flat calm, but the sight of that battered, tiny excuse for a boat skimming the water in a cloud of spray, occasionally jumping up and down with fearsome thuds, cause me to shut my eyes in apprehension. One more thump and that thing was bound to disintegrate! It didn't and soon disappeared into the distance, leaving me with the conviction that those Americans were wonderfully stark, raving mad."

"Talk about nuts! I wouldn't have taken that thing across the Thames."

◆

After all the talk from the start about landing in Miami, the plan developed at the last minute in radio communications between John and his team on the ground in South Florida that a better spot for his arrival would be closer to Fort Lauderdale, some 30 miles to the north.

As it was a Saturday and local news reports had been following Fairfax's impending arrival for the past five or more days, crowds of people were on the beaches and lined up in their cars along Highway A1A to see him come in. By noon *Britannia* was surrounded by a small armada of sloops, ketches, power cruisers, and other yachts. Even the great British passenger liner *Queen Elizabeth*, which was passing nearby on its way out to sea, blew its whistle in honor of John and *Britannia*. "Hail *Britannia*, indeed," John wrote in his log. "We have conquered, and Florida is, at last, ours."

Also there, cozying up to *Britannia*, was an elegant 83-foot-long superyacht named the *Dragon Lady*. Aboard it was what John called his "reception committee," which was made up of all his friends and associates, including Martin Cowling and his wife, Morag; his agent, John Austin; John Crutchlow, a stringer for a British newspaper; plus a team of reporters and broadcasters from ITN and the *Daily Sketch* and an assortment of other journalists. Also on the *Dragon Lady*—though she hardly qualified as one herself—was "my adorable Sylvia." She couldn't wait to throw her arms around her "bronzed muscleman," though Martin Cowling (and even his wife) pretended around the press that "they did not know me" because it was "bad for John's image."

A few miles short of Fort Lauderdale, John spotted a beautiful beach that also appeared to be quite crowded with people waiting to see him and his rowboat. To him that looked like a great spot—with delightful smooth white sand and excellent public access. He headed toward it. It turned out to be Hollywood Beach.

About a half a mile from the beach, he pulled alongside *Dragon Lady* and asked to be towed in: "It was hot; I was tired and practically dying to lie down in a soft, comfortable bed." In John's mind there was "absolutely no need to go on" and yet, amid all the cheers, there were also catcalls. People, including his own friends and associates, rightfully wanted to see him row to the finish, not be given a tow. If he had rowed 4,500 miles, as the media was saying, shouldn't he row the last 2,640 feet? Everyone badly wanted—and totally expected—to see him actually beach *Britannia* all on his own—not with assistance.

This time John had no chance of giving to temptation. The crowds on the water, sands, docks, and sidewalks, and nearby hotels and restaurants at Hollywood Beach were just not going to let him.

He later called his row to shore the "the hardest, longest, most irritating half-mile" he had rowed the entire trip. To the press who asked him about it, his only printable comment in reply was "Bloody stupid." The landing occurred at 1:15 P.M. EDT. It was the first time that any human being had ever rowed solo across one of the world's oceans.

Actually, John did not row all the way to the beach. He stopped some 50 yards away, got out of *Britannia*, and walked in the rest of the way. Sylvia had been dropped off by the *Dragon Lady* so she could be there when he came ashore. "I ran out into the water in my dress and jumped into his arms. He picked me up and we had a big cuddle, and that was it," she remembers. "He was absolutely jubilant."

A drenched, happy Sylvia clinging to him, the conquering hero went straight up to the waiting reporters to shake their hands, accept their congratulations, and start answering their questions.

The very next day, July 20, 1969, at 3:17 P.M. EDT, the US spacecraft *Eagle*, as part of the Apollo 11 mission, with two astronauts on board (Neil Armstrong and Buzz Aldrin) and a third vigilant astronaut in lunar orbit (Michael Collins), made the world's first successful manned landing on the surface of the Moon. Behind their great space enterprise was a large, complex, and expensive team of over 400,000 Americans (and many non-Americans), in government, industry, and universities—including engineers, scientists, technicians, technology managers, business officers, public affairs staff, secretaries, and many others—that enabled the Apollo program to be so successful.

While those historic achievements were taking place on the weekend of July 19–20, British paratrooper Tom McClean, in his dory *Super Silver*, was still fighting his way across the North Atlantic, with a few hundred rough miles yet to row to get to the rocky Irish coast. To the very end Tom's commitment was very different from Fairfax's, as he would do nothing less than complete his journey totally unassisted. He would not be first across the Atlantic alone in a rowboat, but his uncompromising achievement may seem to posterity to merit the greater acclaim.

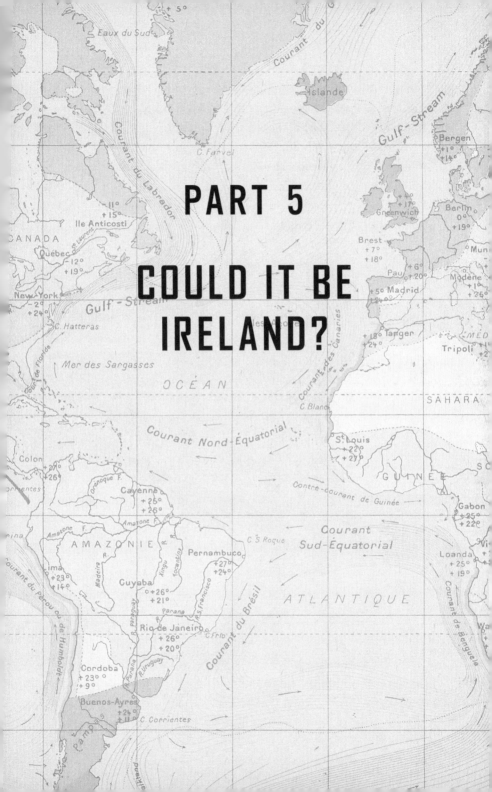

PART 5

COULD IT BE IRELAND?

24

A Goner

Meeting the SS *Hansa* left Tom with a most extraordinary bag of mixed emotions. He felt great, of course. He still felt that way the next morning, Tuesday, July 15: "I couldn't feel anything else, knowing how close I was to success." But he wanted to talk to someone: "You can get used to loneliness. But once it has been broken, no matter how briefly, that is when you begin to feel it."

Tom just wanted to talk to someone, anyone. He wanted to talk about the excitement of being only 600 miles from Ireland. He wanted to talk about how long those 600 miles would take to cover. In short, he wanted to talk about anything at all.

The funny thing is that when Tom had had the chance with the *Hansa* alongside, he'd almost waved them on their way, as if he'd wanted to get rid of them. Now that it was too late, he recalled he'd wanted a time check. He had also meant to ask them how the Moonshot was going; he hadn't heard a thing since his radio blinked out.

He also wanted to ask how John Fairfax was getting along.

As he thought of Fairfax, Tom's mind raced back to that day a few weeks back when he had chosen Fairfax as his "hate target," when he beamed in on John to boost his own "all-important competitive spirit." Tom still wanted to beat him. Although he seriously doubted he now would, he was still determined to try. But hate him? How can you hate a man who is taking the same chances as yourself? How could he hate a man who, for all he knew, might be dead?

If Fairfax was still at sea, it was just a matter of time and his luck holding out: "I hoped it would be for both of us. For me, at least, things were going very smoothly. The weather was still calm, the winds still westerly and still light. Life was as near perfect as it had been at any period during the trip."

Such a change in Tom's fortunes deserved a toast. Out came the rum bottle. He drank to his luck holding for the rest of the voyage. "Let it be smooth," he said, "and let it be quick."

And so it was, for a short while. The Atlantic behaved perfectly, as if apologizing for past mischief. And how gracious that ocean was in its apologies!

Light northerly winds on Wednesday were just what Tom wanted. He was aiming to drop to the south a little, and he couldn't have hoped for better conditions if he had been able to plan them. He rowed all day with a will and a spirit "as buoyant as a rubber duck in a bathtub."

Tom coasted along that day without a care in the world. Even the sun deigned to appear, albeit fleetingly, shyly peeping now and then from behind the white clouds overhead. Yet even without the sun it was a bright day. The sea was so clear and green that Tom would not have been surprised if he had discovered that it had emptied itself overnight and refilled with clean water.

For once the smell of the sea did not remind him of drying seaweed and rotting driftwood. For once it was the sort of aroma that had to be inhaled deeply, filling the lungs and recharging the body with sharp, fresh, and pure oxygen. He could taste the iodine, almost feel the ozone. In short, he had, at last, fallen in love with the sea. It had become a friend he felt could be trusted.

At nightfall the sea was once again a fairyland of phosphorous lights. It sparkled away as far as the eye could see. Each wave top was a miniature city at night with streetlamps and windows all ablaze, and as each little city disappeared there was another swooping gently upward to take its place.

Just ahead of him *Silver*'s bow threw up sparks of dainty fire as she slid through the night toward the east. Surrounded, as Tom was, by one of nature's most beautiful moments, it was easy to discount the tortured memories of the past few weeks as nothing more than a bad dream.

Small wonder that by Thursday, July 17, Tom found himself actually singing once again: "I think the cue for song came with the 12 jetliners that overflew me that day. I saw them all, some winging their way to the west, some winging in the same direction as *Silver* and me." How wonderful they looked as they threaded in and out of the clouds, leaving their vapor trails like brushstrokes across the patches of blue sky. No wonder he felt like singing. He could not remember all the lyrics, so he hopped from song to song, popping in the words where he could remember them and humming the rest. He ran through "Over the Sea to Skye," "Danny Boy," "Shoals of Herring," and "Wild Colonial Boy." He strung them all together as if they were one song. "I doubt very much if it sounded at all tuneful," Tom admitted, "for my voice sounds more like a cracked cup than anything else, but there was nobody to object and it made me feel great."

The last jet of the day flew by at about 6 P.M. Tom had been wondering about the passengers in those planes all day. Where were they going? Did he perhaps know any of the passengers? What would they have made of little *Silver* and of Tom, if they could see them? Maybe they were off on holiday, searching for sun and fun. Most of them would no doubt be heading for the nearest beach as soon as they reached their destination. Tom hoped that he would not land on a crowded holiday beach. There would be too much fuss and bother if they saw "a wild-looking scarecrow trundling out of nowhere."

If he had the choice he'd have *Silver* pitch up onto the shelf of a remote and deserted cove with just one little crofter's hut perched on the cliff above. But he had no choice. He would be more than happy to latch on to any piece of land that was kind enough to allow *Silver* to rest her weather-beaten boards.

Even when the sea began to build up, Tom's feeling of well-being was not interrupted. By 10 P.M. the sea was running high and heavy. He felt he would be facing another night of pumping sessions, and he was right: an hour later he was on the pumps. "It is all part of the job," he said to himself, undaunted. In between those sessions he managed to snatch a couple of catnaps, well alert now to the need to conserve his energy and plan ahead for moments of stress.

Sometime in the early morning—he didn't really know the time but later figured it must have been around 2:30 A.M.—Tom was in his shelter trying to snooze a little when it happened. In the very first second he thought he was "a goner." There was no time to think of anything but survival.

There was a long rumbling crash, and his little world literally turned upside down. Tom flung out his arms and feet in a frantic attempt to steady himself, but he was completely out of control. It happened so fast he didn't have time to figure out why, what, or how. All he knew was that he was experiencing "the most incredible sensation of spinning round" inside his shelter, rather like clothes in a washing machine.

Although he could not see in the darkness, he was most acutely conscious of being bumped around from floor to roof and from side to side, and all the while loose articles were falling about him, on him, and around him.

He had absolutely no idea of whether or not he turned once, twice, or more. The overall impression was that he was being spun round and round in a locked cupboard. Even as he was going round, the sea was pouring in until he was utterly covered. It came in with a rush that, in the confusion, he was sure that he had been swept overboard.

His eyes were shut and his cheeks extended to bursting point as he held his breath. It was so "fantastically eerie" to feel the water over his face and head, filling his ears and pressuring in between his clothes and body, that "panic was merely a hair's-breadth away." It was "the most chaotic and utterly bewildering moment of my life."

Tom's arms and legs were still thrashing about as he fought to find something tangible in a world gone suddenly mad. His hand struck the canvas covering of his shelter. Sodden as it was and weighted down by gallons of water, it seemed as heavy as lead. Tom wrestled with it, but did not seem able to shift it. "Christ, oh my Christ!" he pleaded. Those words ran through his brain over and over again in desperate, frantic repetition.

Tom discovered that his heavy folded inflatable life raft had jammed the free side of the canvas. The spinning had stopped by now, and he was able to wrench it to one side and wriggle out of the shelter. He thought he'd had it—he was still underwater. Then his head broke the surface.

There was just enough light for Tom to gaze with disbelieving eyes at the scene around him. *Silver* was completely filled with water. And yet, incredibly, defying all logic, she was still afloat. The fore and aft turtle decking was showing just above the water, but the gunwales were about six inches under the surface. Tom was sure that *Silver* was being helped up by the buoyancy components, stuffed with blocks of polystyrene, beneath that turtle decking.

He cursed at the top of his voice. He cursed the Atlantic, the weather, himself, and his stupidity in ever starting out on this blasted trip, in a long string of savage, bitter oaths. In some odd way the stream of filthy language propped him up—and he was badly in need of some support. It was a show of bravado, for he had been shaken to his very roots. Yet he had no time to be frightened. He had to survive or die.

He sat first on one gunwale amidships, pushing downward with all his weight until he could feel *Silver's* side dipping slightly, then he moved quickly to the other side to catch the boat at the start of the downward dip. He kept repeating this routine as quickly as he could until he had *Silver* fairly rocking from side to side.

Gradually his maneuvering got each gunwale in turn to break the surface. Then he cut the lashing on his bailing bucket and, as he continued to move from side to side, started heaving the water out five gallons at a time. Slowly, so slowly it seemed like forever, each gunwale began to rock higher and higher above the water. The progress was practically imperceptible, but eventually the water began to clear and the gunwales were no longer under the water.

By the time *Silver's* sides were about six inches above the surface level, Tom had managed to get rid of about a quarter of the water. Then he sat on his rowing seat and began bailing like hell. He had no recollection of time, but by the time he had gotten the water down to about six inches above the floorboards a new day was being born in the eastern sky.

It was Friday, July 18, and Tom was alive to see it. He actually pinched himself to make sure. Then he prayed his eternal thanks as he bailed some more. His feelings at the time can best be summed up in the words of John Millington Synge, the Irish dramatist, who in his book *The Aran Islands* wrote: "A man who is not afraid of the sea will soon be drowned, for he will be going out on a day he shouldn't. But we do be afraid of the sea, and we do only be drowned now and again."

Once *Silver*'s floorboards were clear of water, Tom turned to the pumps and worked at them nonstop until he heard the most welcome sound of sucking on air. He and his dory were back in business.

But what had caused the capsize? That was a question Tom had to answer. The sea had been rough, but *Silver* had survived worse. Checking out everything, he focused on his sea anchor: one of the lines to which it had been attached was broken at the swivel. It seemed that with the anchor off to one side of the boat, *Silver* had swung across the waves and had been rolled by a larger one than the others; perhaps Tom's weight on the side away from the wind and waves added to the process. Once flipped over and filled with water, the boat was like a rubber ball, the same weight as the sea—weightless, in fact—and unstable. *

By the time the boat was finally dry, Tom was in a state of virtual collapse, trembling with a combination of shock, effort, fear, and tiredness: "As I sat down for the first time in hours, I was panting for breath. My mouth lolled open and my eyes were closed as I sank back against the seat. I felt as weak as a wet paper handkerchief. Sweat poured from me in what was very nearly a cloud of steam. I was practically out for the count." Now that it was all over, he just wanted to lie down.

---

*   McClean's capsizing involved some complicated mechanics. The capsizing was caused by his boat's sea-anchor rope, which was attached to the bow, breaking away, leaving the secondary rope—which was tied from the gunwale midships to his sea anchor—lying underneath the boat and situated in the wrong way. When a large wave hit the side of the boat, it pushed the boat hard while, at the same time, the sea anchor started pulling it underneath, capsizing the boat.

But his condition got worse. Beginning with a slight tremble that set all of his muscles twitching, it rapidly developed into a fit of the shakes jerking his body from head to foot. Try as he would, the shakes could not be stopped.

"I don't know how long they lasted, but it seemed as if I would never be still again. I lay there letting my nerves play out their own little drama until I was finally somewhere near normal again." Then he opened his eyes. It was like coming out of a long, dark, narrow tunnel. His throat was parched and his tongue swollen to twice its size. "I wanted to gulp down pints, gallons of cold water. Instead, I forced myself to sip slowly, first rinsing out my mouth, gargling, and then allowing myself to swallow a couple mouthfuls."

Rowing was out of the question that morning. He had to rest, no matter what else happened. Yet he could not bring himself to crawl back into the shelter, which, for him, still represented a sort of "chamber of horrors." The memory of the night's frantic turmoil was far too vivid.

Still in the same clothes and sopping wet, he propped his head up on one of *Silver*'s wooden ribs, curled up on the boards between the shelter entrance and his rowing seat, and tried to sleep. It was a long, long time coming, but finally he drifted off in to a blessedly deep sleep.

Tom awoke in the dark early hours of Saturday morning to yet another blustery bout of weather. It was coming in from the southwest at about 25 MPH but caused him little discomfort. What really troubled him was the cold. The night air was eating into him. Tom was too exhausted to even think of covering himself, and he was shivering again, but this time he knew only the weather was to blame.

Another good sign was that he was ravenously hungry. He had not eaten a thing the day before. He had been without food or hot drink for nearly 24 hours.

Before he could prepare a meal, he had to find his flashlight. It must have been lost overboard in the capsizing, because Tom could not find it anywhere. Luckily the plastic box containing the spare had been firmly lashed down and, despite the fact that *Silver* had been totally swamped, the contents of the box were bone-dry.

He had to wait a little longer for his food. In the violence of the night before, his cooker had been uprooted from the deck. The holding screws had been torn out of the floorboards, and the cooker had been flung to one side and jammed under a gunwale. Tom heaved a sigh of relief to see it lying there, dented, rusting, but still all in one piece: "If that had gone overboard, I would have been in a pickle." He screwed it back to the deck.

He made himself a banquet meal. First course: porridge with honey. Second course: sardines. Main course: curry. Dessert: canned fruit, marmalade, biscuits with margarine, a couple of Mars bars. He washed it all down with a mug of instant coffee heavily laced with rum. Then to celebrate his deliverance, he knocked back a large neat rum.

With the aid of the flashlight, Tom began the anxious task of checking over *Silver*. She was okay. There were absolutely no signs of a leak anywhere in her tough little frame. Then came the tidying-up session. Everything that was loose and by some peculiar chance still in the boat was wiped and lashed down. Everything that was lashed down was untied and relashed.

After that came the job of ensuring that the sea anchor was properly and firmly secured. That was quite a job. Tom crawled up onto the turtle decking, tucked a foot around the samson post, and sprawled forward on his belly, wishing he had suction pads like a fly as *Silver* heaved about in the heavy swell.

He had to lean out and over the bow and tuck his head down as far as possible to get at the shackle bolt, which was fixed about one foot down the stem. He had to use both hands to unscrew the shackle. This was a laborious job, which, in the dark, had to be handled with extreme care, as Tom did not want to lose that shackle—it was the only one he had.

Finally, after having to stop several times to stretch cramped muscles, Tom had the shackle unshipped. The end of the broken sea anchor rope was spliced onto it, and then he screwed the shackle back into place. After that he bound the shackle and rope splice with wire in an effort to give it greater strength. The whole operation, which under normal circumstances would have taken no more than 20 minutes, took him close to an hour to complete. By the time he finished, he was aching with the strain of it from head to toe. "But that did not matter one jot," declares Tom. "I felt happier that the job was done—happier because I felt more secure."

There was one last chore: a check on what was lost overboard during the Thursday night upset. Strangely enough, it was not very much, but it was nevertheless "damned annoying." One two-gallon container of drinking water was missing. Gone were six days' supply of food, a kettle, and a cup. Also, somewhere in the sea were all Tom's charts except the main Atlantic one and one of the Irish coast.

Not too bad at all, considering the mess Tom had been in. He still had food for a couple more weeks. *Silver* was still all in one piece, and so was Tom. What more did he need? What more could he ask?

25

Blacksod Bay

I f Tom had known, it still would not have seemed possible that this Sunday, July 20, was the beginning of the last week of his Atlantic ordeal. Although by dead reckoning he made his position 52°N, 17°W—just about 400 miles to go—there was nothing tangible to go on. No sign of change. Nothing to give him a hint.

The leaden skies that had become so much a part of Tom's everyday world were still glowering down from all sides of the compass. There was nothing to be seen but the raging, turbulent seas—an all-too-frequent view in the past weeks. Tom was so much a part of it by then that it was well-nigh impossible to comprehend any impending change.

Winds building up to 40 MPH pounded into *Silver*, even now striving to drive her in the wrong direction. She was far too light to be bounced about so freely. More than half of Tom's food and water supplies were gone by this time, and he had maintained a fair level of water in her bilges to prevent her riding too high in these conditions.

Trying to trim her in that sort of weather was virtually impossible, but as rowing was out of the question, Tom was glad to have something else on which to concentrate. When he had managed to get her leveled off as much as he possibly could, he settled down to his Sunday letter.

It was from the quartermaster back at the SAS base in Hereford. He told Tom to "stick at it." Oh, brother, Tom thought, "I have no option!"

Tom and his dory stuck at it right through Monday's southeast winds and into a midday darkness of threatening black clouds, which seemed to be heralding the end of the world. By dawn on Tuesday the wind decided to befriend him once again. Slanting in from due west, it surged *Silver* along in gusts reaching to in excess of 30 MPH. Working out a rough position, Tom placed himself at about 14°20'W. "No more, it couldn't possibly be any more, than 240 miles left," Tom chanted to himself. The orphan who became a paratrooper spent several hours at the oars, urging *Silver* toward that unseen coast.

Under such conditions the days began to speed by. The westerlies stayed with him, coaxing him along, nursing him, ushering him; all the time they seemed to be whispering: "You're all right now. Do you hear? You're all right now. Don't worry anymore. It's nearly over."

Were they really being friendly? Or were they trying to lull him into a false sense of security? For it was not all plain sailing by a long shot yet.

From this point all the current flowed northward. Unless Tom took some counteraction and tried to drop south a little, he could be swept away, missing the Irish and the Scottish coasts altogether. "What a stupid ending that would be!" thought Tom, surprised that pondering the possibility didn't bother him much. At long last "my old cussedness was back at full strength" and he was feeling as "stubborn as a mule."

Thursday, July 24, dawned like a public holiday. The sun he'd yearned for and so seldom seen came out with a vengeance. By 11 A.M. the paintwork of his shelter's roof was too hot to touch. He wallowed in the sunshine "like a happy hippopotamus." He stripped to his swimming shorts, which he had washed down in a bucket half full of cold clear drinking water, and reveled in it all. He could feel new life surging through his body. "To blazes with them all!" he said out loud. When he thought of Shackleton and his men spending 18 months in the Antarctic, he felt ashamed of his "petty complaints" about two months in the Atlantic.

A sight of the Irish coast was all he needed to make the perfect day. "Where, or where, is that Irish coast?" he sang. Wherever it might be, Tom was utterly sure that he could smell it. And what a wonderful smell it was! As if to convince him, jet planes appeared about 20 miles to his north and still rising, as if they had not fully completed their takeoff. That surely could mean only one thing: Tom couldn't be too far off Shannon and its international airport. "Maybe it was my imagination," Tom ventured, "but I don't think I had ever rowed so well since I had left St. John's." Apart from meal breaks, he rowed steadily until 10 P.M. Then he slept like a baby.

The wind had swung against him by the morning of Friday, July 25. It came racing in from the southeast, absolutely the opposite of what Tom wanted and needed. Long before midday it built up to nearly 50 MPH and nixed any hope of rowing. In a desperate bid to keep *Silver* from being driven too far to the northwest, Tom heaved two sea anchors overboard and from then on could only hope they would do the trick.

As Tom and his dory sat it out, two fishing boats appeared ahead of them about two miles away. They obviously had not spotted *Silver* and were too far away for Tom to hail. Not for even a brief moment did Tom dicker with the idea of sending up a flare, but rather let the boats go without bothering them. "My decision not to attract their attention," Tom confesses, "was partly governed by doubts about my ability to resist an offer of a tow or help in some way." That had been the plan, and it had to be played out until the bitter end, or "I would betray myself."

Judging from the appearance of those fishing boats, Tom figured he had three or maybe four more days to go. It was time to get his "emergency landing kit" ready. Into an empty waterproof flare container went his logbooks, food rations, medical kit, some small hand flares, his camera, and some rolls of film that he had taken on the trip. Fate was due to be kinder than he imagined.

A steaming cup of coffee at 6:30 A.M. on Saturday, July 26, set him up for what he thought would be another uneventful day. It certainly began as such. Then things started to happen. At 9:30 he spotted a ship off his starboard beam. Again, he tied his red anorak to the telescopic radio aerial, but she failed to spot him. Shortly after 10 o'clock, far away to the east, a long, low, dark shadow appeared on the horizon.

"Could it be Ireland?"

Tom stared at it for quite a while, but it changed shape and then slowly disappeared. Disappointed, Tom told himself it must have been a cloud or smoke from a ship.

The next hour and a half passed without incident. There was very little wind, and Tom rowed steadily to the southeast. At 11:30 in the morning he threw a glance over his shoulder and instantly stopped rowing. It was land, land, land. Definitely land. Tom had just seen, positively beyond all doubt, land for the first time in over two months. This was not a shadow, cloud, or smoke. This was the real McCoy. It could not be too far away, either. Tom reckoned it would take eight hours to reach—just eight hours.

"I wanted to dance. Instead, I just yelled with delight."

For two more solid hours he rowed to the southeast. Over a second coffee, he took a look at his chart of the Irish coast. He was sure that he was off the Mullet Peninsula of County Mayo in northern Eire. But how far now? A quick estimation gave him ten miles to go. A mere ten miles after more than 2,000! Bursting with excitement, Tom rowed on and on. At 3:30 a fishing trawler called the *Ebba Victor* came steaming toward him.

Curious fishermen stared at Tom: "Are you all right?" they called.

"I'll say I'm all right! Never been better."

Tom pointed to the land and asked: "Is that Mullet?"

"It is," they replied.

Tom waved his thanks and turned back to his oars. He wondered if they would ask him if he needed a tow. That was the last thing he needed right now.

But they didn't.

Without another word they steamed off about their own business.

At five o'clock he stopped for tea and a reconsideration of his previous calculation. It was taking longer than he had thought it would to get to that coastline. His guess of eight hours and 10 miles had been off the beam. Half an hour later the wind was strengthening from the south and pushing him away from the land. Perhaps it was just as well at that moment. From what he could make out, the coast was treacherously rocky. White foam was boiling along the edge. It was a pretty hairy sight.

The wind started edging round to the west, setting Tom on a fair easterly course, but not head-on to land. It came at the right time, for it gave him a chance to look for a suitable landing spot—a sandy beach or a river entrance—before darkness fell.

By 10 P.M. Tom still had not spotted what he needed. By then he was four to five miles off a rocky headland, trying to slide downwind and aiming to get behind that rock mass, as he was sure he would at least find shelter from the weather there. He fought hard to make it, but the wind grew too strong for him.

He knew right then he was not going to make it that night. He certainly did not want to take the risk of landing in the dark. By 1 A.M. the wind and sea had swept him right past that headland. Tom grimly settled down to an all-night session at the oars, "paddling away to keep me off those damned rocks." The Atlantic was not going to let him get away from her too easily.

A little earlier he had spotted what he took to be the glow of a lighthouse beam. It had appeared faintly away to the northeast. As he headed *Silver*'s nose out to sea to maintain a safe distance from the land, he kept a lookout for that beam. He saw it sharp and clear at 2 A.M. But his work was still hard labor. The wind had swung round to the south and was running at about 30 MPH. He had no alternative but to keep *Silver* heading north. Within a short time, he could see that he was at the entrance of what appeared to be a large bay.

It was now or never. Tom headed into the center of the bay, rowing like mad to escape the pull of the wind. Slowly, grueling stroke after stroke, he edged in until he was getting some protection from the land. It was much easier from then on. Shortly after 3 A.M., dawn began to lighten the sky, and Tom made a beeline for the lighthouse. He knew he was off Mullet but did not know exactly where, and this was not the time to look, for the wind was almost dead astern of him.

Silver drew closer to the lighthouse with agonizing slowness, and by 4:30 it was light enough for Tom to see a great range of rocks beneath it. It was going to be a tricky, even dangerous, landing. "My main chance," Tom decided, "was to grab my landing kit ready to jump clear as *Silver* humped on to those rocks. I didn't want to see her smashed to pieces, but there was no alternative. I couldn't go on looking for a soft sandy beach forever. If I was going to get ashore it had to be now."

There were just a few yards to go when he made a quick check on his wristwatch. It was 5:30. Seconds later *Silver* hit with a juddering bump. The water was boiling beneath her, heaving her up. The noise of the surging surf was almost deafening. "I have to admit I did not spare any thoughts for *Silver*," Tom explains, more than a bit ashamed. "I was in the air, leaping towards the rocks, at almost the identical moment she struck."

"I staggered, bumped my right knee, and straightened out for the next incoming wave to knock me right off balance. The water carried me onward and upward to a higher ledge of the rock."

Tom wallowed about on his backside like a stranded porpoise, then scrambled back to his feet. Looking down, he could see *Silver* being pounded on the jagged edges of a stepped, slab-like formation of rocks. The dory had turned broadside on and was in imminent danger of being smashed.

Watching *Silver* surging back and forth on those rocks Tom felt as "guilty as hell." How could he let her down after all she had meant to him—after the magnificent performance she had given? "I just could not leave her there like that while I headed for safety," thought Tom, gritting his teeth. "We had come through it all together. We should be safe together."

Even as he thought about it, Tom moved toward her. He slung his landing kit on board and jumped into the water up to his chest: "I had to get *Silver* off those rocks." He got his shoulder under his boat's bow and manhandled her nose out of the water again. It took nearly an hour to do it. All the time they were both being pushed, pounded, and pummeled by the tormenting sea.

"But we made it. Once I had her bow on to the sea, I managed to hold her steady long enough to wait for the next receding wave, and as *Silver* began to slip out with it, I jumped aboard."

Frantically he unshipped a par of oars, slammed them into the rowlocks, and started to row like a mad. For nearly half an hour they moved so slightly that they were almost at a standstill. There were times when Tom's oars struck the rocks just beneath them. Finally, he got her moving. Tom pushed her out about 250 yards, past the split of rocky shore on which the lighthouse stood and around to the other side of the rocks.

Suddenly everything was dead calm. The force of the wind was almost nil as Tom rocked gently in the shelter of the rocks, staring at the scene ahead of him. He could not believe his eyes. Before him was a large sandy cove with hundreds of yards of gently shelving beach. The sand looked soft as a baby's bottom. "My dream landing had come true," Tom marveled. "There was not a soul in sight."

Slowly he walked with *Silver* to that marvelous, glorious, peaceful beach. He kept pulling until his dear dory nosed her way on to the sand. Tom did not stop until the boat was tucked tightly and safely.

They had made it.

It was 7 A.M. on Sunday, July 27, 1969.

Tom jumped out, heaved his vessel as far up on the beach as he could, and tied a rope around a large boulder. Then he stood and looked at *Silver*. For the first time he realized he was actually standing on dry land. His legs felt firm, not a sign of the wobbles he believed would hit him.

Looking at *Silver*, Tom was overwhelmed with pride and affection for her: "She had truly become a part of me."

Suddenly he realized she looked a bit of a mess: "I couldn't leave her like that exposed to the eyes of strangers." Tom pulled as much of the sea grass as he could off her hull, then scrubbed her down with an old brush. Jumping aboard, he squared away everything until she was as shipshape as possible, "until she could feel respectable."

As Tom headed for the roadway above the beach, he felt "lively as a cricket." Standing in the doorway of a nearby cottage was an elderly woman who had obviously seem him land on the beach. Tom waved at her and called out:

"Good morning, ma'am. I've just rowed the Atlantic. Can I take your photograph?"

The woman quite obviously thought the tattered, disheveled, scruffy man before her was "utterly mad." Edging back into her house, she shook her head no.

Before she disappeared, Tom asked, "Then can you please tell me where I am?"

The man who had just rowed the Atlantic solo caught her reply just before she closed her front door. She replied faintly: "Blacksod Bay, County Mayo."

Tom was home.

All he needed was sleep . . . deep, undisturbed sleep. But maybe he would have a drink first. Just 400 yards away he spotted the only pub in the tiny village.

He stepped out toward it. But not before looking back at *Silver*.

Epilogue

T echnically, according to the record books, John Fairfax won the race—to the extent it even was a race. He was the first to cross a complete span of the Atlantic, from continent to continent, solo in a rowboat.

Fairfax arrived on the beach at Hollywood, Florida, eight days before Tom McClean landed on the shore of Blacksod Bay on the northwest coast of Ireland. It didn't matter that Fairfax left the Canary Islands a full four months—117 days—earlier than McClean left Newfoundland. It also didn't matter that it took Fairfax 180 days to navigate the south-central Atlantic in *Britannia*, compared to only 70 days for McClean to make his way across the North Atlantic in *Super Silver*. Nor did it matter that Fairfax received significant in-voyage material assistance—meals, rations, cold drinks, hot showers, fuel, time off his boat, cheers, hand-shakes, a kiss from buxom Svetlana, and more—from several passing ships, 10 of them, whereas McClean made his entire trip completely unassisted. The only thing Tom ever took from anybody while at sea was a fix on his position.

The bottom line was that Fairfax made it across the ocean on July 19, 1969, while McClean did not make his landing until July 27, 1969. In the records of the Ocean Rowing Society International, Fairfax comes at the top of the list of "Historic Oceanrows: Solo." McClean's achievement stands on the line below.*

To the victor go the spoils, as the saying goes. The problem for Fairfax—and more so for second-place finisher McClean—was that there really were no rich spoils. There was no prize or reward for being the first across alone in a rowboat like there had been for aviator Charles Lindbergh (the $25,000 Orteig Prize, equivalent to $375,000 in 2020 dollars) when he became the first to fly the Atlantic nonstop. Besides the congratulatory telegram that John received from the Apollo 11 astronauts and a flurry of tabloid items mostly in British and Florida papers, news of Fairfax's achievement was largely subsumed by the comprehensive coverage given to the first Moon landing, a globally momentous event that occurred barely 24 hours after John came ashore on Hollywood Beach. That coverage continued virtually unabated through the iconic first step onto another world by Neil Armstrong on July 20 and for the next four days to the splashdown and safe return of the astronauts on July 24. To the extent that international media mentioned Fairfax's Atlantic row during that stretch of days, it did not register with most people as much more than a blip on the screen.

Not that the two men didn't enjoy what might be called some "niche celebrity"—the niche audience being the people visiting select British boat shows where Fairfax and McClean shook hands, exhibited their rowboats, gave presentations on their voyages, and, after their books were published in late 1969, signed autographed copies. The largest affair

---

*   *Historic Oceanrows* is the precise term used by the Ocean Rowing Society International (ORSI) to categorize the first 14 completed rows across an ocean. To qualify, the ocean rows had to have been undertaken without water makers, without satellite phones, and without the Global Positioning System (GPS), Emergency Position-Indicating Radio Beacon (EPIRB) stations, or life rafts. In the view of one ORSI director, the 14 Historic Oceanrows, all made before 1982, were "done under conditions that were not much different from the days of Columbus." Another ORSI veteran has described the rowers who made the 14 trips as "test pilots, but without a parachute." For transoceanic trips completed from 1982 on, the ORSI record book uses the categorization "Modern Day Oceanrows."

they attended together was the Earl's Court boat show held in London in January 1970. One of the major exhibits stood under a large banner Atlantic Rowers: West to East ►◄ East to West and the prows of *Super Silver* and *Britannia* facing each other almost nose to nose. Tom manned the stand for 10 long days, whereas John only stayed for two, which was long enough for him to meet "the most important people," such as Princess Margaret; her husband, Lord Snowden; and their two children David and Sarah Armstrong. Tom stayed for the entire show, but not because he enjoyed being with the crowds—in fact, "the more people I saw the more I wanted to escape from them." He remembers a couple of chaps dropping by who had stayed too long at the "famous Boat Show Guinness stand" who declared so everyone nearby could hear that "they did not believe that I had done the trip." Tom came to take that sort of declaration as a great compliment, knowing that Neil Armstrong and the other Apollo lunar astronauts got the same challenge for the rest of their lives.

The two men barely spoke to each other. One might have thought that they would have exchanged experiences, given what both had gone through. But there was none of that. They were hardly kindred spirits. Tom felt absolutely no feelings of resentment, but he sensed that Fairfax did, even though he had "won the race," almost as if Tom did not belong in his company. Basically, each man did what was needed for press and public and did not interact privately. In the photographs that were taken of the two men at the boat show, it seems that Fairfax and McClean always stood as far away from each other as they could.

One reason that Fairfax skipped out early on the Earl's Court boat show was that he was scheduled for an interview in the London studio of Thames Television. After arriving, John was surprised to find that he was being featured on an episode of the popular BBC biographical program *This Is Your Life*, which was based on the 1952 American show of the same title. Hosted by a 47-year-old Irish—but primarily British-employed—TV program host, Eamonn Andrews, the episode brought several people onto the stage to talk about their relationship to John and what they knew about John's adventurous life. The primary "surprise" friend who appeared on the show was John's mother, Mary. Also there for John was Sylvia Cook, now 29 years old. On air John told the British audience that he and Sylvia had just gotten engaged to be married. He also declared his intention to row the Pacific Ocean, across its widest expanse, from San Francisco to Australia, and that Sylvia would be joining him. When asked by the show host if she didn't fear making such a long and perilous trip, Sylvia said the 10,000-mile trip, which likely meant spending more than a year at sea, did not frighten her.

It surprised Fairfax himself that he decided to get back to ocean rowing so soon, let alone take on the vast Pacific. For the first few months after crossing the Atlantic, John felt that if he never rowed a boat again, it would be too soon. But things had not gone so well for him following giving the famous victory sign on the beach in Florida by crossing his oars high above his head making a big *V*. Certainly it had not been anything like a bonanza financially. Furthermore, not all of the press that he got was positive. The *Miami Herald* published one article, in fact, that positively angered him. It reported that, according to some unnamed experts, "it was impossible for a man to sink a knife underwater into a shark's belly, the skin of a shark being too rough for it." To John, that was tantamount to calling him a liar: "Naturally I did not take kindly to that and challenged them, or any other newspaper who thought along the same lines, to put up a shark of their own choice—except a Great White—anywhere, anytime, and I would fight it under the same conditions I had experienced at sea, for £10,000."

The *Miami Herald* did not reply, nor did John hear from any other taker. But John couldn't give it up. He made a deal with a South Florida film photographer to come with him to Nassau and record him underwater fighting a shark. The idea was then to have a short documentary made from the footage and make $10,000 from it. John thought his idea was "brilliant." Not only would he be getting back at the *Miami Herald*, but he would also get "all the money I needed to finance the Pacific row."

"I did my bit, off the Bahamas, killing an 8-foot 2-inch Hammerhead." More than that, John had "the great satisfaction" of towing the dead shark all the way back to Florida and dumping it on the doorstep of the *Miami Herald*'s headquarters "so that they could check that the shark had not been drugged and had no wounds other than those caused by my knife." Unhappily, the photographer's film did not turn out to be good enough for a documentary—that was John's assessment of the situation, anyway. Returning to London, he was able to sell the story of what he done to the *Sunday People*, a British tabloid Sunday newspaper, but the fee he got for it barely covered his expenses.

But John was never short of brilliant ideas: "Fight another shark and convince somebody to give me $10,000 to film another documentary." This time he wouldn't try to hawk his idea in South Florida; he would go to New York City. But with bills stacking up quickly, John didn't have the money for a New York trip. Somebody else would need to give him the means to go.

Once again Sylvia came to his rescue. She was already working hard to finish his book manuscript, which was already past due to the publisher. Now she approached an American firm, Great American Industries, a major international distributor of skin-diving equipment, and persuaded it to give John a one-way airline ticket to New York. There he would meet with company's advertising department to discuss his idea for his man-fighting-shark documentary. "Utterly broke," John also borrowed £50 from Sylvia's dad for the trip.

John got money from Great American Industries, but it was not a great deal. After hearing his pitch—John could be a very persuasive pitchman—the company agreed to lend him the money on the condition that if he didn't produce what the firm's executive council judged to be a good documentary, John would have to return all the money.

Once again, the Fairfax "shark movie" didn't get out of the water. Returning to Nassau, the boat he chartered broke down. The weather was foul, and not a single shark agreed to cooperate. The most exciting moment came when a tiny nurse shark, about four feet long, bit John in the arm. It would have been some dramatic footage if only John's photographer had been around at the time.

There appeared to be only one thing that he could do to impress people—and perhaps only one thing that could impress himself. That was again, to do something that had never been done. "How could I even *dream* of going through it all again?" John reflected. "Yet, dream I did and, as usual, I found that from dreams to actions, as far as I was concerned, was but one short step."

For Sylvia, it took a few more steps than that. First, she had to oversee John's money situation, which was much more red than black. She had to keep him out of the casinos as best she could. She had to assure John's literary agent, George Greenfield, that she would help him (Greenfield had John's power of attorney) untangle John's very tangled financial affairs. She had to make sure that Clare Allow, the boat builder, got paid. She had to arrange for the boat, *Britannia II*, to be shipped—free of charge (thanks to Holland America Line)—to San Francisco, which John insisted had to be the place where the trans-Pacific trip started because he loved the city so much. It was also her assignment to get a free trip for John and herself to San Francisco, which she arranged as a luxury cruise on the P&O Lines (the *Chusan*). Dozens of tasks, major and minor, fell to Sylvia, all while she was getting herself ready to go on a trip that would be her own wild adventure of a lifetime.

She loved John so dearly that there was never any doubt in Sylvia's mind that she would go with him, to the end of the earth if necessary. Her entire family thought it was crazy for her to go. Not just her mother and father disapproved; the strongest disapproval came from Sylvia's brother, who disliked John intensely. According to Sylvia, he thought "the whole project was suicidal" and "would do nothing that might possibly be construed as encouraging the escapade."

Nonetheless, her family came to San Francisco to see them off.

The date was April 26, 1971.

◆

The immediate aftermath of Tom McClean's Atlantic crossing of 1969 was, characteristically, in striking contrast to Fairfax's.

Not looking for any spotlight, after rowing the Atlantic, Tom almost immediately returned to the army in Hereford. He received a hero's welcome that was embarrassing to him: "I seemed to have become quite famous. I was made a freeman of the City of Hereford at a welcome-home ceremony attended by most of the members of the SAS stationed at Hereford at the time. I was also asked to give lectures at Rotary Clubs, but this was not really my idea of fun."

In his 1983 book *Rough Passage*, Tom titled the chapter on this part of his life "A Hunt for Home." It was exactly that. He'd had two homes in his life to this point: the orphanage and the army. After crossing the Atlantic, he was intent on finding a new home—a home in which he could build a rewarding and pleasing rest of his life.

He decided to leave the army. Numerous jobs in civilian life were being offered to him unsolicited, but none of them seemed right to him. He needed to give himself time to think out what he really wanted to do, so he thought he would head for the Venns' farm in Buckinghamshire, which during his teens had been as close to a real home as he'd ever had.

He never got to the Venns', but in his Cooper Mini car, he got just about everywhere else, especially if it was a remote location. First, he drove into North Wales, but finding it "too crowded," he headed upward into Scotland, never getting too far from its wild spectacular northwestern coast, well north of Glasgow. Tom was especially taken with the Isle of Mull, a tremendously beautiful island in the Inner Hebrides. One noteworthy feature of Mull for Tom was that it had a nice castle, Caisteal Dhubhairt in Scottish Gaelic, dating back to the 13th century, which was the seat of Clan Maclean. That made it worth a look even if Tom had not had the opportunity to get reacquainted with Lord Sir Charles Maclean (who happened to be Queen Elizabeth II's lord chamberlain), whom he had met at a Clan Maclean reunion in London a few years earlier.

After he had made friends with a few of the local people, word that Tom McClean, the Atlantic ocean rower, was in Mull was sent to Duart Castle, resulting in Tom getting a chance to stay there for a couple of nights. Furthermore, Lord Maclean asked one of his employees to show Tom around the magnificently diverse island, the second largest in the Inner Hebrides, with its colorful burghs, three other castles, mountainous core, 300 miles of coastline, vast moorlands, numerous scenic peninsulas, and surrounding small islands.

Seeing the Isle of Mull made concrete a notion that had been forming in Tom's mind for some time. "I decided to buy some land, as remote as possible, and build cabins on it so that all sorts of people could come along and use it as a base for expeditions, climbing, canoeing, or simply to get away from the rush of modern life."

In the meantime, other offers came Tom's way. One was to a buy a bar and restaurant. Another was to become part of "a one-off military operation abroad." Becoming a paid mercenary would have earned him a very respectable sum of money, and he did look into it back in London, where he found that a number of former Paras and ex-SAS troopers were involved. But he felt in his bones that his days as a soldier were over. Mercenary service was too insecure, covert, and risky for his liking. "I preferred to control my own life rather than have it controlled by secretive people who were obviously going to make more out of my skills than I was. It was time to stop being a solider and start trying to make an honest go of civilian life."

Tom went back north on his quest to find just the right tract of remote wilderness where he could build what he had come to call an "adventure centre." His heart was set on it, but the question was how to afford the land and the cost of building on it. He would need several thousand pounds, and he just didn't have it.

Determined, he called Lieutenant Colonel Sir Archibald David Stirling, the founder of the SAS, a legendary British soldier who had gone out of his way to congratulate Tom personally upon Tom's return to London following his Atlantic crossing. Tom told Colonel Stirling about his idea for an adventure center and asked David if he knew of any nice land for the purpose that might be available. Indeed, Stirling did. He told Tom that his cousin, Lord Lovat (Simon Christopher Joseph Fraser, the 15th Lord Lovat and head of Clan Fraser), who was a famous British commando in World War II, owned land in western Scotland that might suit Tom. As soon as Stirling ended the call with Tom, he called his cousin, and then phoned Tom right back. All was worked

out for Tom to come take a look. Like a shot Tom was off, heading to
Glasgow, onto Fort William, and then to the fishing port of Mallaig on
the west coast of the Highlands at the entrance to the Sound of Sleat.
Across the narrow channel lay the legendary Isle of Skye, the largest
and northernmost of the major islands in the Inner Hebrides, with its
dramatic mountain scenery.

Immediately Tom knew that he had found one of the last great wilderness paradises in the British Isles: incomparable scenic beauty, stunning
coastline, white sand beaches, rugged mountainous grandeur, few roads
(thus the need for boat transport), two of the deepest freshwater lakes (Loch
Morar and Loch Nevis) in the British Isles, enchanting islands such as the
Isle of Skye lying just off the coast, and fish and wildlife galore.

He couldn't wait to start exploring. He took the local ferry from
Mallaig to Inverie, on Loch Nevis, and then made a long walk, about
eight miles, until he reached Airor, on the coast overlooking the Sound
of Sleat and Isle of Skye. There he borrowed a small Seagull outboard
and motored a further five miles around the coast until he found a man,
a doctor from Mallaig on holiday, who had been recommended to Tom
for knowing many of the landowners throughout the Morar and Nevis
regions.

The doctor (whose unlikely name was Dr. Donald Duck) was friendly
enough but not at all enthusiastic about Tom's idea of setting up an
adventure center. Apparently there had been such a place established a
few years earlier on the Camusrory Estate, at the head of Loch Nevis,
run primarily for children. The doctor admitted that it had been built
in a windswept, rain-beaten spot that caught every piece of weather
that passed up and down the loch, hardly the ideal place for a bunch of
town children used to parks, pavements, and considerable comforts. It
had failed miserably and been abandoned. All the locals knew about the
failure and so were "guarded against another newcomer to the area who
probably did not appreciate just how bad things could be up there." If
that venture had failed, even with the benefit of significant local financial
backing, which it had been, how could Tom expect to make a go of it,
an outsider, all on his own?

Hearing all the reasons why an adventure center would not work made Tom even more determined to build and operate one successfully. "Who dares wins," after all. "If someone says that something cannot be done," says Tom, "then my attitude was, and still is, to turn around and have a damned good try." Furthermore, he knew that people in remote parts of a country were naturally careful and canny, especially when it came to arrival of new ideas from outsiders. Tom had the type of personality that knew instinctively how to interact with them: quietly, politely, and with respect. But he also knew that positive change through hard work and solid opportunity was ultimately welcome everywhere, especially "if I paid my bills on time and didn't push my southern accent!"

He continued scouting the region, particularly on the two shores of Loch Nevis and the north shore of Loch Morar to Nevis's south. One thing that he liked about Loch Morar was that, like Loch Ness, it had its own monster, Morag. After Nessie, Morag was the most famous of Scotland's legendary monsters, with sightings reported as far back as 1887 (and many of them since then involving multiple witnesses). Having a monster in the loch could draw more campers to his adventure center, Tom thought.

In the end Tom chose "a derelict place" on the south shore of Loch Nevis. Called Ardintigh, the property was situated on a bay directly opposite the Knoydart Estate, a 125,270-acre protected national scenic area on a peninsula that dipped into Loch Nevis from the north. To the Scots, Knoydart formed the northern part of what traditionally was known as Na Garbh Chriochan, or the Rough Bounds, due to its remoteness and harsh terrain. It was accessible only by boat or by a 16-mile walk through rough country, which gave Knoydart Estate a justifiable claim to being "Britain's last wilderness." Being an area already popular with hill walkers, mountaineers, sailors, and wildlife enthusiasts, having Knoydart so close by fit Tom's purposes perfectly.

Yet, Ardintigh needed a great deal of work even to make it a minimally suitable spot for an adventure center. When Tom first saw it, there was the remains of a field, a broken-down croft with a Rowan tree growing within the ruined building and a small stone beach. To look the place over, even though it was the month of December and very cold, Tom stayed in a tent for a few days. It was not long before news got around Nevis and Morar that "a mad Irishman" had spent his Christmas camping out in Ardintigh. It certainly fit the bill for being remote. Mallaig and Morar could be easily reached by roadway or rail, but from there on it was tough going. There were no roads to Ardintigh Bay. If there were to be an adventure camp there, it would be accessible only by boat from Mallaig or on foot by walking for two to three hours alongside Loch Morar. Tom saw the location as an advantage, not a disadvantage, because it would attract truly dedicated outdoors folk.

In early 1971 he purchased the rights from the Lovat Estate to use the land at Ardintigh for his adventure center. He bought a boat ("an 18-foot conventional clinker-built, good and solid"), which he named *Moby Dick*, and, while living in a tent, began the multitude of backbreaking labors needed to ready the place, starting with the task of building of a septic tank big enough to serve a camp of up to 24 people. Several months later came the building of a lodge—made of stone and timber and located practically on the beach—comprised of a main building, fully equipped kitchen, a dining/recreation room, two separate toilet/shower rooms, and a drying room for "wet kit" (combs, razors, deodorants, and the like) followed by the assembly of bunkhouses for 24 people in five wooden huts ("prefabricated timber cabins"). Tom also built a toilet block and designed a simple hydroelectric power system, which provided limited electricity in the evenings by harnessing the power from Ardintigh burn. For some of the work he received help from a handful of local people "who had by now become friends and realized I meant business" as well as from the SAS carpenter, Bernie Franks, who had helped him build and modify *Silver* at Hereford. Also helping occasionally on odd jobs were a few units of the Paras and SAS, who "came in small groups and camped rough in the huts, cooking for themselves on open fires and living a very rugged, open-air life."

It took until the summer of 1973 before Ardintigh Highland Outdoor Centre was ready for its first group of campers. Early on, Tom catered to various British Army and Territorial Army units who were looking to "Retreat and Recharge!" For them, Tom built what he called the "Cave," a rectangular structure made of dry-stone walls and a flat sloping roof in which he placed government-surplus two-tiered bunks and mattresses and made accommodation for 18 men. This—and the fact that groups of soldiers had helped with the construction of the Cave and a couple other facilities at Armintigh—gave some of the more cynical locals the mistaken impression that Tom had used the army "to feather my nest," when in fact Tom had paid every penny of the cost of building the entirety of the camp. Nor was Tom's place ever used as a training center for military activities—another local rumor. There were no weapons allowed at the camp (other than his own licensed hunting rifle), and all the activities were "leisure-oriented"—climbing, abseiling, canoeing, swimming, anything that the wild countryside could offer. According to Tom, "The decision as to what the army did at Ardintigh always rested with themselves, their instructors, or the officers in charge."

Ardintigh continued to attract a number of military and ex-military groups, including the Royal Irish Rangers, but as word spread, the camp, though its conditions stayed very spartan, welcomed corporate groups as well as various youth and adult organizations, including school and scout troops. Needing a bigger boat for bringing stores and campers coming in through Mallaig (as most did), Tom bought the *Sea Otter*, a 26-foot wooden clinker built with an inboard two-cylinder diesel engine. For the use of his customers he also needed a small fleet of canoes. He found a dealer in Aviemore, southeast of Inverness, who specialized in boats for shooting the rapids in the Scottish and Welsh rivers. Tom called them "the battleships," they were so strong.

It took a while but, by the late 1970s, his Ardintigh operation became a staple of the Western Highlands. "The Highlanders take a year or two, maybe longer, to accept a newcomer," Tom explains, "but once they have accepted you as one of their own, they are the kindest, warmest friends you could ever hope to meet. They had every reason to think I was just another madman on the run from the real world, but as the adventure center grew, I began to notice passing boats slow a little as they looked at the huts, the lodge, the clearing on the beach."*

Although Tom doesn't make too much of it, another factor that surely broke the ice for him with the local folk was the fact that this particular McClean had rowed across the Atlantic alone, though many of them likely thought he was crazy to have done it. Virtually everyone living on the west coast of Scotland was connected with the sea, be they fishermen or ferry crew, or in fish marketing or marine engineering. Of course, Tom said little or nothing to any of them about his historic voyage and was genuinely embarrassed when the word spread around the local villages that they had an epic oarsman in their midst.

That made him that much more likable to the Highlanders and Islanders. They were happy to add him to the list of legendary Macleans.

Once Tom got his Highland Outdoor Centre "chugging along at full steam," he couldn't stop his mind from turning toward other adventures into far horizons.

One of his most ambitious—again, many would say crazy—ideas was to climb Mount Everest and, not surprisingly, to do it all on his own—no team, no guide, no Sherpa. Thinking out a plan, Tom started designing what he called his "Moby house box." These were boxes six feet long, three feet wide, and three feet high, which could be dropped on Mount Everest at various heights, ten of them, one at every 1,000 feet from a base camp at 12,000 feet. In the boxes would be stores, oxygen, spare climbing gear and clothing, and a relay radio. He thought he could live in one of the boxes until the weather allowed him to move on to the next one. He bought plans and maps of the mountain, read books about it,

---

*   Furthermore, Clann MhicIllEathain was Scottish Gaelic. Clan Maclean was not only a Highlands Scottish clan, it was one of the oldest clans in the Highlands, owning large tracts of land in Argyll as well as the Inner Hebrides. Many early Macleans were legendary for their honor, strength, and courage in battle. Some of them, it is written, fought in support of Robert the Bruce in support of Scottish independence at the Battle of Bannockburn in 1314; in 1513, during the Anglo-Scottish Wars, Lachlan Maclean of Duart was killed—as was Scottish king James IV—at the Battle of Flodden.

and wrote letters to a couple of veteran British climbers. He was "really keen to give it a try" but, after beginning training in the winter on the mountains around Ardintigh, he learned that he couldn't just go climb the world's most famous mountain. There was a waiting list of people wanting to climb Everest. He would have to register his climb with the Nepalese government and then, if the authorities approved his plan, wait for a slot. Tom was not the sort of person to join a queue to climb a mountain. He gave up the idea.

What about the South Pole? he thought. Tom had never been much of a reader but as a young soldier he had read a book about the Antarctic expeditions of Robert Falcon Scott (1901–1904 and 1910–1913); Tom was especially taken by the story of Scott's second expedition in which he and his companions died in their attempt to beat the Norwegian explorer Roald Amundsen to the Pole (which Amundsen achieved in January 1912). He grew even more enamored by Sir Ernest Shackleton, reading Shackleton's autobiographical account of the truly remarkable story of his Antarctic expedition of 1914–1916, in which his ship *Endurance*, with all its crew and sledge dogs, became hopelessly trapped in ice floes for nine months, their ship eventually being crushed by the ice, and Shackleton and his crew of 27 men doggedly finding ways through sheer determination to survive for 497 days, eventually—heroically—managing rescue for all of the men (but unfortunately for none of the dogs).

For Tom, the South Pole became a serious destination. He began to make detailed lists of equipment for the journey. He researched the types of dogs he would want to pull his sledge, a lightweight "Moby house sledge" of his own design and construction. He studied maps and charts of the Antarctic. He knew with the right planning he could do it: "I wanted a success, not a heroic failure." He studied the problems of navigation on the southern icecap that covered the Antarctic land mass, which were considerable. He wrote to the British Antarctic Survey headquarters at Cambridge, explaining his plan and asking for advice. "They were not at all pleased," Tom remembers, "giving me the firm impression that not only did they operate in the Antarctic, but they had invented it and owned it." The BAS "did not welcome solitary explorers roving around their patch, pointing out that if I became stuck in the middle of nowhere they would be the ones who would have to come and get me out."

Tom was not the argumentative type—he was more the type to do what he wanted, the way he wanted, or he would not do it at all. "I regarded the trip to the Antarctic in the same way as the transatlantic row," Tom explains. "If I got myself into trouble, I would have to get myself out. If I disappeared, I wouldn't expect anyone to go out of his way to spend time and money looking for me."

He was also not the type to give up easily. Having been rebuffed by the British Antarctic Survey, he spoke to David Stirling, the SAS founder, who contacted the Americans. They had a research station on McMurdo Sound at the south tip of Ross Island (about 810 miles from the South Pole) but could not help. No one wanted to accept a lone explorer.

Tom had spent almost two years trying to mount, first, his solo climb of Mount Everest and, second, his expedition to the South Pole. Neither worked out. Looking for another outlet for his restless spirit, he began to paint, mostly landscapes. Never in his life had he done anything so artistic or instinctual. But he came to love it. It tapped new sources of awareness, vision, and feeling. "I became very inward looking, introspective," reflects Tom. "Painting was a way of getting out of myself." Most of his works were wild seascapes taken from around Mallaig, or scenes from his imagination—the Antarctic, the oceans. He painted one picture of the small boat, the *James Caird*, that Shackleton and four select men sailed (and rowed) from Elephant Island in the South Shetlands to South Georgia, a tiny dot of land in a vast and hostile cold ocean, 300 miles away, to get help from a whaling station for the rest of the crew of *Endurance*, which had been stranded in ice and abandoned in the Weddell Sea.

Painting, too, was an adventure—and good therapy for all the time he spent alone at Ardintigh.

That particular "alone-ness" was soon to end, however. In 1976 he married a pretty young Yorkshire woman named Jill Stacey. The two had first met in the spring of 1974: Jill was on holiday in Arisaig, a small village on the west coast of the Highlands south of Loch Morar, and Tom was visiting friends in the community. Their meeting was pure happenstance: "As I drove towards the village I saw a girl walking along the road in the direction I was driving. I stopped, offered her a lift, and began talking to her." That night they went out for a drink: "She had a level head on her shoulders, talked a great deal of sense and had a wonderful sense of humor. I asked her for her home address, told her that I would call for her when next in England."

For the time being, that was the end of it. But Tom kept thinking about Miss Jill Stacey and the fact that she lived in Yorkshire. The Venn family farm where he spent such happy times as a teenager was in Buckinghamshire, and they were due for a visit from him. He did visit the Venns, but first he found Jill's home, near Rotherham, and knocked on the door. Over the next eight months they saw each other as much as they could, either in England or Scotland. In the spring of 1975, Tom proposed and Jill accepted. They married in October 1976. Jill joined Tom happily at Ardintigh and became a great partner in business and in life. Marriage also helped to further crack the ice with the local folk: "The solitary madman up the loch had now acquired a pretty girl whom they immediately took to. After our wedding in Yorkshire we had another reception in Inverie, during which the doors were really thrown open in the most Highland of ways. The Knoydart Estate gave a party for us at the village hall with a band from Fort William: Fergie Macdonald and the Highland Band. It was a great *ceilidh* with everyone from the oldest inhabitant to the smallest children dancing the night away. People came from far and wide, some from far across the loch by boat."

The angry boy from the orphanage had found love, a home, an altogether happy life—one soon to be blessed with two sons, James and Ryan, and two granddaughters, Grace and Daisy.

Yet adventure, for Tom McClean, was part of life, coming in a wide variety of ways, but which, like his Atlantic crossing and Highland Outdoor Centre, required solid planning. As Tom would often say, "Risk has no real part in adventure. Planning has. Racing drivers may be regarded by some as adventurers, and perhaps they are, but they face risk, unavoidable risk sometimes, and that, to me, is unacceptable." A debatable proposition coming from a man that had had no experience with ocean rowing, deciding, in an instant, almost on a dare, to row a boat across the Atlantic, alone.

Tom recognized that in that essential respect perhaps he was, indeed, a madman. If not Mount Everest or the South Pole, there was always the Atlantic, right there in his side yard. Maybe there was some other sort of ocean voyage to make.

He started thinking about the possibility. But now there was also Jill to consider, and their infant child, and a second one on the way around Christmastime 1981. "I told Jill of my plan, but she was not too enthusiastic. She seemed to think it was just another hare-brained scheme which would eventually fold up and disappear." If it didn't do that, if it materialized, Tom was sure Jill would come around and support him.

He wasn't at all sure about the people of the Western Highlands living around him. He wasn't about to tell any of them that the little madman in their midst might soon be crossing the ocean again.

Alone.

John Fairfax

Once was not enough for Tom McClean or John Fairfax. Mountain climbers don't stop after reaching one summit. Marathon runners don't run just one race. Skydivers don't jump just out of one airplane. And ocean rowers and sailors who have crossed oceans and set or broken records doing it typically don't call it quits after one voyage. The sort of adventurous, risk-taking, goal-oriented men and women who are driven to push their ambitions and capacities to the limit and beyond are continually on the lookout for their next great challenge.

Tom called it "getting itchy feet." John, typically, was more bombastic: "By the very nature of my life I am, of necessity, a gambler. I'm after a battle with nature, primitive and raw."

In April 1972, John Fairfax and his fiancé, Sylvia Cook, became the first people to row across the Pacific.

In making the trip, Sylvia became the first woman to row any ocean.

Their crossing began in San Francisco and ended on Hayman Island, Australia, off the coast of Queensland, an 8,000-mile trip.

The trip took 361 days—from April 26, 1971, to April 22, 1972—almost a full year, with "brief" halts at Ensenada on Mexico's Baja Peninsula (June 3–July 31, 1971); Teraina, aka Washington Island (October 6–November 12, 1971), a coral atoll a few hundred miles south of the Hawaiian Islands; and the tiny island of Onotoa (January 9–February 7, 1972), an atoll in the Gilbert Islands.

Their boat, *Britannia II*, was 36 feet long and five feet abeam—compared to 25 feet long and four foot nine inches for *Britannia I*. Both were designed by Uffa Fox and built at Lallows boatyard at Cowes. Compared to *Britannia I*, *Britannia II* appeared quite streamlined but also looked so large that it would be hard to row. In fact, the boat proved to be easy to row despite its size and solidity.

A meat grinder of near disaster, their voyage faced storms, shipwrecks (off Onotoa), and, most terrifying of all, a shark bite (while spearfishing in the Coral Sea), which took a big chunk of John's arm, nearly killing him.

For much of their journey, the ocean was very rough. At one point, their boat's rudder was snapped clean off. *Britannia II* was frequently swamped. At night there were times when John and Sylvia did not know if their boat was the right way or wrong way up.

In the closing days of their trip, they were caught off the northeastern coast of Australia (Queensland) in Severe Tropical Cyclone Emily. The couple lashed themselves to their boat until the storm subsided. Unreachable by radio for a time, they were presumed lost. Eight lives were lost at sea during the cyclone.

Their Pacific crossing attracted even more publicity and media attention than John's Atlantic crossing in 1969. A major stimulant for the coverage was the fact—titillating for society and culture in the early 1970s—that a yet-unmarried attractive young man and pretty young divorcée were traveling across the ocean together, on a small boat, alone for months at a time, and were surely having sex in their small boat.

Their Pacific crossing inspired the memoir *Oars Across the Pacific*, coauthored by Fairfax and Cook and published in 1972 by John Farquharson Limited in Britain and in 1973 by W. W. Norton & Company in the United States.

In the mid-1970s, Fairfax went back to the Pacific, again with Sylvia, to try to salvage a cache of lead ingots from a downed ship they had spied on their crossing. The plan proved unworkable and was not attempted.

John and Sylvia never married. Their relationship became more and more volatile, then distant. They ended their relationship in the late 1970s.

John never returned to sea. Nor did Sylvia.

In the 1980s John moved to the Miami Beach area and married Tiffany Alisha, a professional astrologer. In 1992, after losing their house to the catastrophic winds accompanying Hurricane Andrew, the couple moved to Henderson, Nevada, near Las Vegas.

John became a professional gambler, spending at least five nights a week in the Vegas casinos. His preferred game in his younger years had been craps but was now baccarat, the tension-filled card game also favored by James Bond.

John died at his home in Nevada of an apparent heart attack on February 8, 2012. His wife, Tiffany, was his only immediate survivor.

Over 50 obituaries appeared internationally announcing Fairfax's death and remembering his life, including notices and stories in the *Times, Daily Mail, Guardian, New York Times, Wall Street Journal, Los Angeles Times, Miami Herald, Philadelphia Inquirer, Chicago Sun-Times, Village Voice*, and *Sydney Morning Herald*, and *Brisbane Times*. News and feature stories about John were released by Reuters, Associated Press, United Press International, ABC News, Sky News Australia, Turkish Press, among others. Typical of many of the published stories was the one that appeared in the American news aggregation website *Newser*; it was titled "One of World's Most Interesting Men Is Dead: John Fairfax, 74, Had a Resume That Almost Defies Belief."

Sylvia Cook later married and had a son. She spent the rest of her life in the Surrey area, near London, becoming a talented upholsterer who worked part-time at a branch of B&Q, a British multinational home improvement retailing company. When asked, she has politely told reporters that she remained a close friend of Fairfax right up to the time of his death.

To celebrate the 50th anniversary of Fairfax's Atlantic crossing, the City of Hollywood, Florida, sponsored a reenactment of Fairfax's landing on Hollywood Beach, staging it on July 20, 2019, though Fairfax had actually arrived on the beach on July 19. (July 20 was a better day for the public celebration, as it was a Saturday. Also, July 20 was being celebrated as the 50th anniversary of the Apollo 11 Moon landing.) The city installed a plaque commemorating Fairfax's landing at its community center on the beach at Garfield Street and presented John's widow, Tiffany, a key to the city. To local reporters that day, Tiffany Fairfax said about John: "Not only was he a super-achiever, a superman, but he was my king. He was the kindest, most generous, sweetest man you could possibly meet (and) romantic in every way. He wasn't after it for money or fame or anything like that. It was personal."

Also present at the anniversary event was a young film producer, John Goodrich, who announced his intention of making a feature film based on John's extraordinary life. "We're in very active development," Goodrich told the press. "John's legacy was unlike any other. There will not be another man on this Earth like him." According to IMDb in 2023, the project was still in development.

POSTSCRIPT

Tom McClean

n the summer of 1982, during Britain's National Maritime Year, Tom McClean set the world record for the smallest boat to ever cross the Atlantic. Called *Giltspur* (named after the British packaging and transportation company sponsoring the trip), his tiny sloop measured a mere 118 inches (3 meters) long. Tom built the sailboat with marine plywood on oak frames and nylon sheathing over the hull; some who saw it cynically remarked "it's a raft, really." Equipped with four radios, a small outboard emergency motor, and 60 days of food and water, *Giltspur* was incredibly heavy, weighing in at about a ton. As the food and freshwater were consumed, McClean replaced their weight by taking on seawater ballast. With nearly all the ship's weight below the floorboards, it was nearly impossible for the craft to capsize. The entire length of the short boat was cabin, with just a small hatch at the stern where Tom could stand to tend the sails. Space inside the boat—to live, eat, and sleep—was extremely tight: an area only 24 inches wide by 42 inches long and 18 inches high. As in 1969, Tom navigated only with a sextant. The trip, leaving once again from St. John's, Newfoundland, on June 22, and landing in Falmouth, on the south of Cornwall, England, on August 15, took 54 days. This was 16 days less than when Tom rowed transatlantic in *Super Silver* in 1969, but this time the 3,000-mile journey confronted truly grueling and ferocious conditions, including a full Atlantic gale and significant other storms, all with high waves, some as high as 60 feet.

Unfortunately, the record that Tom set in August 1982 for the smallest boat ever to cross the Atlantic was snatched away from him just three weeks later when an American sailor, Bill Dunlop, sailed from Maine to Falmouth in a sailboat, *Wind's Will*, a mere eight inches shorter. Dunlop actually left on June 13, nine days earlier than McClean, but did not finish his crossing until August 30, 15 days later.

At the next London Boat Show at Earl's Court, in January 1983, McClean and Dunlop met for the first time. At a friendly meeting, the two men compared notes on their trips. Of course, both checked out each other's sloops, which had been put alongside each other as a special Atlantic sailing exhibit. Seeing firsthand how Dunlop's boat was eight inches shorter than *Giltspur*, which gave him the record for shortest boat to cross the Atlantic, Tom got an idea, which for the time being he kept to himself: "Suppose I saw nine inches off the stern of *Giltspur*, making her one inch shorter than *Wind's Will*, and do the voyage again. That would get the record back for Britain, but it had to be a secret in case some other sailor, or even Bill himself, had it in mind to do something similar. Anyway, no alterations could be made until the London Boat Show was over because they wanted the boat as she had been for the voyage."

For Tom, there really was no "supposing" about it. In fact, taking no chances, he chain-sawed a bit more than two feet off *Giltspur*, making her only 93 inches long. Again, he shipped the boat to Newfoundland and in the summer of 1983 crossed the Atlantic all over again. Naturally, his journey—3,360 miles in 62 days and 10 hours—had its share of danger and adventure. This time he headed for Portugal. His mast and steering snapped off in the Bay of Biscay during an electric thunderstorm. Ignoring people on the radio telling him to give up, Tom overlapped the mast and tied it together, shortened the sails, cut them up, and floated in the last 400 miles. By the time he drifted into the estuary of the Rio Douro and on into the port city of Porto (aka Oporto), Tom had lost three stone—42 pounds—and was virtually out of food and water. His record with *Giltspur II* as the smallest boat ever to cross the Atlantic still stands.

(It deserves mention that Bill Dunlop disappeared in the South Pacific in his tiny nine-foot sailboat in 1984, never to been or heard from again. The native of Mechanic Falls, Maine, was 41 years old when he vanished.)

One might think that McClean could do nothing "madder" than crossing the ocean solo—three times (to this point)—twice in boats that were not even as long as many of the marble-topped islands found in today's modern kitchens. But the type of brilliant calculated madness exemplified by Tom knows no bounds.

In the early summer of 1985, Tom spent 40 days living alone on a dot on the map known as Rockall, a pillar of granite rock sticking out of the Atlantic a couple of hundred miles west of the Hebrides. Critics called Tom's enterprise "a self-directed and largely fruitless attempt to assert Britain's territorial claim to the islet." The United Kingdom had claimed Rockall in 1955 and incorporated it as a part of Scotland in 1972. However, three nearby countries—Ireland, Iceland, and Denmark—did not recognize the UK's right to Rockall, citing the United Nations Convention on the Law of the Sea, which stated that "rocks which cannot sustain human habitation or economic life of their own shall have no exclusive economic zone or continental shelf." Given the controversy, McClean sought to establish that Rockall could, in fact, sustain habitation, which thereby would justify Britain's claim not just to Rockall but, more importantly, to an "exclusive economic zone" whose "special rights" included use of that zone's surrounding marine resources, including energy production from water and wind. Tom's plan was to get himself to Rockall—whose closest inhabited neighbor of any sort was North Uist, an island in Scotland's Outer Hebrides some 230 miles away—plant himself on it, build a shelter, and live on it for up to six months (his original plan), thereby defending and reestablishing Britain's claim.

Tom lived on Rockall from May 26 to July 4, 1985, but the whole affair proved quite difficult from start to finish. Just getting onto the rock was the most significant challenge. Battered for centuries by gales and swamped by waves, nothing survives on Rockall save lichen, seaweed, and a few invertebrates. Seabirds use it as a temporary staging post. In Tom's first attempt to get on the rock, bad weather defeated him, and the mainsail of his sloop snapped off in high winds before he even got close. Then he chartered a trawler, the *Vision*, to get him out to the gnarly islet via a rubber dinghy. Doing his best to jump onto the rock, Tom injured his leg badly. It looked to the men watching from the trawler that Tom was at serious risk of drowning. The crew of the dingy did heroic work to drag him off Rockall's treacherous flank as Tom struggled to keep himself out of the rocks and crashing surf. More than once Tom disappeared into the churning ocean, weighed down by his kit and crampons. Reemerging bruised but undaunted, Tom was rescued by the dingy crew, who hauled him back on board. But Tom again threw himself onto Rockall, bellowing "back off" to those trying to keep him in the dingy. His next attempt at getting onto and staying on the rock succeeded.

For 40 days McClean lived in a homemade flat-pack box crafted from marine plywood—it was basically the same "Moby box" design that he had planned for his climb of Mount Everest. He assembled his box on Rockall, glued and drilled its base to a high ledge, and eventually managed to drag his entire store of supplies—80 gallons of water and more than 330 pounds of food and supplies—up to it. Inside his box (five by four by three feet), Tom slept diagonally from corner to corner, right on top of his water and food supplies. His only link to the outside world was a shortwave radio, which he used to talk to passing fishing boats and navy vessels. At the end of his successful 40-day stay, his wife, Jill, came out on the fishing boat that brought him back. In discussing his stay on Rockall, Tom was always clear about his objective: it was political and territorial. Always considering himself to be a great "patriot," he was doing his best to cement the UK's claim to the ownership of Rockall by being the first civilian to live there.

In 1987, McClean crossed the ocean again, alone, for the fourth time. This time, at age 44, he was again manning a pair of oars. What provoked him to do it—and *provoke* is the right word—was the fact that a Frenchman had been credited for setting the record for the shortest time for any solo row across the Atlantic. In 1980, 35-year-old Gérard d'Aboville in a 20-foot wooden boat, *Captaine Cook*, crossed from Cape Cod (Chatham, Massachusetts) to the French coast of Brittany, a 2,735-mile trip he completed in 71 days and 23 hours (July 10–September 20, 1980). That was more than a day longer than it had taken McClean to cross the North Atlantic in 1969. But, the newly established Ocean Rowing Society, on a technicality, gave d'Aboville the record because he had passed Lizard Point, the most southerly point on mainland Great Britain, more than a day earlier than the record set by McClean in 1969. Furthermore, d'Aboville, before he started his voyage, had reportedly announced his destination to be the "Lizard Meridian," a name given by Dutch and British cartographers to the longitude line passing through Lizard Point, because the first step in oceanic navigation via the dead reckoning method depended on the last point of land sighted. For ships leaving for America from Britain and northern Europe, the starting point for dead reckoning was Lizard Point (or for the Spanish and Portuguese, more usually from the Teide volcano on Tenerife—the so-called Tenerife longitude). An argument could then be made that d'Aboville, when he got to Lizard Point, had reached his intended destination and had technically crossed all the way across the Atlantic, even though his voyage continued on, taking a few more days, to the French port of Brest. (In 1991, d'Aboville would row across the Pacific Ocean, taking 134 days from Japan to the State of Washington. His 26-foot boat, *Sector*, represented a new era of advanced technology in ocean rowing, as his vessel was made out of Kevlar, had solar panels attached to charge the batteries of his radio, and included a video camera and an up-to-date portable stove. The Frenchman faced 40-foot waves and winds speeds of 80 MPH during his 6,000-mile trip. Upon completing his Pacific voyage, d'Aboville became the first person to row both oceans solo.)

McClean was not the only member of the British maritime community who thought the decision to credit d'Aboville with the record—which the ORS did not determine until 1985—was hogwash. But Tom was no complainer. He preferred to do something about it. So, he began planning for an Atlantic crossing in 1987 that would wrest the Atlantic solo speed record for a rowboat away from d'Aboville and claim it for British rowing.

In a 20-foot dory named *Skol 1080*, Tom heaved his way from Newfoundland to the Bishop's Rock Lighthouse on tiny island off the southwestern tip of Cornwall (*The Guinness Book of Records* lists Bishop's Rock, in the Isles of Scilly, as the world's smallest island with a building on it.) And wrest it away he did, by a considerable margin, surviving his boat turning upside down in the middle of the night in 50-foot waves and emptying essential equipment into the ocean, to make the 1,732-mile crossing in 54 hard days at sea (June 16–August 10, 1987). That voyage still stands today as the world record.

Interestingly, another man was rowing the Atlantic solo that very same summer of 1987. He was 49-year-old Englishman Don Allum. Sixteen years earlier, Allum had rowed the Atlantic for the first time with his cousin Geoff Allum in their boat *QE 3*. On January 12, 1971, they departed from Las Palmas in the Grand Canaries, as John Fairfax had done, and finished 73 days later, on March 26, in Barbados in the West Indies, a trip of 2,370 miles. The Allums became the first pair to ever row the Atlantic from east to west—and only the third duo to have rowed the ocean at all. The following year they sought to complete the first-ever circuit of the Atlantic in a rowboat by traveling eastward from Newfoundland and heading toward Ireland. They left St. John's on June 4, 1972, but after only five days, Geoff became so severely seasick and dehydrated that he had to be picked up by a passing oil tanker. Don continued on his own for 71 days, during which he was met by strong headwinds that kept pushing him back to the west roughly half the time. On the evening of his 75th day at sea, his boat was swamped by a large wave. Don lost his oars, his spare clothes, and most of his food. The next day he was found by a passing ship and rescued. After their failed attempt, Geoff decided to never try again; Don waited 14 years before giving it another go.

On January 30, 1986, Don Allum set out from the Grand Canaries in a slightly modified *QE3* and headed solo for the West Indies. It was a torturous 2,715-mile trip lasting 114 days (January 30–May 23, 1986). For the last two weeks of his voyage Don was completely out of drinking water. When he landed on the island of Nevis, both his eyesight and hearing were failing and he had lost half his body weight. It took months for him to recuperate.

That should have been the end of Don Allum's career in ocean rowing. But, at the age of 50, he was determined to make the full circuit of the Atlantic that he and his cousin Geoff had failed to complete 15 years earlier. Having convinced himself, if nobody else, that he was healthy enough to go, Don, in the spring of 1987, shipped the *QE3* to St. John's for the return voyage. What he ultimately faced on his 1,720-mile voyage (June 21–September 5, 1987)—several capsizes of his boat, a severe gash to his head when the compass hit him as the boat went over—would have been enough to defeat a man half his age. When just 80 miles west of Ireland, an early fall storm caught up with him and almost totally overwhelmed the boat. Hours later, the people of the village of Dooagh on Achill Island in Ireland's County Mayo, unbeknownst to him, were down on the beach to help bring him in safely in any way they could, having kept up with his situation on the radio. Not only did the villagers shine their car headlights out to sea to spot the *QE3*, but many of them waded right into the sea, fetching an exhausted Don Allum from his shipwrecked boat and carrying him to medical attention. Don stayed in Dooagh for weeks with the locals nursing his body and reviving his spirit. Later, the village folk built a large monument down near the beach to commemorate his voyage, which made him the first person to row the Atlantic in both directions.

Sadly, Allum never regained his health. Through two bouts of kidney failure and several warnings of heart trouble, and despite the pleadings of family and friends to seek medical help, he refused to get treatment. "I have done everything I want to do," Don told them. He died on November 2, 1992, from a heart attack at his flat in Heston, Middlesex.

Tom McClean, who spent some time with both Allums over the years, agreed with those in the British nautical community who felt that "Don Allum was the bravest of us all." McClean and Allum had spent time together in Newfoundland in the spring of 1987 when both were preparing their boats for launch from St. John's. Additionally, Geoff Allum, in a handwritten letter to McClean dated February 10, 2014, told McClean that his Atlantic voyage of 1969 in *Super Silver* was "a great inspiration to us" at the time when Geoff and Don were planning to row the Atlantic from west to east in 1971.

It was the story of Don Allum that so inspired the British progressive rock group Marillion in 2004 to write an epic song about Don's ocean journeys, titled "Ocean Cloud."

In 1990, McClean carried out one of his "wackiest" adventures. He designed a 37-foot-long boat in the shape of a beer bottle. Dubbed the *Typhoo Atlantic Challenger*—Tom had arranged financing for his boat and voyage from Typhoo Tea, a popular British tea brand since 1903—he sailed what had to be one of the strangest vessels ever to ply the open seas from New York Harbor to Falmouth. With more panache than usual, McClean equipped his bright red boat (the color of the Typhoo Tea brand) with a four-poster bed and more sophisticated navigational equipment than he had ever employed before.

The same year Tom started building another highly unusual boat meant for a solo transatlantic crossing. It was a vessel matching the actual size and shape of an adult sperm whale: 65 feet long and 25 feet high. To make the vessel as realistic as possible, Tom painted it to have a mouth and eyes, covered it in a skin-like foam, and put a "blowhole" on top that could shoot water high into the air. Not surprisingly, it was dubbed *Moby*—Tom's own nickname from his army days. The large boat was not designed to be rowed, for not even Tom could imagine managing that, but rather was powered by two diesel engines. While designing the boat himself ("Why would you go to a boat builder when they'll charge you ten times?"), a nautical engineer told Tom that his plans were crazy—one of many times over the course of his life that he had heard that about his plans and ambitions.

Moby was quite an attention-getter. During the sea trials, when Tom, from his controls "inside the belly of the beast," put it through its paces in the Moray Firth, the "whale boat," *Moby, Prince of Whales*, attracted the curiosity not only of a flotilla of other boats but also of more than one school of dolphins. For further sea trials, he chose to take *Moby* out on a 2,000-mile voyage around Britain. With the wide publicity it got around the British Isles, the whale boat attracted excited attention from coastal boats and people on the passing seashores.

He was never a political person, but his years in close touch with the sea nonetheless turned Tom—as it has a number of other ocean rowers and sailors—into a dedicated environmentalist. "You go so slow rowing across the ocean that you see everything that is going on. You literally can touch the ocean with all its life—and not just with your oars. That changes a person. Ocean rowing in general has changed a lot in terms of the psychology, philosophy, and ambitions of us rowers, because we've seen the pollution build up, the volume of plastic grow like a cancer on different parts of the sea. It's disgusting, and we need to stop it now."

Unfortunately, *Moby* has been mostly stranded for the past few years on Tom's beach at his center on the shores of Loch Nevis. He has used the time to give his whale boat "a new and better life"—one based on clean energy. Tom plans to replace his boat's diesel engines with sleek electric motors to make it more environmentally friendly. "You won't have the dirty old diesels thumping around," he explains. "I really like the idea of a company getting involved, and saving the planet, and doing good. I've put a big, big, effort into it all. A lot of people have a great pipe dream. They run out of money and it all fizzles out. But I've kept going."

Today, Tom McClean, at age 81, is as active as ever. He looks ahead to new projects, not behind; to more hard work, not relaxation; to more adventures, not a rocking chair. He and his wife, Jill, still tend to their Ardintigh center and enjoy spending time with their two sons and with their grandchildren.

It's surprising that Tom isn't more of a national figure, particularly in a nation that so reveres its sailors and explorers. The audaciousness of his achievements seems to match and exceed the record of many other British adventurers who have actually accomplished less. His relative obscurity may be an unfortunate consequence of the English class system. Had he been from "the right family"—like Scott of the Antarctic, Sir Ranulph Twisleton-Wykeham-Fiennes, Sir Wilfred Patrick Thesiger, or even Sir Richard Branson, all household names in Britain despite their shortcomings and their failures—and not an orphan from Ireland, Tom McClean, too, would likely be more renowned and given a national award. (I believe he should, in fact, be knighted.) But Tom was a down-to-earth working-class chap, which perhaps explains some of the silence about his amazing life and achievements. Unlike so many other British sailors, adventurers, and record breakers, he has never received an official honor. Not a single one.*

Tom sees this as an honor in itself—that is the great thing about him, that he honestly could not care less for such attention and honors. He's a genuine patriot, but he is also an outsider who has never played the celebrity game. Although he happily welcomes groups to Loch Nevis and has done after-dinner speaking and motivational talks all over the country, he'd rather stay home with Jill, take a boat ride on the loch, or a walk up into the mountains.

If you are lucky enough to sit down in the sitting room of the stone cottage he built himself and have a chat over a mug of coffee and ask him where he found the grit and determination to take on the extraordinary challenges of his life, he will answer you simple and direct: "It's not a case of gritting your teeth and saying, 'I'm not gonna give in.' It's in your body. It's in your being. I don't think you can train for that. That comes from when I was in the orphanage. I'm Dublin-born of Irish parents, but

---

*   A friend of mine who is British does not think that the British class system is at fault in Tom McClean not receiving any national award. "Yes, definitely at one time," my friend has commented to me privately, "and to some extent now. But the OBE and MBE awards go to people from very ordinary walks of life who accomplish things (look at the UK astronauts, for example). I would guess it is more likely because his major accomplishment was one in which he came in second—for whom the big awards don't happen. And knighthood would be a huge leap—much more likely to have been given an OBE or MBE (and again, only had he been first)." My British friend continued: "Britons LOVE plucky working-class people from disadvantaged backgrounds who struggle against the odds—especially if they don't come first—look at the Olympic ski jumper Eddie the Eagle as an example. But if they don't want to be public figures, they fade back to being forgotten, usually as they wish to be. It is very British to do as Tom did—which is not to care at all—hence this being more your opinion, Jim, than even his own. Nevertheless, I love how you point out how Tom should be remembered more officially and otherwise." I want to thank my British friend, who I am keeping anonymous, for sharing these thoughts for my book. My main rejoinder, as readers of the book now understand, is that Tom *deserves to be considered the first* to cross the Atlantic solo because he accomplished it totally unassisted compared to the numerous times Fairfax got out of his rowboat, was resupplied, and got liberal assistance from passing ships.

they felt it would be better for someone else to raise me. As a boy I had a lot of anger. I had a strong streak of stubbornness. I certainly don't think of myself as a hero. I wanted to amount to something. I wanted to make my mark. I did know, however, that one day I would find the answer."

If you want to pay Tom McClean a great compliment, tell him you think he was "completely mad" to row alone across the ocean five times.

He will give you a broad smile and a quick answer: "Sure, why not! If someone calls me a big-headed bastard or tells me I'm stark, staring mad, I just feel good."

Paraphrasing Herman Melville, author of *Moby Dick*, Tom's namesake: "My motives and my objects may seem mad to some, but all of my means have been sane."

Essay on Sources

The original source of inspiration for my writing this book was a song. Not just any song, but a powerful elegiac hymn to which I was introduced during the preproduction of the 2018 motion picture *First Man*, the story of Neil Armstrong, based on my 2005 biography of the same title. The song "Ocean Cloud" by the British neo-progressive rock group Marillion had nothing to do with the film, but its filming by Universal Pictures and director Damien Chazelle was indirectly responsible for the song coming to my attention. For with me consulting on the making of *First Man* was Neil Armstrong's eldest son, Rick Armstrong, whom I had met and interviewed for my book about his father some 15 years earlier, but I had not chatted with him about our love of music. Spending time with Rick for many days while the movie was being made, I learned that Rick was an even more ardent fan of rock music than I was. In fact, Rick played the guitar semi-professionally and was a member of Edison's Children, a science fiction- and space-oriented progressive rock trio that also featured guitarist and singer Eric Blackwood and bassist Pete Trewavas. Most importantly for the eventual writing of this book, Rick Armstrong was a devoted fan—maybe the number one biggest fan—of Marillion, for which Pete Trewavas chiefly played.

As popular and long-lasting as Marillion had been since their emergence as a bridge between punk rock and classic progressive rock in the 1980s, I was not familiar with their music. But my friendship with Rick Armstrong turned me on to Marillion's music. I became a huge fan, ordering several of their many albums and listening to them frequently. Although I came to love many of the group's songs, none captivated me more than "Ocean Cloud," an 18-minute song—dolorous yet uplifting and inspiring—on the 2004 album *Marbles*. The song (the longest ever produced by a group known for its long songs) told the remarkable and poignant story of Englishman Don Allum, who in 1986–1987 became the first person ever to row the Atlantic solo in both directions. (The significant achievements and heroic spirit of Don Allum are discussed in this book's "Postscript: Tom McClean.")

I listened to "Ocean Cloud" and watched its beautiful music video dozens of times from 2017 to 2020. I looked up, and came to know very well, its mournful yet wistful lyrics of challenge, loneliness, escape, defiance, perfect solitude, and finality that so brilliantly told the story of Don Allum's final brave Atlantic row. I watched an interview, posted on YouTube, in which Marillion leader Steve Hogarth explained why he wrote the song and how and why he thought the song touched the hearts of so many of the group's fans. I managed to Skype with Hogarth to ask him questions about the song and get contact information for the Allum family (Don had died in 1992, at age 55.) Through social media, I met and chatted with other devotees of the song. For many of them, as with me, their love of Marillion began with "Ocean Cloud." For us, the song is very special in that it brings goosebumps, tears, and, finally, a tender smile. At every live concert a large part of the crowd asks the group to play the song. Fans know that good music takes one on a journey. For the 1,080 seconds of "Ocean Cloud," the listener is away from Earth—or as one line of the song's lyrics say:

> *Between two planets*
> *In between the points of light*
> *Between two distant shorelines*
> *Here am I*

Listening to "Ocean Cloud," we, too, are in a rowboat, alone, on the open sea. When the song ends, we have fallen in love with Don Allum and with the ocean. Some of us who really cherish the song feel like we have become a better person.

By early 2020, in the middle of the COVID-19 pandemic, I became seriously interested in writing the story of Don Allum. I exhausted the internet, reading everything I could find about him. The best source was the website of the Ocean Rowing Society International. Founded in 1983, it is the governing body for international ocean rowing and the official adjudicator of ocean rowing records. The ORSI website, I found, had some great material, including the logbook entries from Don Allum's two ocean crossings. There was also an excellent short biographical sketch of Don written by Geoff Allum, a younger cousin who had rowed the Atlantic with Don in 1971 and who together in 1972 had started the return eastward until they ran into such troubles midocean that they both nearly lost their lives. The terrible watery travail left Geoff committed to never trying such an ocean crossing ever again, while it left Don in such bad shape that he had to wait 14 years before his body and mind were ready to make a second hack at the Atlantic, this time all by himself, and successfully, both ways.

As informative as Geoff's account of his cousin's maritime adventures was, it was nothing close to offering a complete biography. Not even with the help of Don's journal—posted on the ORSI website—could I have managed the type of full story I wanted to tell.

Meanwhile, I continued looking into the history of epic rowing of the world's oceans, focusing on the earliest feats, especially the Atlantic crossings.

The first crossing to succeed occurred in 1896, when Norwegian-born immigrants to the United States George Harbo (né Gottlieb Harbo Ragnhildrød) and Frank Samuelsen (né Gabriel Samuelsen) made a two-man row across the Atlantic. Harbo and Samuelsen, veteran mariners and fishermen who lived along the New Jersey coast, set out in their 18-foot-long clinker-built oak rowboat from the Battery in New York City with no other means of propulsion but oars, hoping to arrive in the port at Le Havre, France, but were lucky, 55 days later, to find the Isles of Scilly, at the southernmost tip of England, 3,250 miles from New

York. The duration of their crossing, 55 days, remained a record time for rowing the Atlantic for 114 years, until 2010, when it was finally broken by a boat rowed not by two men but by four.

Though several other attempts were made, the next successful crossing of the Atlantic in a rowboat, dubbed *English Rose III*, did not happen until 1966, when two British soldiers, Captain John Ridgway and Sergeant Chay Blyth, teamed up and rowed from Cape Cod, Massachusetts, leaving June 4, landing on the Aran Islands off the coast of Ireland 92 days later. I ordered a copy of their remarkable autobiographical account of the grueling journey, *A Fighting Chance* (published in London the same year as their arrival), and devoured the book in one day. Once Ridgway and Blyth got their 20-foot dory into the water (Blyth having had virtually no sea experience), I had to see them the rest of the way. Theirs was truly an epic journey, in which they braved vicious storms, two hurricanes, huge waves, whales bigger than their boat, as well as extreme fatigue and far less than substantial rations.

As soon as I opened their book, I realized that Ridgway and Blyth were not just British soldiers; they were British Army paratroopers. Where had I heard that before? Oh, yes, I recalled that Neil Armstrong had mentioned to me over lunch during my interviewing him for *First Man* some 15 years earlier that, not just John Fairfax, but a British paratrooper had rowed the Atlantic solo in the summer of 1969 simultaneous with the first Moon landing. Neil couldn't recall the paratrooper's name, but he knew it was not Ridgway or Blyth. It was another man.

I looked first to see if Ridgway and Blyth mentioned the man in question in their book—they had not. But it only took an internet search for me to discover who he was. The other paratrooper, who had also crossed the Atlantic in a rowboat in the summer of 1969, was Tom McClean. Apparently McClean had Ridgway as his commanding officer in the British Army's elite Parachute Regiment and Blyth was Tom's sergeant, before Tom moved on from the Paras to the SAS special forces unit. It was the inspiration of the bold transatlantic enterprise of Ridgway and Blyth in 1966 that gave McClean the crazy notion of endeavoring something even more daring—to row the Atlantic alone. It was a crazy notion because McClean had no previous experience at all in ocean rowing.

By this time—besides being stuck in extreme social distancing inside my Alabama home with my wife of 44 years and my 92-year-old mother-in-law—I was in a quandary. Do I continue to pursue the Don Allum story so dear to my heart because of my love of "Ocean Cloud" and because the fact that Don's achievement of being the first to cross the Atlantic solo in both directions (1986–1987) was so incredible? If so, I definitely needed more source materials, potentially through the assistance of Don's cousin Geoff, for whom I still had no address. Or do I write a book about John Fairfax, who is credited as the first person to cross the Atlantic solo in a rowboat successfully and doing it from west to east and arriving in Florida—Florida, from where the astronauts launched!—just one day before Apollo 11 landed on the Moon? How do you beat that? Or do I write the story of Tom McClean, who, as I got to know more and more about him, seemed the person most overlooked in the annals of ocean rowing, even though he nearly beat Fairfax across the Atlantic, going west to east, and Tom did it totally unassisted—that is, without getting supplies or other material help from any passing ships—whereas Fairfax's trip, though completed eight days before McClean's—was greatly assisted and had the advantage of starting five months earlier?

I ordered three more books: Fairfax's *Britannia: Rowing Alone across the Atlantic: The Record of an Adventure* (published by Simon & Schuster in 1972 and reissued as a leather-bound collector's edition by Easton Press in 1988) and McClean's two memoirs, *I Had to Dare: Rowing the Atlantic in Seventy Days* (published in 1971 by Jarrolds of London), and *Rough Passage: A Life of Adventure* (coauthored with Alec Beilby and published in the United Kingdom in 1983 by Hutchinson/Stanley Paul). I read all three books, one right after another, in five days, absolutely enthralled by each man's remarkable story. It was not just the solo ocean rows themselves that fascinated me. It was their entire life stories that were so extraordinary and captivating.

Finishing the three books, I learned there was a fourth that I needed to read: *Oars Across the Pacific* (New York: W. W. Norton & Company, 1972) told the first-person story of the historic first crossing of the Pacific Ocean by rowboat made by John Fairfax and his British girlfriend and associate Sylvia Cook, from San Francisco to Australia. Their incredible voyage started on April 26, 1971, and finished on April 22, 1972, a journey of 363 days. In the process, Sylvia Cook became the first woman to row not only the Pacific Ocean but *any* ocean. Furthermore, Cook, who coauthored *Oars Across the Pacific*, had played a pivotal role in helping Fairfax plan and prepare for and carry out his Atlantic crossing in 1969. She was a central character in the overall story of the "race" between Fairfax and McClean to be first across the Atlantic solo.

The idea of a "race" having taken place between John Fairfax and Tom McClean became the driving force in my planning of the book. Outside of the ocean rowing community, however, very little about this drama was at all well known, which made it even more important for me to bring the extraordinary story to the wider world.

Critically important was whether there was sufficient source material for telling the story of their race across the Atlantic in 1969. Though the shutdowns brought on by COVID-19 would make it impossible for me to conduct the necessary research abroad, I became convinced that there was a way to do it.

I exhausted what could be found via the internet. That research started by scouring the website of the Ocean Rowing Society International. Since its establishment in 1983, the ORSI had documented all known ocean rows while adjudicating records and firsts in consultation with Guinness World Records. For several years the ORSI operation was in the hands of British adventurer Kenneth Crutchlow (1944–2016), the ORSI founder and its longtime president. With the help of his wife, Ukrainian artist Tatiana Rezvoy, Crutchlow kept notes that laid the basis for a compilation of worldwide rowing statistics. Those stats made up the majority of contents in the original ORSI website, which was developed in the early 1990s by Tom Lynch and maintained by Theodore Rezvoy and Tatiana Rezvoy. It was a groundbreaking website for its time, but it could only be maintained manually, meaning that using it was unwieldy, having reached nearly 1,000 entries, with the required human-processed statistical work. By the time I started visiting their website in 2018, Crutchlow had died, but his successors—notably ORSI's Fiann Paul, himself a multiple record holder in ocean rowing—were committed to creating a brand-new website and database through which users could find and cross-reference virtually everything the ORSI had recorded. The new database consisted of various interactive and interrelated statistics, notably tables of expeditions, explorers, vessels, an interactive map that displayed expeditions in any given area and period, a page where two expeditions could be fully compared, and an outline page that summarized all the facts as numbers on one page. The inspiration for the new database came from Fiann Paul's interest in working with geodatabases, sophisticated databases of geographic data, very useful for the new ORSI website's identification of locations showing, among other things, the precise routes taken by all the rowers that had made ocean voyages.

The ORSI website would prove immensely useful to me. More than the database, it also held short biographies of many of the rowers, descriptions of their vessels, photos, and facsimiles of logbooks and journals kept by some of the record setters. As for John Fairfax, the database helped in profiling his ocean crossing(s), and it also published a well-done short biographical stretch written by Crutchlow and veteran rower Steve Boga for their book *The Oceanrowers*. (Learning of the book, I immediately tried to order it but could not find when or where it was published.) Although not as helpful about Tom McClean, the website did have information about him as well.

Naturally, besides the ORSI website, I found numerous articles on the World Wide Web about both of my men, including news articles, feature stories, a few interviews and video clips, and obituaries (in the case of Fairfax, as he had died in February 2012, five months before Neil Armstrong passed away). My research materials were quickly building up.

But I needed to go to the source.

As I knew from writing the Neil Armstrong biography and many of my other book projects over the years, it was essential to include firsthand personal testimony; in other words, oral history through one-on-one interviews directly with the historical actors was vital to accuracy, filling in unrecorded details, and adding color, tone, and vibrancy.

Unfortunately, as stated above, John Fairfax was no longer alive. Although a number of feature stories dealing with Fairfax had appeared in print media over the years—often with illuminating quotes from John—no one had done an extensive interview with him. So that important element of his biography was missing—and that gap was especially important because there were many aspects of John's life, especially his early years as an only child in Rome, Italy, during World II, and his adolescence in Juan Perón's Argentina, which John had never said much about and no one writing about him had ever adequately covered. His mother, Mara Penev, had died years earlier, and with no other siblings or close relatives, it seemed impossible to fill in the holes in John's story by interviewing other people.

But there was Sylvia Cook. She came into John Fairfax's life in 1967, as his girlfriend, lover, secretary, assistant, and ultimately his partner in ocean adventures. With a little effort, I found that Sylvia, born in 1947, was still alive and living in retirement in Surrey, outside London. It was not easy to find her contact information. Finally, I emailed a British journalist, Simon Usborne, who had written an article about Sylvia titled "The Pensioner Next Door Who Rowed across an Ocean for Love," published in the *Independent* on February 8, 2012. Usborne kindly provided me with Sylvia's phone number, and I telephoned her the same day. I explained to her who I was and what I was hoping to do. Understandably a bit wary of my "cold call," she agreed to look at a list of questions about Fairfax, about her years with him, and, mostly, about his 1969 solo crossing of the Atlantic. As readers have seen in this book, Ms. Cook's replies to my questions were honest, candid, and totally fascinating. Thanks to her well-thought-out and complete replies—many of them to questions to which only she would know the answer—I was able to flesh out Fairfax's life story up to and through his 1969 ocean crossing very effectively. The result changed the narrative that had been established about him—both by John himself and by the journalists who write about him—in some very fundamental ways.

That left Tom McClean—and here the promise of my project got richly awarded.

Born in 1943, Tom McClean in 2019 was then 77 years old and very much alive. He still is today, at age 83. He has resided for the past 50-plus years on the far northwestern coast of Scotland, in the small village of Morar (three miles south of Mallaig, if that helps orient anyone unfamiliar with Scottish geography). His simple cottage residence is on a raw but extremely beautiful piece of land lying between Loch Morar (the deepest freshwater body in the British Isles) and the mouth of the Morar River. With his wife of 46 years, Jill Stacey McClean, Tom has been operating a Highland Adventure Centre at Ardintigh on the south shore of nearby Loch Nevis. Situated amid the spectacular scenery of mountains and lochs, his camp has been enjoyed by military groups for adventure training and R&R, nature lovers, and many other groups wishing to escape to what Tom calls "Britain's last great wilderness" for a half century.

For four months, I conducted weekly 90-minute-long interviews with Tom McClean over the internet. Having read both of his books carefully, my questions were designed to elicit additional information and get Tom to comment on some subjects not covered, or not covered in great depth, in his books. I sent him my questions for each week's interview at least a few days in advance, so he could think them over and pull out any files or other materials that might help to amplify his answers. I had a wonderful time getting to know Tom through these interviews, and his wife, Jill, as well. Tom also gave me free and unlimited use of all material in his two books, as he holds the copyrights for them exclusively. For the book he freely provided all the photographs illustrating his ocean row and his life. He also reviewed for accuracy my entire manuscript, as Neil Armstrong had done with my book about him. Both men had the integrity to offer changes without demanding that they be made.

As for the photographs showing Fairfax's row, a few of them were provided by Sylvia Cook, and the rest were made available by letter of authorization from The Easton Press, publisher of Fairfax's book *Britannia*.

With most of the sources that I thought I would need in hand, I started writing the book. Ultimately, I had to make a decision about how to reference my sources. In the end, I decided not to utilize any standard style of referencing all the quotations in the book. As a great many of the quotes came from Fairfax and McClean via their books, I determined that detailed referencing of those quotes was unnecessary. Instead, I would direct my readers to pick up those four books, if interested, and read the full firsthand accounts penned by the two men themselves. I doubted that anyone would benefit greatly from a standard set of source notes similar to those one would find in any of my other books.

As for my Skype interviews with Tom McClean, with Tom's permission my plan has been to offer them for publication on the website of the Ocean Rowing Society.

The only source materials that might be in question are the emails I received from Sylvia Cook in response to the questions I asked her about John Fairfax. The dates of those emails are August 17, 21, 22, and 30, 2020; September 18 and 22, 2020; October 22, 2020; December 4, 2020; and February 26, 2021. If a reader wishes to see a copy of any of these emails, I shall consider providing it, if the request—i.e., the reason for it—is judged to be credible.

Although Ms. Cook provided me with highly valuable insights into John Fairfax and to his mother and family background, I certainly wish that I had been able to gain access to more materials about John's life.

Regrettably, I had no success in reaching John's widow, Tiffany Alisha Fairfax, who, according to the scant information I could discover about her, married John in 1979; lived with him as she does today in Henderson, Nevada; is considered a professional astrologer; wrote a column "Cosmic Jackpot" for the *Vegas Voice* and another for *Las Vegas* magazine; privately consulted for celebrity and everyday clients; and followed the astrological events surrounding such high-profile crimes and court cases as the trial of O. J. Simpson and the slaying of child beauty queen JonBenét Ramsey. She did not meet John until well after his ocean rows, but likely could have offered some important insights into his character and later life as a professional gambler.

To sum up: I have done the best I could with source materials that were available, given the restrictions of the pandemic. Even with their limitations, I believe those sources have been sufficient for me to tell this remarkable double story reliably and with a richness of detail.

Bibliography

PRIMARY SOURCES

BOOKS

Fairfax, John. *Britannia: Rowing Alone Across the Atlantic*. Norwalk, CT: The Easton Press, 1971.

Fairfax, John and Sylvia Cook. *Oars Across the Pacific*. New York: W. W. Norton, 1972.

McClean, Tom. *I Had to Dare: Rowing the Atlantic in Seventy Days*. London: Jarrolds Publishers, 1971.

McClean, Tom. *Rough Passage: A Life of Adventure*. London and Melbourne: Hutchinson/Stanley Paul, 1983.

NEWSPAPERS AND PERIODICALS

John Fairfax, "How I Rowed the Atlantic and Found Florida," *Esquire*, April 1, 1970, accessed at https://classic.esquire.com/article/1970/4/1/how-i-rowed-across-the-atlantic-and-found-florida.

INTERVIEWS CONDUCTED BY AUTHOR

Cook, Sylvia, Sussex, England (by telephone)
July 14, 2020
August 4, 2020
McClean, Tom, Morar, Scotland (via Skype)
June 18, 2020
June 24, 2020

July 2, 2020
July 16, 2020
August 14, 20202
September 4, 2020
November 18, 2020
December 17, 2020
January 21, 2021
March 18, 2021
April 1, 2021
July 8, 2021
August 20, 2021
June 30, 2022
August 4, 2022
September 16, 2022
December 14, 2022

E-MAIL CORRESPONDENCE WITH AUTHOR
Cook, Sylvia, Sussex
>This correspondence between the author and Ms. Cook took place beginning August 14, 2020 and continuing intermittently until July 31, 2022. Email exchanges occurred on 20 different dates with several of them involving strings of multiple messages on the same day. Some of them involved attachments in which Ms. Cook answered a list of questions provided to her by the author.

McClean, Tom, Morar, Scotland
>This correspondence amounts to several dozen email messages between the author and Tom McClean over the time span from May 23, 2020, up to January 12, 2023. Many of these emails occurred directly in advance of a Skype interview and involved the scheduling of the upcoming interview. The emails also included the author's questions for the upcoming interview, conversations with McClean (and sometimes with his wife Jill) which were audio-recorded and transcribed. Several of the messages gave additional thoughts from McClean to the subject matter discussed in the past interview. The emails come from more than 50 individual dates.

WEBSITES
Tom McClean, Motivational/Inspirational Speaker: http://www.motivationspeaker.co.uk/index.asp.
"Tom McClean, Public Figure," Facebook, https://www.facebook.com/pages/Tom-McClean/111093492275845.
Ocean Rowing Society International: http://www.oceanrowing.com/ors_menu.htm

SECONDARY SOURCES

BOOKS

Anthony, Irving. *Voyagers Unafraid*. New York and Chicago: A.L. Burt Company, 1936.

Campbell, Joseph. *The Hero With a Thousand Faces*. Third Edition. Navato, CA: New World Library, 2008.

Crutchlow, Kenneth and Steve Boga. *The Oceanrowers*. Dorset, England: Ocean Rowing Society International (ORSI) website: www.oceanrowing.com /Oceanrowers/index.htm.

Davison, Ann, David Lewis, and Hannes Lindemann. *Great Voyages in Small Boats: Solo Transatlantic*. New York: John de Graff, 1982.

Ferguson, Gregor. *The Paras: British Airborne Forces 1940-1984*. London: Osprey Publishing, 1984.

Goñi, Uki. *The Real Odessa: How Perón Brought the Nazi War Criminals to Argentina*. Revised edition. London and New York: Granta Books, 2002.

Hammick, Anne. *The Atlantic Crossing Guide*. Camden, ME: International Marine, 1992.

Rackley, Adam. *Salt, Sweat, Tears: The Men Who Rowed the Oceans*. New York: Penguin Books, 2014.

Ridgway, John and Chay Blyth. *A Fighting Chance*. London: The Companion Book Club of London, 1966; Philadelphia, PA: Lippincott, 1967.

Shaw, David W. *Daring the Sea: The True Story of the First Men to Row Across the Atlantic Ocean*. New York: Citadel Press, 1998.

ARTICLES

"A Chance Encounter with Tom McClean," *A Bolas About*, March 29, 2018, https ://abolasabout.wordpress.com/2018/03/29/a-chance-encounter-with-tom-mcclean/.

Bernstein, Adam. "'Professional adventurer' John Fairfax dies at 74," *Washington Post*, February 13, 2012, https://www.washingtonpost.com/sports/professional -adventurer-john-fairfax-dies-at-74/2012/02/13/gIQAAiy7BR_story.html.

"Adventurer John Fairfax dies at 74; rowed across the Atlantic and Pacific oceans," *Los Angeles Times*, February 22, 2012, https://www.latimes.com/local /obituaries/la-me-john-fairfax-20120222-story.html.

"Atlantic oarsman John Fairfax dies," *ABC News*, February 19, 2012, https://www .abc.net.au/news/2012-02-20/atlantic-rower-fairfax-dies/3839122.

Banks, Joe. "The 73-Year-Old Adventurer Sailing a 60ft Steel Whale Across the Atlantic Ocean," *Vice Newsletter*, February 18, 2016, https://www.vice.com/en_uk /article/gqmzbj/tom-mcclean.

Beckman, Leah. "John Fairfax Loved Hookers: Ten 'Juicy' Stories Omitted From His NYT Obit," Gawker, February 20, 2012, https://gawker.com/5886695 /john-fairfax-loved-hookers-ten-juicy-stories-omitted-from-his-nyt-obit.

"Bottled-Up Sailor Sets Records," *Washington Post*, August 18, 1990, https://www.washingtonpost.com/archive/lifestyle/1990/08/18/bottled-up-sailor-sets-records/c9580c51-6448-4fb4-aca2-acadb751787c/.

Carrell, Severin. "King of Rockall Tom McClean gets ready to hand over his crown," *Guardian*, May 28, 2013, https://www.theguardian.com/uk/2013/may/28/rockall-nick-hancock-tom-mcclean.

Childs, Martin. "John Fairfax: Adventurer who became the first man to row solo across the Atlantic Ocean," *Independent*, February 25, 2012, https://www.independent.co.uk/news/obituaries/john-fairfax-adventurer-who-became-the-first-man-to-row-solo-across-the-atlantic-ocean-7440623.html.

"Fegan's boys—where are they now? Tom McClean," n.d., http://clutch.open.ac.uk/schools/watlingway99/Where-Now.html.

Fox, Margalit. "John Fairfax, Who Rowed Across Oceans, Dies at 74," *New York Times*, February 18, 2012, https://www.nytimes.com/2012/02/19/us/john-fairfax-who-rowed-across-oceans-dies-at-74.html?pagewanted=1&_r=1.

Gibson, Dan. "RIP, John Fairfax, Totally Amazing Guy," *The Range*, February 20, 2012, https://www.tucsonweekly.com/TheRange/archives/2012/02/20/rip-john-fairfax-totally-amazing-guy.

"Hollywood Celebrates 50th Anniversary of the Landing of John Fairfax, First Rower to Cross the Atlantic—Hollywood Gazette," *Sports Commentary*, June 26, 2019, https://www.sportscommentary.net/watersports/hollywood-celebrates-50th-anniversary-of-the-landing-of-john-fairfax-first-rower-to-cross-the-atlantic-hollywood-gazette/.

"Hollywood honors John Fairfax, a rowing legend," *South Florida Sun Sentinel*, July 20, 2019, https://www.sun-sentinel.com/local/broward/hollywood/117154775-132.html.

Ivall, Stephen. "Museum exhibition pays tribute to first solo rower," *The Packet*, August 2, 2006, https://www.falmouthpacket.co.uk/news/cornwall_news/860020.museum-exhibition-pays-tribute-first-solo-rower/.

Jefferies, Chris. "Whale boat aims for carbon-neutral Atlantic crossing," *Motorboat & Yacht*, March 8, 2016, https://www.mby.com/news/whale-boat-carbon-neutral-atlantic-crossing-51826.

"John Fairfax," *Telegraph*, February 17, 2012, https://www.telegraph.co.uk/news/obituaries/9089905/John-Fairfax.html.

"John Fairfax and Sylvia Cook," *The Coracle*, October 13, 2017, http://thecoracle.blogspot.com/2017/10/john-fairfax-and-sylvia-cook.html.

"John Fairfax dies at 74," ESPN, Fevruary 19, 2012, https://www.espn.com/espnw/news-commentary/story/_/id/7593672/john-fairfax-crossed-oceans-rowboats-dies.

"John Fairfax: First Solo Atlantic Ocean Rower, Dies at 74," *The Log: California's Boating & Fishing News*, February 28, 2012, https://www.thelog.com/snw/john-fairfax-first-solo-atlantic-ocean-rower-dies-at-74/.

"John Fairfax Never Dies . . . ," *Hear the Boat Sing*, February 22, 2012, https ://heartheboatsing.com/2012/02/22/john-fairfax-never-dies/.

"John Fairfax: Pirate in a Rowboat," *American Digest*, February 19, 2012, http ://americandigest.org/mt-archives/driveby/pirate_in_a_rowboat.php.

"John Fairfax, who crossed oceans in rowboats dies," *Sydney Morning Herald*, February 21, 2012, accessed at https://www.smh.com.au/world/john-fairfax -who-crossed-oceans-in-rowboats-dies-20120220-1tjg3.html.

"John Fairfax, who rowed Atlantic alone, dies," CBS News, February 19, 2012, https ://www.cbsnews.com/news/john-fairfax-who-rowed-atlantic-alone-dies/.

Lange, Jeva. "The forgotten adventurer who made history in Apollo 11's shadow," *The Week*, July 18, 2019, https://theweek.com/articles/853544/forgotten -adventurer-who-made-history-apollo-11s-shadow.

Long, Brent. "Why Hollywood Should Make a Movie About John Fairfax—Rower, Pirate's Apprentice and Gambler," Reuters, February 19, 2012, https://www .reuters.com/article/idUS258393619220120219.

"Man who crossed oceans, dead at 74," *UPI*, February 19, 2012, https://www.upi.com /Top_News/US/2012/02/19/Man-who-crossed-oceans-dead-at-74 /55251329672731/?spt=hs&or=tn&cur3=1.

Miller, Stephen. "A Solo Seafarer, Armed Only With Oars," *Wall Street Journal*, February 15, 2012, https://www.wsj.com/articles/SB100014240529702040627 04577221703971002824.

Moag, Jeff. "Historical Badass: John Fairfax, Shark Hunter and Gunfighter, Also Rowed Across Oceans," *Adventure Journal*, May 14, 2020, https://www .adventure-journal.com/2020/05/john-fairfax-shark-wrestler-and-gunfighter -also-rowed-across-oceans/.

"'Moby', the whale-shaped boat that will cross the Atlantic," *Surfer Today*, March 9, 2016, https://www.surfertoday.com/environment/moby-the -whale-shaped-boat-that-will-cross-the-atlantic.

Ranzulli, Melanie. "How to Row Across the Ocean," *Gadling*, Februrary 21, 2012, https://gadling.com/2012/02/21/how-to-row-across-the-ocean/.

Rutherford, Nichola, "Rockall: The adventurers who lived on a craggy outcrop," BBC News, June 11, 2019, https://www.bbc.com/news/uk-scotland-48582267.

Savage, Roz. "Devastation: John Fairfax Rowed a Different Ocean," Februrary 26, 2012, https://www.rozsavage.com/devastation-john-fairfax-rowed-a-different-ocean/.

Seamans, Kate. "One of World's Most Interesting Men is Dead; John Fairfax, 74, had a resume that almost defies belief," Newser, February 20, 2012, https://www .newser.com/story/140095/one-of-worlds-most-interesting-men-is-dead.html.

Serpell, Nick. "Been and Gone: Farewell to ocean 'adventurer' Fairfax," BBC News, March 1, 2012, https://www.bbc.com/news/magazine-17203352.

Smith, C. Brian. "True Grit: The John Fairfax Story," February 24, 2016, https ://cbriansmith.com/2016/02/24/true-grit-the-john-fairfax-story/.

Smith, Kirsty. "Master and Commander: One Man and His Whale," *Scottish Field*, February 28, 2020, https://www.scottishfield.co.uk/outdoors/master-and -commander-one-man-and-his-whale/.

Thompson, Melissa. "The extraordinary adventurer who lived wild in the jungle, fought sharks and became a pirate," *Mirror*, February 24, 2012, https://www .reuters.com/article/idUS258393619220120219.

Thring, Oliver, "A salty swansong for the SAS veteran and 'Moby', his iron whale," *Sunday Times*, March 6, 2016, https://www.thetimes.co.uk/article/a-salty -swansong-for-the-sas-veteran-and-moby-his-iron-whale-qwct3trwt.

Usborne, Simon. "The pensioner next door who rowed across an ocean for love," *Independent*, February 27, 2012, https://www.independent.co.uk/news /uk/home-news/the-pensioner-next-door-who-rowed-across-an-ocean-for -love-7441165.html.

"Who owns Rockall? A history of disputes over a tiny Atlantic island," *GeoGarage Blog*, June 12, 2019, http://blog.geogarage.com/2019/06/who-owns-rockall -history-of-disputes.html.

"You couldn't script it: world loses its most interesting man," *Brisbane Times*, February 21, 2012, https://www.brisbanetimes.com.au/world/you-couldnt -script-it-world-loses-one-of-its-most-interesting-men-20120221-1tkfb.html.

TERTIARY SOURCES

Books Read by Author in Conjunction with Preparing *Completely Mad*

Abbey, Edward. *Desert Solitaire: A Season in the Wilderness*. Ballantine, 1971.

Balf, Todd. *The Darkest Jungle: The True Story of the Darien Expedition and America's Ill-Fated Race to Connect the Seas*. Crown, 2003.

Bergreen, Laurence. *Over the Edge of the World: Magellan's Terrifying Circumnavigation of the Globe*. Perennial/HarperCollins, 2004.

Brashears, David. *High Exposure: An Enduring Passion for Everest and Unforgiving Places*. Simon & Schuster, 2000.

Callahan, Steven. *Adrift: 76 Days Lost at Sea*. Mariner Books, 2002.

Chichester, Frank. *Gipsy Moth Circles the World*. Coward-McCann, 1967.

Dugard, Martin. *Farther Than Any Man: The Rise and Fall of Captain James Cook*. Washington Square Press, 2002.

Fletcher, Colin. *The Man Who Walked Through Time: The Story of the First Trip Afoot in the Grand Canyon*. Vintage Reissue Edition, 1989.

Grann, David. *The Lost City of Z: A Tale of Deadly Obsession in the Amazon*. Vintage, 2010.

Henderson, Bruce. *True North: Peary, Cook, and the Race to the Pole*. W. W. Norton, 2006.

Heyerdahl, Thor. *Kon-Tiki: Across the Pacific in a Raft.* Rand McNally, 1950.

Hillary, Edmund. *High Adventure: The True Story of the First Ascent of Everest.* Oxford University Press, 2003.

Junger, Sebastian. *The Perfect Storm: A True Story of Men Against the Sea.* W. W. Norton, 2009.

Krakauer, John. *Into the Wild.* Anchor, 1997.

Krakauer, John. *Into Thin Air: A Personal Account of the Mt. Everest Disaster.* Anchor, 1999.

Lansing, Alfred. *Endurance: Shackleton's Incredible Voyage.* Basic Books, 1959, 1986, 2014.

Larsen, Erik. *Isaac's Storm: A Man, a Time, and the Deadliest Hurricane in History.* Vintage, 2011.

Newby, Eric. *A Short Walk in the Hindu Kush.* HarperCollins, 2010.

Philbrick, Nathaniel. *Into the Heart of the Sea: The Tragedy of Whale Ship Essex.* Penguin, 2001.

Ralston, Aran. *Between a Rock and a Hard Place.* Atria Books, 2005.

Rousmaniere, John. *The Deadliest Storm in the History of Modern Sailing.* W. W. Norton, 2000.

Shackleton, Ernest. *South: Shackleton's Last Expedition—Illustrated 100th Anniversary Edition.* Seawolf Press, 2020.

Slocum, Captain John. *Sailing Alone Around the World.* Leonaur, 2010.

Strayed, Cheryl. *Wild: From Lost to Found on the Pacific Coast Trail.* Vintage, 2013.

Tenzing, Jamling. *Touching My Father's Soul: A Sherpa's Journey to the Top of Everest.* HarperOne, 2002.

Thesiger, Wilfred. *Arabian Sands.* Penguin Classics Reprint, 2008.

Winchester, Simon. *Krakatoa: The Day the World Exploded.* Harper, 2005.

Acknowledgments

J ust as I would never consider rowing a boat solo across the Atlantic Ocean, neither would I ever want to write a book all by myself without the active help and support of colleagues, friends, and family.

If I ever made any such daring ocean voyage, it would have to be in a large outrigger canoe like those that the ancient Austronesian people took across the South Pacific, in the long process (from 1500 BCE to 1200 CE) populating the islands of Oceania from Formosa and the Philippines to Hawaii and Easter Island. Scholars suggest that the outriggers canoes used in the Austronesian Expansion could hold as many as 80 people with room to spare for some domesticated animals and a good stock of water and food. But the outrigger that I had in mind for my journey did not require such great capacity. In my canoe I only needed a crew of six, leaving plenty of space for drinks and sandwiches.

The critical first person I wanted—nay, needed—in my boat-as-book was Tom McClean. The stout paratrooper and ocean rower became—well, not my captain, as I had to be the author of my own boat—but for me a sort of nautical Gandalf, the wizard from the *Lord of the Rings* trilogy, with his characteristics of veiled power, good intentions, care for all creatures of good, and superb sense of where we were and where we needed to go and not go. Without Tom's full cooperation I could never have written *Completely Mad* (which by the way is also the name of my metaphorical boat). The wizard of a man not only showed me, Jedi-like, how to steer my boat and taught me rowing techniques, he also encouraged me when my energy sapped and my spirits sagged. Such a hobbit as I could not have made the crossing successfully without Tom McClean—in fact, I wouldn't have even tried. It was also a blessing to have his merry wife, Jill, talking to me regularly on our boat's satellite telephone, sharing stories about Tom, cheering us on, and waiting for us at the finish line with biscuits, a huge piping-hot bowl of Tom's favorite chicken curry, and a bottle of my personal favorite Dalmore 25-Year Highland Scotch Whiskey.

For my boat's first mate (I realize that Austronesian outriggers did not have such ranks, at least that we know of, but they must have had something of the like), my choice was Sylvia Cook. After all, she had not only been John Fairfax's girlfriend and assistant at the time of his Atlantic crossing in 1969, three years later she also rowed with Fairfax all the way across the Pacific from San Francisco to Australia, the first to accomplish the unimaginable trip. An expert rower and celestial navigator, Sylvia on our passage could continue telling me stories about Fairfax, the highly astonishing buccaneer, while making sure that I did not diminish his record yet not exaggerate his life story by glorifying John and making him into the heroic figure that he wasn't.

At my side from the first moments of designing my craft to its arrival on the distant shore there had to be Laurie Fox, my longtime sidekick in the business of launching boats, who has served as my literary agent now for over 20 years. Not only is Laurie a very creative and veteran boatbuilder herself and a professional guide who has steered me through the rough waters of several perilous book crossings, she is an also accomplished mariner—truly—having made a number of expeditions into the Pacific aboard different sorts of boats and for a while even living on a boat. Laurie is enchanting and delightful, and in some ways reminds me of Sylvia Cook, and I am sure the two women would not only get along quite well personally, they would be the crew's hardest workers and inspirational leaders. Before embarking, I imagined I would have many long talks with both of them during our trip, listening to them more than I myself talked.

Another member of my crew was my friend: the indomitable, clever, and good-hearted Francis French. Being British, Francis helped me understand some of what I wrongly identified as oddities, peculiarities, or eccentricities in British society and in the character of the British people. I imagined that Francis would get along well with Tom McClean and Sylvia Cooke, as all three of them were British (all, in fact, raised in England, Tom in an orphanage). There is not much Francis French does not know about everything—his knowledge of history and culture is virtually encyclopedic. He is himself also a veteran boatsman—a published author with several books to his name, primarily about astronauts and exploration. Francis was thus well-acquainted with men—and women, too—who would fit right in on a boat named *Completely Mad*. Even before my outrigger made it all the way across the ocean, he gave me a thorough critique of the ocean route I was navigating and making suggestions to correct and improve it.

The toughest decision of who to put on the boat and who to leave on shore came when considering what to do with my wife, Peggy. As it turned out, she had to be on the vessel but at a distance. An outbreak of a new plague called COVID-19 required that *Completely Mad* be conceived, built, and taken across to its destination in an unusual type of ship quarantine. My outrigger had to stay on a very strict navigational course, which restricted me—if I can be rightfully be called "the skipper"—as well as my laptop and books, to an exposed position at the helm (i.e., the island in our kitchen) while all sorts of noisy, intervening actions took place hourly all around me. To block out the noise of the waves and the wind (read, television set), I was forced to put in my ear buds, through which I listened nonstop not to music, per se, but to the sound of ocean waves and breezes on "Ocean Radio," a channel on a broad-band accessed via an apparently nautical-friendly WWW site, with such hypnotic wordless tunes as "Ocean Surf," "Tranquil Ocean Waves," "Water Ambience," "Tropical Ocean Currents," and conversely, "Thrilling Ocean Waves" and "Strong Storms at Sea." Literally, I participated in this audio experience some 90 percent of the time that I was inside my boat, steering it slowly and often not so surely, from St. John's, Newfoundland, to Blacksod Bay, Ireland, or, alternatively, depending on my disposition, from Gran Canaria, Spain to Hollywood, Florida.

Also in the ship quarantine was my dear mother-in-law, Marilyn, who at 92 years old was in failing physical and mental health. She had come to stay with us from her landlocked home in Indiana just as the plague broke out, and stayed as comfortably as we could make her until she slipped away from our vessel a few months before we got our first sight of land.

Occasionally from the vantage point of the boat, I could see other members of my family, assembled outside a portal on the keel, waving at those of us who could be seen on board, shouting out, while riding out their own waves, words of encouragement and love. Sometimes in the mist they looked like to be a mirage, a hallucination, so much time in quarantine at sea made it hard to fathom them as real. But, phantasms of the sea, they were not: Nathan, my son; Jessica; his wife, Luke and Claire, their children; my daughter Jennifer, her husband Cole; their children Isabelle and Mason. They could only be on my boat vicariously, but I planned to tell them all about my adventure when I made it back home.

Finally, I wish to give a hearty thanks to Jessica Case of Pegasus Boats—I mean, Pegasus *Books*—who did a fantastic job as "harbor pilot" maneuvering *Completely Mad* through dangerously shallow waters to its final destination. Harbor pilots, like good editors, are highly skilled professionals in navigation. They are required to know immense details of restricted waterways such depth, currents, natural and man-made structures, as well as hydrodynamic effects and numerous other hazards. They must display expertise in handling ships of all types and sizes. In every way imaginable, Jessica Case demonstrated that she was a marvelously expert ship handler, avoiding collisions with coastal rocks and threading the way through last-minute channel effects. Thanks to her we made it!

May everyone involved in the voyage make myriad magical journeys in the years to come in boats of their own design and construction.

Myself, I am not sure how many more ocean crossings I myself will try. Perhaps one or two. But I am certainly glad I made this one, in the company of Tom and John, and all the rest.

—James R. Hansen
Birmingham, Alabama

About the Author

J ames R. Hansen is professor emeritus of history at Auburn University. A former historian for NASA, Hansen is the author of fourteen books involving air and space and exploration. His 2005 book *First Man*, the only authorized biography of Neil Armstrong, has on two separate occasions appeared on the *New York Times Bestseller* list and has been translated into two dozen languages. In 1995 NASA nominated his book *Spaceflight Revolution* for a Pulitzer Prize, the only time the U.S. space agency has ever made such a nomination. His 2009 book, *Truth, Lies, and O-Rings: Inside the Space Shuttle Challenger Disaster*, has been called by reviewers "the definitive study" of the Challenger accident. He lives in Birmingham, Alabama.